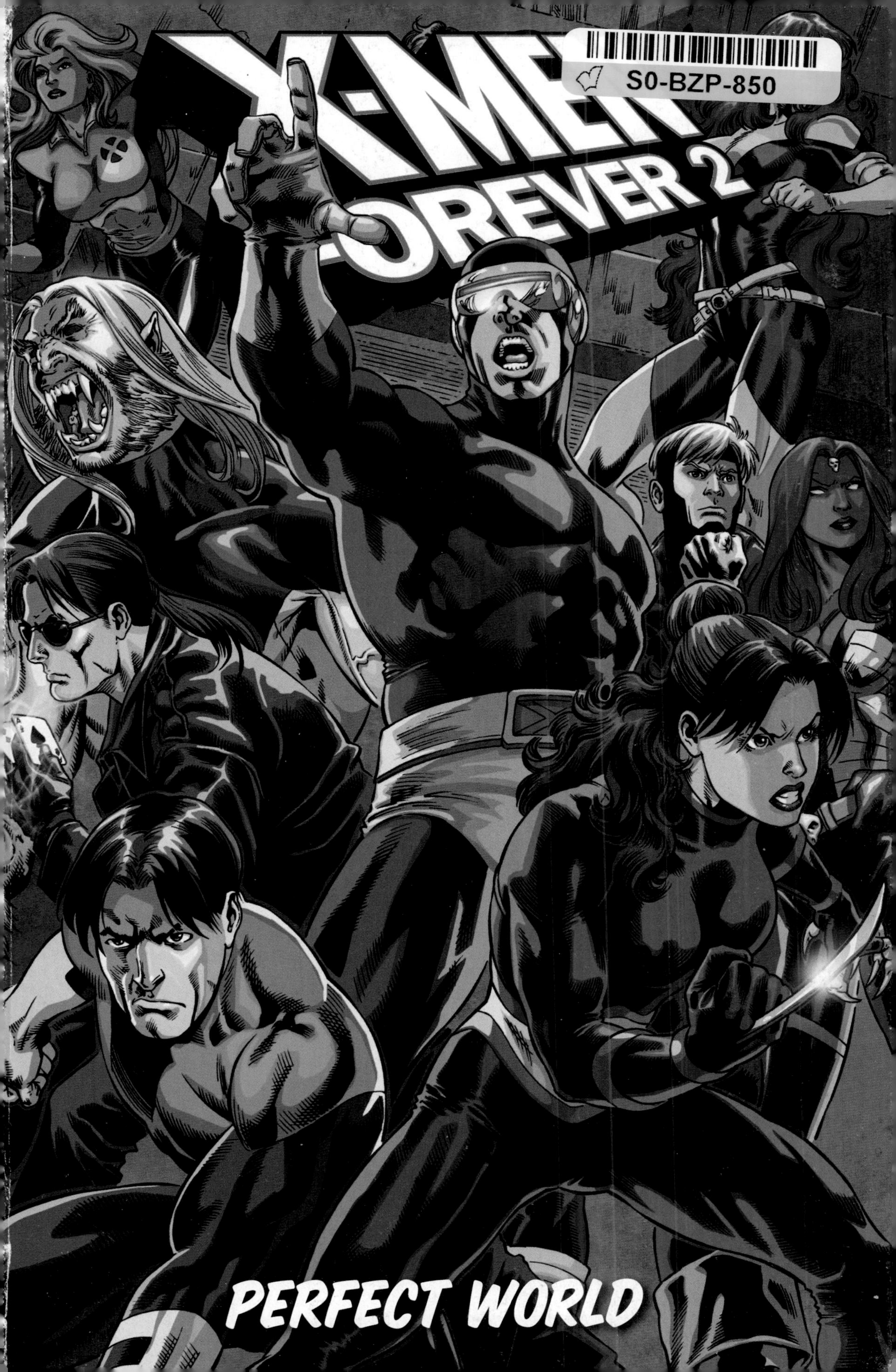
X-MEN
FOREVER 2
PERFECT WORLD

X-MEN FOREVER 2

PERFECT WORLD

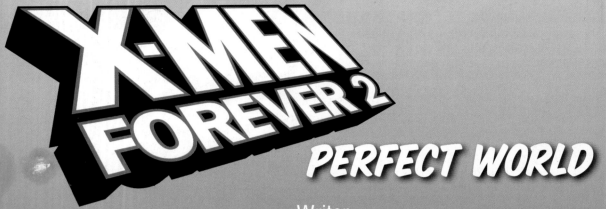

Writer
CHRIS CLAREMONT

Pencilers
RODNEY BUCHEMI (ISSUES #11-12), ROBERT ATKINS (ISSUE #13), ANDY SMITH (ISSUES #14-15), & RAMON ROSANAS (ISSUE #16)

Inkers
GREG ADAMS (ISSUES #11-12), RICK KETCHAM WITH SANDU FLOREA (ISSUE #13), CORY HAMSCHER (ISSUES #14-15) & RAMON ROSANAS (ISSUES #16)

Colorists
WIL QUINTANA (ISSUES #11-15) & RAMON ROSANAS (ISSUE #16)

Letterers
TOM ORZECHOWSKI (ISSUES #11-12 & #14-16) & DAVE SHARPE (ISSUE #13)

Cover Art
TOM GRUMMETT WITH CORY HAMSCHER, MORRY HOLLOWELL, WILFREDO QUINTANA, CHRIS SOTOMAYOR, MATT MILLA & BRAD ANDERSON

Editors
MICHAEL HORWITZ & JORDAN D. WHITE

Consulting Editor
MARC SUMERAK

Senior Editor
MARK PANICCIA

Collection Editor: **JENNIFER GRÜNWALD** • Editorial Assistants: **JAMES EMMETT & JOE HOCHSTEIN**
Assistant Editors: **ALEX STARBUCK & NELSON RIBEIRO**
Editor, Special Projects: **MARK D. BEAZLEY** • Senior Editor, Special Projects: **JEFF YOUNGQUIST**
Senior Vice President of Sales: **DAVID GABRIEL**

Editor in Chief: **AXEL ALONSO** • Chief Creative Officer: **JOE QUESADA**
Publisher: **DAN BUCKLEY** • Executive Producer: **ALAN FINE**

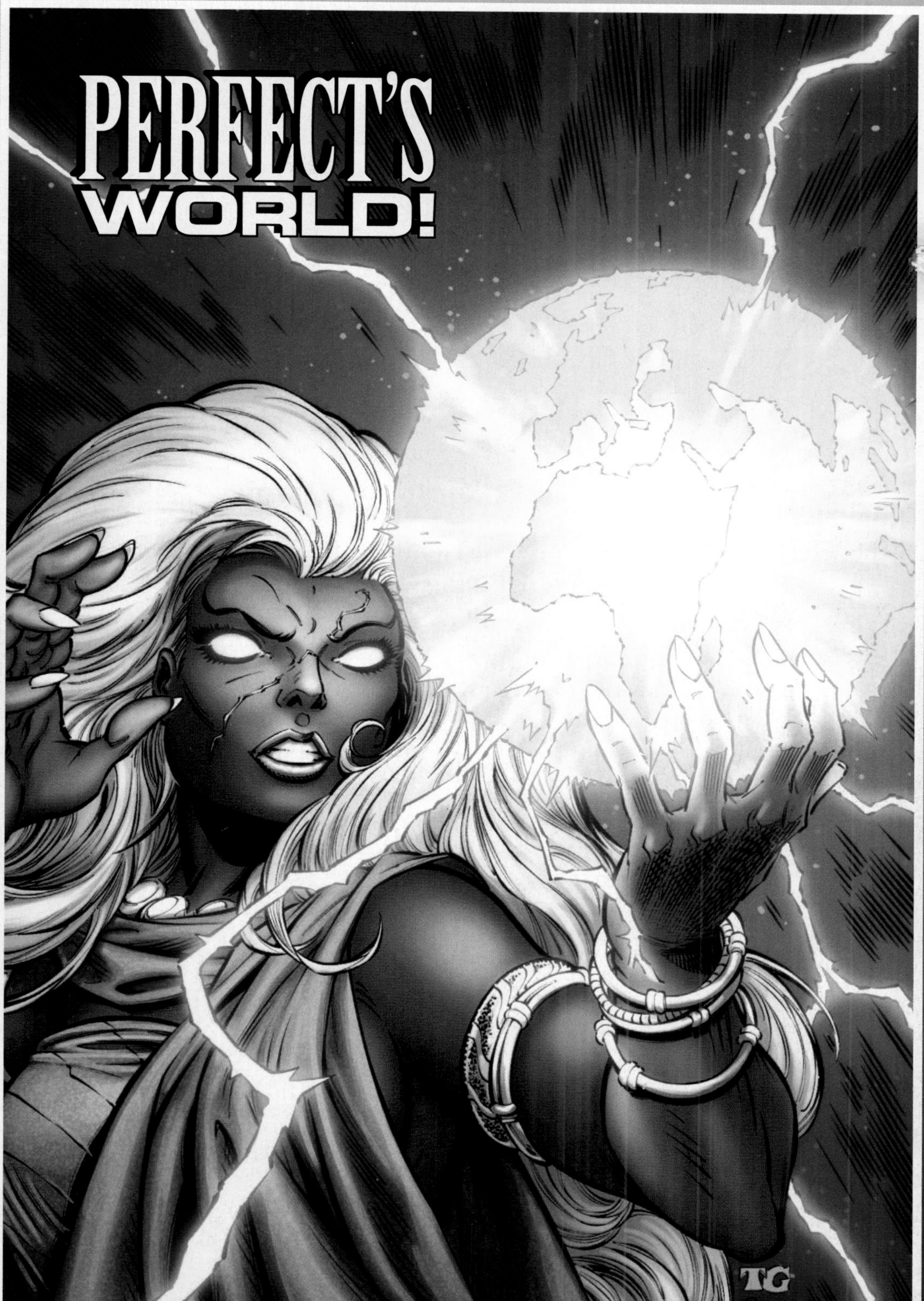
PERFECT'S
WORLD!
TG

ELEVEN

mics legend Chris Claremont had an epic 16-year run on **X-MEN**, which conclude
n **X-MEN: MUTANT GENESIS** *#1-3 in 1991. Now, in an unprecedented comics even*
Claremont returns to his iconic run on the **X-MEN**.

Previously, in

X-MEN FOREVER

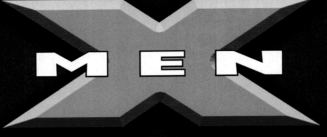

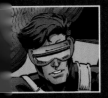

CYCLOPS
Scott Summers

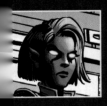

ROGUE
na Marie Raven

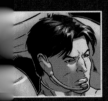

NIGHT-CRAWLER
Kurt Wagner

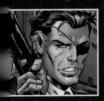

NICK FURY
Director of S.H.I.E.L.D.

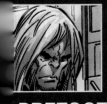

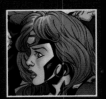

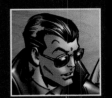

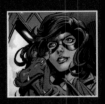

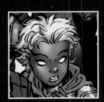

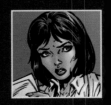

The X-Men's efforts to cure Mutant Burnout – a condition that sentences mutants to an early death – have placed them in opposition to the anti-mutant cabal known as the Consortium, with both Wolverine and Beast among the casualties of their conflict... or so it seemed...

Mr. Sinister's evil clone of Logan has returned, and he wants Kitty Pryde dead! After narrowly escaping an attack by the crazed clone, Kitty and 'Ro find themselves arrested in Tokyo, and quickly released on the orders of Mariko, the leader of the Yashida Clan and controller of The Consortium!

Mariko betrays them and they are ambushed by a squadron of S.H.I.E.L.D. agents. They are joined in the battle by the timely interference of Gambit and Jean Grey, who help them to fend off their attackers.

When the dust clears however, they discover that their ranks have been diminished. Ro has been captured to be taken before the Hand's newest ally:

JEAN GREY

GAMBIT
Remy Picard

SHADOWCA
Kitty Pryde

LIL' 'RO
Ororo Munroe?

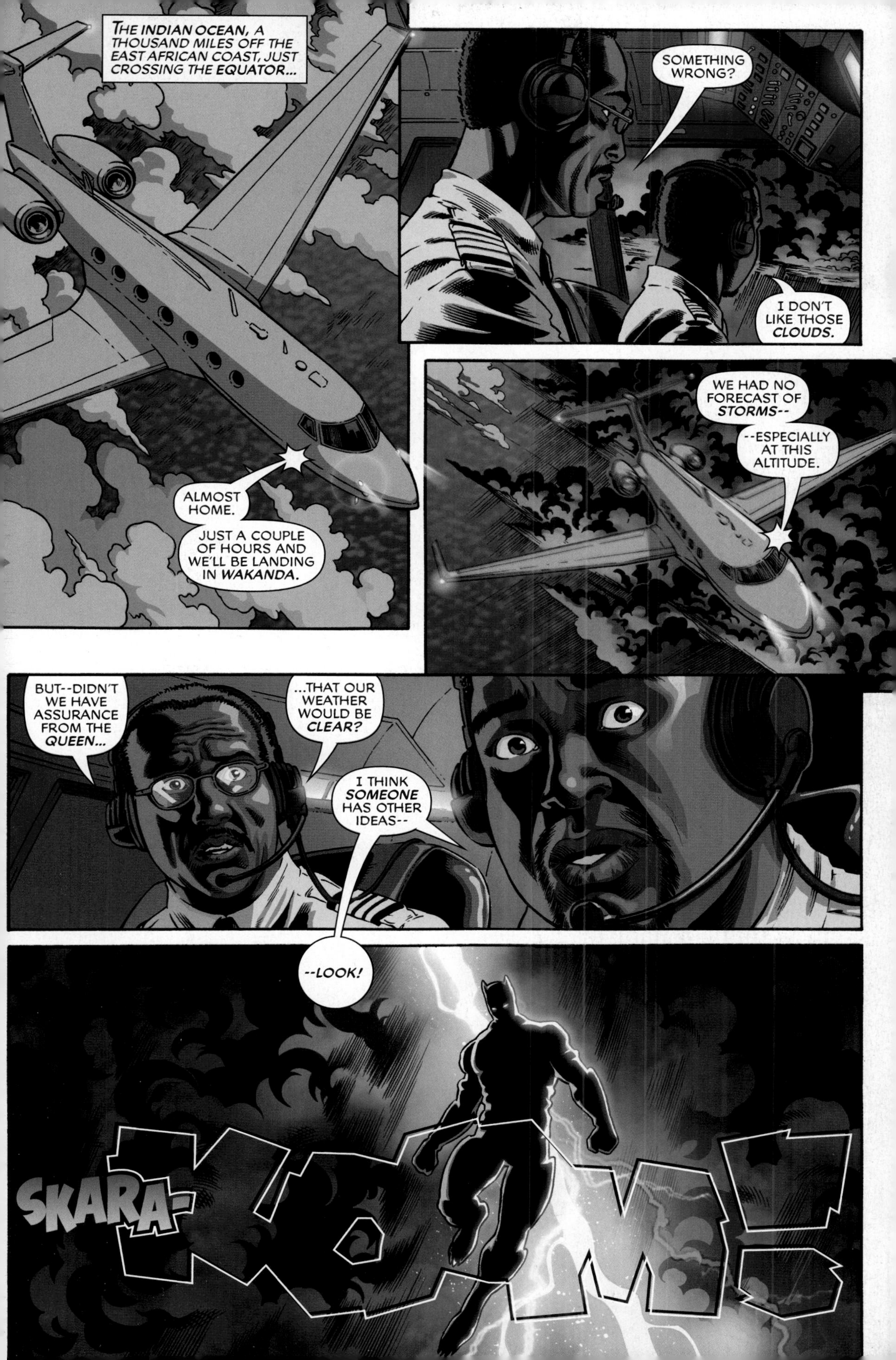
THE INDIAN OCEAN, A THOUSAND MILES OFF THE EAST AFRICAN COAST, JUST CROSSING THE EQUATOR...
SOMETHING WRONG?
I DON'T LIKE THOSE CLOUDS.
ALMOST HOME.
JUST A COUPLE OF HOURS AND WE'LL BE LANDING IN WAKANDA.
WE HAD NO FORECAST OF STORMS--
--ESPECIALLY AT THIS ALTITUDE.
BUT--DIDN'T WE HAVE ASSURANCE FROM THE QUEEN...
...THAT OUR WEATHER WOULD BE CLEAR?
I THINK SOMEONE HAS OTHER IDEAS--
--LOOK!
SKARA-KOOM!

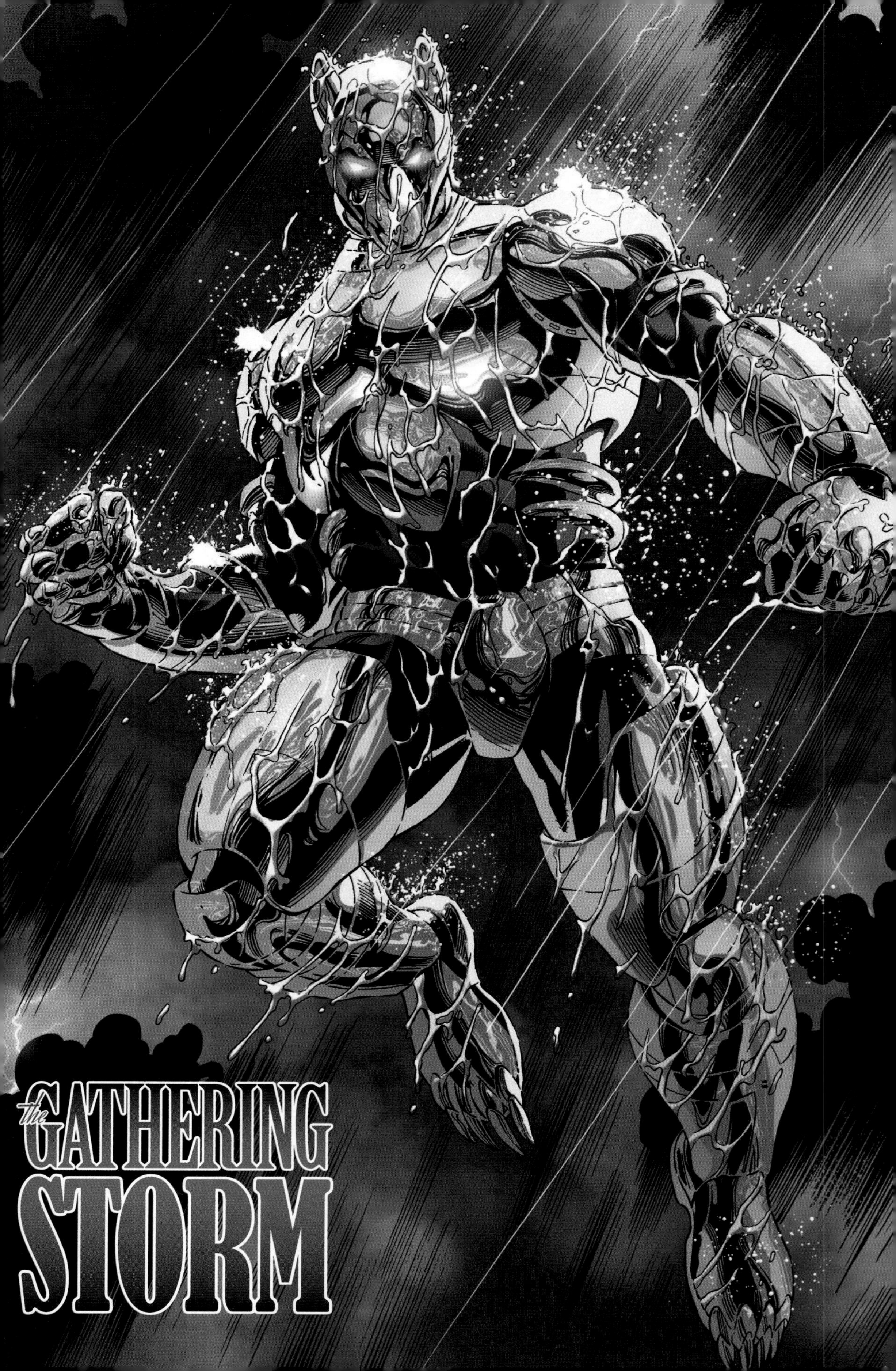
the GATHERING
STORM

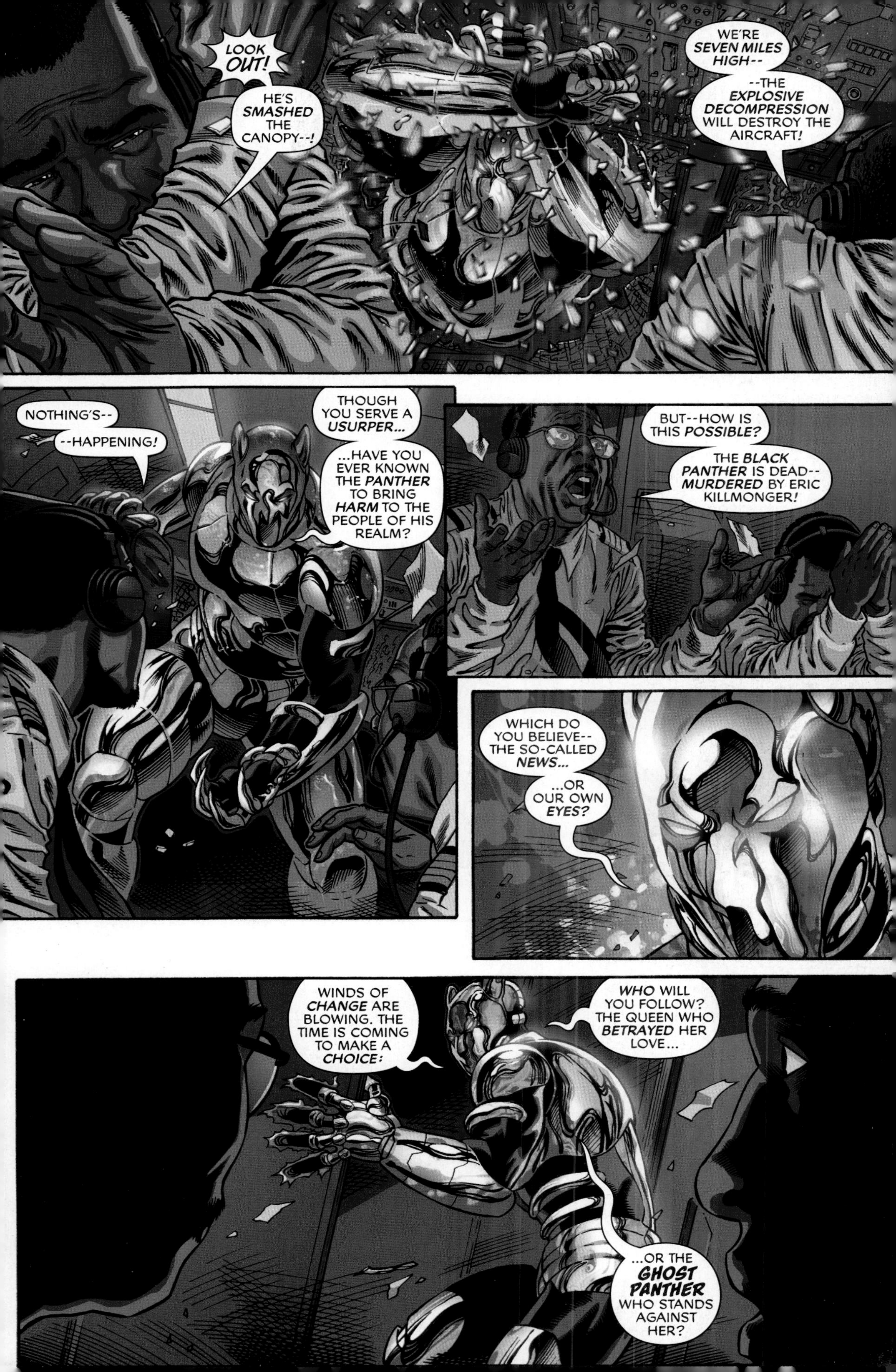
LOOK OUT!
HE'S SMASHED THE CANOPY--!
WE'RE SEVEN MILES HIGH--
--THE EXPLOSIVE DECOMPRESSION WILL DESTROY THE AIRCRAFT!
NOTHING'S--
--HAPPENING!
THOUGH YOU SERVE A USURPER...
...HAVE YOU EVER KNOWN THE PANTHER TO BRING HARM TO THE PEOPLE OF HIS REALM?
BUT--HOW IS THIS POSSIBLE?
THE BLACK PANTHER IS DEAD--MURDERED BY ERIC KILLMONGER!
WHICH DO YOU BELIEVE--THE SO-CALLED NEWS...
...OR OUR OWN EYES?
WINDS OF CHANGE ARE BLOWING. THE TIME IS COMING TO MAKE A CHOICE:
WHO WILL YOU FOLLOW? THE QUEEN WHO BETRAYED HER LOVE...
...OR THE GHOST PANTHER WHO STANDS AGAINST HER?

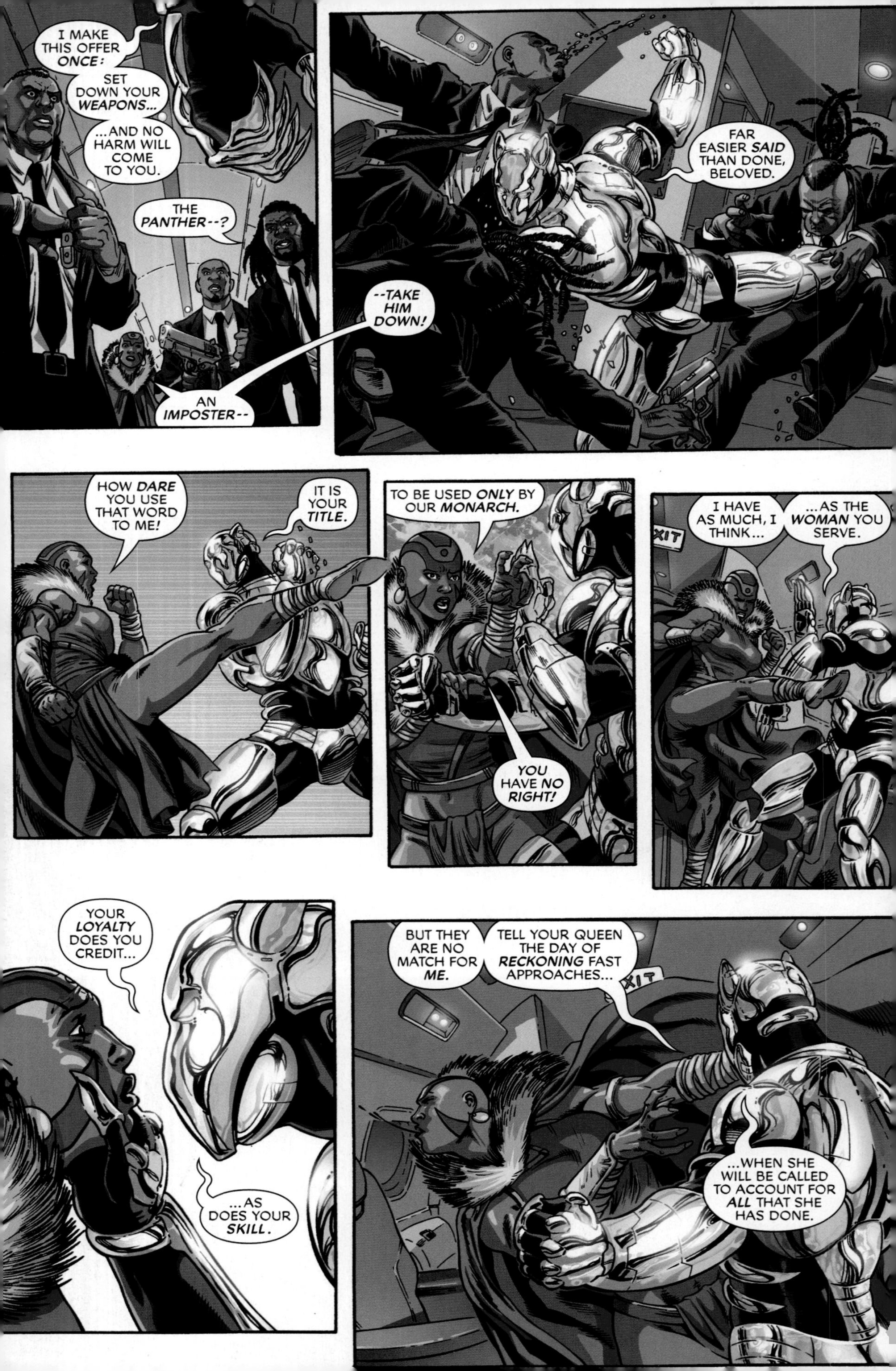
I MAKE THIS OFFER ONCE:
SET DOWN YOUR WEAPONS...
...AND NO HARM WILL COME TO YOU.
THE PANTHER--?
AN IMPOSTER--
--TAKE HIM DOWN!
FAR EASIER SAID THAN DONE, BELOVED.
HOW DARE YOU USE THAT WORD TO ME!
IT IS YOUR TITLE.
TO BE USED ONLY BY OUR MONARCH.
YOU HAVE NO RIGHT!
I HAVE AS MUCH, I THINK...
...AS THE WOMAN YOU SERVE.
YOUR LOYALTY DOES YOU CREDIT...
...AS DOES YOUR SKILL.
BUT THEY ARE NO MATCH FOR ME.
TELL YOUR QUEEN THE DAY OF RECKONING FAST APPROACHES...
...WHEN SHE WILL BE CALLED TO ACCOUNT FOR ALL THAT SHE HAS DONE.

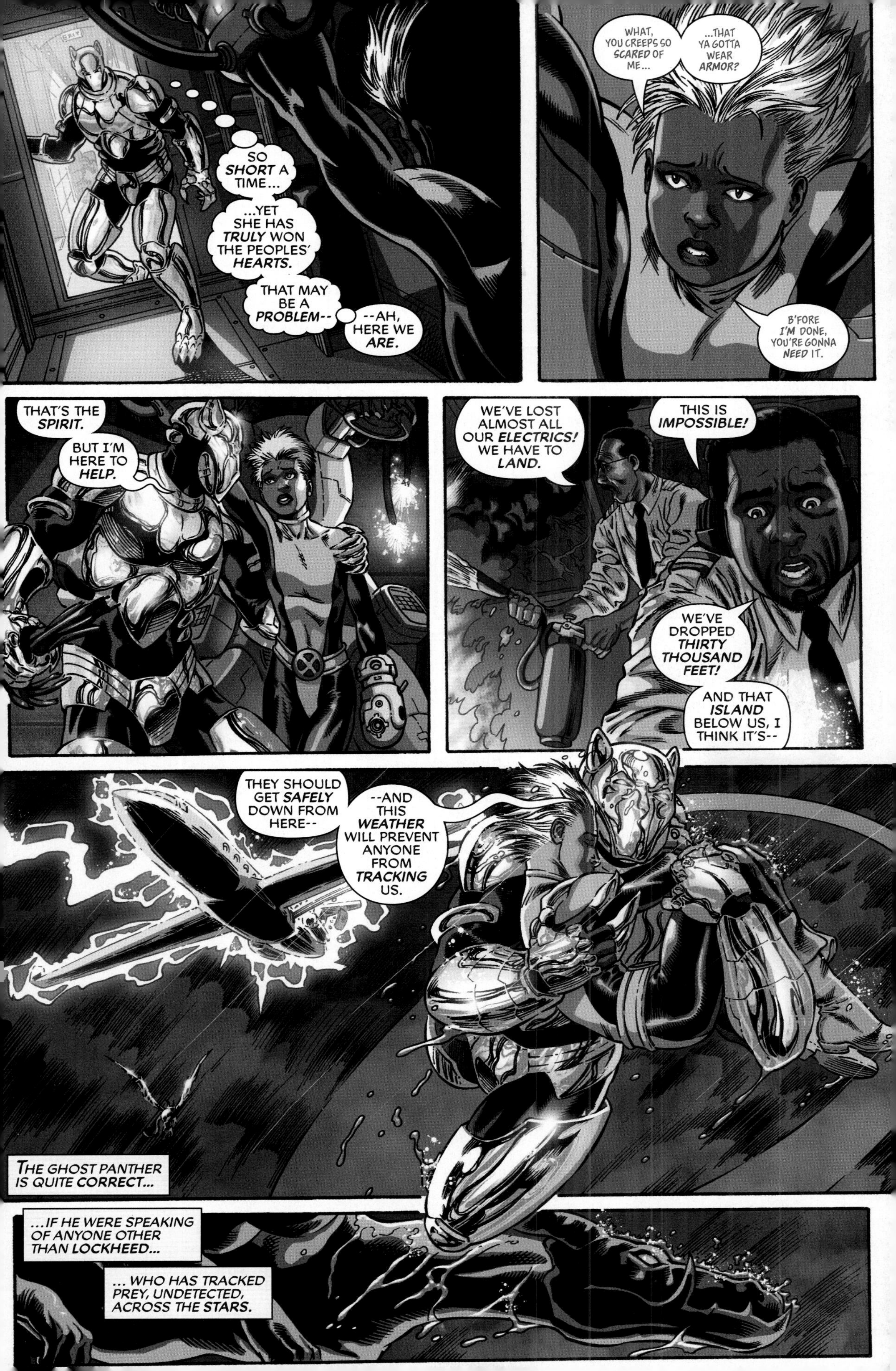
SO SHORT A TIME...
...YET SHE HAS TRULY WON THE PEOPLES' HEARTS.
THAT MAY BE A PROBLEM--
--AH, HERE WE ARE.
WHAT, YOU CREEPS SO SCARED OF ME...
...THAT YA GOTTA WEAR ARMOR?
B'FORE I'M DONE, YOU'RE GONNA NEED IT.
THAT'S THE SPIRIT.
BUT I'M HERE TO HELP.
WE'VE LOST ALMOST ALL OUR ELECTRICS! WE HAVE TO LAND.
THIS IS IMPOSSIBLE!
WE'VE DROPPED THIRTY THOUSAND FEET!
AND THAT ISLAND BELOW US, I THINK IT'S--
THEY SHOULD GET SAFELY DOWN FROM HERE--
--AND THIS WEATHER WILL PREVENT ANYONE FROM TRACKING US.
THE GHOST PANTHER IS QUITE CORRECT...
...IF HE WERE SPEAKING OF ANYONE OTHER THAN LOCKHEED...
...WHO HAS TRACKED PREY, UNDETECTED, ACROSS THE STARS.

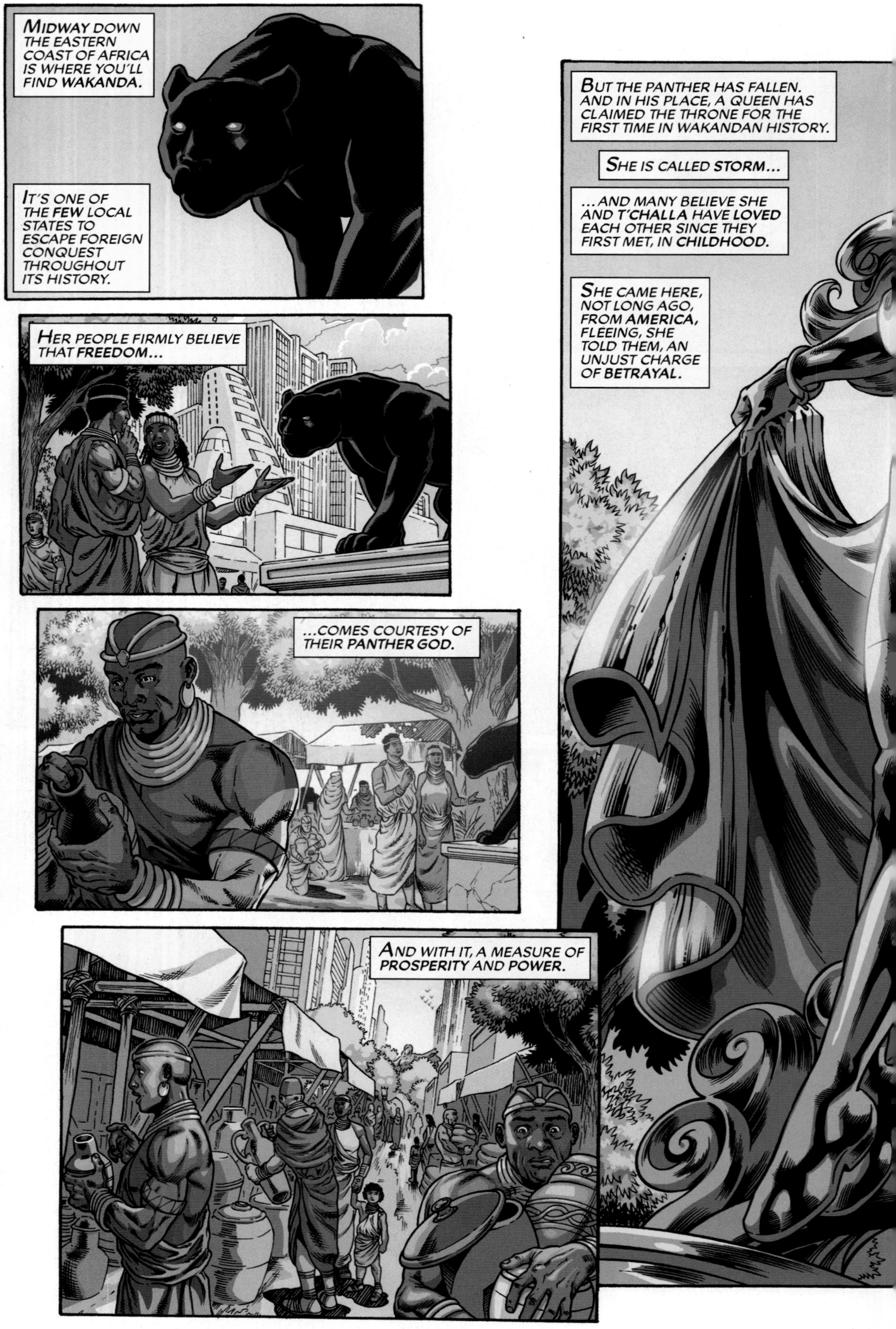
MIDWAY DOWN THE EASTERN COAST OF AFRICA IS WHERE YOU'LL FIND WAKANDA.
IT'S ONE OF THE FEW LOCAL STATES TO ESCAPE FOREIGN CONQUEST THROUGHOUT ITS HISTORY.
HER PEOPLE FIRMLY BELIEVE THAT FREEDOM...
...COMES COURTESY OF THEIR PANTHER GOD.
AND WITH IT, A MEASURE OF PROSPERITY AND POWER.
BUT THE PANTHER HAS FALLEN. AND IN HIS PLACE, A QUEEN HAS CLAIMED THE THRONE FOR THE FIRST TIME IN WAKANDAN HISTORY.
SHE IS CALLED STORM...
...AND MANY BELIEVE SHE AND T'CHALLA HAVE LOVED EACH OTHER SINCE THEY FIRST MET, IN CHILDHOOD.
SHE CAME HERE, NOT LONG AGO, FROM AMERICA, FLEEING, SHE TOLD THEM, AN UNJUST CHARGE OF BETRAYAL.

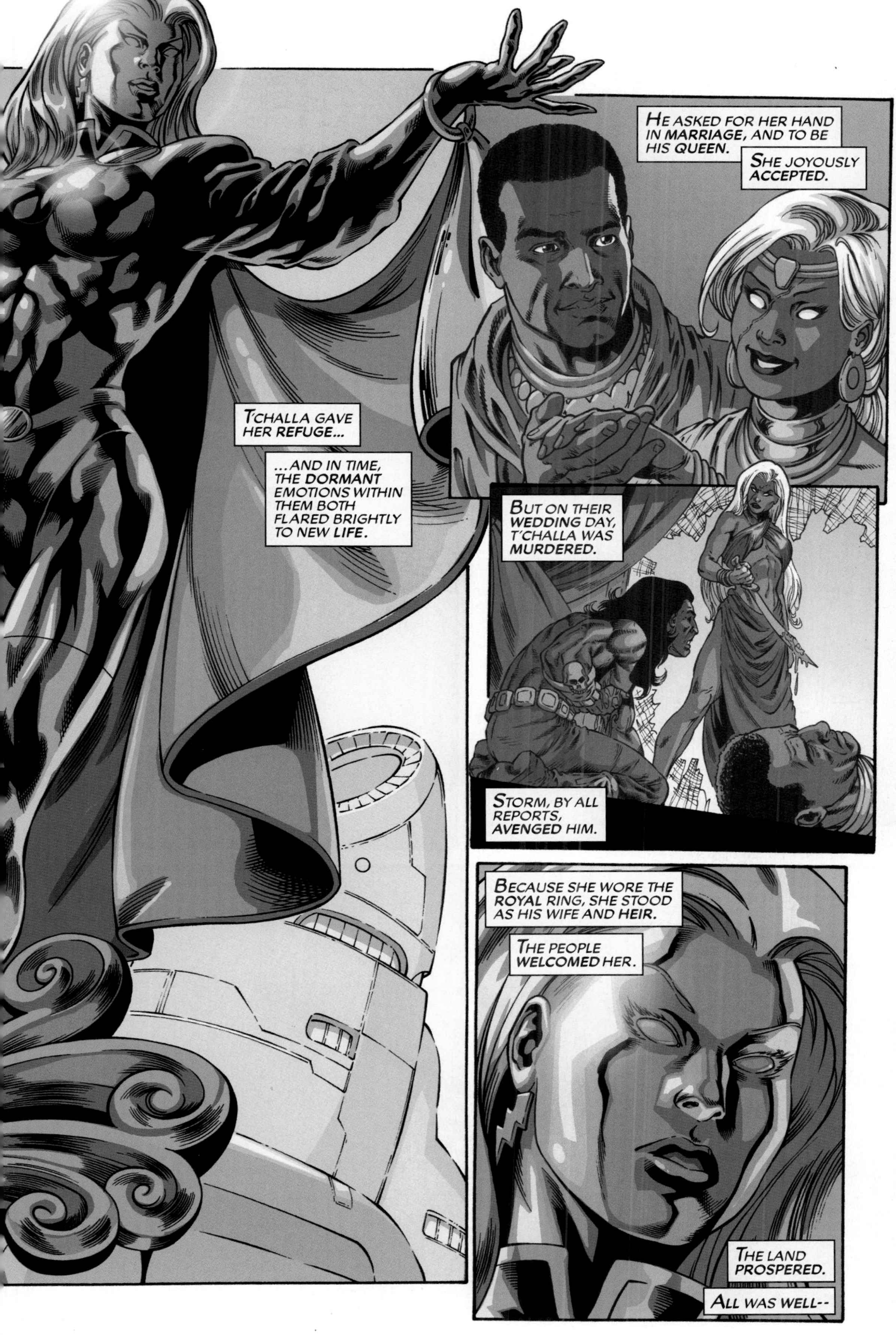
T'CHALLA GAVE HER REFUGE...
...AND IN TIME, THE DORMANT EMOTIONS WITHIN THEM BOTH FLARED BRIGHTLY TO NEW LIFE.
HE ASKED FOR HER HAND IN MARRIAGE, AND TO BE HIS QUEEN.
SHE JOYOUSLY ACCEPTED.
BUT ON THEIR WEDDING DAY, T'CHALLA WAS MURDERED.
STORM, BY ALL REPORTS, AVENGED HIM.
BECAUSE SHE WORE THE ROYAL RING, SHE STOOD AS HIS WIFE AND HEIR.
THE PEOPLE WELCOMED HER.
THE LAND PROSPERED.
ALL WAS WELL--

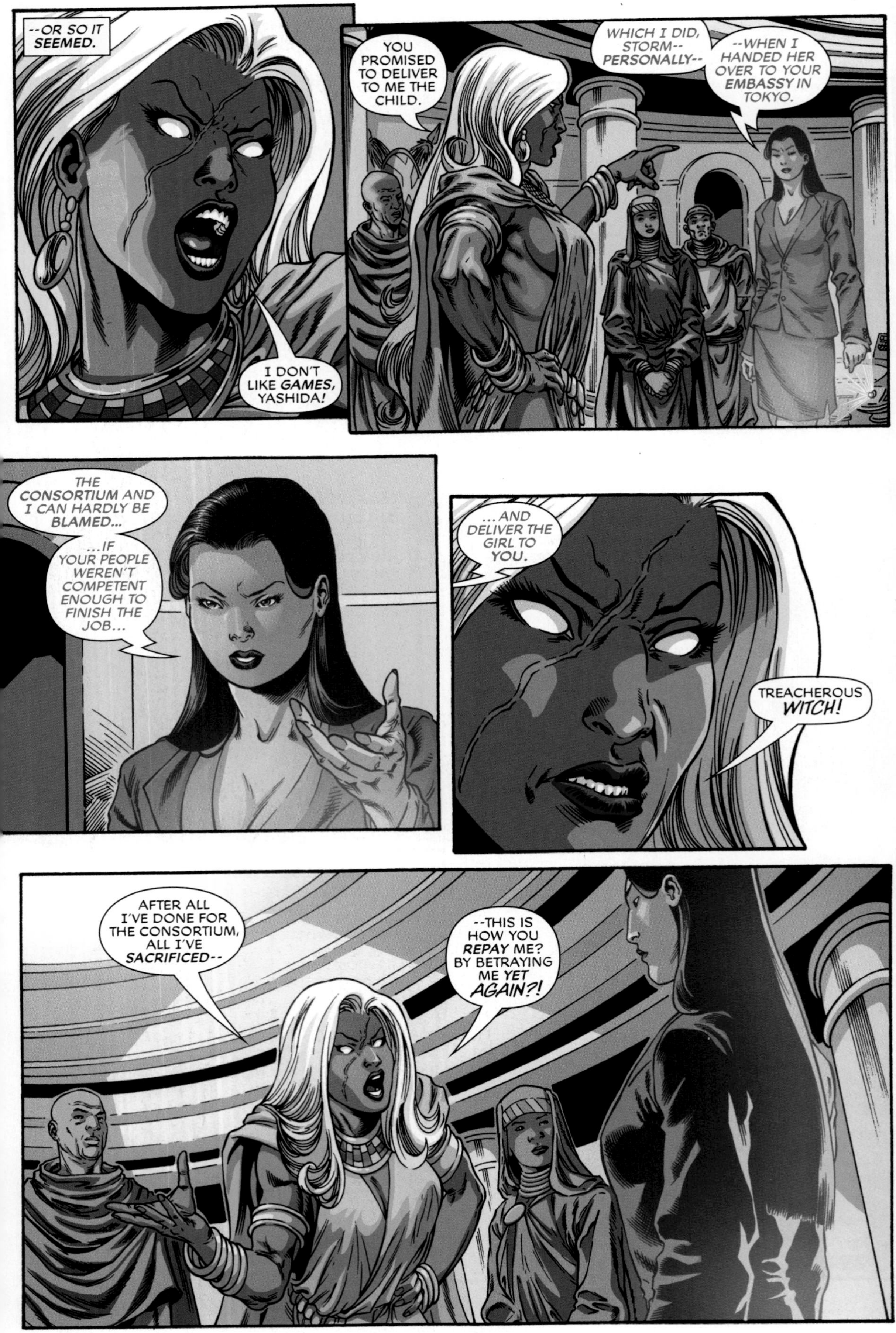
--OR SO IT SEEMED.
I DON'T LIKE GAMES, YASHIDA!
YOU PROMISED TO DELIVER TO ME THE CHILD.
WHICH I DID, STORM-- PERSONALLY--
--WHEN I HANDED HER OVER TO YOUR EMBASSY IN TOKYO.
THE CONSORTIUM AND I CAN HARDLY BE BLAMED...
...IF YOUR PEOPLE WEREN'T COMPETENT ENOUGH TO FINISH THE JOB...
...AND DELIVER THE GIRL TO YOU.
TREACHEROUS WITCH!
AFTER ALL I'VE DONE FOR THE CONSORTIUM, ALL I'VE SACRIFICED--
--THIS IS HOW YOU REPAY ME? BY BETRAYING ME YET AGAIN?!

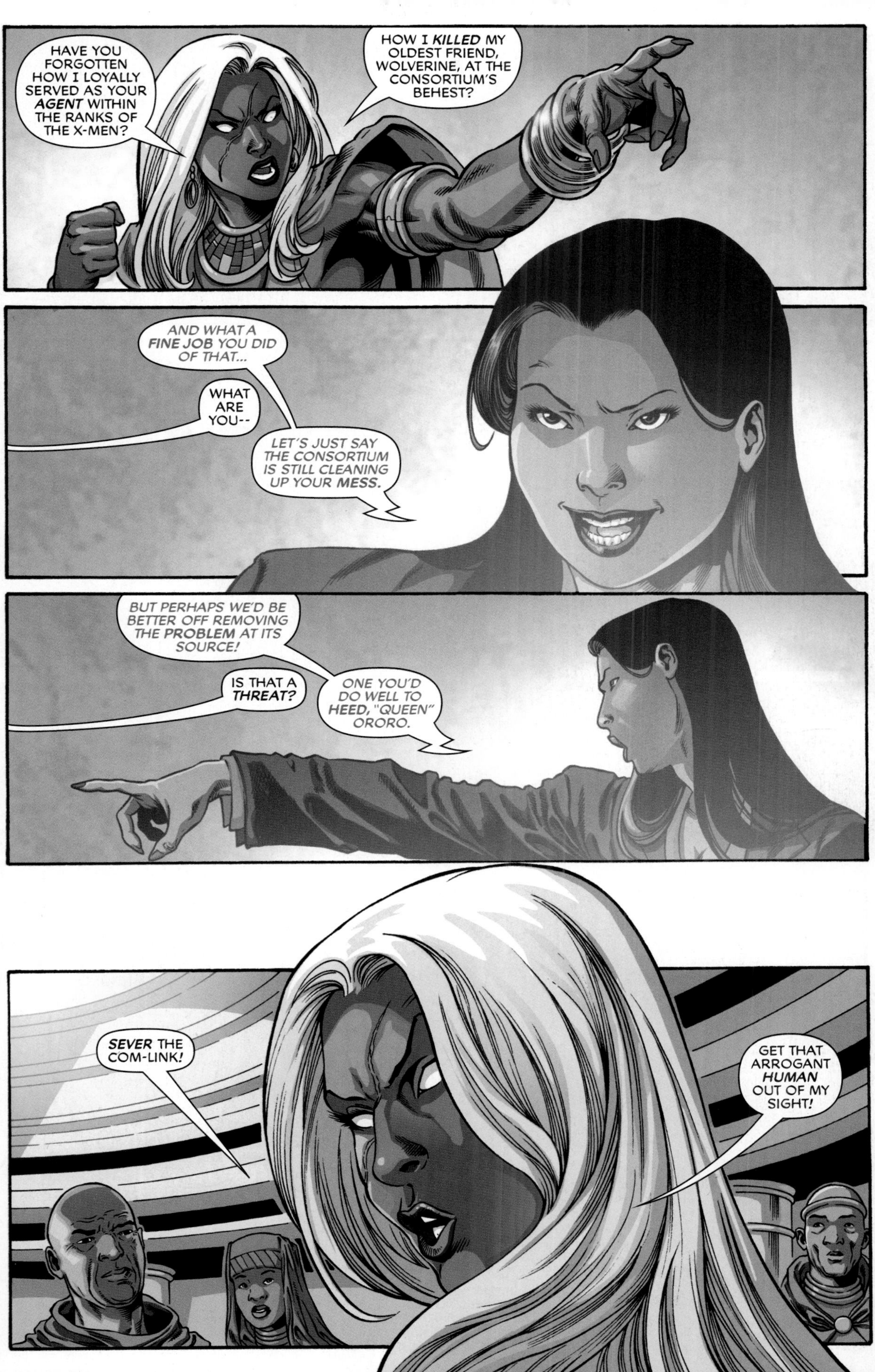
HAVE YOU FORGOTTEN HOW I LOYALLY SERVED AS YOUR AGENT WITHIN THE RANKS OF THE X-MEN?
HOW I KILLED MY OLDEST FRIEND, WOLVERINE, AT THE CONSORTIUM'S BEHEST?
AND WHAT A FINE JOB YOU DID OF THAT...
WHAT ARE YOU--
LET'S JUST SAY THE CONSORTIUM IS STILL CLEANING UP YOUR MESS.
BUT PERHAPS WE'D BE BETTER OFF REMOVING THE PROBLEM AT ITS SOURCE!
IS THAT A THREAT?
ONE YOU'D DO WELL TO HEED, "QUEEN" ORORO.
SEVER THE COM-LINK!
GET THAT ARROGANT HUMAN OUT OF MY SIGHT!

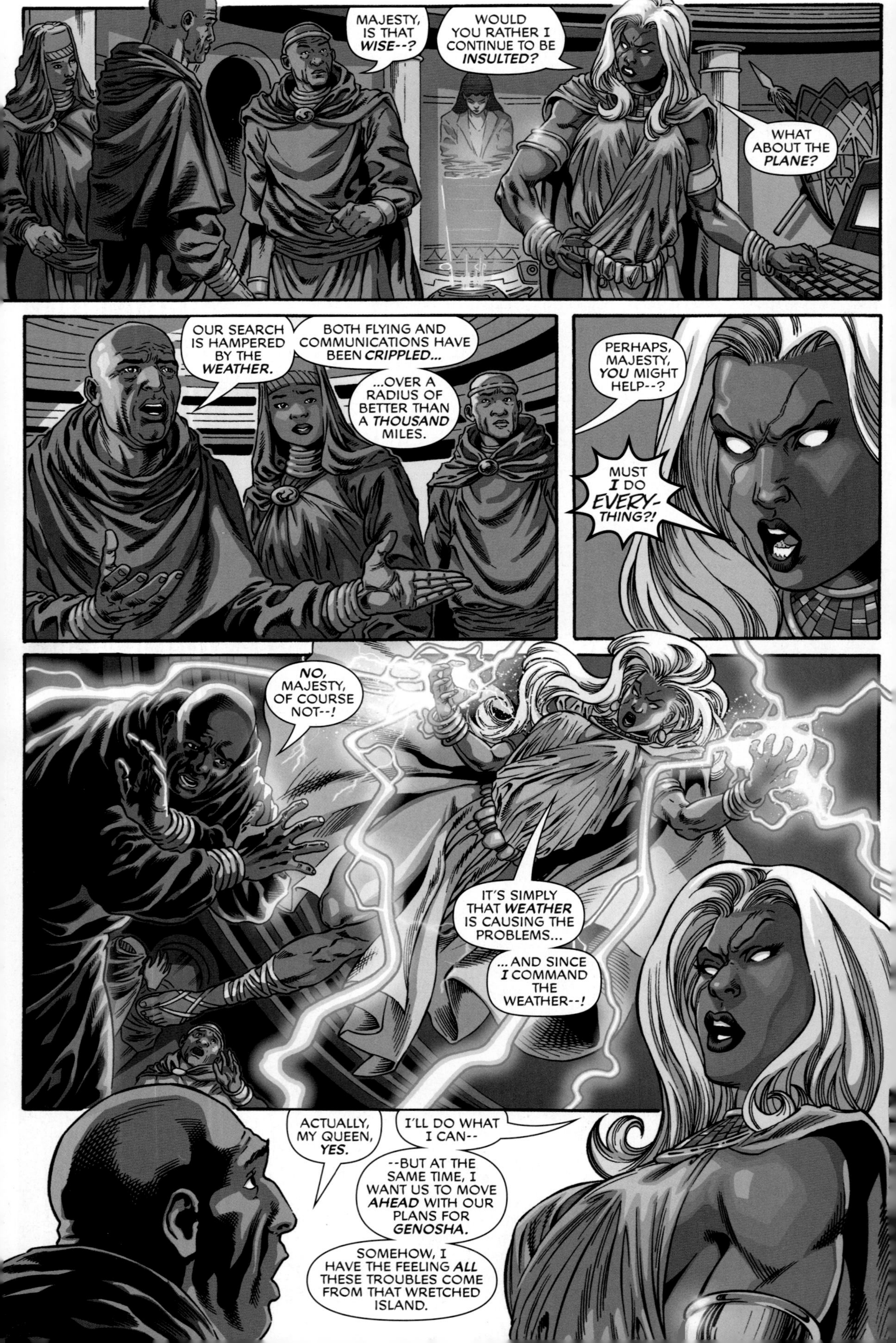
MAJESTY, IS THAT *WISE--?*
WOULD YOU RATHER I CONTINUE TO BE *INSULTED?*
WHAT ABOUT THE *PLANE?*
OUR SEARCH IS HAMPERED BY THE *WEATHER.*
BOTH FLYING AND COMMUNICATIONS HAVE BEEN *CRIPPLED...*
...OVER A RADIUS OF BETTER THAN A *THOUSAND* MILES.
PERHAPS, MAJESTY, *YOU* MIGHT HELP--?
MUST *I* DO *EVERY-THING?!*
NO, MAJESTY, OF COURSE NOT--!
IT'S SIMPLY THAT *WEATHER* IS CAUSING THE PROBLEMS...
...AND SINCE *I* COMMAND THE WEATHER--!
ACTUALLY, MY QUEEN, *YES.*
I'LL DO WHAT I CAN--
--BUT AT THE SAME TIME, I WANT US TO MOVE *AHEAD* WITH OUR PLANS FOR *GENOSHA.*
SOMEHOW, I HAVE THE FEELING *ALL* THESE TROUBLES COME FROM THAT WRETCHED ISLAND.

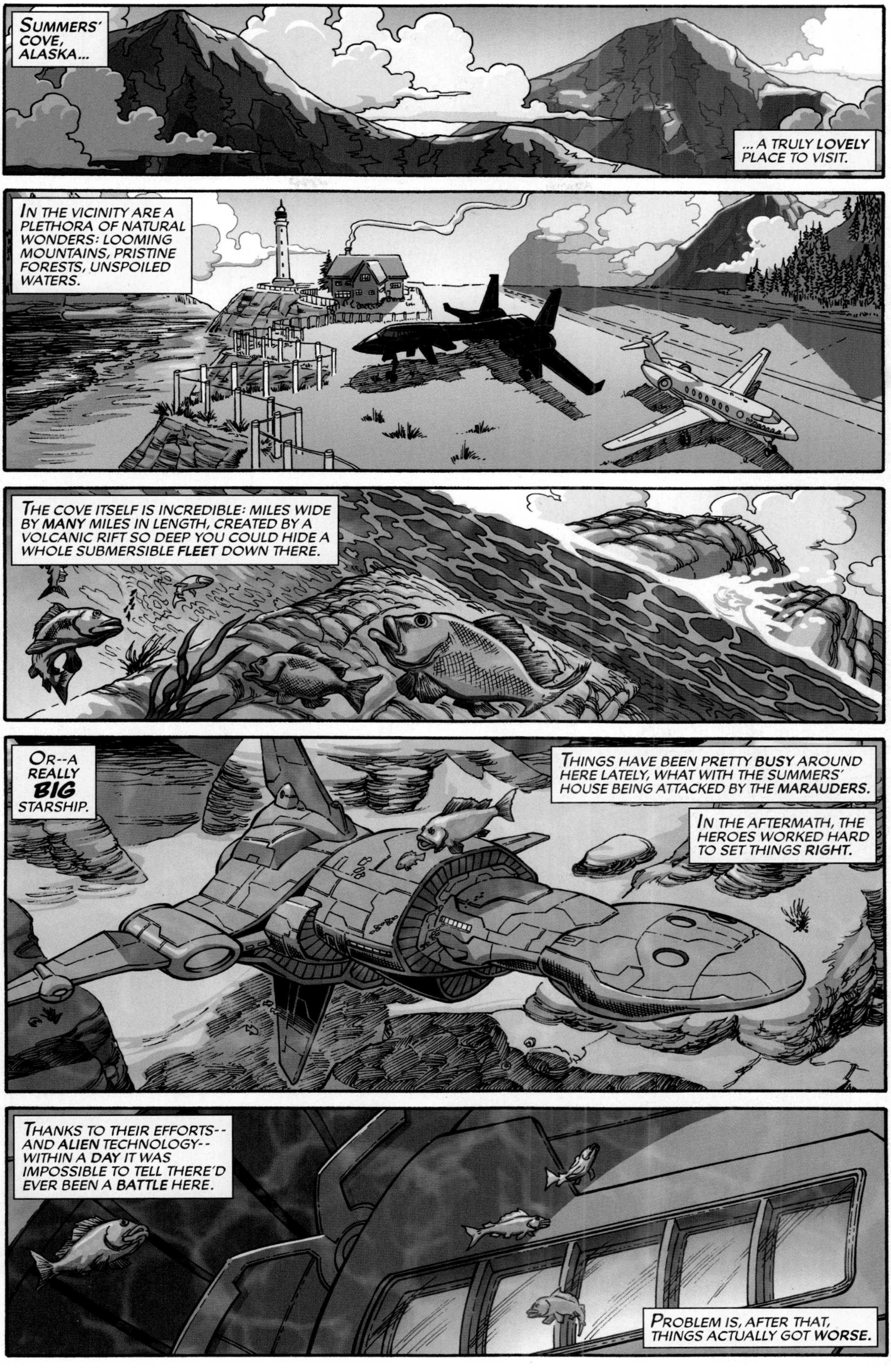

SUMMERS' COVE, ALASKA...
...A TRULY LOVELY PLACE TO VISIT.
IN THE VICINITY ARE A PLETHORA OF NATURAL WONDERS: LOOMING MOUNTAINS, PRISTINE FORESTS, UNSPOILED WATERS.
THE COVE ITSELF IS INCREDIBLE: MILES WIDE BY MANY MILES IN LENGTH, CREATED BY A VOLCANIC RIFT SO DEEP YOU COULD HIDE A WHOLE SUBMERSIBLE FLEET DOWN THERE.
OR--A REALLY BIG STARSHIP.
THINGS HAVE BEEN PRETTY BUSY AROUND HERE LATELY, WHAT WITH THE SUMMERS' HOUSE BEING ATTACKED BY THE MARAUDERS.
IN THE AFTERMATH, THE HEROES WORKED HARD TO SET THINGS RIGHT.
THANKS TO THEIR EFFORTS-- AND ALIEN TECHNOLOGY-- WITHIN A DAY IT WAS IMPOSSIBLE TO TELL THERE'D EVER BEEN A BATTLE HERE.
PROBLEM IS, AFTER THAT, THINGS ACTUALLY GOT WORSE.

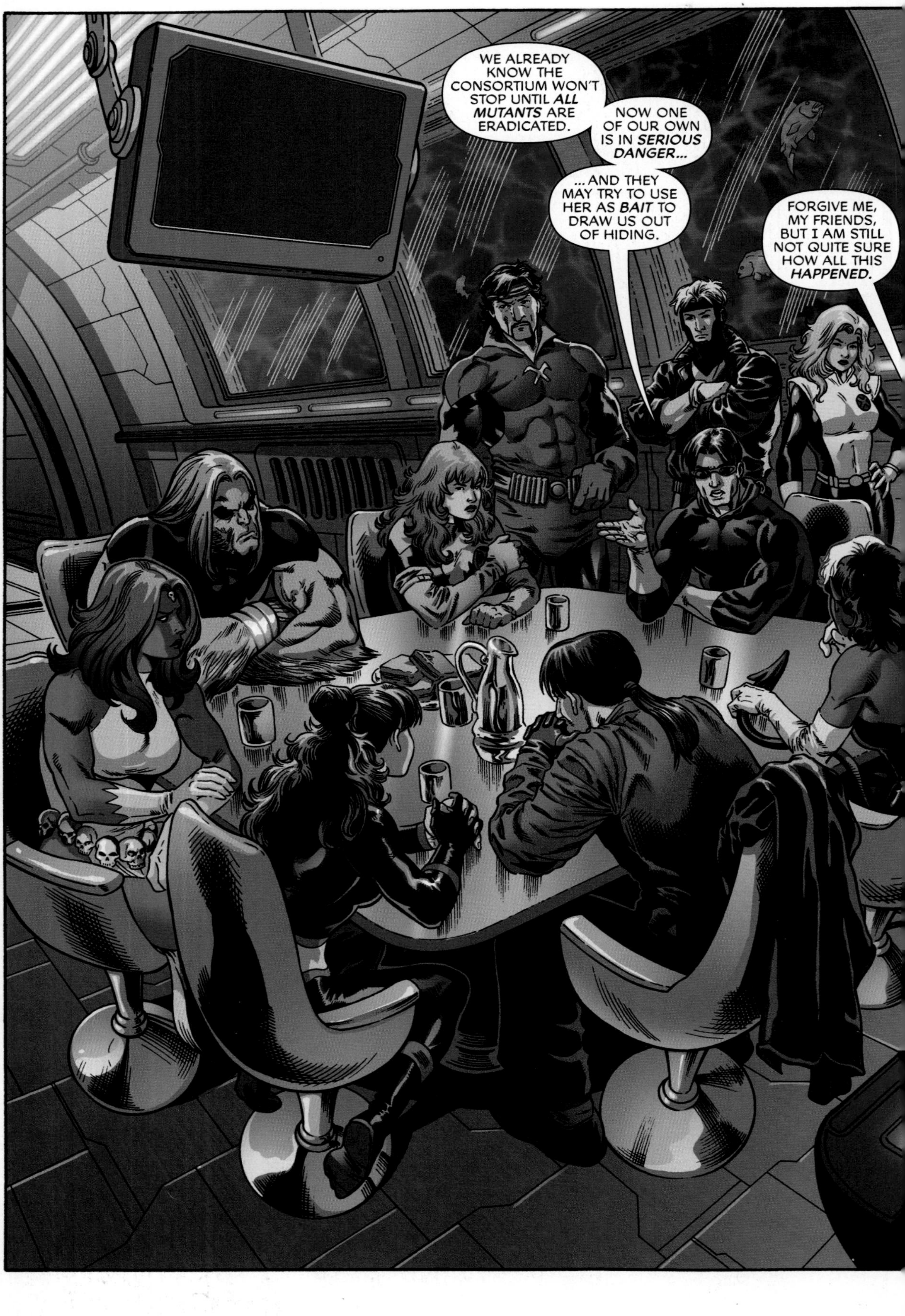
WE ALREADY KNOW THE CONSORTIUM WON'T STOP UNTIL ALL MUTANTS ARE ERADICATED.
NOW ONE OF OUR OWN IS IN SERIOUS DANGER...
...AND THEY MAY TRY TO USE HER AS BAIT TO DRAW US OUT OF HIDING.
FORGIVE ME, MY FRIENDS, BUT I AM STILL NOT QUITE SURE HOW ALL THIS HAPPENED.

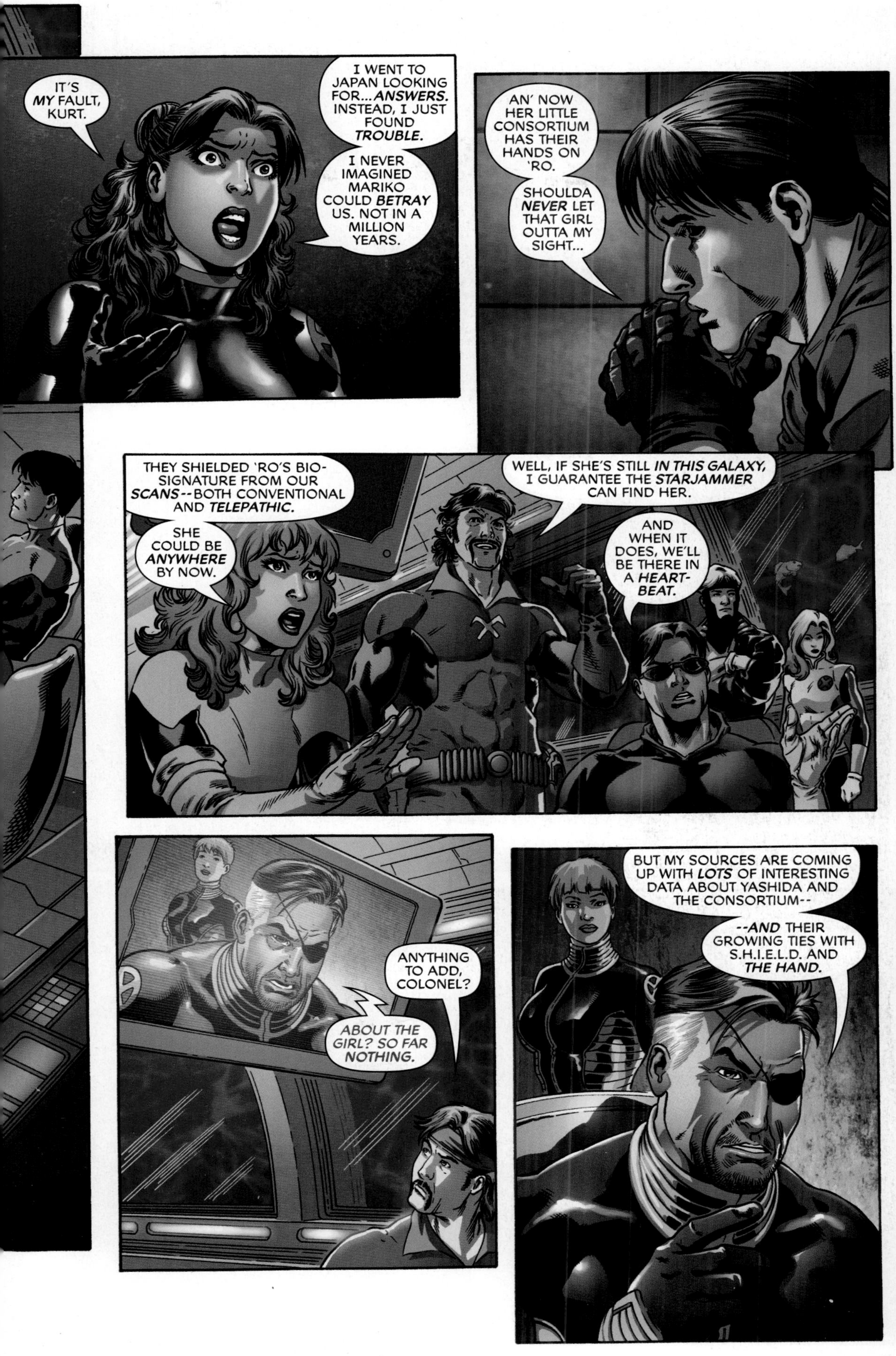
IT'S *MY* FAULT, KURT.
I WENT TO JAPAN LOOKING FOR... *ANSWERS.* INSTEAD, I JUST FOUND *TROUBLE.*
I NEVER IMAGINED MARIKO COULD *BETRAY* US. NOT IN A MILLION YEARS.
AN' NOW HER LITTLE CONSORTIUM HAS THEIR HANDS ON 'RO.
SHOULDA *NEVER* LET THAT GIRL OUTTA MY SIGHT...
THEY SHIELDED 'RO'S BIO-SIGNATURE FROM OUR *SCANS*--BOTH CONVENTIONAL AND *TELEPATHIC.*
SHE COULD BE *ANYWHERE* BY NOW.
WELL, IF SHE'S STILL *IN THIS GALAXY,* I GUARANTEE THE *STARJAMMER* CAN FIND HER.
AND WHEN IT DOES, WE'LL BE THERE IN A *HEART-BEAT.*
ANYTHING TO ADD, COLONEL?
ABOUT THE GIRL? SO FAR NOTHING.
BUT MY SOURCES ARE COMING UP WITH *LOTS* OF INTERESTING DATA ABOUT YASHIDA AND THE CONSORTIUM--
--*AND* THEIR GROWING TIES WITH S.H.I.E.L.D. AND *THE HAND.*

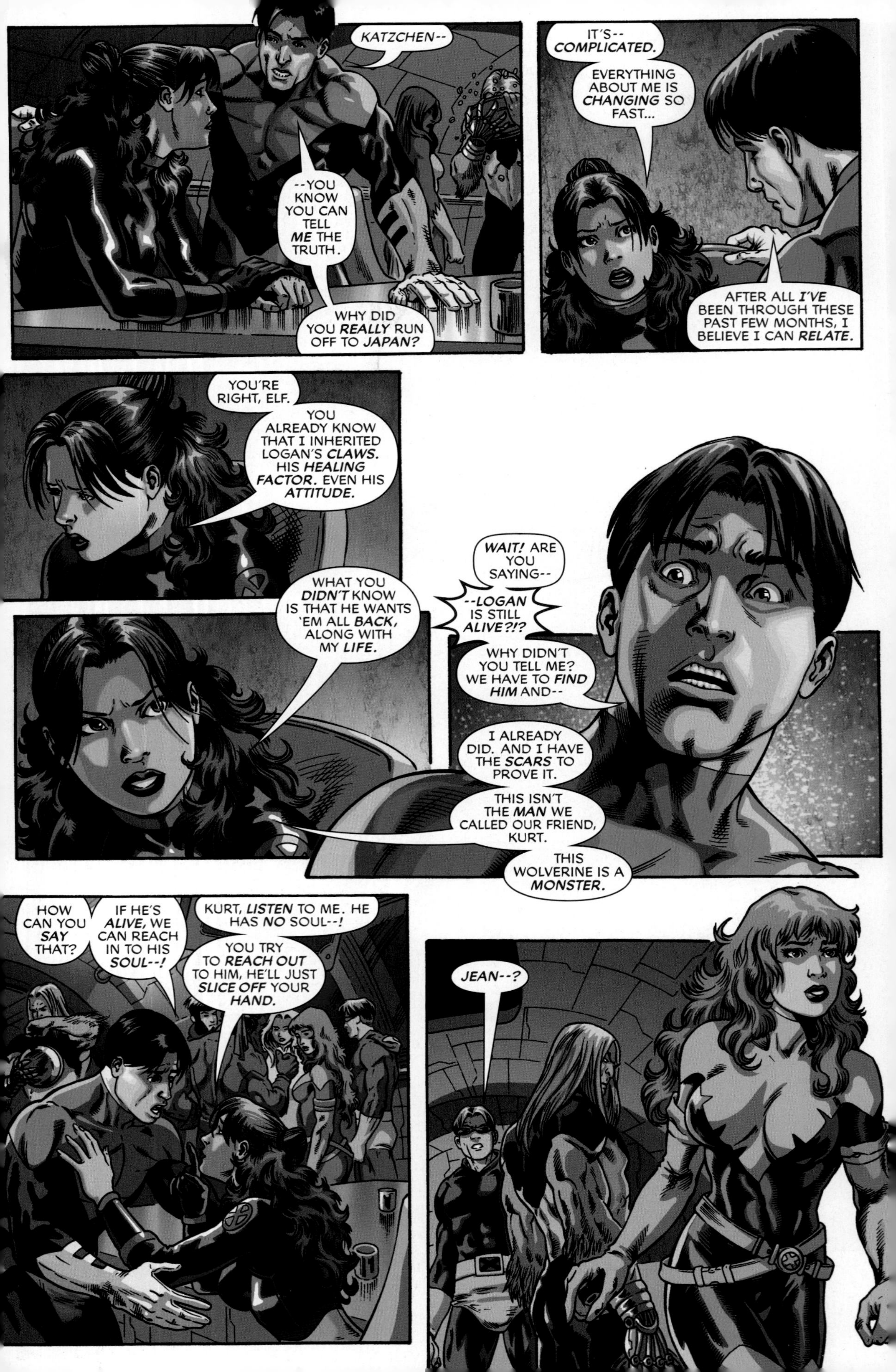
KATZCHEN--
--YOU KNOW YOU CAN TELL ME THE TRUTH.
WHY DID YOU REALLY RUN OFF TO JAPAN?
IT'S--COMPLICATED.
EVERYTHING ABOUT ME IS CHANGING SO FAST...
AFTER ALL I'VE BEEN THROUGH THESE PAST FEW MONTHS, I BELIEVE I CAN RELATE.
YOU'RE RIGHT, ELF.
YOU ALREADY KNOW THAT I INHERITED LOGAN'S CLAWS. HIS HEALING FACTOR. EVEN HIS ATTITUDE.
WHAT YOU DIDN'T KNOW IS THAT HE WANTS 'EM ALL BACK, ALONG WITH MY LIFE.
WAIT! ARE YOU SAYING--
--LOGAN IS STILL ALIVE?!?
WHY DIDN'T YOU TELL ME? WE HAVE TO FIND HIM AND--
I ALREADY DID. AND I HAVE THE SCARS TO PROVE IT.
THIS ISN'T THE MAN WE CALLED OUR FRIEND, KURT.
THIS WOLVERINE IS A MONSTER.
HOW CAN YOU SAY THAT?
IF HE'S ALIVE, WE CAN REACH IN TO HIS SOUL--!
KURT, LISTEN TO ME. HE HAS NO SOUL--!
YOU TRY TO REACH OUT TO HIM, HE'LL JUST SLICE OFF YOUR HAND.
JEAN--?

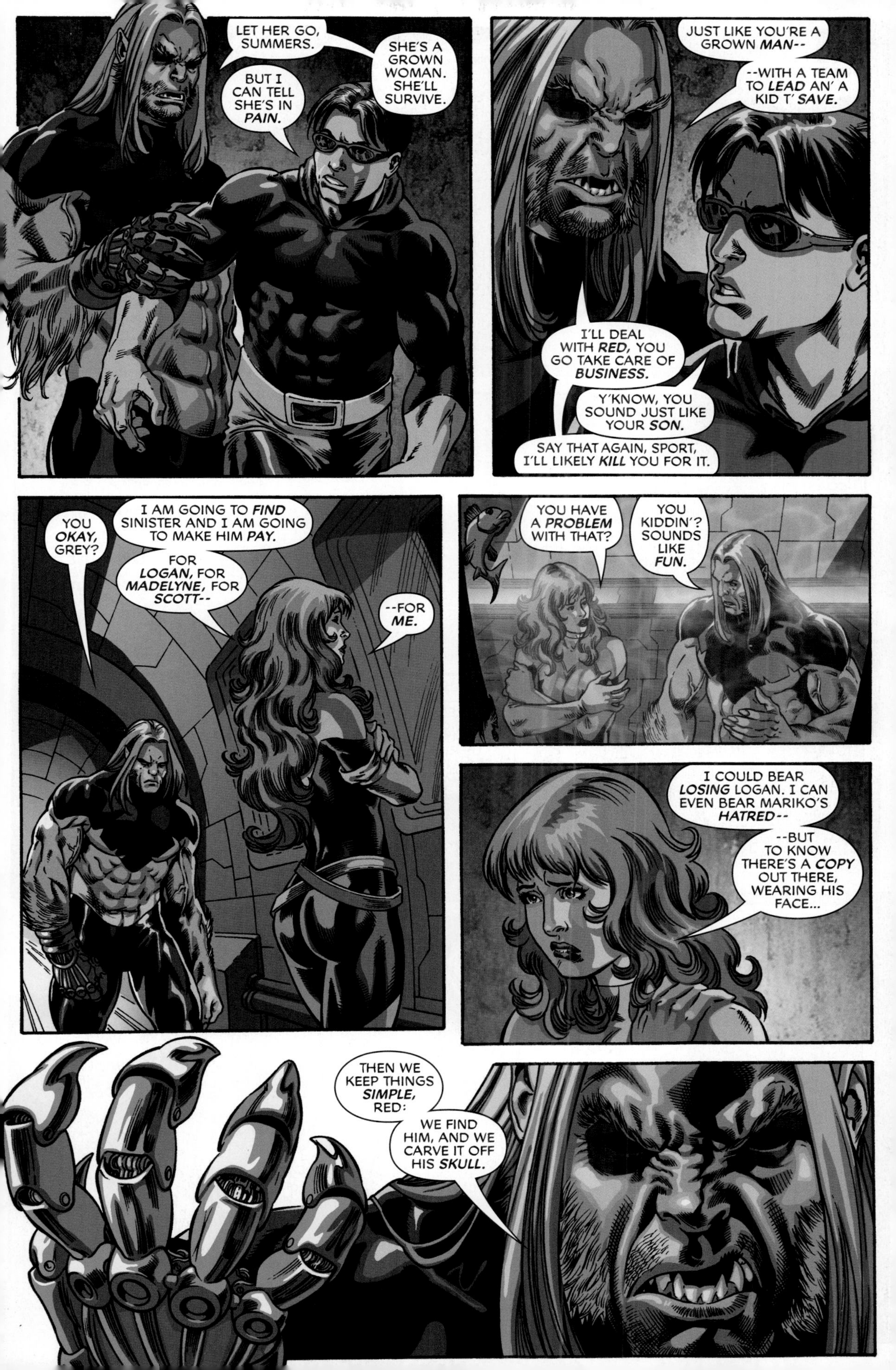
LET HER GO, SUMMERS.
SHE'S A GROWN WOMAN. SHE'LL SURVIVE.
BUT I CAN TELL SHE'S IN PAIN.
JUST LIKE YOU'RE A GROWN MAN--
--WITH A TEAM TO LEAD AN' A KID T' SAVE.
I'LL DEAL WITH RED, YOU GO TAKE CARE OF BUSINESS.
Y'KNOW, YOU SOUND JUST LIKE YOUR SON.
SAY THAT AGAIN, SPORT, I'LL LIKELY KILL YOU FOR IT.
YOU OKAY, GREY?
I AM GOING TO FIND SINISTER AND I AM GOING TO MAKE HIM PAY.
FOR LOGAN, FOR MADELYNE, FOR SCOTT--
--FOR ME.
YOU HAVE A PROBLEM WITH THAT?
YOU KIDDIN'? SOUNDS LIKE FUN.
I COULD BEAR LOSING LOGAN. I CAN EVEN BEAR MARIKO'S HATRED--
--BUT TO KNOW THERE'S A COPY OUT THERE, WEARING HIS FACE...
THEN WE KEEP THINGS SIMPLE, RED:
WE FIND HIM, AND WE CARVE IT OFF HIS SKULL.

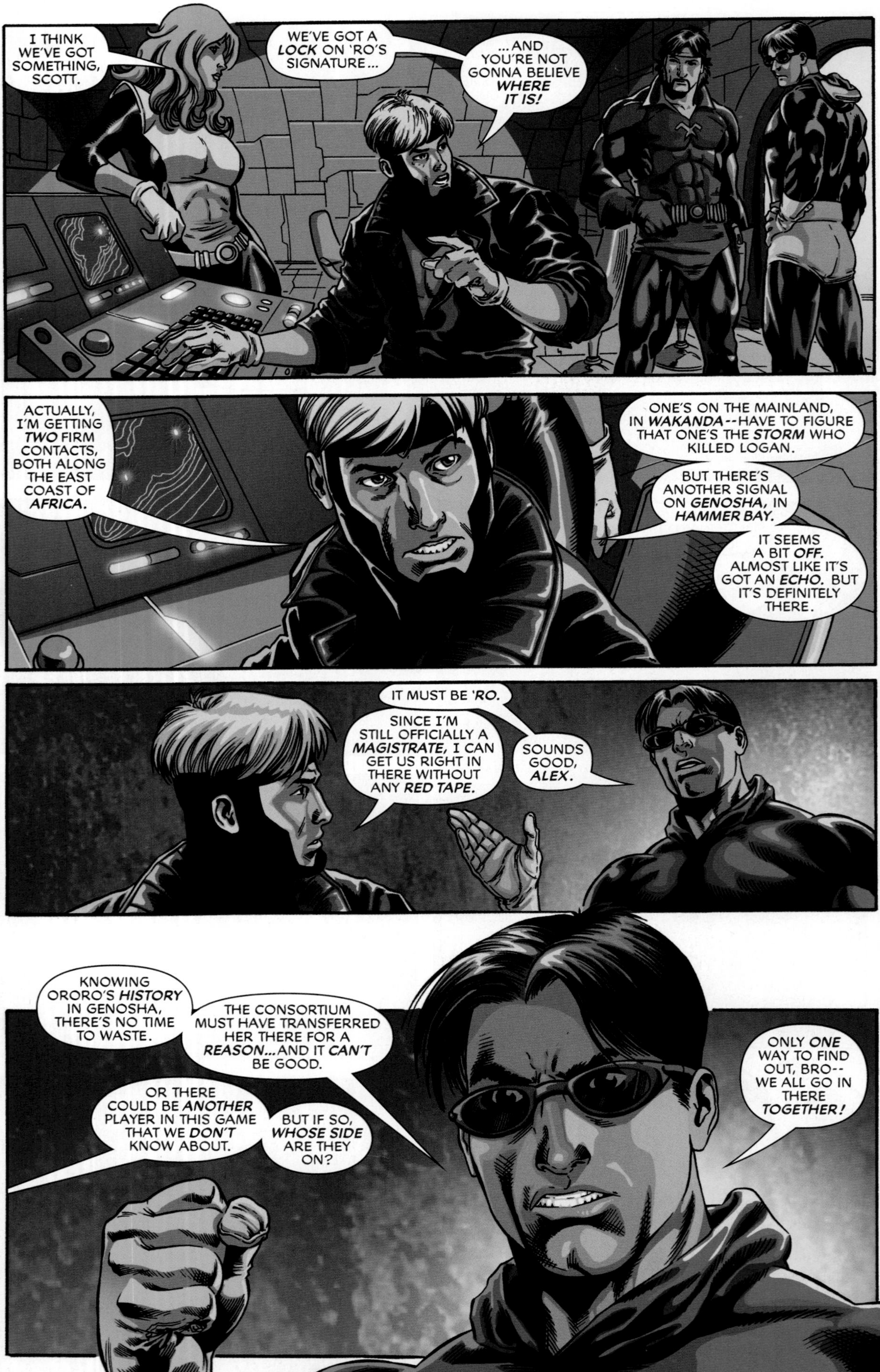

I THINK WE'VE GOT SOMETHING, SCOTT.
WE'VE GOT A LOCK ON 'RO'S SIGNATURE...
...AND YOU'RE NOT GONNA BELIEVE WHERE IT IS!
ACTUALLY, I'M GETTING TWO FIRM CONTACTS, BOTH ALONG THE EAST COAST OF AFRICA.
ONE'S ON THE MAINLAND, IN WAKANDA--HAVE TO FIGURE THAT ONE'S THE STORM WHO KILLED LOGAN.
BUT THERE'S ANOTHER SIGNAL ON GENOSHA, IN HAMMER BAY.
IT SEEMS A BIT OFF. ALMOST LIKE IT'S GOT AN ECHO. BUT IT'S DEFINITELY THERE.
IT MUST BE 'RO.
SINCE I'M STILL OFFICIALLY A MAGISTRATE, I CAN GET US RIGHT IN THERE WITHOUT ANY RED TAPE.
SOUNDS GOOD, ALEX.
KNOWING ORORO'S HISTORY IN GENOSHA, THERE'S NO TIME TO WASTE.
THE CONSORTIUM MUST HAVE TRANSFERRED HER THERE FOR A REASON...AND IT CAN'T BE GOOD.
OR THERE COULD BE ANOTHER PLAYER IN THIS GAME THAT WE DON'T KNOW ABOUT.
BUT IF SO, WHOSE SIDE ARE THEY ON?
ONLY ONE WAY TO FIND OUT, BRO--WE ALL GO IN THERE TOGETHER!

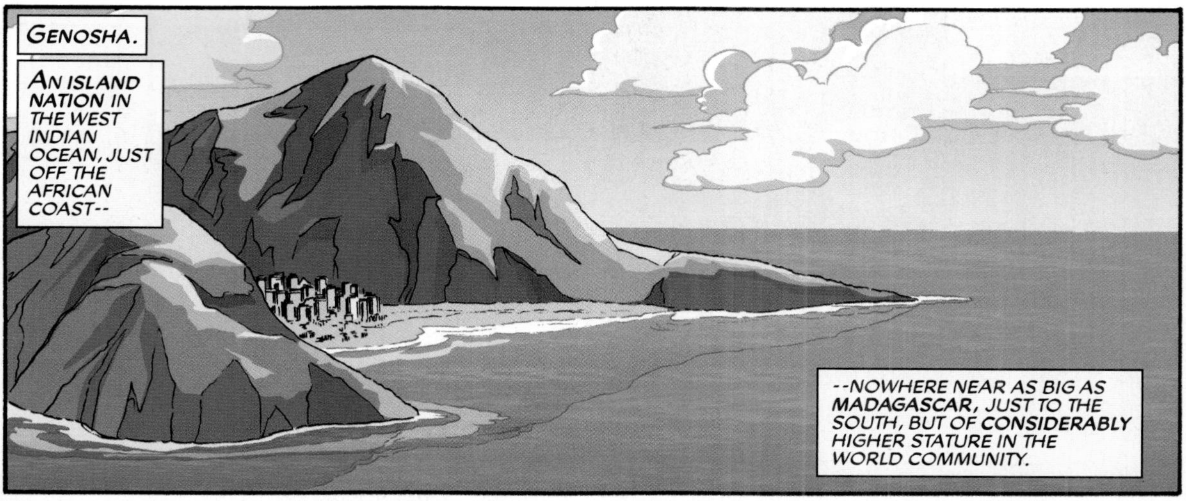
GENOSHA.
AN ISLAND NATION IN THE WEST INDIAN OCEAN, JUST OFF THE AFRICAN COAST--
--NOWHERE NEAR AS BIG AS MADAGASCAR, JUST TO THE SOUTH, BUT OF CONSIDERABLY HIGHER STATURE IN THE WORLD COMMUNITY.

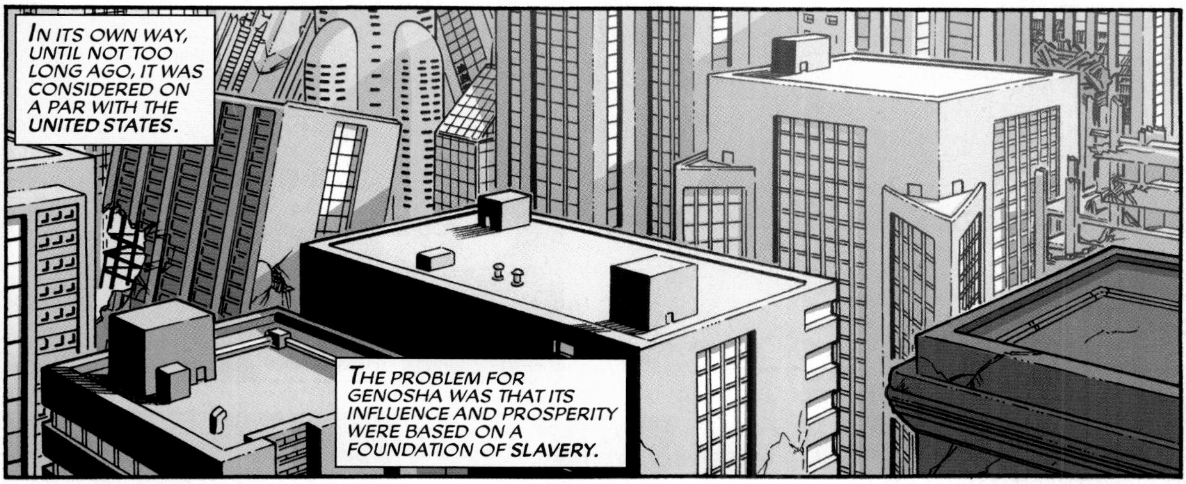
IN ITS OWN WAY, UNTIL NOT TOO LONG AGO, IT WAS CONSIDERED ON A PAR WITH THE UNITED STATES.
THE PROBLEM FOR GENOSHA WAS THAT ITS INFLUENCE AND PROSPERITY WERE BASED ON A FOUNDATION OF SLAVERY.

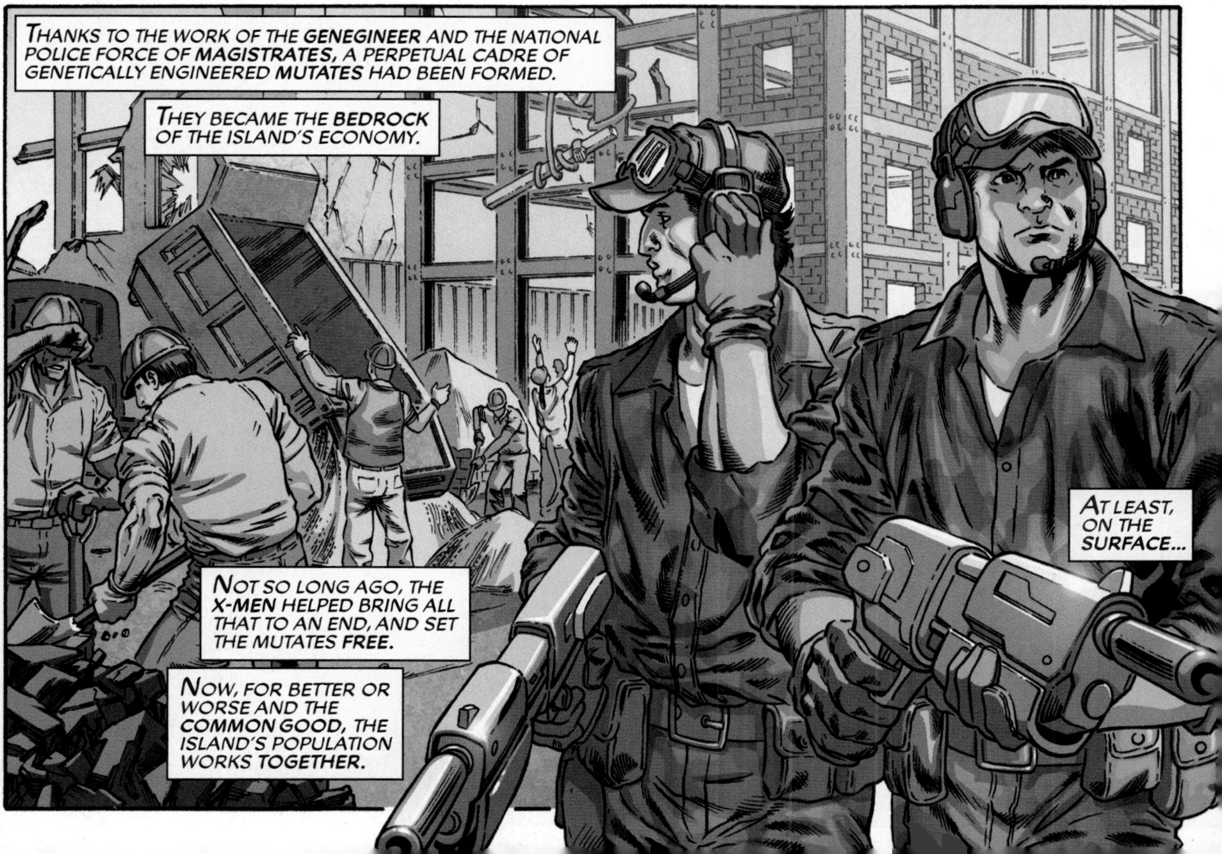
THANKS TO THE WORK OF THE GENEGINEER AND THE NATIONAL POLICE FORCE OF MAGISTRATES, A PERPETUAL CADRE OF GENETICALLY ENGINEERED MUTATES HAD BEEN FORMED.
THEY BECAME THE BEDROCK OF THE ISLAND'S ECONOMY.
NOT SO LONG AGO, THE X-MEN HELPED BRING ALL THAT TO AN END, AND SET THE MUTATES FREE.
NOW, FOR BETTER OR WORSE AND THE COMMON GOOD, THE ISLAND'S POPULATION WORKS TOGETHER.
AT LEAST, ON THE SURFACE...

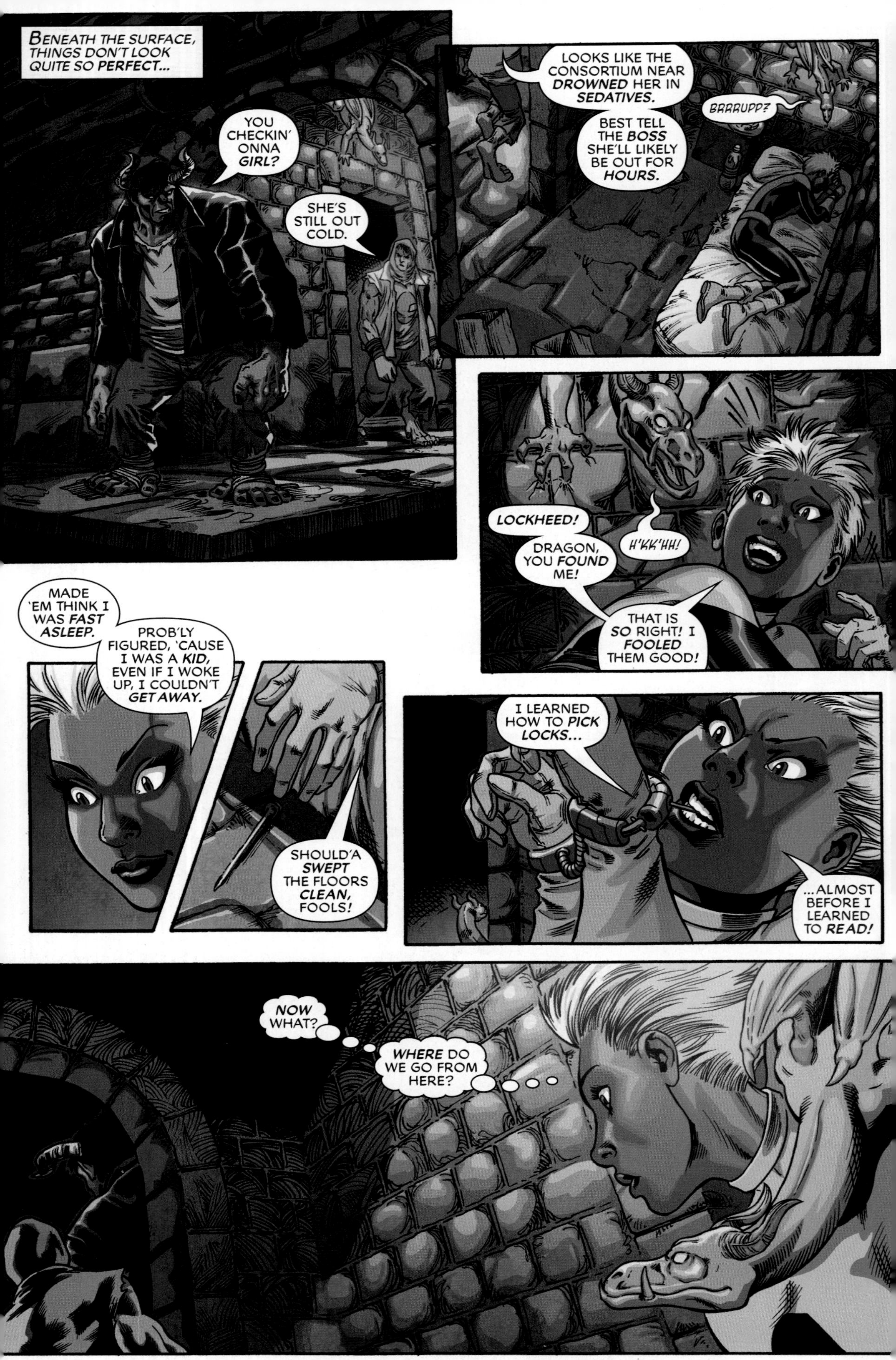
BENEATH THE SURFACE, THINGS DON'T LOOK QUITE SO PERFECT...
YOU CHECKIN' ONNA GIRL?
SHE'S STILL OUT COLD.
LOOKS LIKE THE CONSORTIUM NEAR DROWNED HER IN SEDATIVES.
BEST TELL THE BOSS SHE'LL LIKELY BE OUT FOR HOURS.
BRRRUPP?
LOCKHEED!
DRAGON, YOU FOUND ME!
H'KK'HH!
THAT IS SO RIGHT! I FOOLED THEM GOOD!
MADE 'EM THINK I WAS FAST ASLEEP.
PROB'LY FIGURED, 'CAUSE I WAS A KID, EVEN IF I WOKE UP, I COULDN'T GET AWAY.
SHOULD'A SWEPT THE FLOORS CLEAN, FOOLS!
I LEARNED HOW TO PICK LOCKS...
...ALMOST BEFORE I LEARNED TO READ!
NOW WHAT?
WHERE DO WE GO FROM HERE?

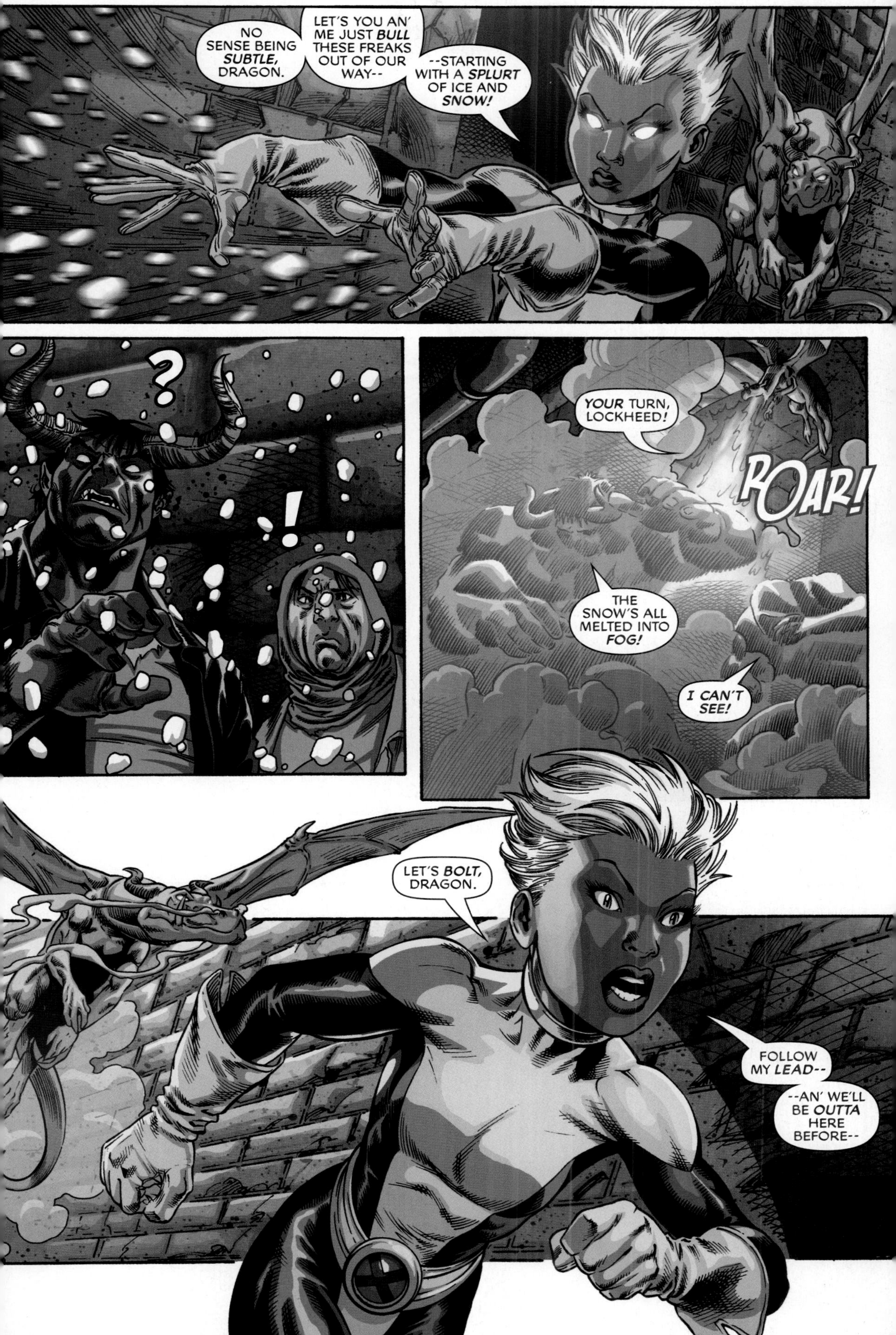

NO SENSE BEING *SUBTLE,* DRAGON.
LET'S YOU AN' ME JUST *BULL* THESE FREAKS OUT OF OUR WAY--
--STARTING WITH A *SPLURT* OF ICE AND *SNOW!*
?
!
YOUR TURN, LOCKHEED*!*
ROAR!
THE SNOW'S ALL MELTED INTO *FOG!*
I CAN'T SEE!
LET'S *BOLT,* DRAGON.
FOLLOW MY *LEAD*--
--AN' WE'LL BE *OUTTA* HERE BEFORE--

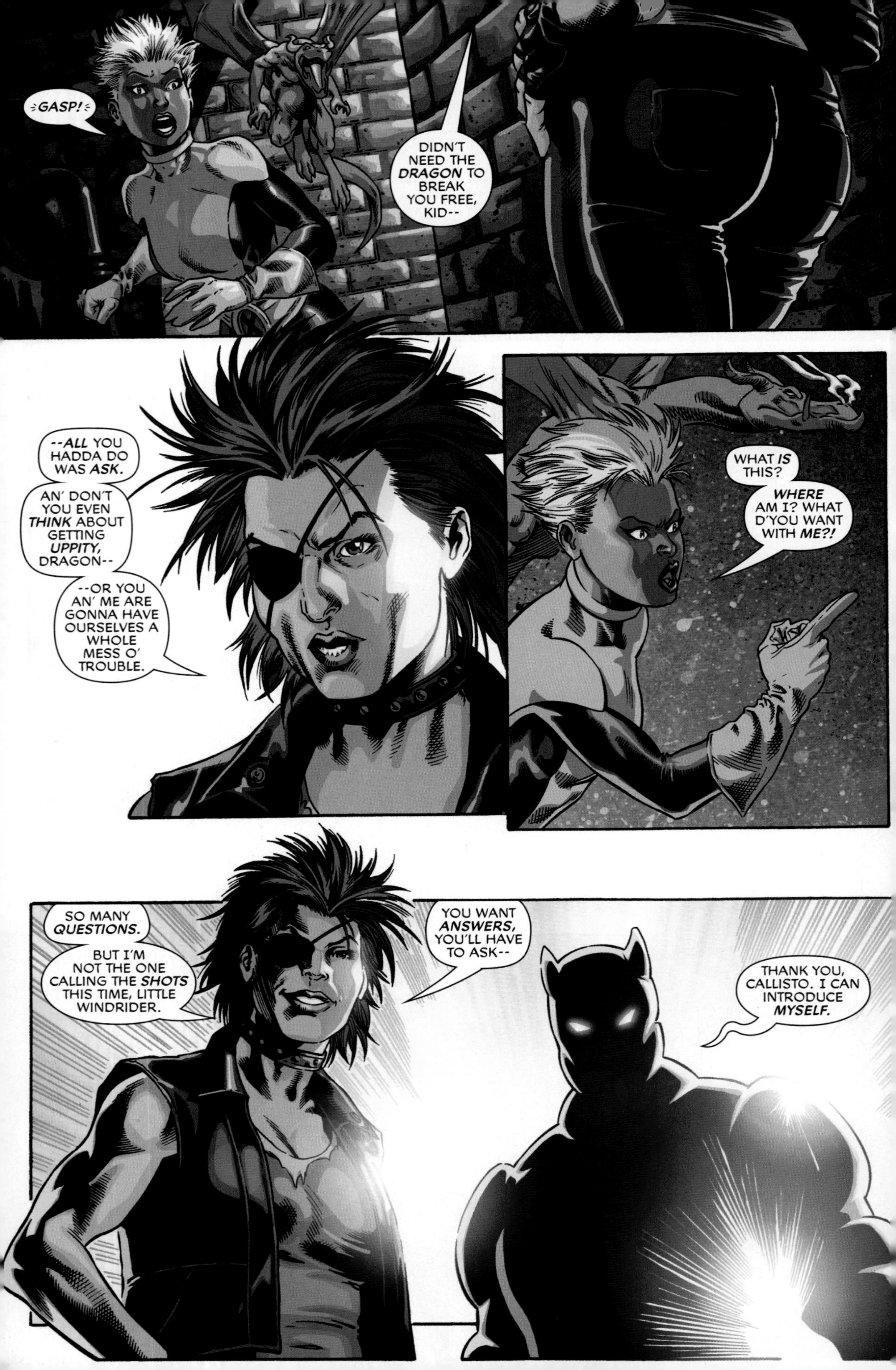
GASP!
DIDN'T NEED THE DRAGON TO BREAK YOU FREE, KID--
--ALL YOU HADDA DO WAS ASK.
AN' DON'T YOU EVEN THINK ABOUT GETTING UPPITY, DRAGON--
--OR YOU AN' ME ARE GONNA HAVE OURSELVES A WHOLE MESS O' TROUBLE.
WHAT IS THIS?
WHERE AM I? WHAT D'YOU WANT WITH ME?!
SO MANY QUESTIONS.
BUT I'M NOT THE ONE CALLING THE SHOTS THIS TIME, LITTLE WINDRIDER.
YOU WANT ANSWERS, YOU'LL HAVE TO ASK--
THANK YOU, CALLISTO. I CAN INTRODUCE MYSELF.

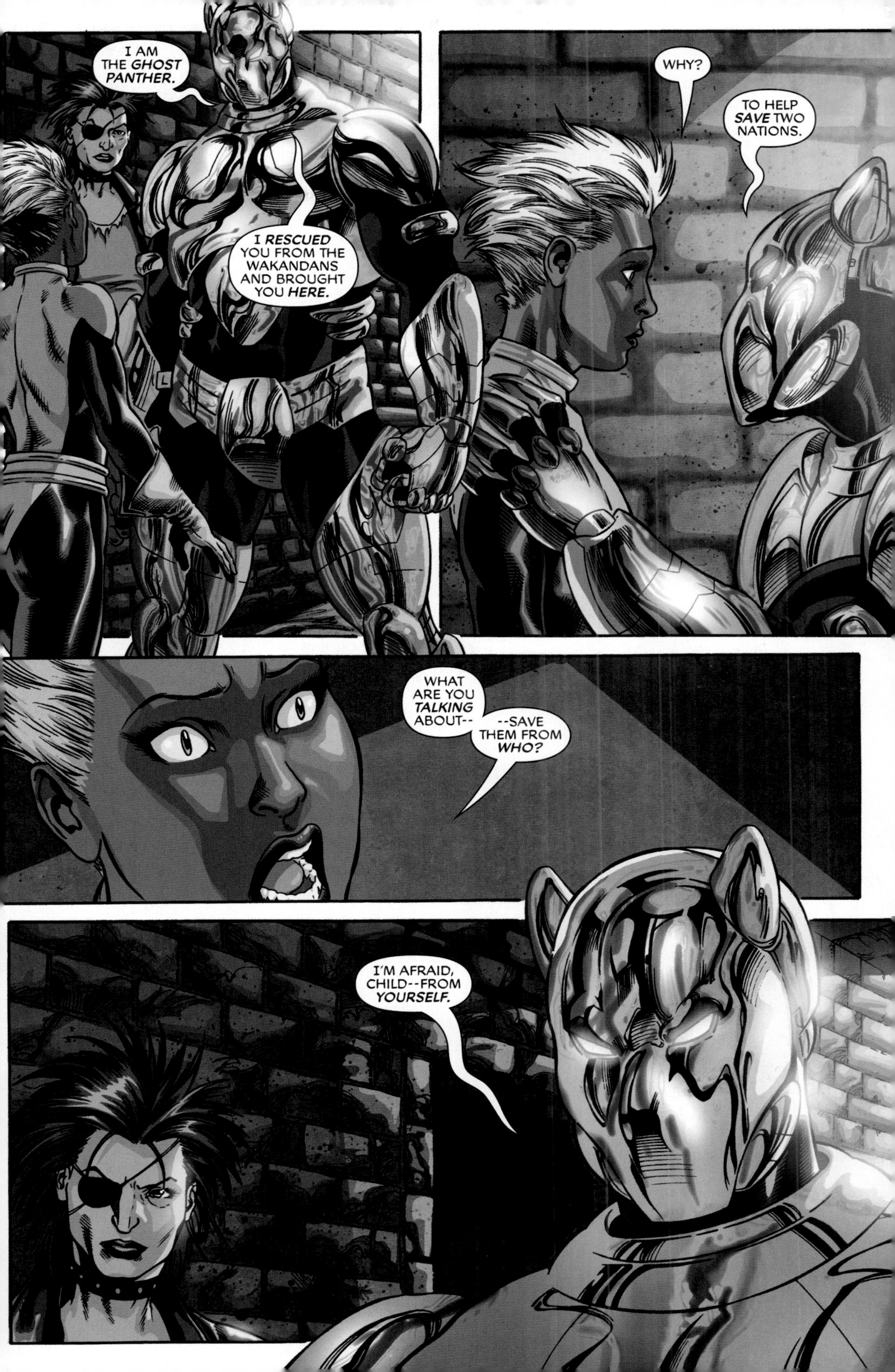
I AM THE GHOST PANTHER.
I RESCUED YOU FROM THE WAKANDANS AND BROUGHT YOU HERE.
WHY?
TO HELP SAVE TWO NATIONS.
WHAT ARE YOU TALKING ABOUT--
--SAVE THEM FROM WHO?
I'M AFRAID, CHILD--FROM YOURSELF.

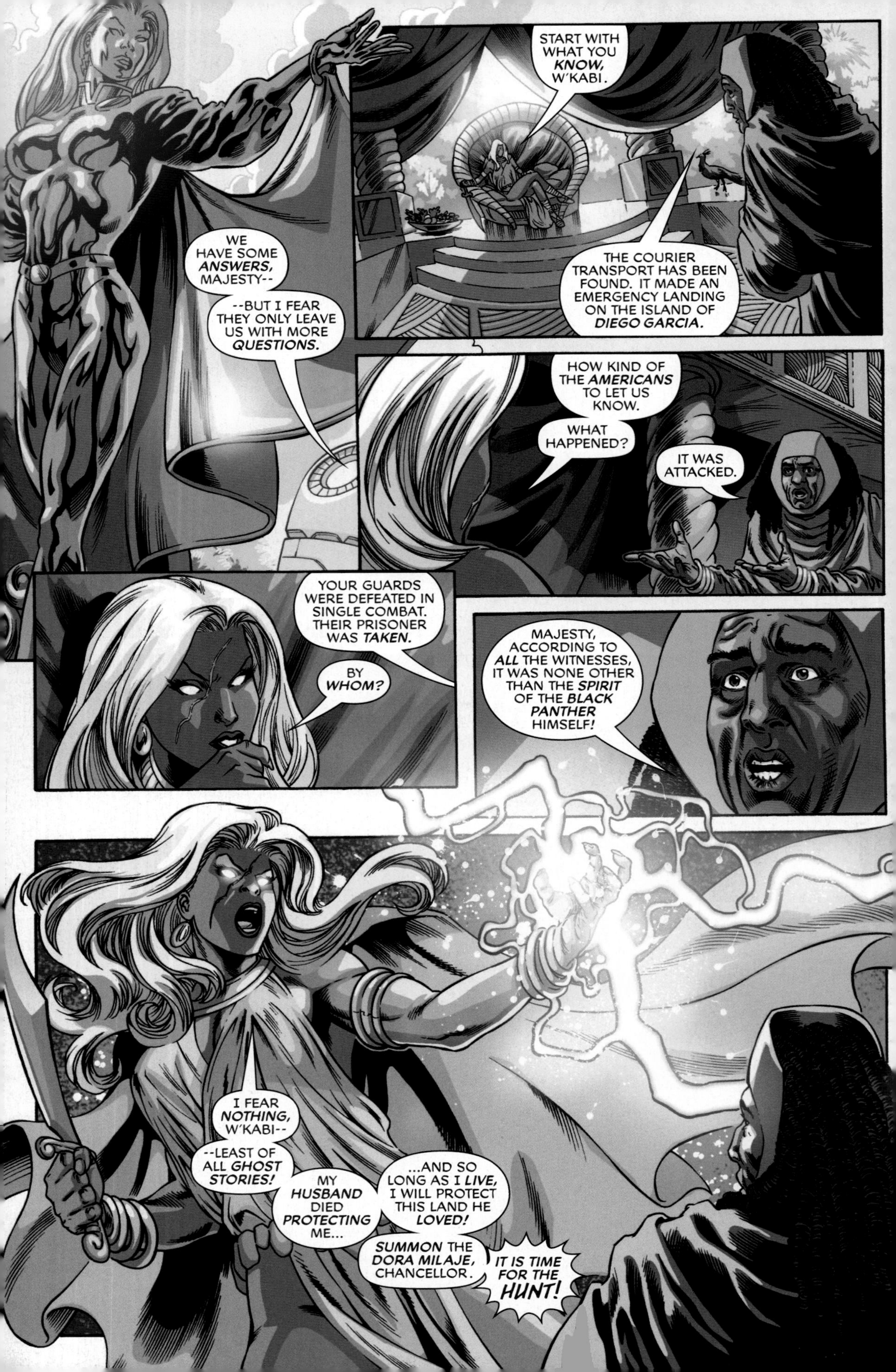
START WITH WHAT YOU KNOW, W'KABI.
WE HAVE SOME ANSWERS, MAJESTY--
--BUT I FEAR THEY ONLY LEAVE US WITH MORE QUESTIONS.
THE COURIER TRANSPORT HAS BEEN FOUND. IT MADE AN EMERGENCY LANDING ON THE ISLAND OF DIEGO GARCIA.
HOW KIND OF THE AMERICANS TO LET US KNOW.
WHAT HAPPENED?
IT WAS ATTACKED.
YOUR GUARDS WERE DEFEATED IN SINGLE COMBAT. THEIR PRISONER WAS TAKEN.
BY WHOM?
MAJESTY, ACCORDING TO ALL THE WITNESSES, IT WAS NONE OTHER THAN THE SPIRIT OF THE BLACK PANTHER HIMSELF!
I FEAR NOTHING, W'KABI--
--LEAST OF ALL GHOST STORIES!
MY HUSBAND DIED PROTECTING ME...
...AND SO LONG AS I LIVE, I WILL PROTECT THIS LAND HE LOVED!
SUMMON THE DORA MILAJE, CHANCELLOR.
IT IS TIME FOR THE HUNT!

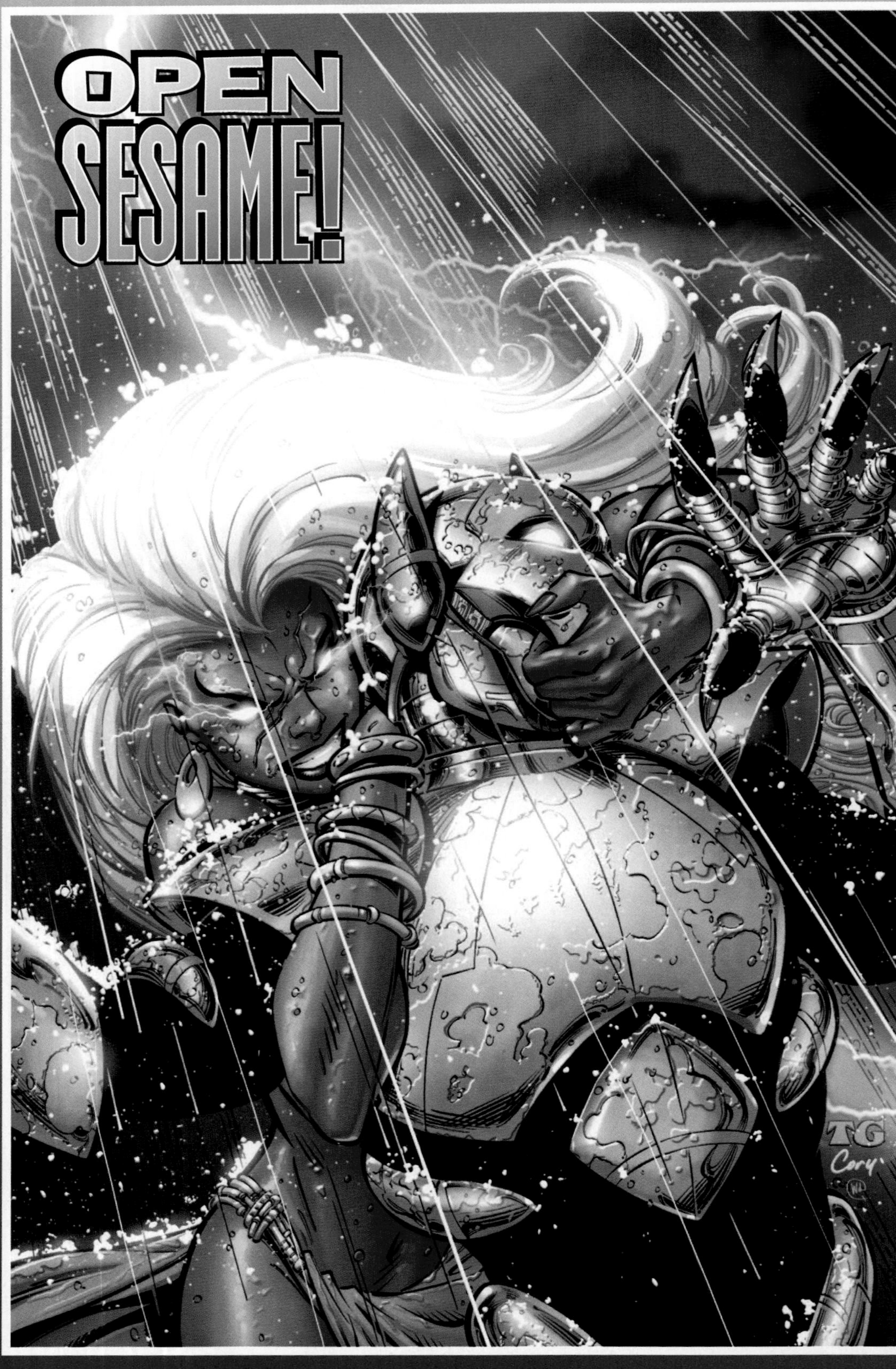
OPEN SESAME!
TG
Cory

TWELVE

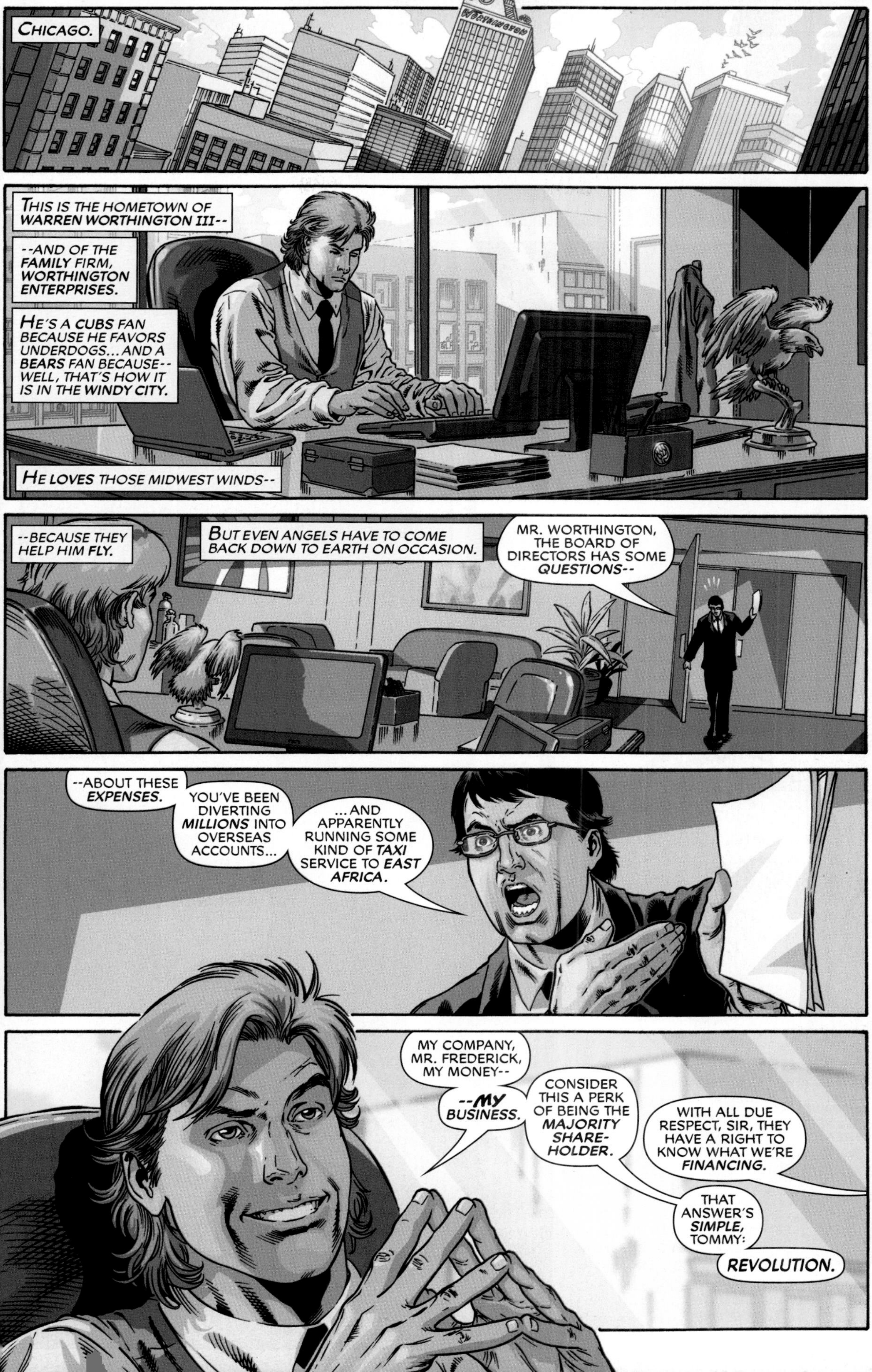
CHICAGO.
THIS IS THE HOMETOWN OF WARREN WORTHINGTON III--
--AND OF THE FAMILY FIRM, WORTHINGTON ENTERPRISES.
HE'S A CUBS FAN BECAUSE HE FAVORS UNDERDOGS... AND A BEARS FAN BECAUSE-- WELL, THAT'S HOW IT IS IN THE WINDY CITY.
HE LOVES THOSE MIDWEST WINDS--
--BECAUSE THEY HELP HIM FLY.
BUT EVEN ANGELS HAVE TO COME BACK DOWN TO EARTH ON OCCASION.
MR. WORTHINGTON, THE BOARD OF DIRECTORS HAS SOME QUESTIONS--
--ABOUT THESE EXPENSES.
YOU'VE BEEN DIVERTING MILLIONS INTO OVERSEAS ACCOUNTS...
...AND APPARENTLY RUNNING SOME KIND OF TAXI SERVICE TO EAST AFRICA.
MY COMPANY, MR. FREDERICK, MY MONEY--
--MY BUSINESS.
CONSIDER THIS A PERK OF BEING THE MAJORITY SHARE-HOLDER.
WITH ALL DUE RESPECT, SIR, THEY HAVE A RIGHT TO KNOW WHAT WE'RE FINANCING.
THAT ANSWER'S SIMPLE, TOMMY:
REVOLUTION.

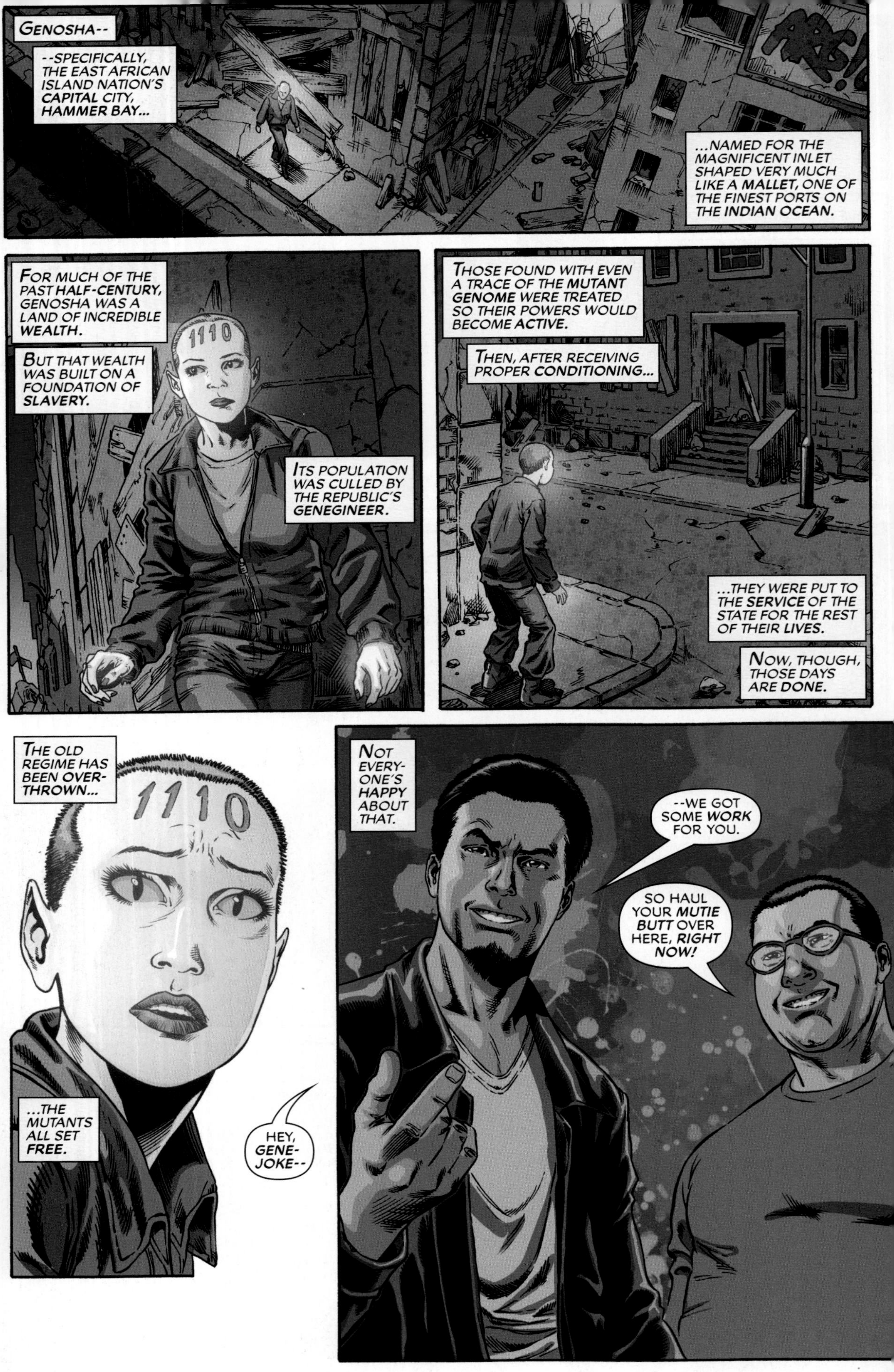
GENOSHA--
--SPECIFICALLY, THE EAST AFRICAN ISLAND NATION'S CAPITAL CITY, HAMMER BAY...
...NAMED FOR THE MAGNIFICENT INLET SHAPED VERY MUCH LIKE A MALLET, ONE OF THE FINEST PORTS ON THE INDIAN OCEAN.
FOR MUCH OF THE PAST HALF-CENTURY, GENOSHA WAS A LAND OF INCREDIBLE WEALTH.
1110
BUT THAT WEALTH WAS BUILT ON A FOUNDATION OF SLAVERY.
ITS POPULATION WAS CULLED BY THE REPUBLIC'S GENEGINEER.
THOSE FOUND WITH EVEN A TRACE OF THE MUTANT GENOME WERE TREATED SO THEIR POWERS WOULD BECOME ACTIVE.
THEN, AFTER RECEIVING PROPER CONDITIONING...
...THEY WERE PUT TO THE SERVICE OF THE STATE FOR THE REST OF THEIR LIVES.
NOW, THOUGH, THOSE DAYS ARE DONE.
THE OLD REGIME HAS BEEN OVERTHROWN...
1110
...THE MUTANTS ALL SET FREE.
HEY, GENE-JOKE--
NOT EVERYONE'S HAPPY ABOUT THAT.
--WE GOT SOME WORK FOR YOU.
SO HAUL YOUR MUTIE BUTT OVER HERE, RIGHT NOW!

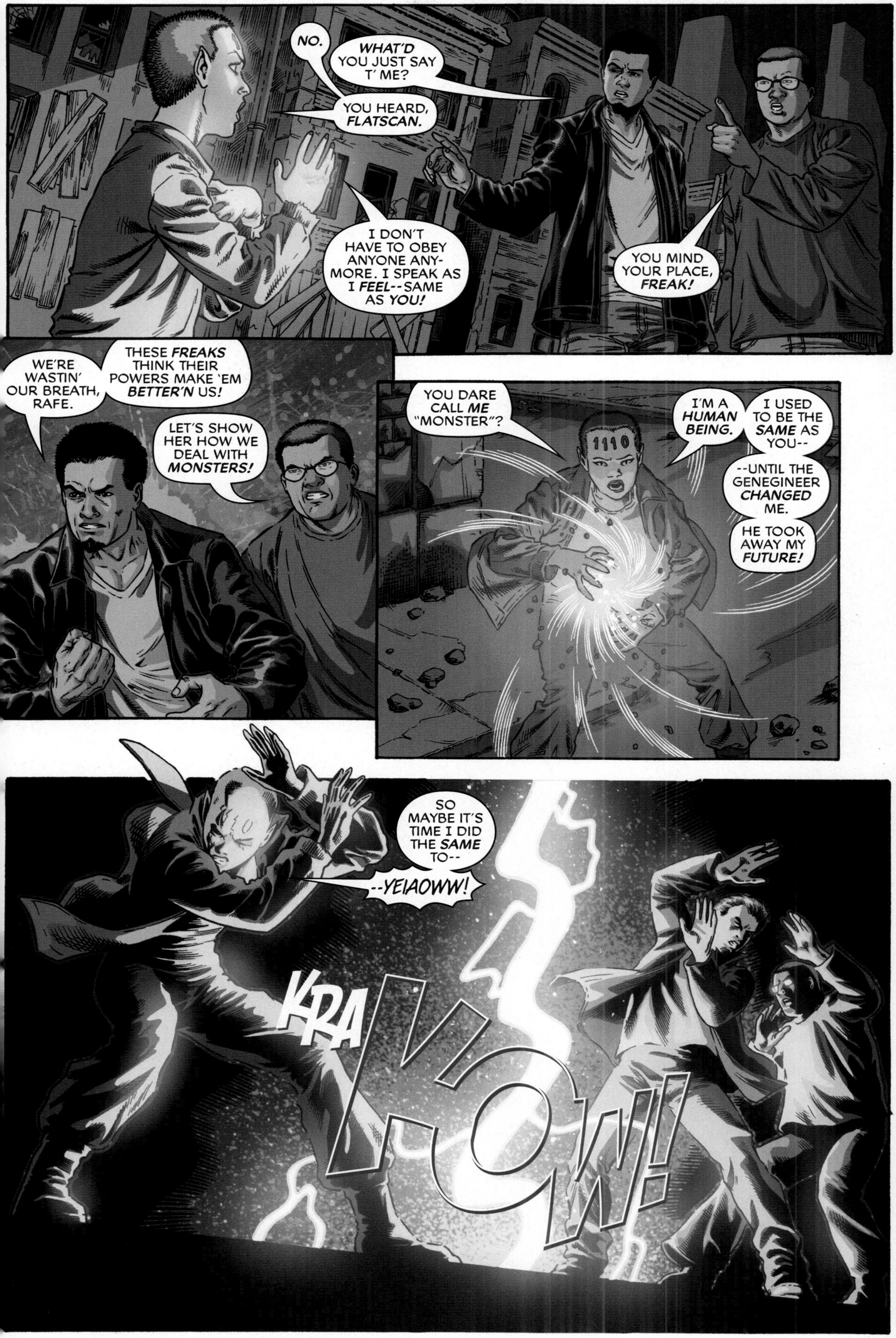

NO.
WHAT'D YOU JUST SAY T' ME?
YOU HEARD, FLATSCAN.
I DON'T HAVE TO OBEY ANYONE ANYMORE. I SPEAK AS I FEEL--SAME AS YOU!
YOU MIND YOUR PLACE, FREAK!
WE'RE WASTIN' OUR BREATH, RAFE.
THESE FREAKS THINK THEIR POWERS MAKE 'EM BETTER'N US!
LET'S SHOW HER HOW WE DEAL WITH MONSTERS!
YOU DARE CALL ME "MONSTER"?
I'M A HUMAN BEING.
I USED TO BE THE SAME AS YOU--
--UNTIL THE GENEGINEER CHANGED ME.
HE TOOK AWAY MY FUTURE!
1110
SO MAYBE IT'S TIME I DID THE SAME TO--
--YEIAOWW!
KRA
KOW!

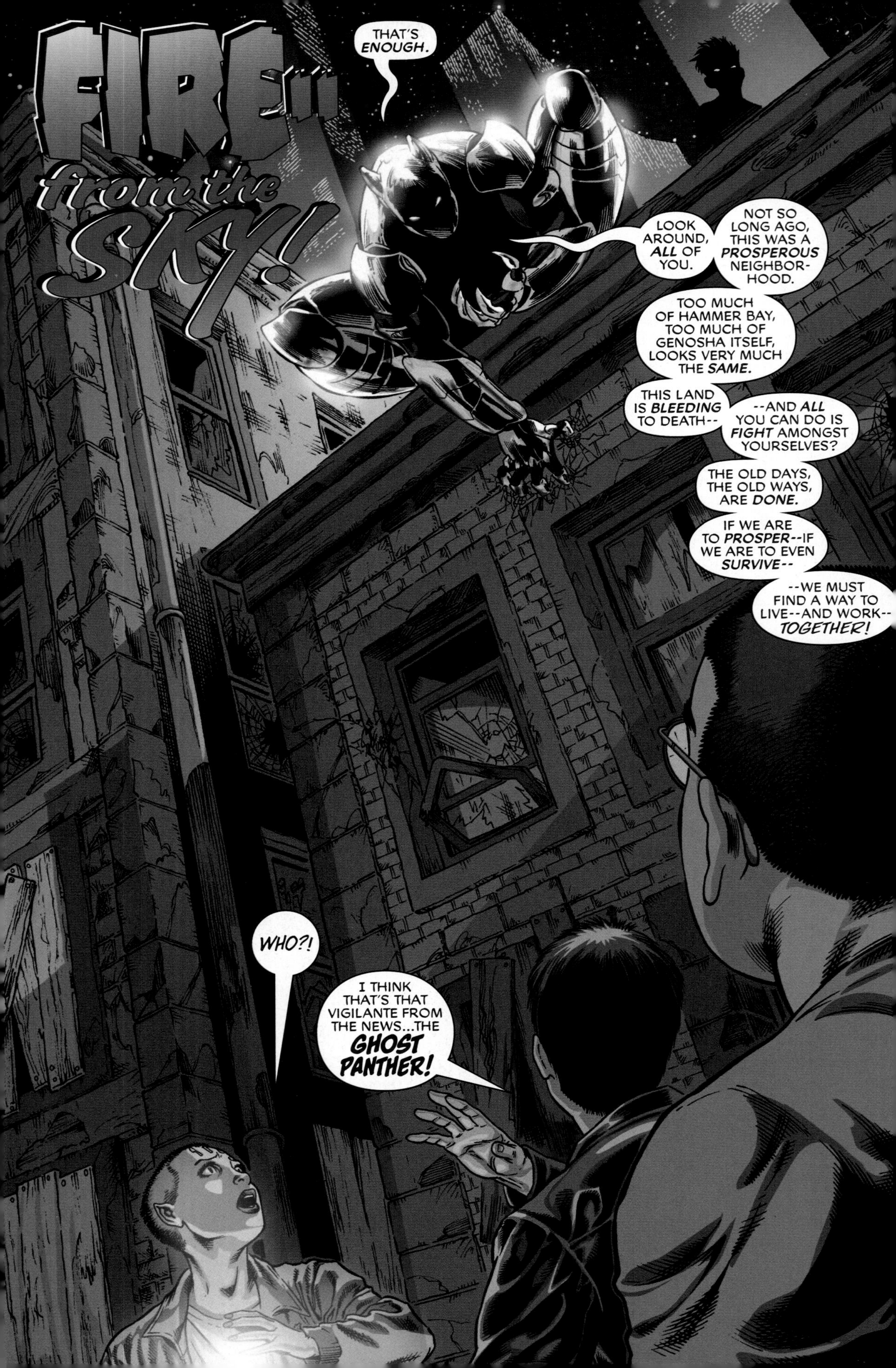
FIRE... from the SKY!
THAT'S ENOUGH.
LOOK AROUND, ALL OF YOU.
NOT SO LONG AGO, THIS WAS A PROSPEROUS NEIGHBOR-HOOD.
TOO MUCH OF HAMMER BAY, TOO MUCH OF GENOSHA ITSELF, LOOKS VERY MUCH THE SAME.
THIS LAND IS BLEEDING TO DEATH--
--AND ALL YOU CAN DO IS FIGHT AMONGST YOURSELVES?
THE OLD DAYS, THE OLD WAYS, ARE DONE.
IF WE ARE TO PROSPER--IF WE ARE TO EVEN SURVIVE--
--WE MUST FIND A WAY TO LIVE--AND WORK--TOGETHER!
WHO?!
I THINK THAT'S THAT VIGILANTE FROM THE NEWS...THE GHOST PANTHER!

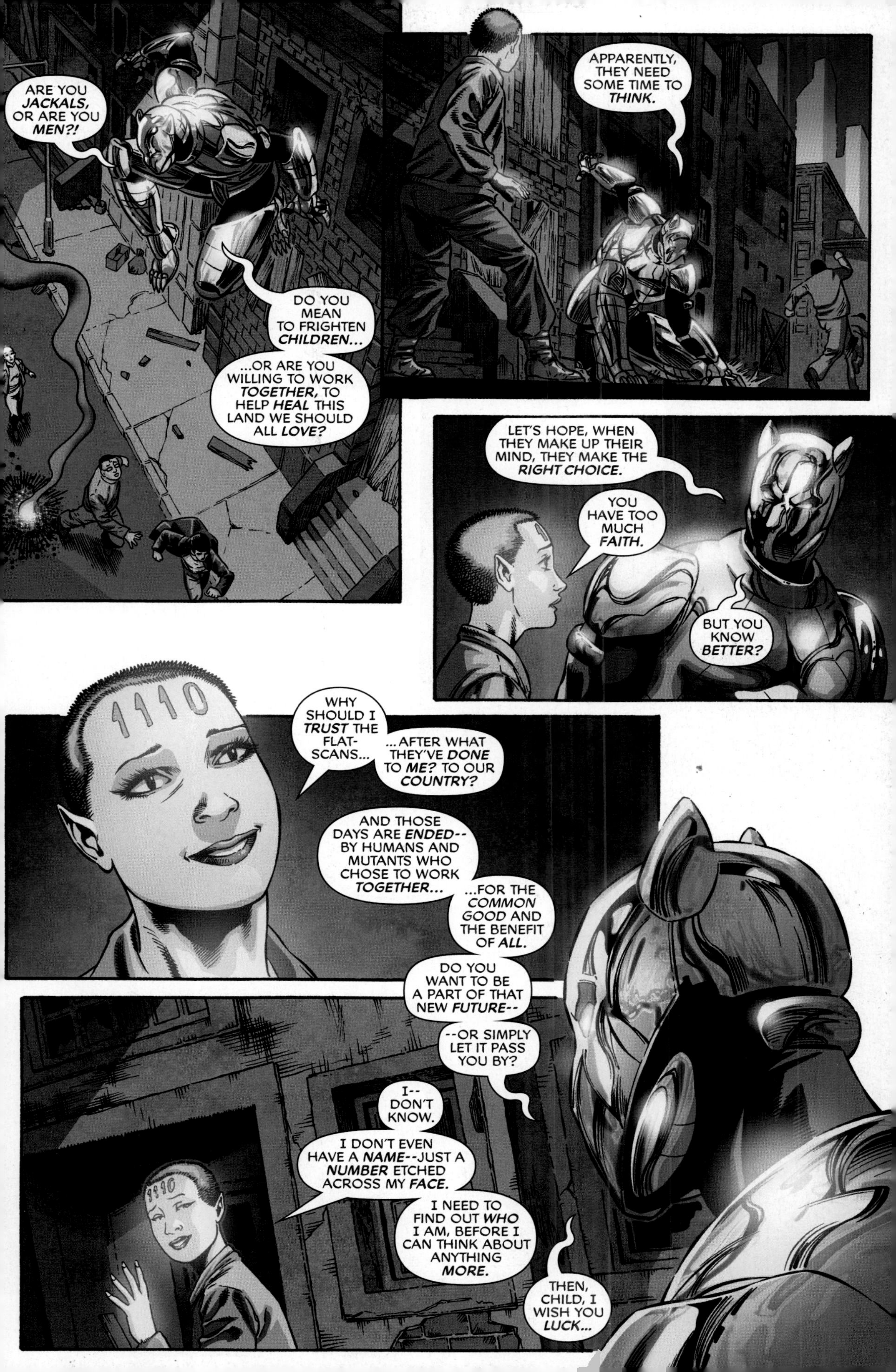
ARE YOU JACKALS, OR ARE YOU MEN?!
DO YOU MEAN TO FRIGHTEN CHILDREN...
...OR ARE YOU WILLING TO WORK TOGETHER, TO HELP HEAL THIS LAND WE SHOULD ALL LOVE?
APPARENTLY, THEY NEED SOME TIME TO THINK.
LET'S HOPE, WHEN THEY MAKE UP THEIR MIND, THEY MAKE THE RIGHT CHOICE.
YOU HAVE TOO MUCH FAITH.
BUT YOU KNOW BETTER?
1110
WHY SHOULD I TRUST THE FLAT-SCANS...
...AFTER WHAT THEY'VE DONE TO ME? TO OUR COUNTRY?
AND THOSE DAYS ARE ENDED-- BY HUMANS AND MUTANTS WHO CHOSE TO WORK TOGETHER...
...FOR THE COMMON GOOD AND THE BENEFIT OF ALL.
DO YOU WANT TO BE A PART OF THAT NEW FUTURE--
--OR SIMPLY LET IT PASS YOU BY?
I-- DON'T KNOW.
I DON'T EVEN HAVE A NAME--JUST A NUMBER ETCHED ACROSS MY FACE.
I NEED TO FIND OUT WHO I AM, BEFORE I CAN THINK ABOUT ANYTHING MORE.
THEN, CHILD, I WISH YOU LUCK...

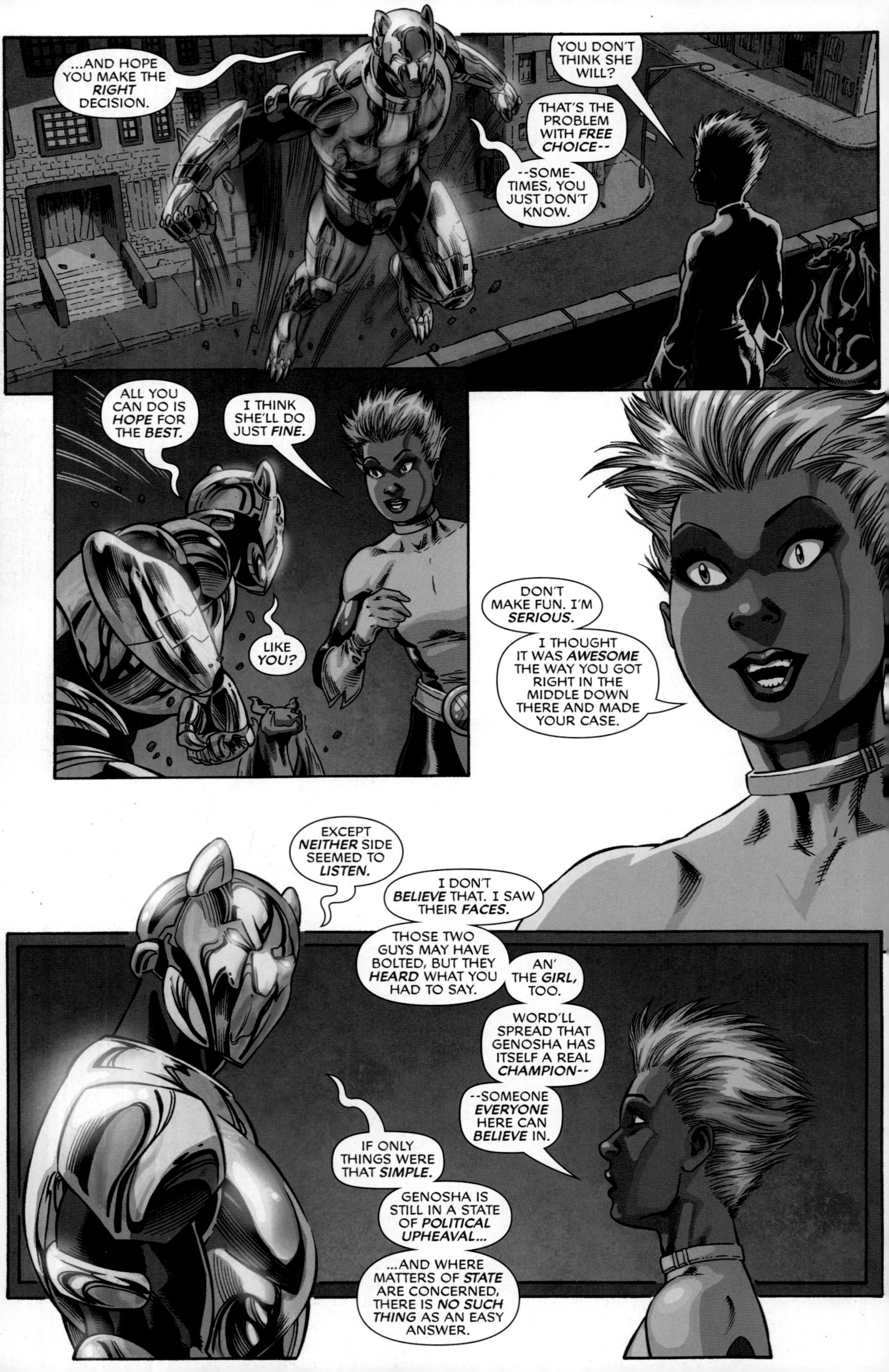
...AND HOPE YOU MAKE THE RIGHT DECISION.
YOU DON'T THINK SHE WILL?
THAT'S THE PROBLEM WITH FREE CHOICE--
--SOMETIMES, YOU JUST DON'T KNOW.
ALL YOU CAN DO IS HOPE FOR THE BEST.
I THINK SHE'LL DO JUST FINE.
LIKE YOU?
DON'T MAKE FUN. I'M SERIOUS.
I THOUGHT IT WAS AWESOME THE WAY YOU GOT RIGHT IN THE MIDDLE DOWN THERE AND MADE YOUR CASE.
EXCEPT NEITHER SIDE SEEMED TO LISTEN.
I DON'T BELIEVE THAT. I SAW THEIR FACES.
THOSE TWO GUYS MAY HAVE BOLTED, BUT THEY HEARD WHAT YOU HAD TO SAY.
AN' THE GIRL, TOO.
WORD'LL SPREAD THAT GENOSHA HAS ITSELF A REAL CHAMPION--
--SOMEONE EVERYONE HERE CAN BELIEVE IN.
IF ONLY THINGS WERE THAT SIMPLE.
GENOSHA IS STILL IN A STATE OF POLITICAL UPHEAVAL...
...AND WHERE MATTERS OF STATE ARE CONCERNED, THERE IS NO SUCH THING AS AN EASY ANSWER.

THE UNITED NATIONS, NEW YORK...

MR. *SECRETARY-GENERAL*, FELLOW DELEGATES, I SPEAK TO YOU TODAY AS A PERSONAL REPRESENTATIVE OF THE *PRESIDENT OF THE UNITED STATES.*

THE SITUATION FACED BY THIS ORGANIZATION, AND, BY EXTENSION, THE *WORLD...*

...IS *GRAVE.*

THE NATION OF *GENOSHA* IS IN *TURMOIL.*

THE RECENT *CONFLICT* THERE HAS BEEN *DEVASTATING.*

AND NOW THEY FACE A *THREAT* BY THE QUEEN OF *WAKANDA* TO *ANNEX* THE ISLAND.

OUTRAGEOUS!

IS THE WOMAN *MAD*?

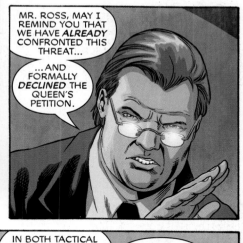

MR. ROSS, MAY I REMIND YOU THAT WE HAVE *ALREADY* CONFRONTED THIS THREAT...

...AND FORMALLY *DECLINED* THE QUEEN'S PETITION.

WITH ALL RESPECT, MR. SECRETARY-GENERAL, SHE HAS *OTHER* IDEAS.

FROM A *STRATEGIC* STANDPOINT, GENOSHA IS *UNIQUE.*

IT HAS AMONG ITS POPULATION THE WORLD'S *LARGEST* CACHE OF *SUPER-POWERED MUTANTS*--

--ALL OF WHOM ARE RECENTLY LIBERATED *SLAVES.*

IN BOTH TACTICAL AND STRATEGIC TERMS, THE POTENTIAL *THREAT* THEY POSE TO THE WORLD IS *IMMEASURABLE.*

I GUESS THE QUESTION *WE* FACE, IS WHETHER OR NOT THE QUEEN CAN BE *TRUSTED.*

IF SHE GAINS CONTROL OF GENOSHA, WILL SHE USE THOSE MUTANTS FOR GOOD OR *ILL*?

AND IF THE REST OF THE WORLD DECIDES TO *STOP* HER...

...IS THAT EVEN *POSSIBLE*?

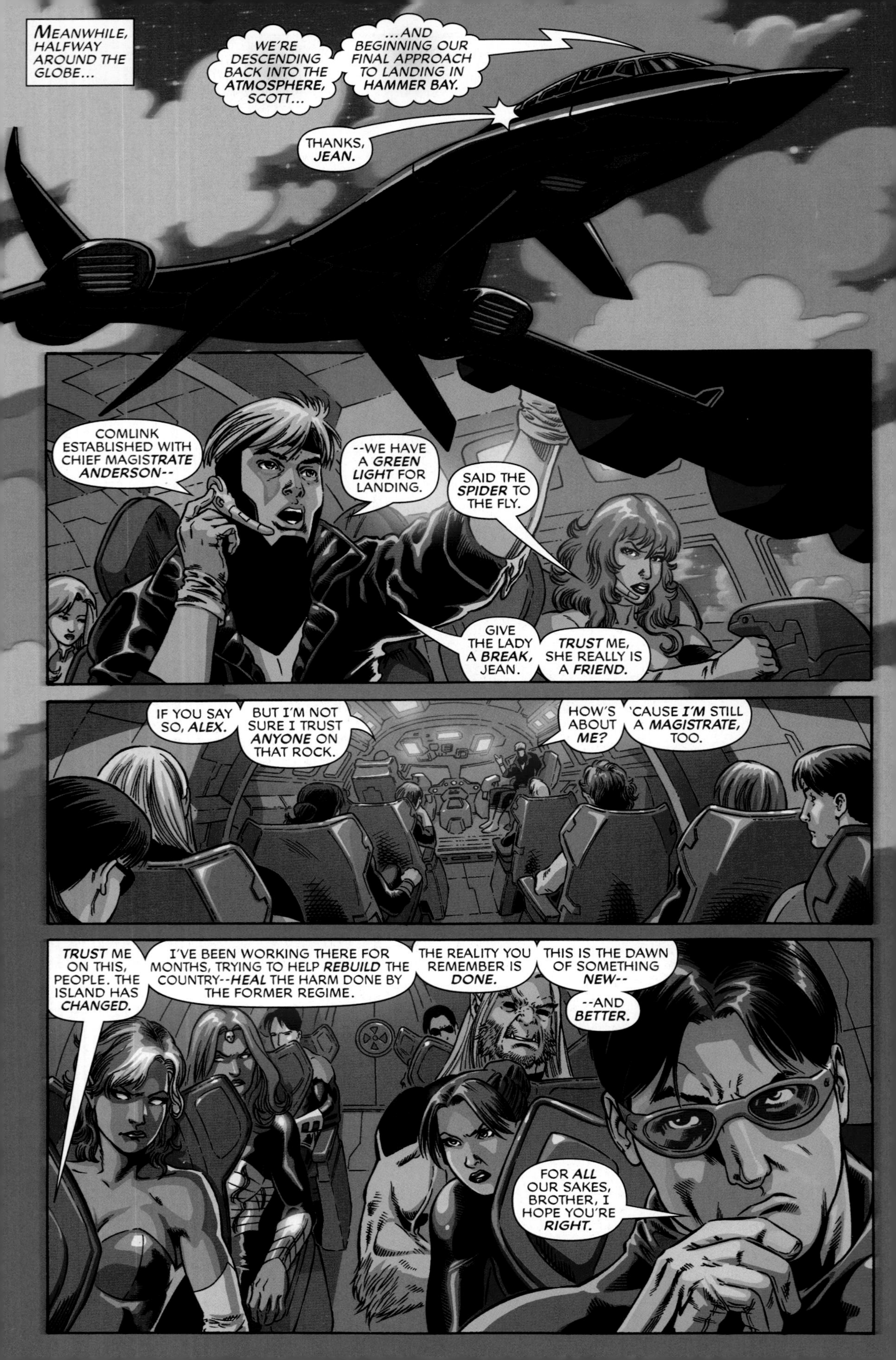
MEANWHILE, HALFWAY AROUND THE GLOBE...
WE'RE DESCENDING BACK INTO THE ATMOSPHERE, SCOTT...
...AND BEGINNING OUR FINAL APPROACH TO LANDING IN HAMMER BAY.
THANKS, JEAN.
COMLINK ESTABLISHED WITH CHIEF MAGISTRATE ANDERSON--
--WE HAVE A GREEN LIGHT FOR LANDING.
SAID THE SPIDER TO THE FLY.
GIVE THE LADY A BREAK, JEAN.
TRUST ME, SHE REALLY IS A FRIEND.
IF YOU SAY SO, ALEX.
BUT I'M NOT SURE I TRUST ANYONE ON THAT ROCK.
HOW'S ABOUT ME?
'CAUSE I'M STILL A MAGISTRATE, TOO.
TRUST ME ON THIS, PEOPLE. THE ISLAND HAS CHANGED.
I'VE BEEN WORKING THERE FOR MONTHS, TRYING TO HELP REBUILD THE COUNTRY--HEAL THE HARM DONE BY THE FORMER REGIME.
THE REALITY YOU REMEMBER IS DONE.
THIS IS THE DAWN OF SOMETHING NEW--
--AND BETTER.
FOR ALL OUR SAKES, BROTHER, I HOPE YOU'RE RIGHT.

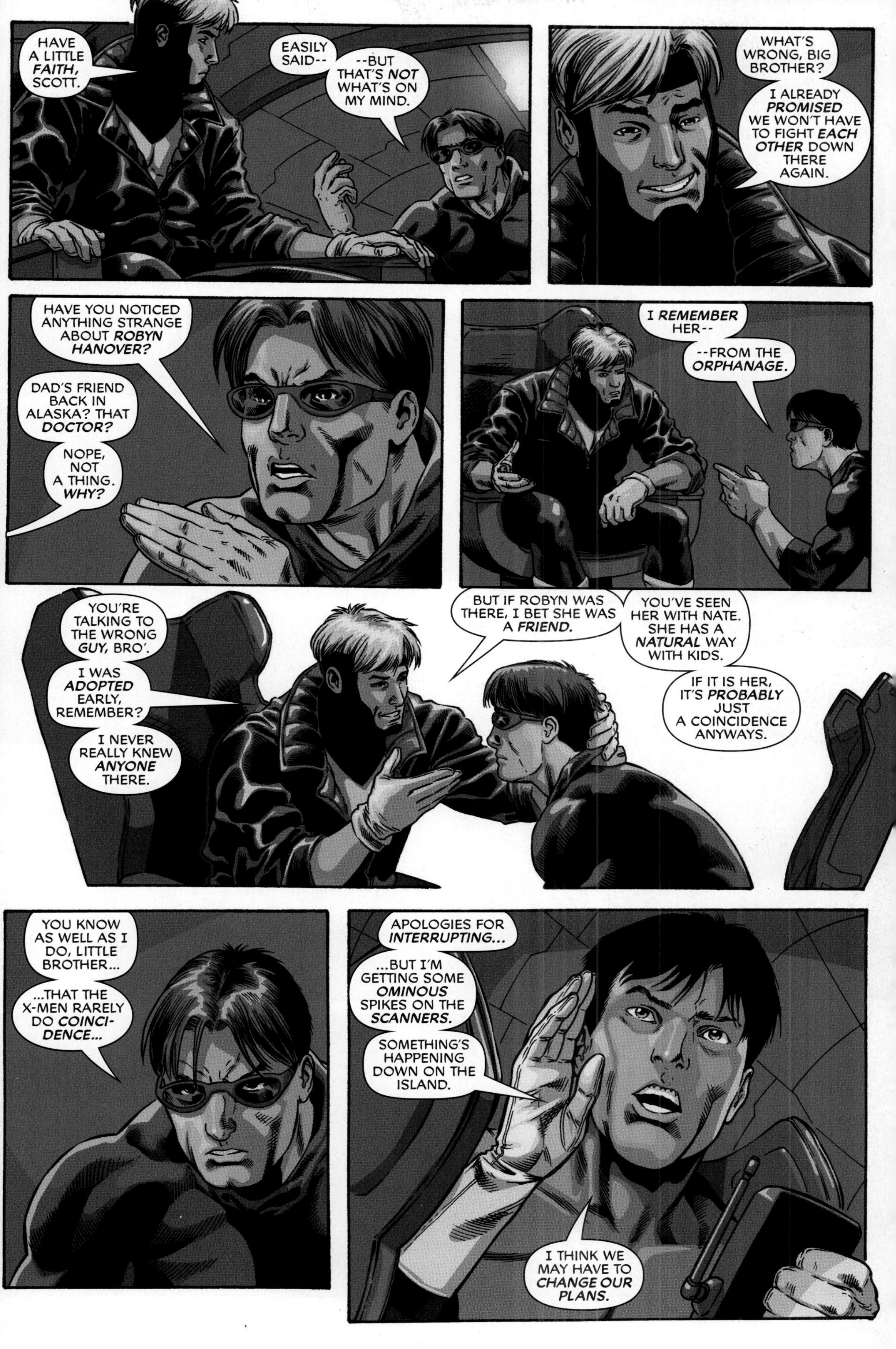

HAVE A LITTLE FAITH, SCOTT.
EASILY SAID--
--BUT THAT'S NOT WHAT'S ON MY MIND.
WHAT'S WRONG, BIG BROTHER?
I ALREADY PROMISED WE WON'T HAVE TO FIGHT EACH OTHER DOWN THERE AGAIN.
HAVE YOU NOTICED ANYTHING STRANGE ABOUT ROBYN HANOVER?
DAD'S FRIEND BACK IN ALASKA? THAT DOCTOR?
NOPE, NOT A THING. WHY?
I REMEMBER HER--
--FROM THE ORPHANAGE.
YOU'RE TALKING TO THE WRONG GUY, BRO'.
I WAS ADOPTED EARLY, REMEMBER?
I NEVER REALLY KNEW ANYONE THERE.
BUT IF ROBYN WAS THERE, I BET SHE WAS A FRIEND.
YOU'VE SEEN HER WITH NATE. SHE HAS A NATURAL WAY WITH KIDS.
IF IT IS HER, IT'S PROBABLY JUST A COINCIDENCE ANYWAYS.
YOU KNOW AS WELL AS I DO, LITTLE BROTHER...
...THAT THE X-MEN RARELY DO COINCI-DENCE...
APOLOGIES FOR INTERRUPTING...
...BUT I'M GETTING SOME OMINOUS SPIKES ON THE SCANNERS.
SOMETHING'S HAPPENING DOWN ON THE ISLAND.
I THINK WE MAY HAVE TO CHANGE OUR PLANS.

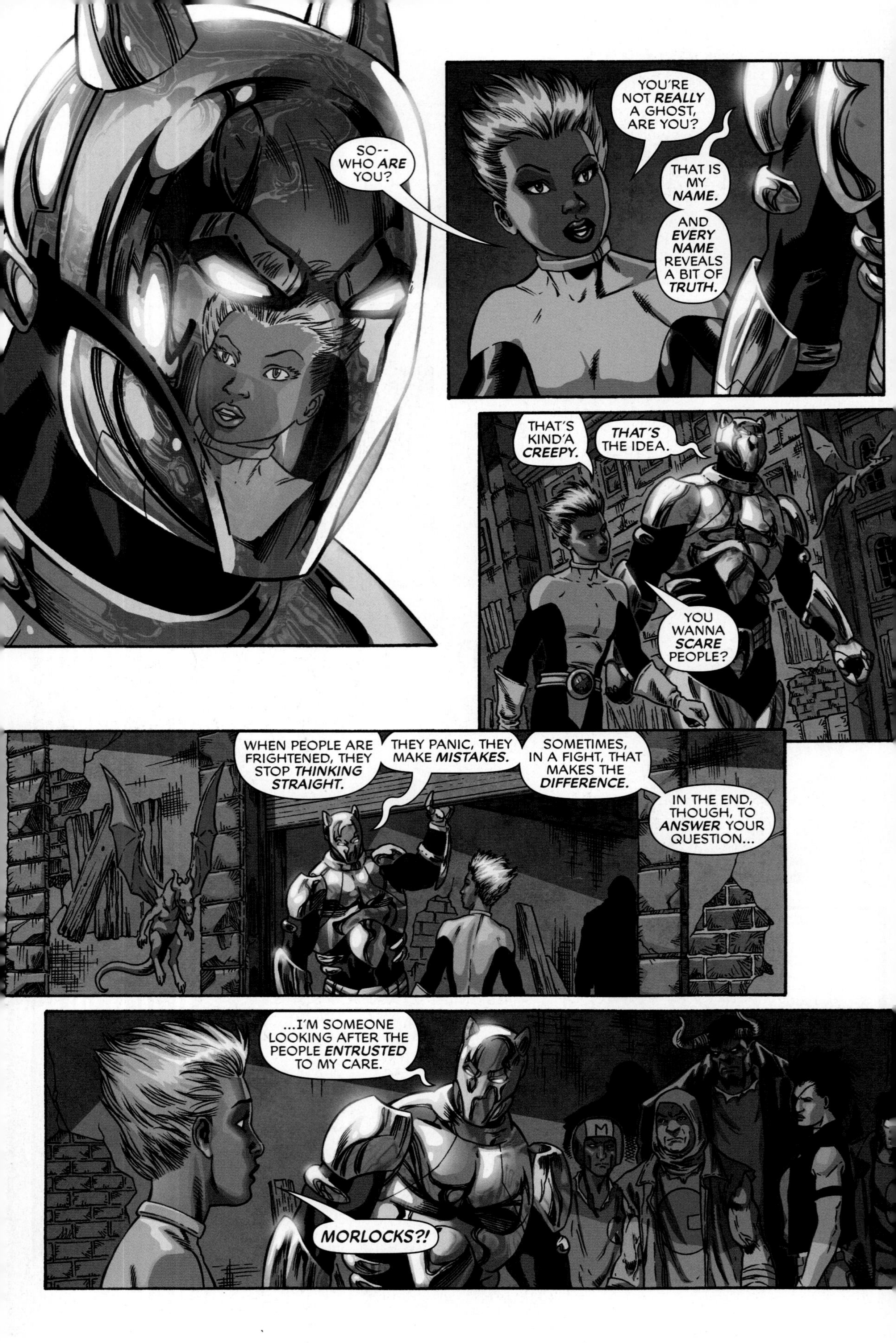
SO-- WHO *ARE* YOU?
YOU'RE NOT *REALLY* A GHOST, ARE YOU?
THAT IS MY *NAME.*
AND *EVERY NAME* REVEALS A BIT OF *TRUTH.*
THAT'S KIND'A *CREEPY.*
THAT'S THE IDEA.
YOU WANNA *SCARE* PEOPLE?
WHEN PEOPLE ARE FRIGHTENED, THEY STOP *THINKING STRAIGHT.*
THEY PANIC, THEY MAKE *MISTAKES.*
SOMETIMES, IN A FIGHT, THAT MAKES THE *DIFFERENCE.*
IN THE END, THOUGH, TO *ANSWER* YOUR QUESTION...
...I'M SOMEONE LOOKING AFTER THE PEOPLE *ENTRUSTED* TO MY CARE.
MORLOCKS?!

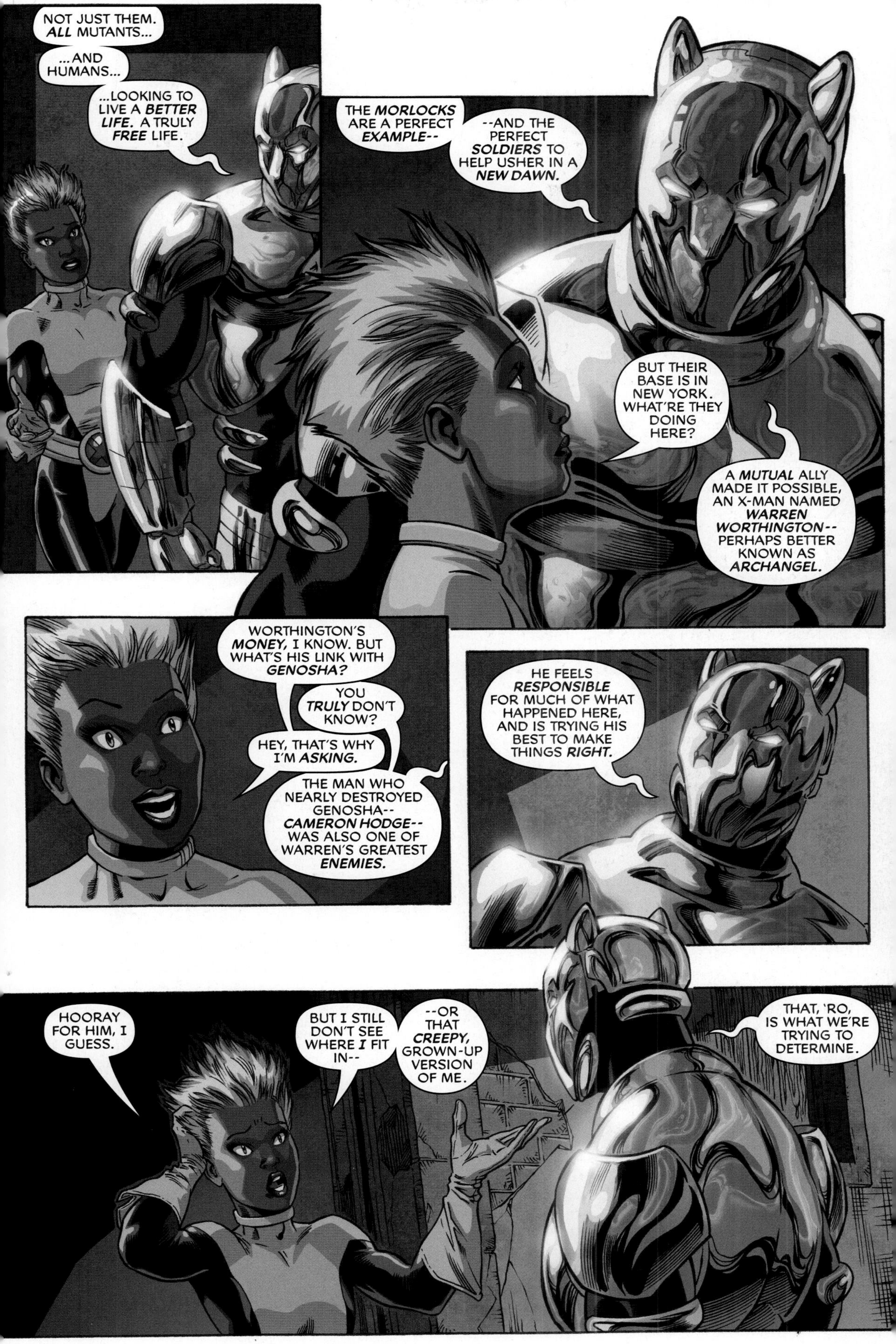
NOT JUST THEM. ALL MUTANTS...
...AND HUMANS...
...LOOKING TO LIVE A BETTER LIFE. A TRULY FREE LIFE.
THE MORLOCKS ARE A PERFECT EXAMPLE--
--AND THE PERFECT SOLDIERS TO HELP USHER IN A NEW DAWN.
BUT THEIR BASE IS IN NEW YORK. WHAT'RE THEY DOING HERE?
A MUTUAL ALLY MADE IT POSSIBLE, AN X-MAN NAMED WARREN WORTHINGTON--PERHAPS BETTER KNOWN AS ARCHANGEL.
WORTHINGTON'S MONEY, I KNOW. BUT WHAT'S HIS LINK WITH GENOSHA?
YOU TRULY DON'T KNOW?
HEY, THAT'S WHY I'M ASKING.
THE MAN WHO NEARLY DESTROYED GENOSHA--CAMERON HODGE--WAS ALSO ONE OF WARREN'S GREATEST ENEMIES.
HE FEELS RESPONSIBLE FOR MUCH OF WHAT HAPPENED HERE, AND IS TRYING HIS BEST TO MAKE THINGS RIGHT.
HOORAY FOR HIM, I GUESS.
BUT I STILL DON'T SEE WHERE I FIT IN--
--OR THAT CREEPY, GROWN-UP VERSION OF ME.
THAT, 'RO, IS WHAT WE'RE TRYING TO DETERMINE.

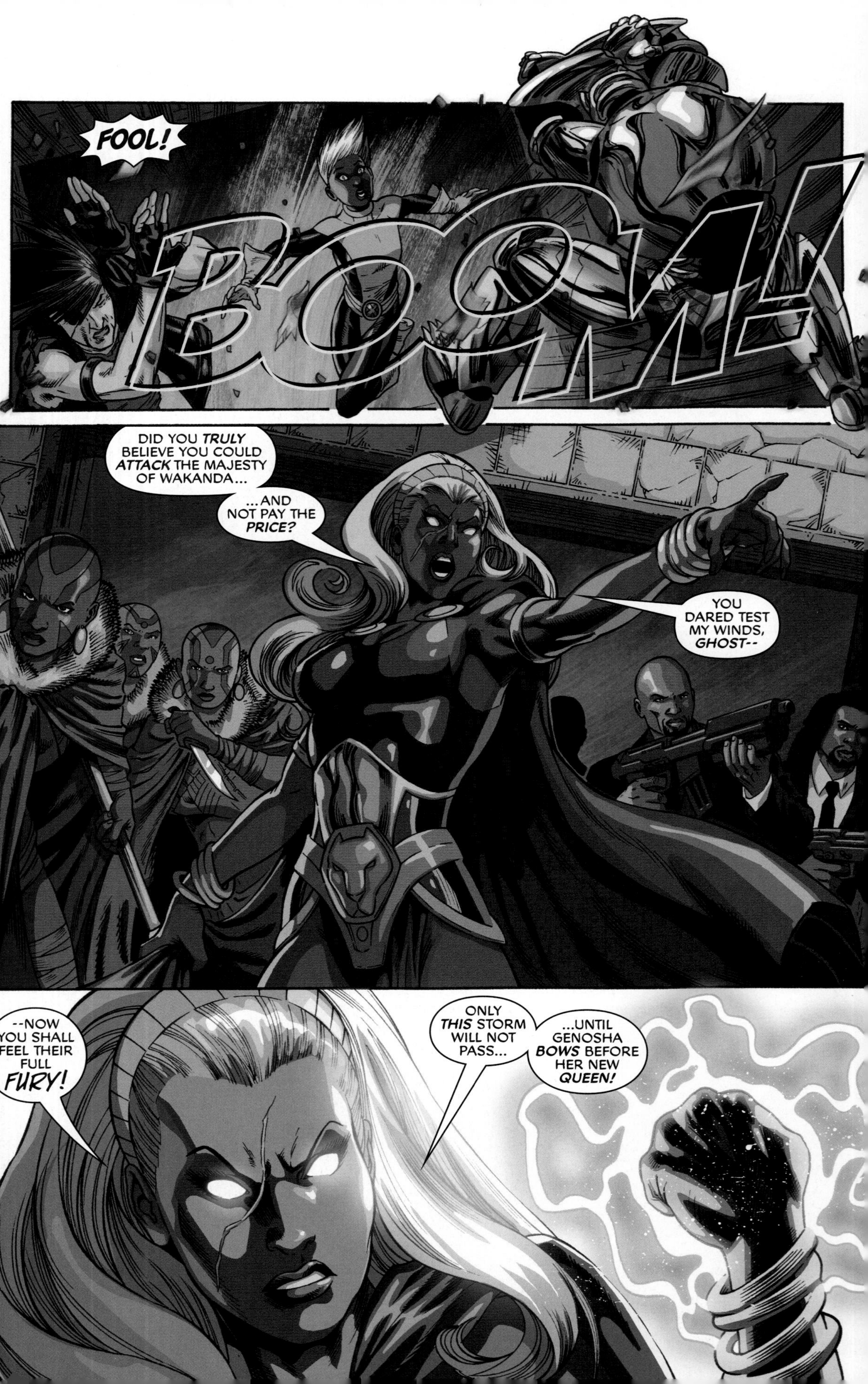
FOOL!
BOOM!
DID YOU TRULY BELIEVE YOU COULD ATTACK THE MAJESTY OF WAKANDA...
...AND NOT PAY THE PRICE?
YOU DARED TEST MY WINDS, GHOST--
--NOW YOU SHALL FEEL THEIR FULL FURY!
ONLY THIS STORM WILL NOT PASS...
...UNTIL GENOSHA BOWS BEFORE HER NEW QUEEN!

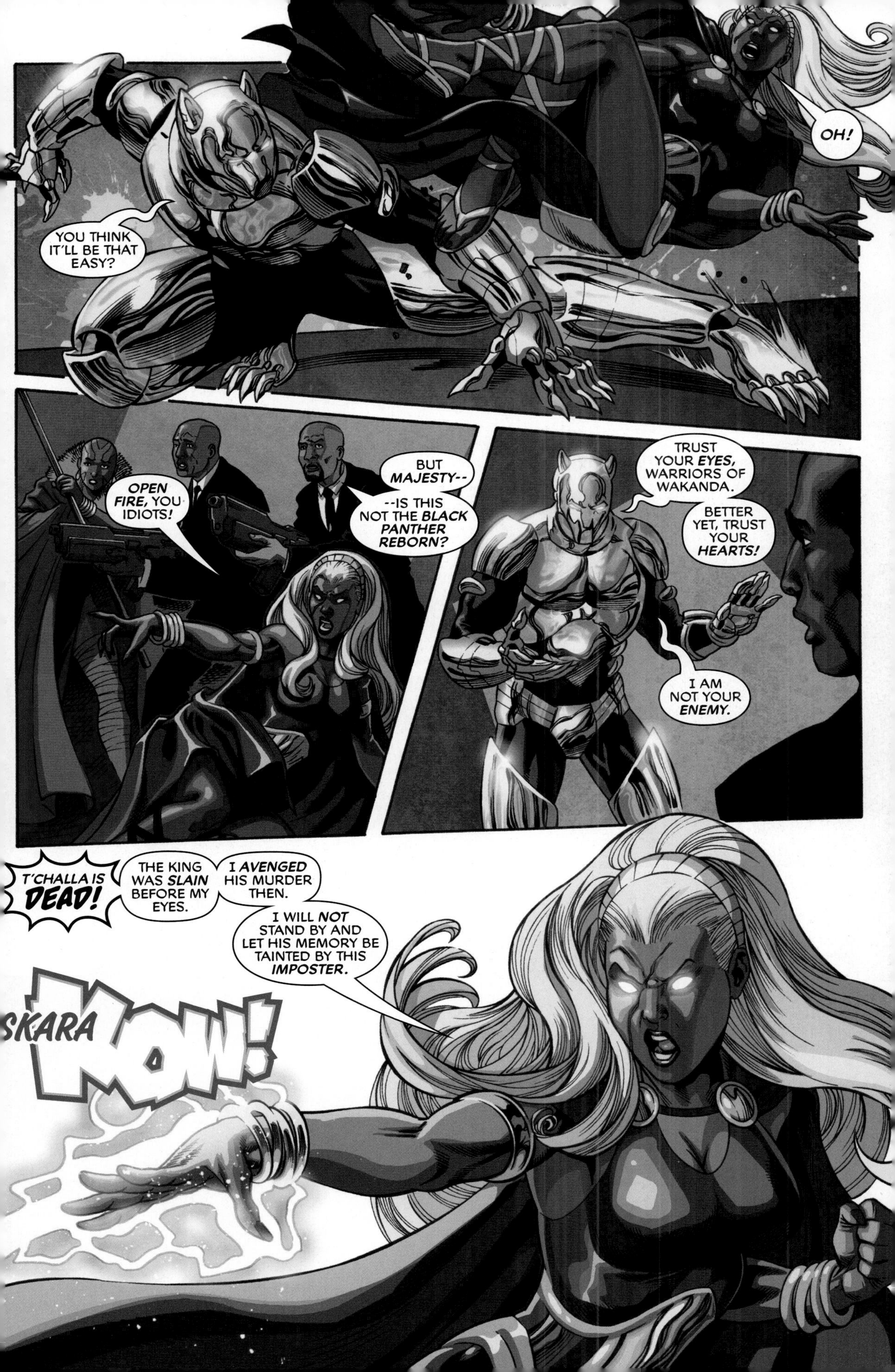
OH!
YOU THINK IT'LL BE THAT EASY?
OPEN FIRE, YOU IDIOTS!
BUT MAJESTY--
--IS THIS NOT THE BLACK PANTHER REBORN?
TRUST YOUR EYES, WARRIORS OF WAKANDA.
BETTER YET, TRUST YOUR HEARTS!
I AM NOT YOUR ENEMY.
T'CHALLA IS DEAD!
THE KING WAS SLAIN BEFORE MY EYES.
I AVENGED HIS MURDER THEN.
I WILL NOT STAND BY AND LET HIS MEMORY BE TAINTED BY THIS IMPOSTER.
SKARA KOW!

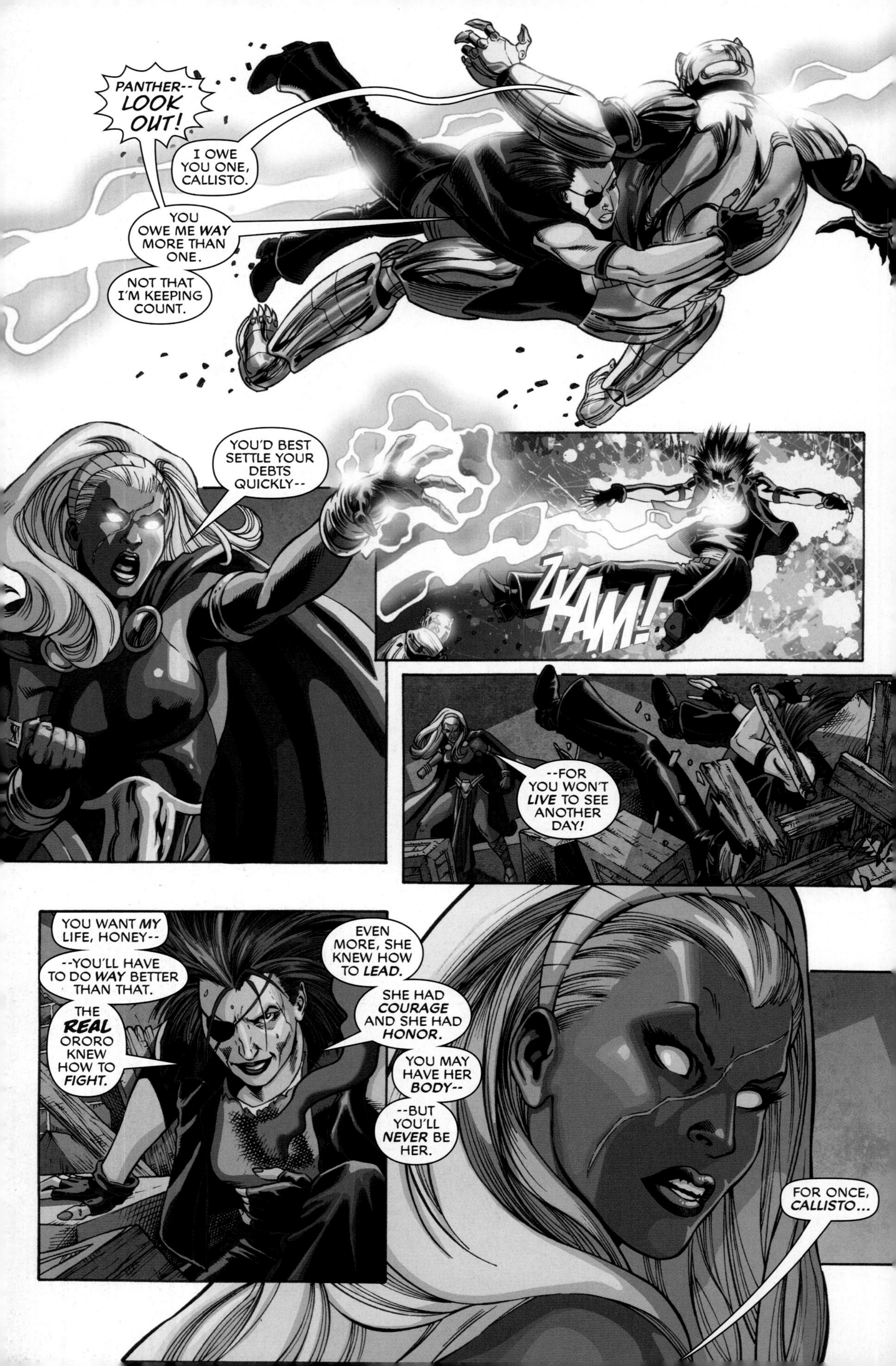
PANTHER-- LOOK OUT!
I OWE YOU ONE, CALLISTO.
YOU OWE ME WAY MORE THAN ONE.
NOT THAT I'M KEEPING COUNT.
YOU'D BEST SETTLE YOUR DEBTS QUICKLY--
ZZKAM!!
--FOR YOU WON'T LIVE TO SEE ANOTHER DAY!
YOU WANT MY LIFE, HONEY--
--YOU'LL HAVE TO DO WAY BETTER THAN THAT.
THE REAL ORORO KNEW HOW TO FIGHT.
EVEN MORE, SHE KNEW HOW TO LEAD.
SHE HAD COURAGE AND SHE HAD HONOR.
YOU MAY HAVE HER BODY--
--BUT YOU'LL NEVER BE HER.
FOR ONCE, CALLISTO...

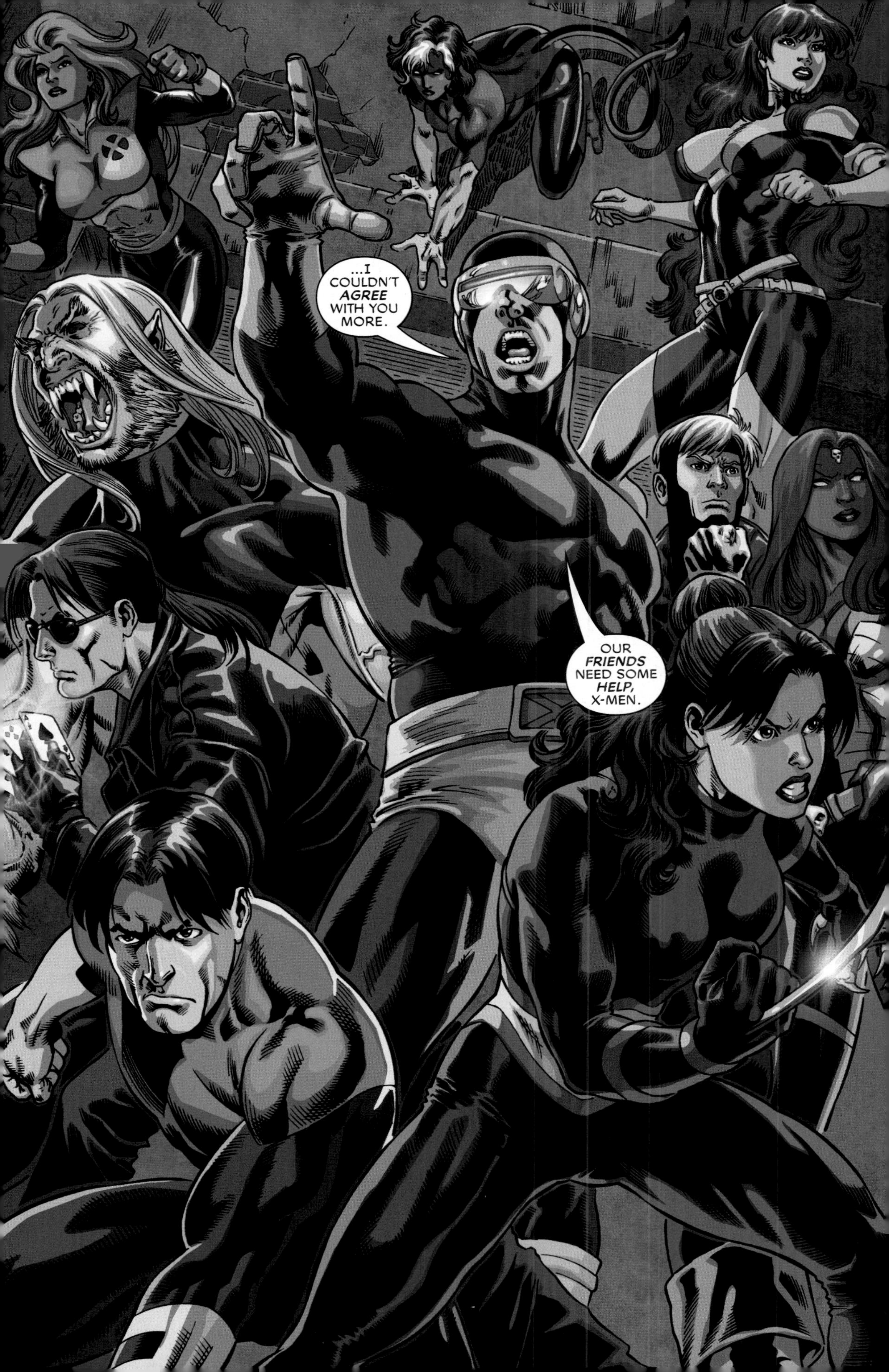
...I COULDN'T AGREE WITH YOU MORE.
OUR FRIENDS NEED SOME HELP, X-MEN.

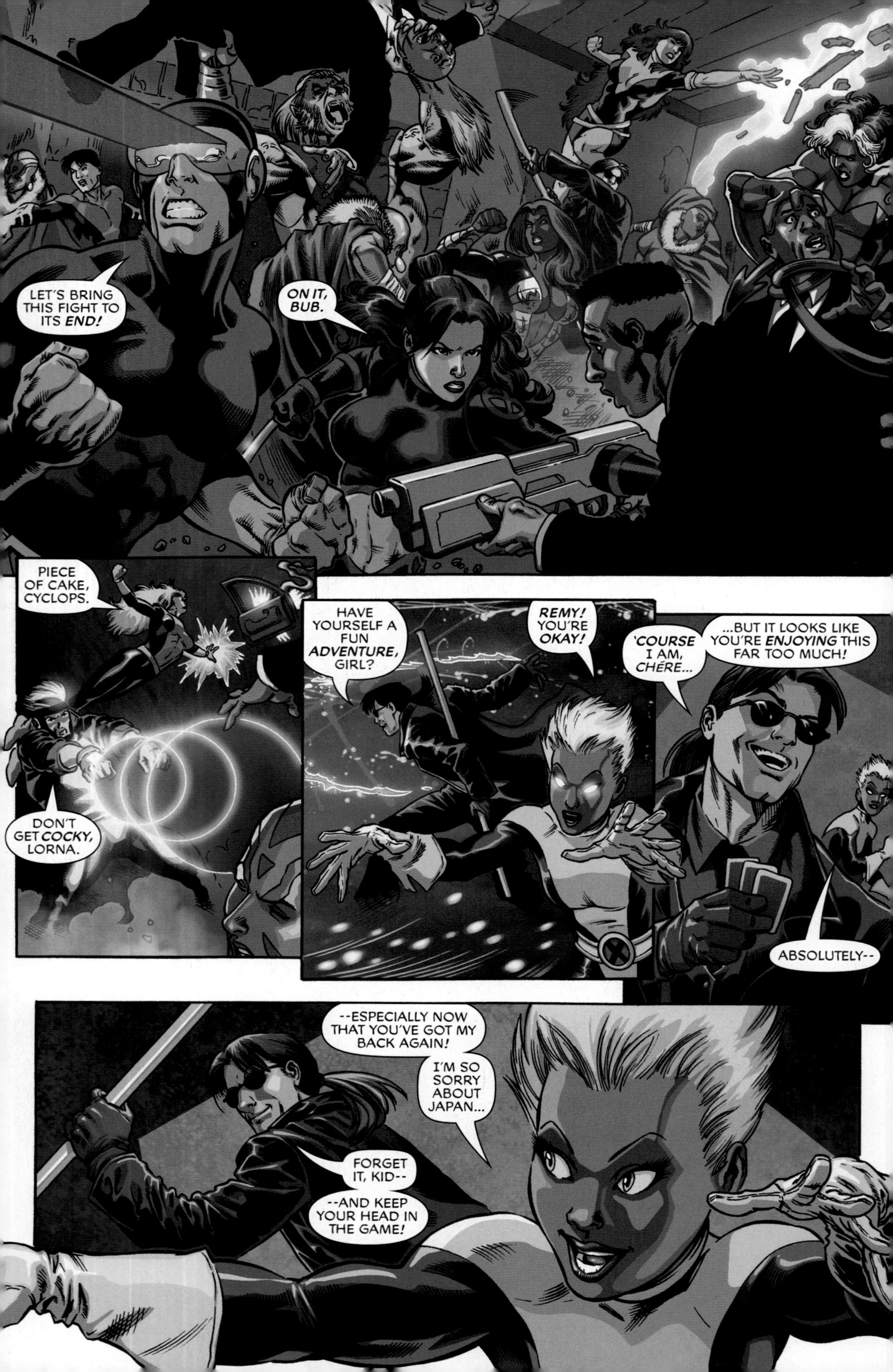
LET'S BRING THIS FIGHT TO ITS END!
ON IT, BUB.
PIECE OF CAKE, CYCLOPS.
DON'T GET COCKY, LORNA.
HAVE YOURSELF A FUN ADVENTURE, GIRL?
REMY! YOU'RE OKAY!
'COURSE I AM, CHÉRE...
...BUT IT LOOKS LIKE YOU'RE ENJOYING THIS FAR TOO MUCH!
ABSOLUTELY--
--ESPECIALLY NOW THAT YOU'VE GOT MY BACK AGAIN!
I'M SO SORRY ABOUT JAPAN...
FORGET IT, KID--
--AND KEEP YOUR HEAD IN THE GAME!

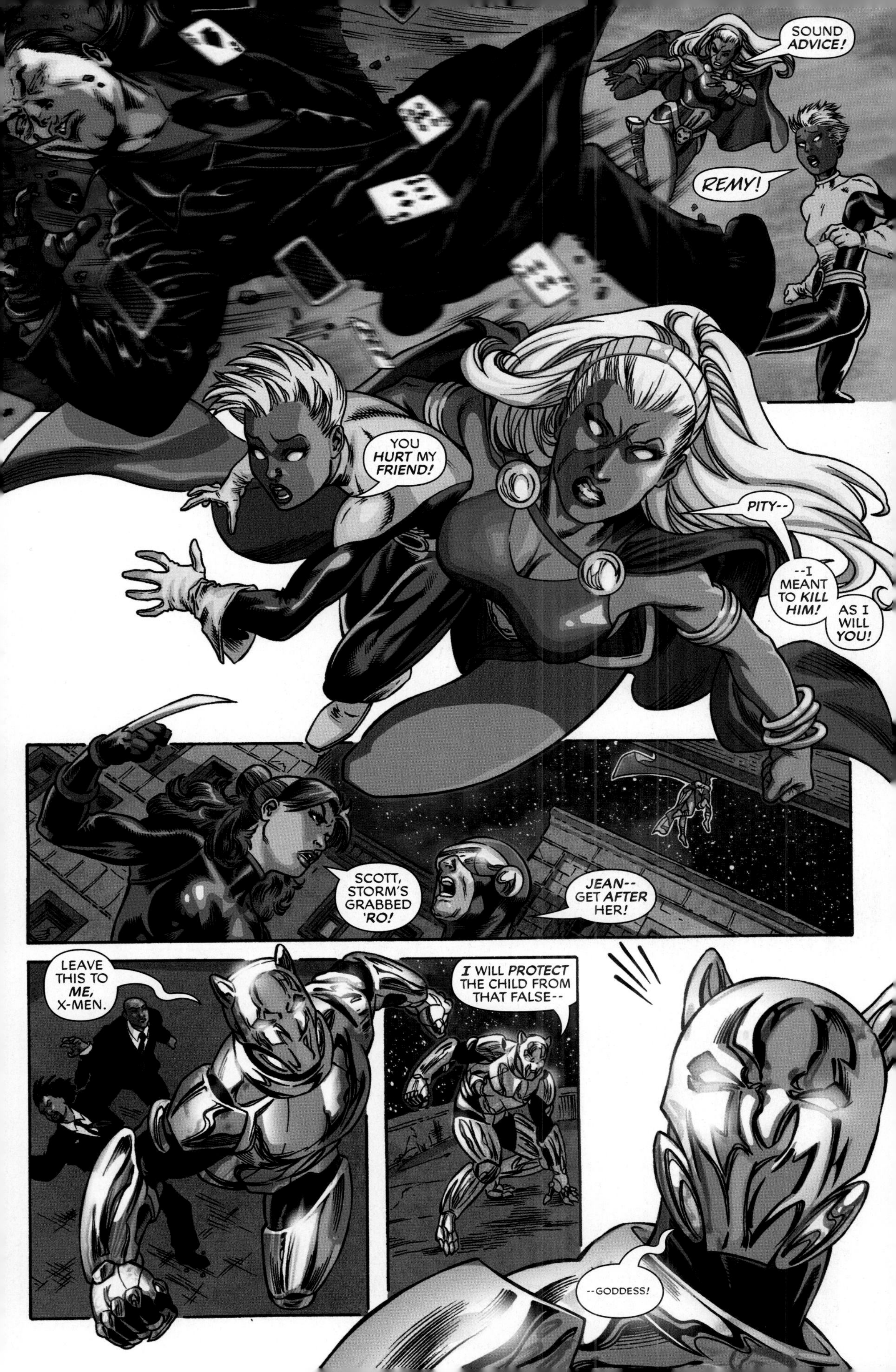
SOUND ADVICE!
REMY!
YOU HURT MY FRIEND!
PITY--
--I MEANT TO KILL HIM!
AS I WILL YOU!
SCOTT, STORM'S GRABBED 'RO!
JEAN-- GET AFTER HER!
LEAVE THIS TO ME, X-MEN.
I WILL PROTECT THE CHILD FROM THAT FALSE--
--GODDESS!

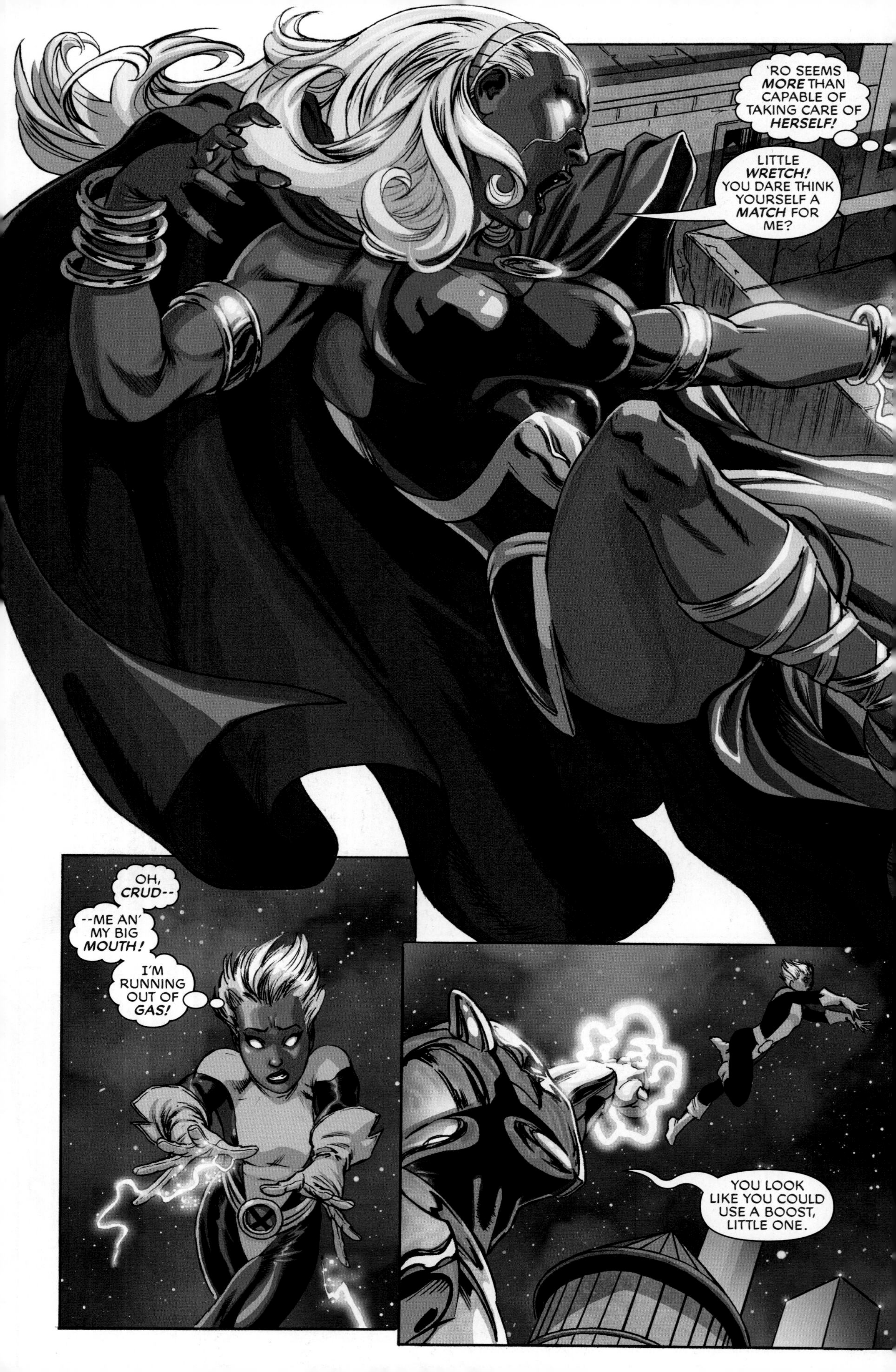
'RO SEEMS MORE THAN CAPABLE OF TAKING CARE OF HERSELF!
LITTLE WRETCH! YOU DARE THINK YOURSELF A MATCH FOR ME?
OH, CRUD--
--ME AN' MY BIG MOUTH!
I'M RUNNING OUT OF GAS!
YOU LOOK LIKE YOU COULD USE A BOOST, LITTLE ONE.

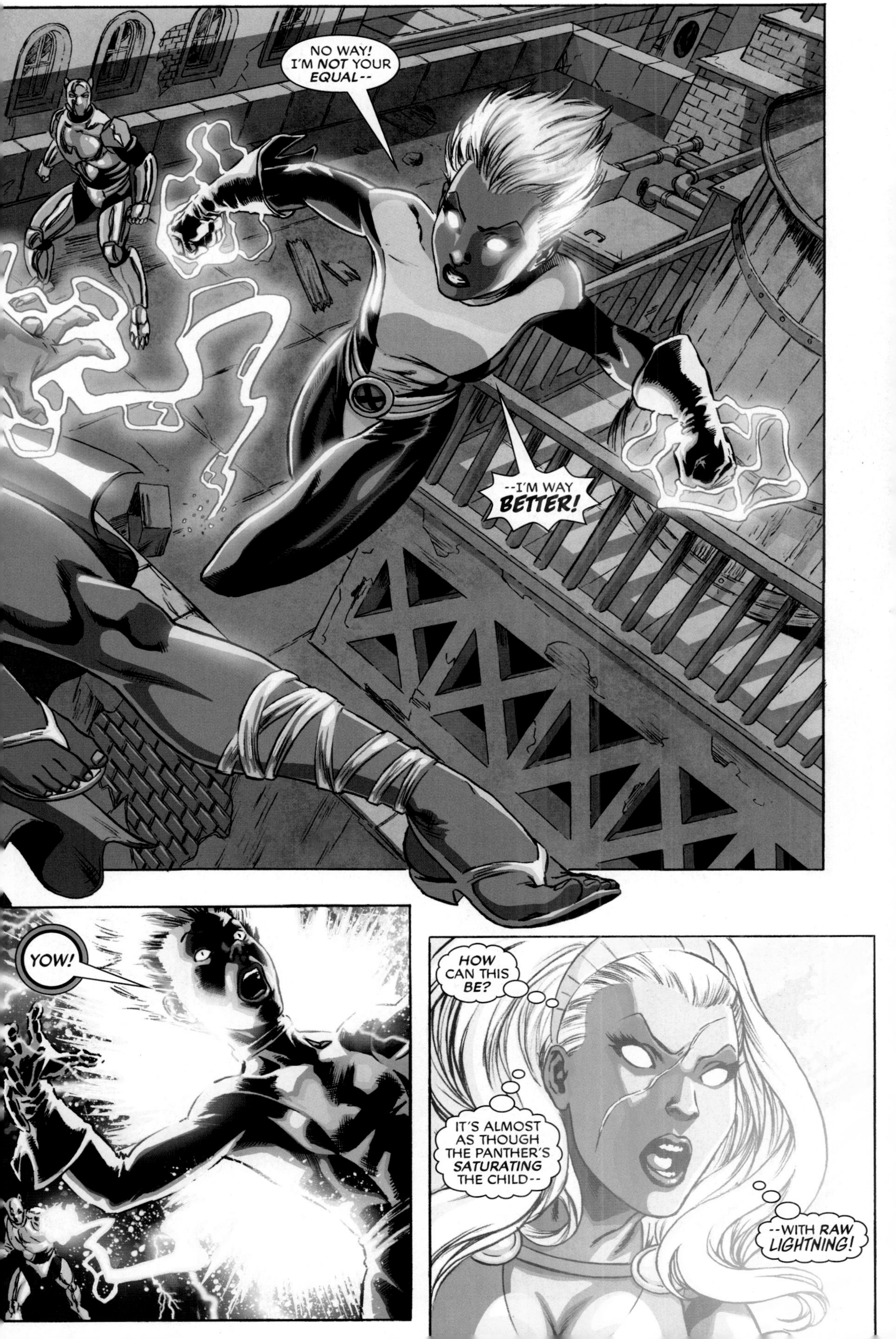
NO WAY! I'M *NOT* YOUR *EQUAL*--
--I'M WAY **BETTER!**
YOW!
HOW CAN THIS *BE?*
IT'S ALMOST AS THOUGH THE PANTHER'S *SATURATING* THE CHILD--
--WITH *RAW LIGHTNING!*

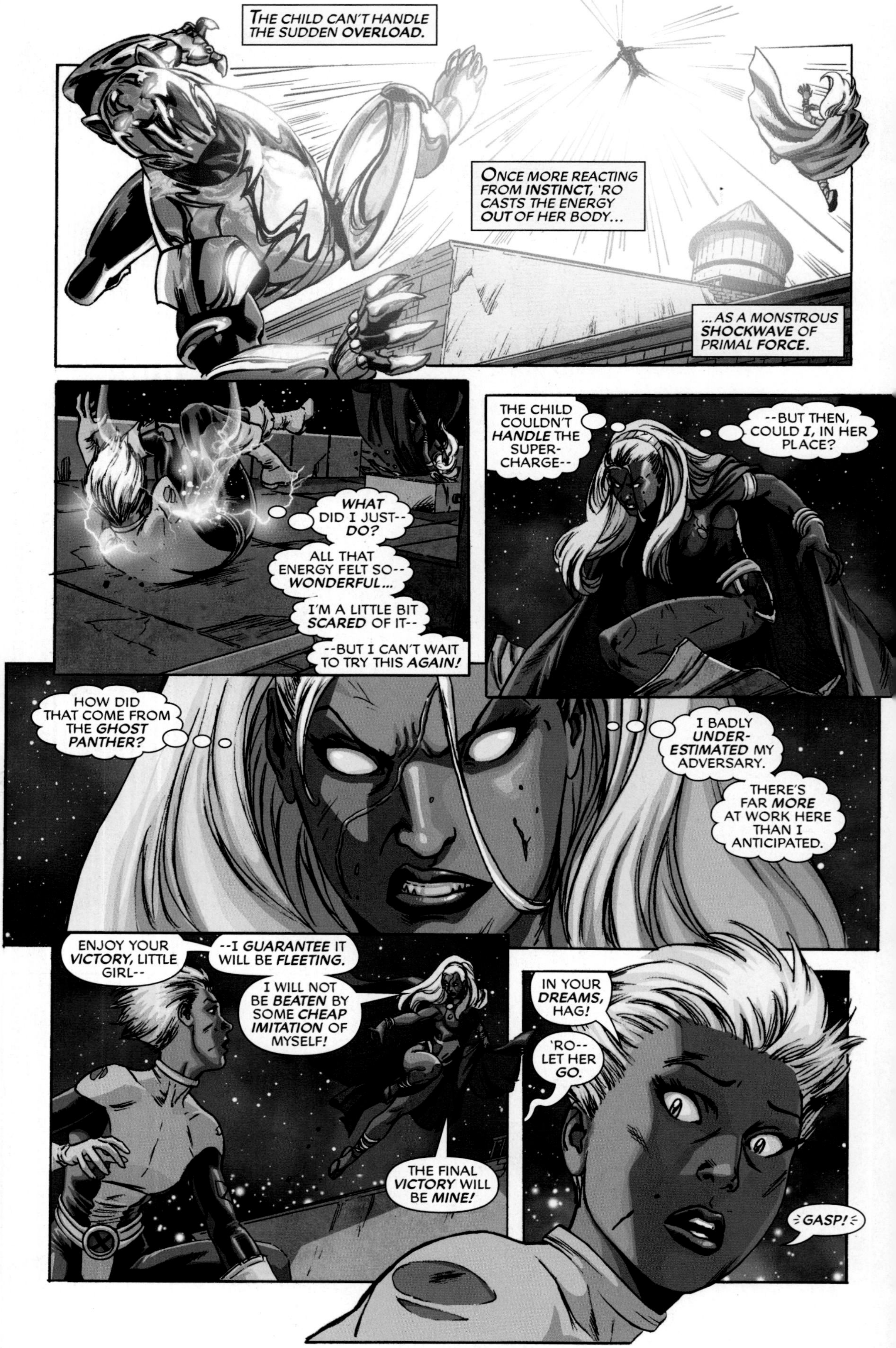

THE CHILD CAN'T HANDLE THE SUDDEN OVERLOAD.
ONCE MORE REACTING FROM INSTINCT, 'RO CASTS THE ENERGY OUT OF HER BODY...
...AS A MONSTROUS SHOCKWAVE OF PRIMAL FORCE.
WHAT DID I JUST--DO?
ALL THAT ENERGY FELT SO--WONDERFUL...
I'M A LITTLE BIT SCARED OF IT--
--BUT I CAN'T WAIT TO TRY THIS AGAIN!
THE CHILD COULDN'T HANDLE THE SUPER-CHARGE--
--BUT THEN, COULD I, IN HER PLACE?
HOW DID THAT COME FROM THE GHOST PANTHER?
I BADLY UNDER-ESTIMATED MY ADVERSARY.
THERE'S FAR MORE AT WORK HERE THAN I ANTICIPATED.
ENJOY YOUR VICTORY, LITTLE GIRL--
--I GUARANTEE IT WILL BE FLEETING.
I WILL NOT BE BEATEN BY SOME CHEAP IMITATION OF MYSELF!
THE FINAL VICTORY WILL BE MINE!
IN YOUR DREAMS, HAG!
'RO--LET HER GO.
GASP!

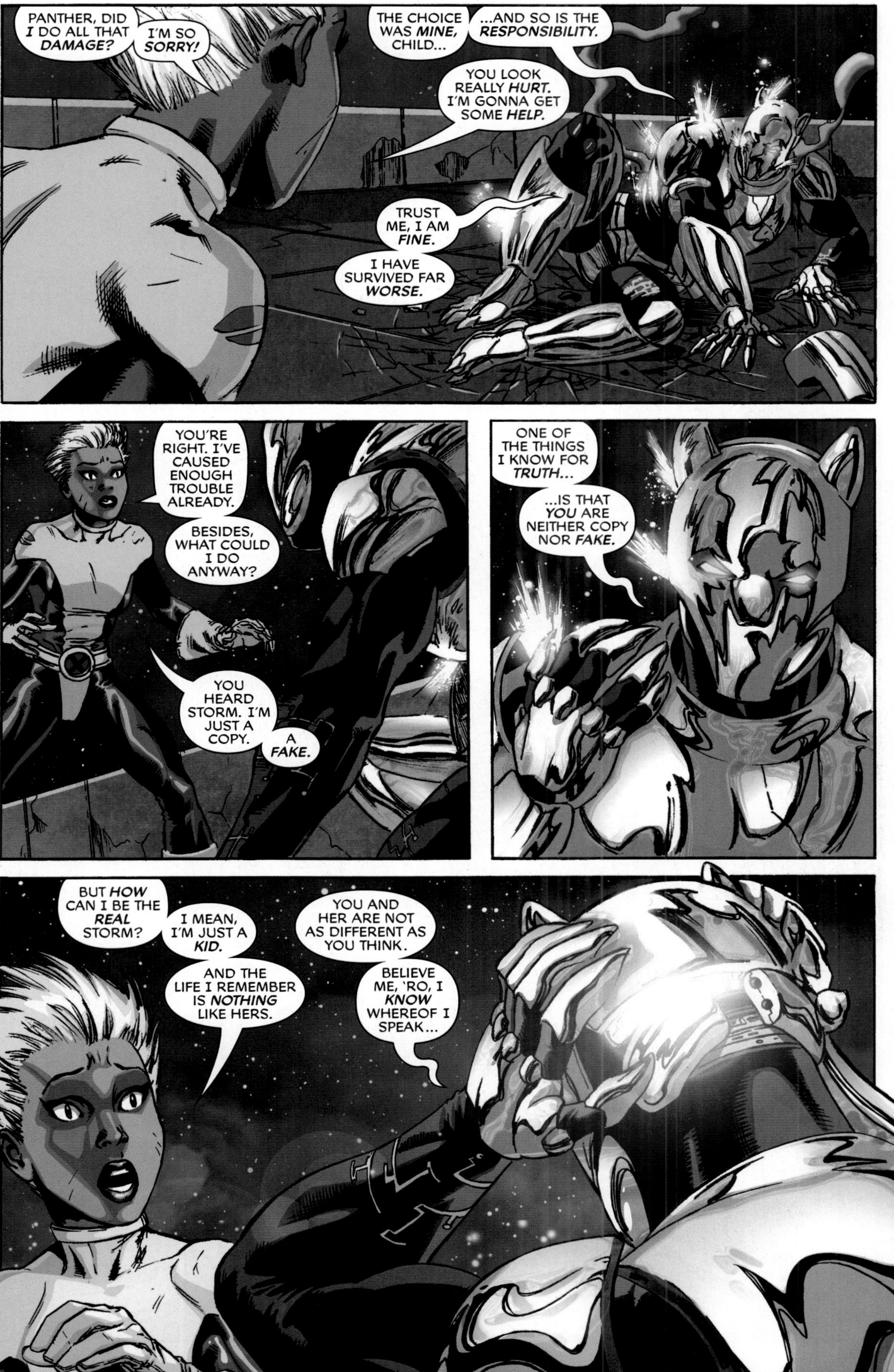
PANTHER, DID I DO ALL THAT DAMAGE?
I'M SO SORRY!
THE CHOICE WAS MINE, CHILD...
...AND SO IS THE RESPONSIBILITY.
YOU LOOK REALLY HURT. I'M GONNA GET SOME HELP.
TRUST ME, I AM FINE.
I HAVE SURVIVED FAR WORSE.
YOU'RE RIGHT. I'VE CAUSED ENOUGH TROUBLE ALREADY.
BESIDES, WHAT COULD I DO ANYWAY?
YOU HEARD STORM. I'M JUST A COPY.
A FAKE.
ONE OF THE THINGS I KNOW FOR TRUTH...
...IS THAT YOU ARE NEITHER COPY NOR FAKE.
BUT HOW CAN I BE THE REAL STORM?
I MEAN, I'M JUST A KID.
AND THE LIFE I REMEMBER IS NOTHING LIKE HERS.
YOU AND HER ARE NOT AS DIFFERENT AS YOU THINK.
BELIEVE ME, 'RO, I KNOW WHEREOF I SPEAK...

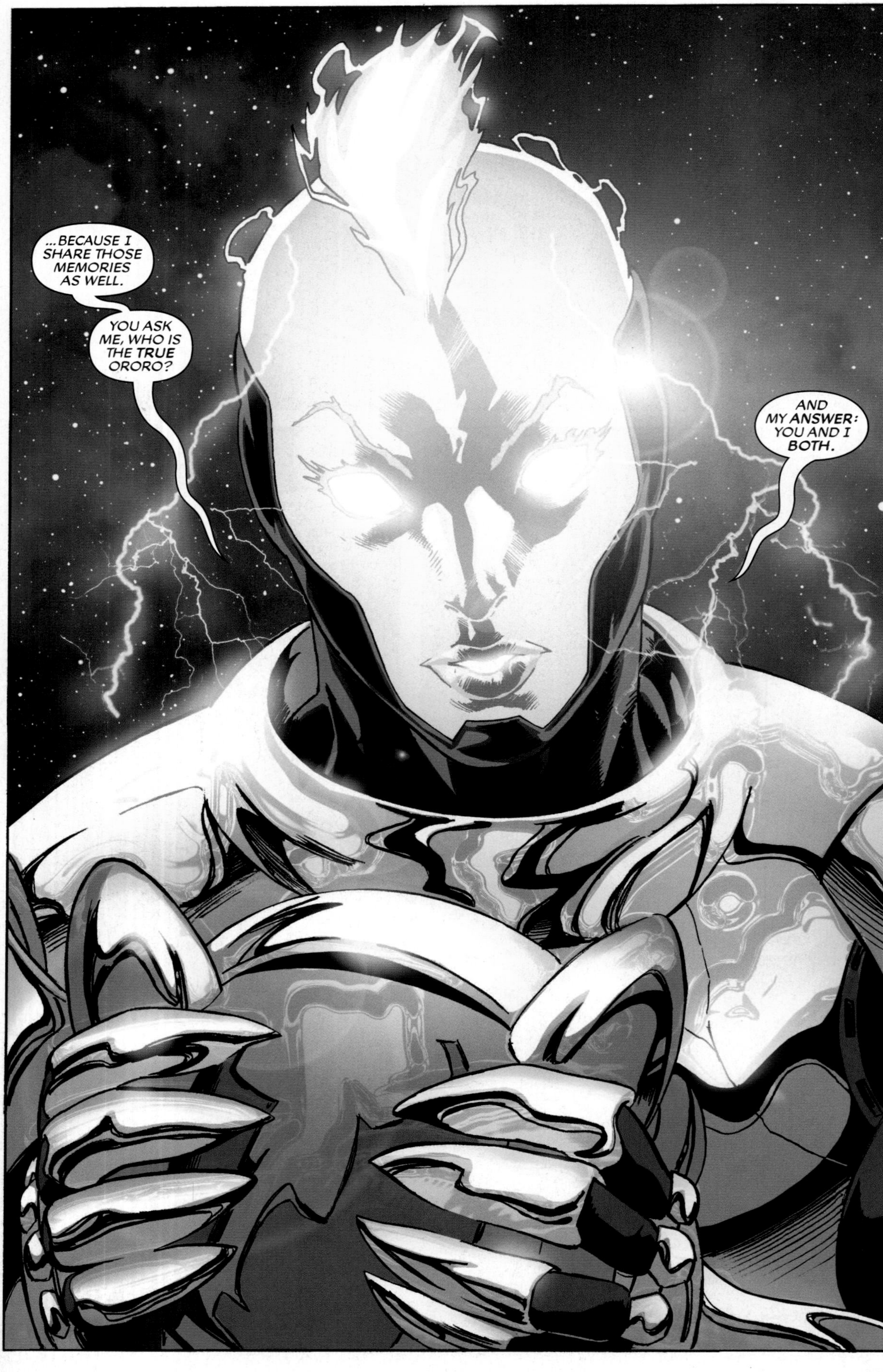
...BECAUSE I SHARE THOSE MEMORIES AS WELL.
YOU ASK ME, WHO IS THE TRUE ORORO?
AND MY ANSWER: YOU AND I BOTH.

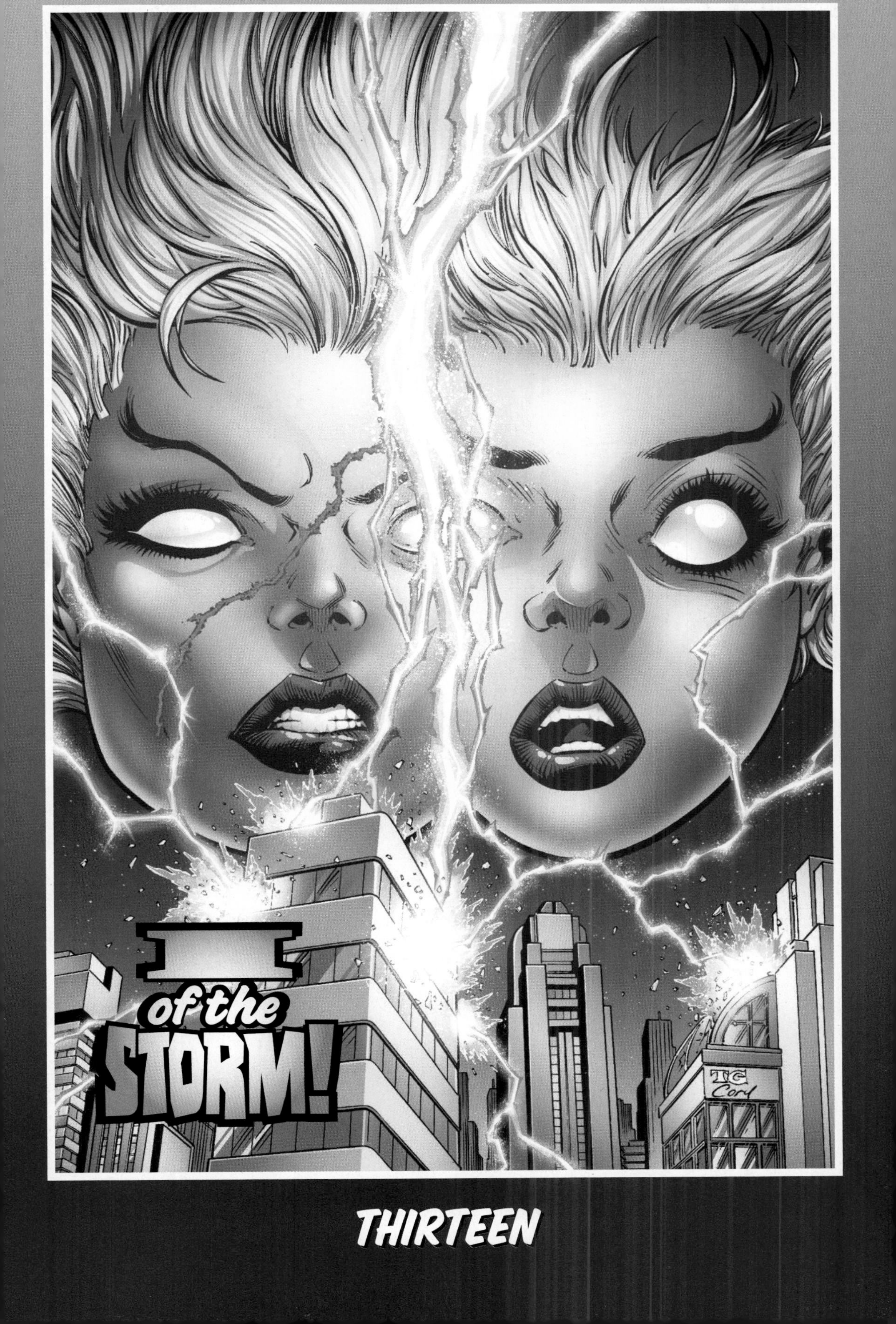
of the
STORM!
TC Corp

THIRTEEN

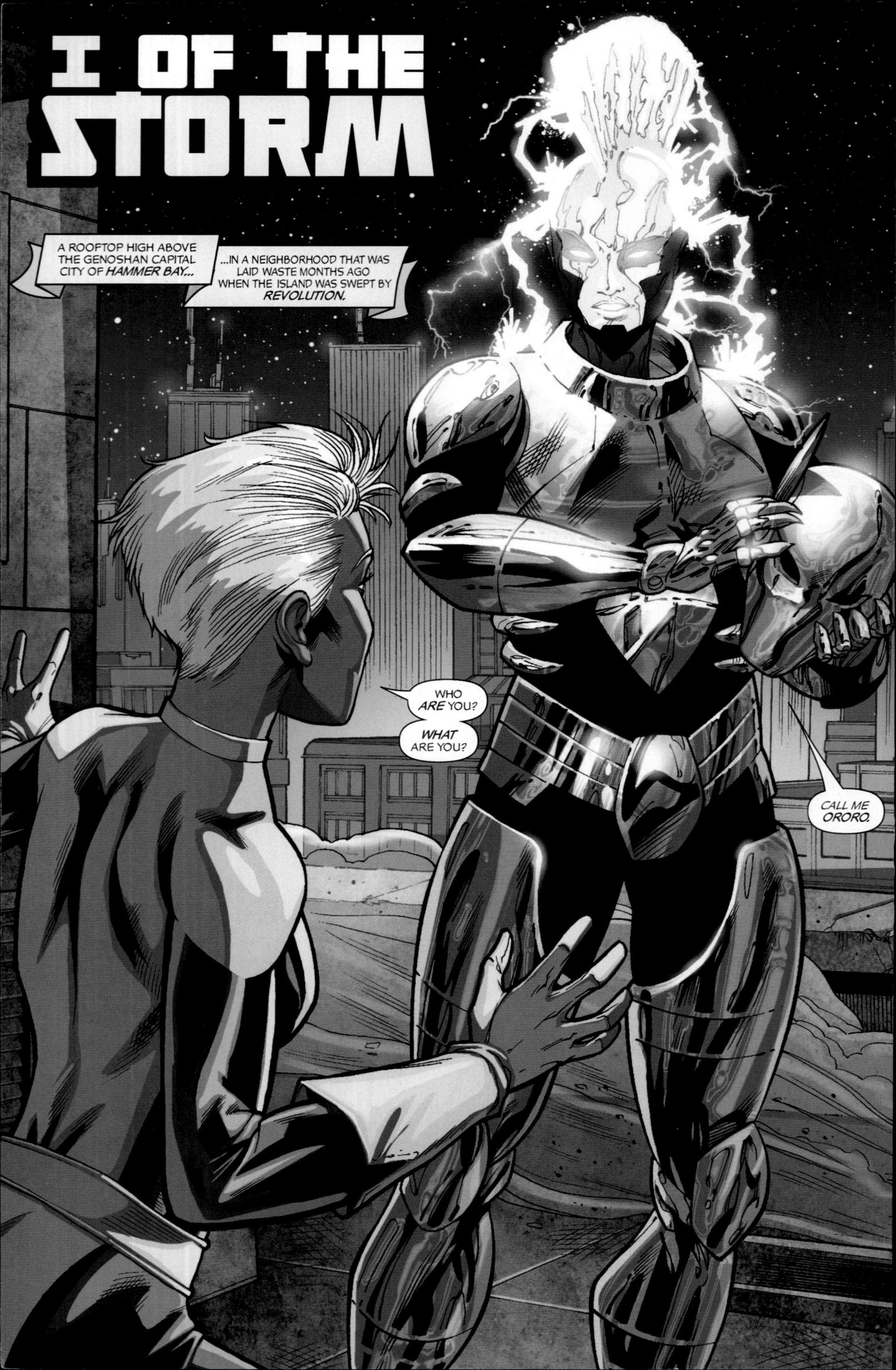
I OF THE STORM
A ROOFTOP HIGH ABOVE THE GENOSHAN CAPITAL CITY OF HAMMER BAY...
...IN A NEIGHBORHOOD THAT WAS LAID WASTE MONTHS AGO WHEN THE ISLAND WAS SWEPT BY REVOLUTION.
WHO ARE YOU?
WHAT ARE YOU?
CALL ME ORORO.

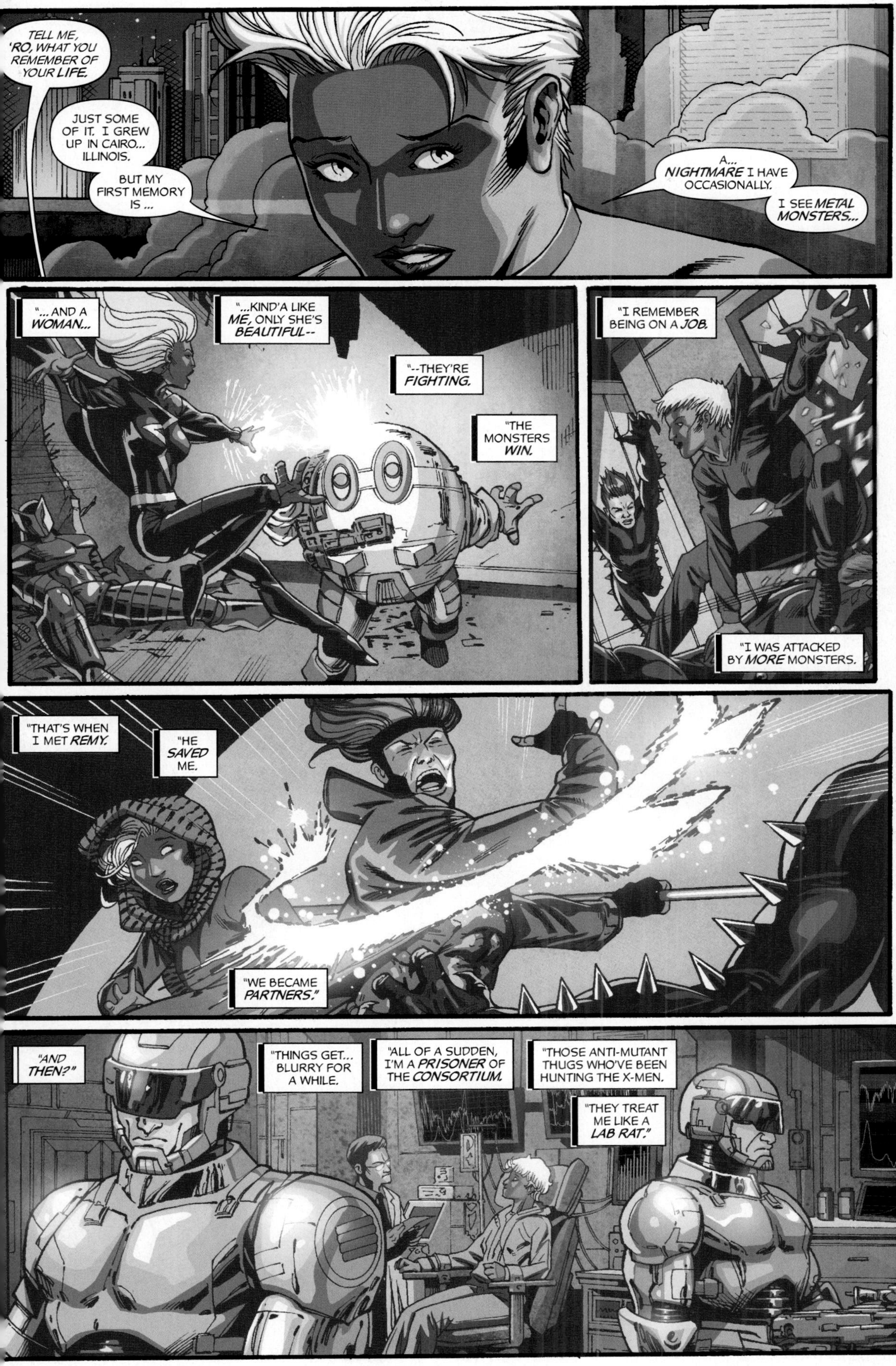
TELL ME, 'RO, WHAT YOU REMEMBER OF YOUR LIFE.
JUST SOME OF IT. I GREW UP IN CAIRO... ILLINOIS.
BUT MY FIRST MEMORY IS ...
A... NIGHTMARE I HAVE OCCASIONALLY.
I SEE METAL MONSTERS...
"...AND A WOMAN...
"...KIND'A LIKE ME, ONLY SHE'S BEAUTIFUL--
"--THEY'RE FIGHTING.
"THE MONSTERS WIN.
"I REMEMBER BEING ON A JOB.
"I WAS ATTACKED BY MORE MONSTERS.
"THAT'S WHEN I MET REMY.
"HE SAVED ME.
"WE BECAME PARTNERS."
"AND THEN?"
"THINGS GET... BLURRY FOR A WHILE.
"ALL OF A SUDDEN, I'M A PRISONER OF THE CONSORTIUM.
"THOSE ANTI-MUTANT THUGS WHO'VE BEEN HUNTING THE X-MEN.
"THEY TREAT ME LIKE A LAB RAT."

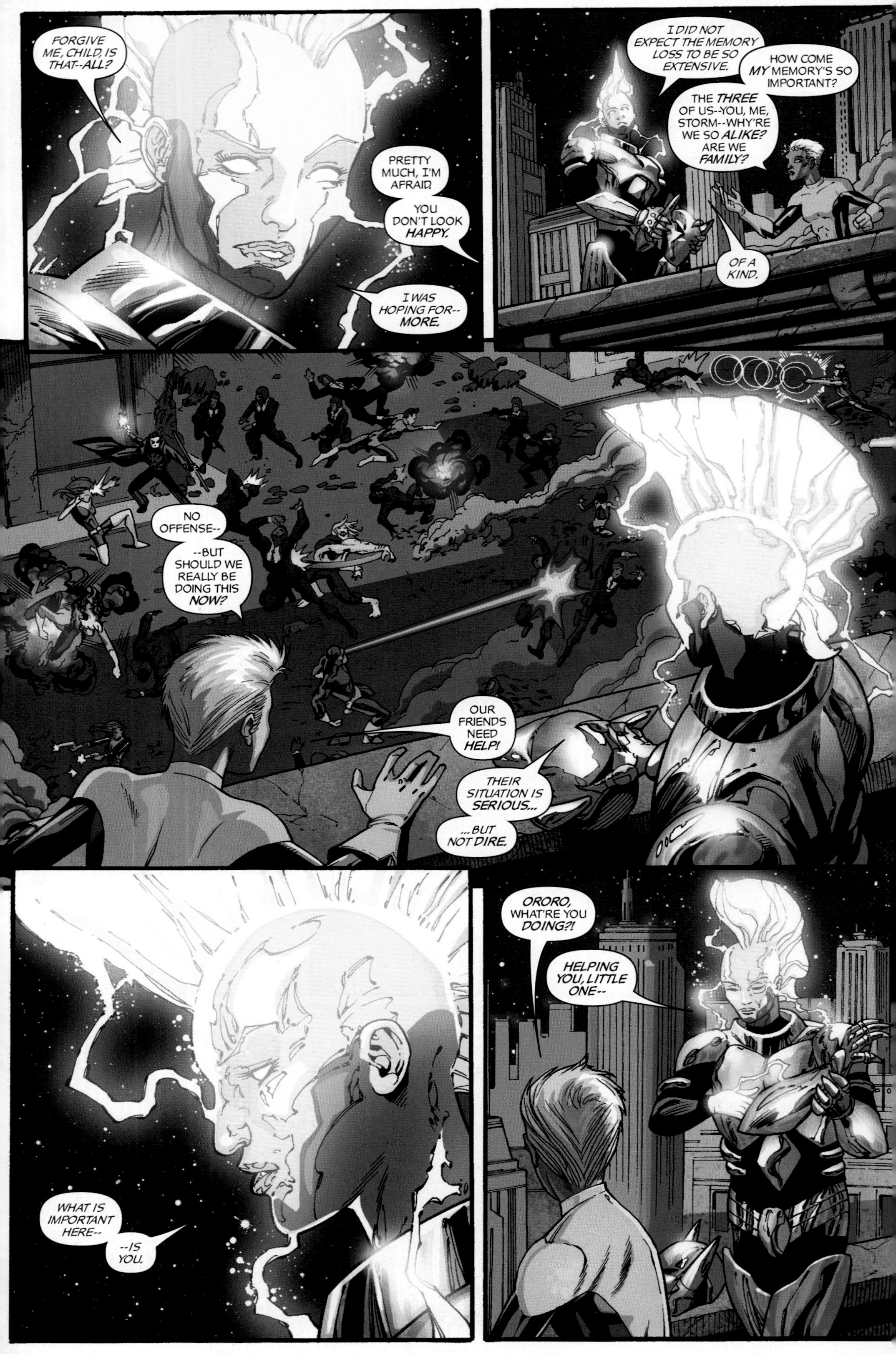
FORGIVE ME, CHILD, IS THAT--ALL?
PRETTY MUCH, I'M AFRAID.
YOU DON'T LOOK HAPPY.
I WAS HOPING FOR-- MORE.
I DID NOT EXPECT THE MEMORY LOSS TO BE SO EXTENSIVE.
HOW COME MY MEMORY'S SO IMPORTANT?
THE THREE OF US--YOU, ME, STORM--WHY'RE WE SO ALIKE? ARE WE FAMILY?
OF A KIND.
NO OFFENSE--
--BUT SHOULD WE REALLY BE DOING THIS NOW?
OUR FRIENDS NEED HELP!
THEIR SITUATION IS SERIOUS...
...BUT NOT DIRE.
WHAT IS IMPORTANT HERE--
--IS YOU.
ORORO, WHAT'RE YOU DOING?!
HELPING YOU, LITTLE ONE--

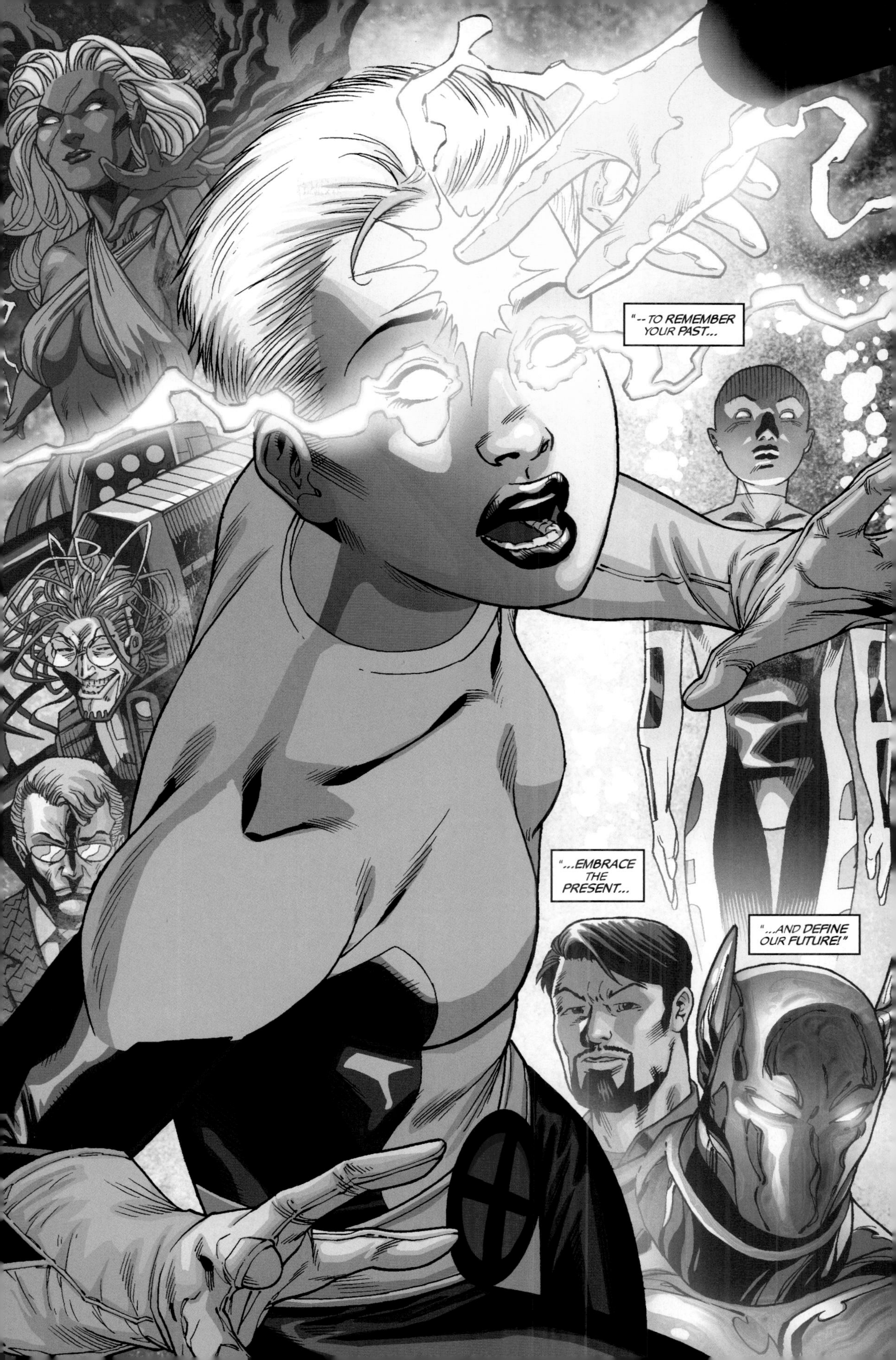
"--TO REMEMBER YOUR PAST...
"...EMBRACE THE PRESENT...
"...AND DEFINE OUR FUTURE!"

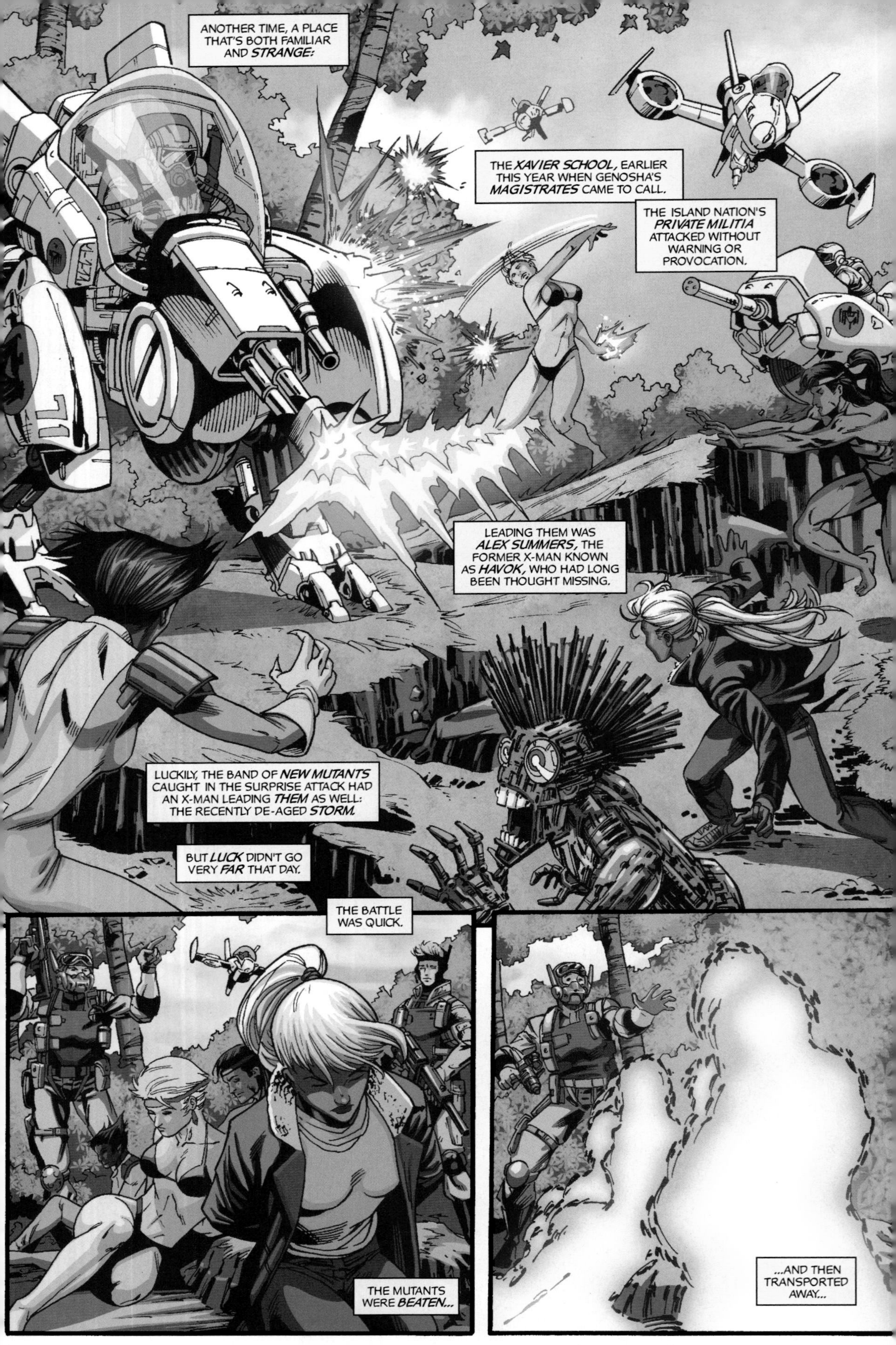
ANOTHER TIME, A PLACE THAT'S BOTH FAMILIAR AND STRANGE:
THE XAVIER SCHOOL, EARLIER THIS YEAR WHEN GENOSHA'S MAGISTRATES CAME TO CALL.
THE ISLAND NATION'S PRIVATE MILITIA ATTACKED WITHOUT WARNING OR PROVOCATION.
LEADING THEM WAS ALEX SUMMERS, THE FORMER X-MAN KNOWN AS HAVOK, WHO HAD LONG BEEN THOUGHT MISSING.
LUCKILY, THE BAND OF NEW MUTANTS CAUGHT IN THE SURPRISE ATTACK HAD AN X-MAN LEADING THEM AS WELL: THE RECENTLY DE-AGED STORM.
BUT LUCK DIDN'T GO VERY FAR THAT DAY.
THE BATTLE WAS QUICK.
THE MUTANTS WERE BEATEN...
...AND THEN TRANSPORTED AWAY...

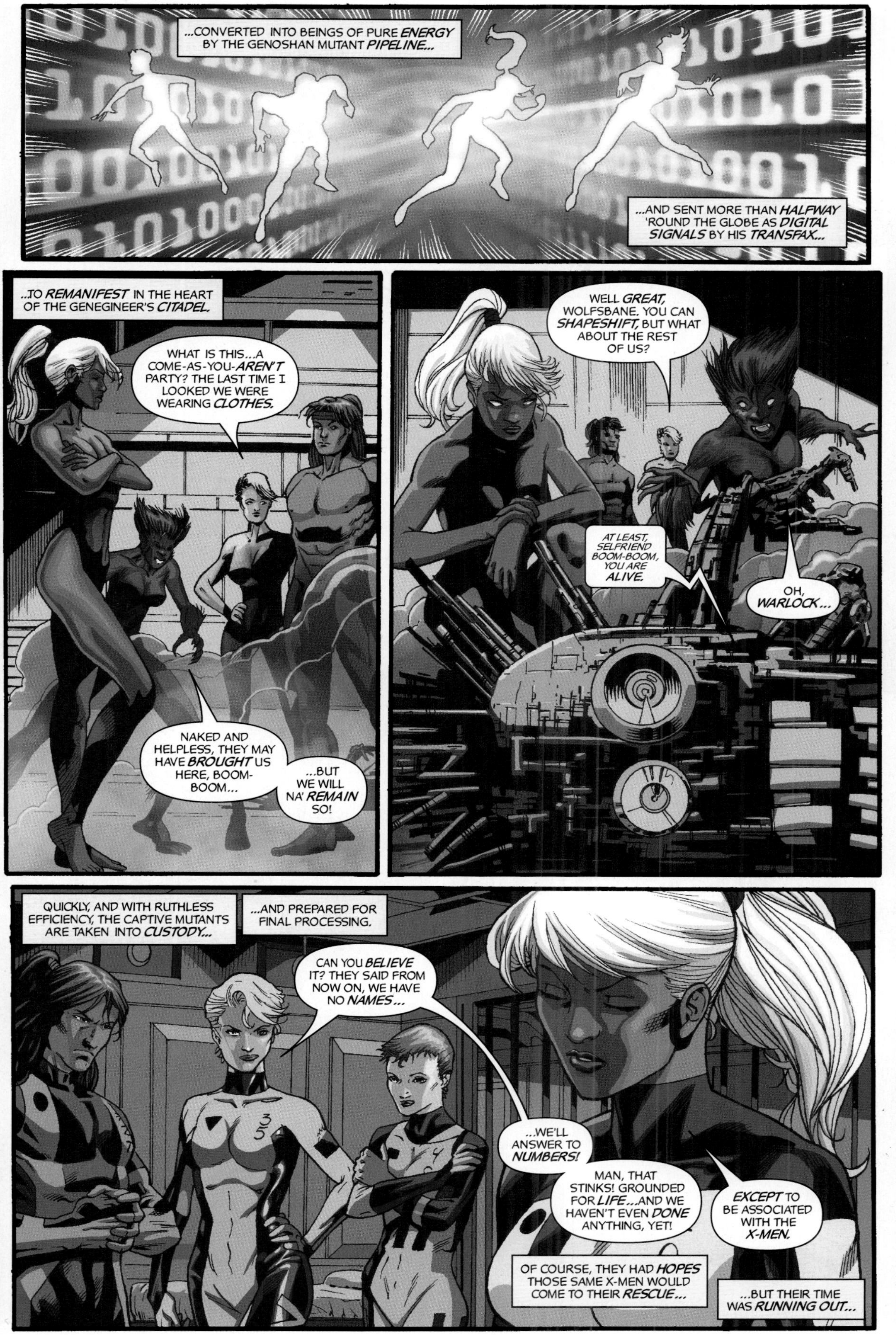

...CONVERTED INTO BEINGS OF PURE ENERGY BY THE GENOSHAN MUTANT PIPELINE...
...AND SENT MORE THAN HALFWAY 'ROUND THE GLOBE AS DIGITAL SIGNALS BY HIS TRANSFAX...
...TO REMANIFEST IN THE HEART OF THE GENEGINEER'S CITADEL.
WHAT IS THIS...A COME-AS-YOU-AREN'T PARTY? THE LAST TIME I LOOKED WE WERE WEARING CLOTHES.
NAKED AND HELPLESS, THEY MAY HAVE BROUGHT US HERE, BOOM-BOOM...
...BUT WE WILL NA' REMAIN SO!
WELL GREAT, WOLFSBANE. YOU CAN SHAPESHIFT, BUT WHAT ABOUT THE REST OF US?
AT LEAST, SELFRIEND BOOM-BOOM, YOU ARE ALIVE.
OH, WARLOCK...
QUICKLY, AND WITH RUTHLESS EFFICIENCY, THE CAPTIVE MUTANTS ARE TAKEN INTO CUSTODY...
...AND PREPARED FOR FINAL PROCESSING.
CAN YOU BELIEVE IT? THEY SAID FROM NOW ON, WE HAVE NO NAMES...
...WE'LL ANSWER TO NUMBERS!
MAN, THAT STINKS! GROUNDED FOR LIFE...AND WE HAVEN'T EVEN DONE ANYTHING, YET!
EXCEPT TO BE ASSOCIATED WITH THE X-MEN.
OF COURSE, THEY HAD HOPES THOSE SAME X-MEN WOULD COME TO THEIR RESCUE...
...BUT THEIR TIME WAS RUNNING OUT...

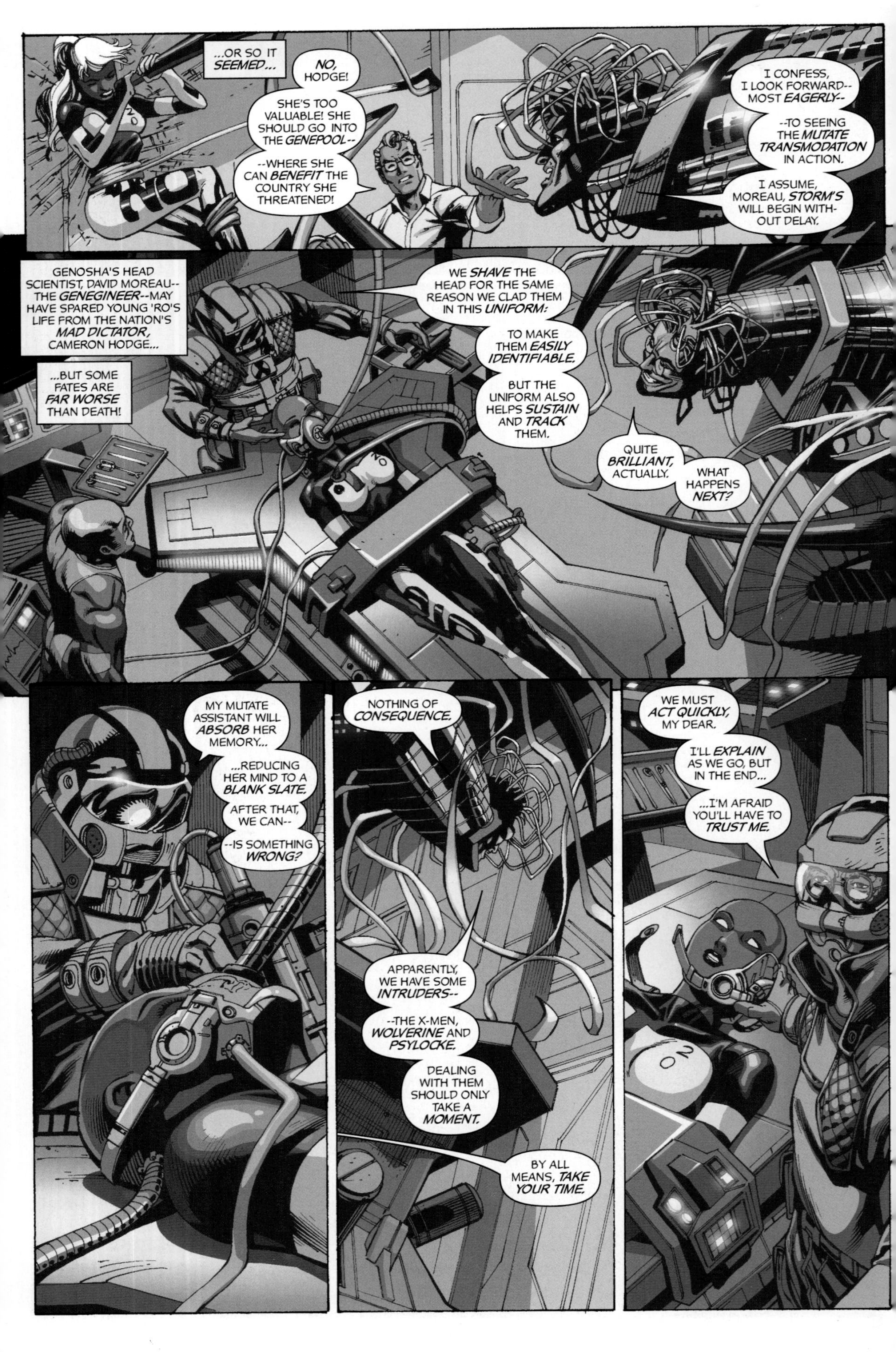
...OR SO IT SEEMED...
NO, HODGE!
SHE'S TOO VALUABLE! SHE SHOULD GO INTO THE GENEPOOL--
--WHERE SHE CAN BENEFIT THE COUNTRY SHE THREATENED!
I CONFESS, I LOOK FORWARD-- MOST EAGERLY--
--TO SEEING THE MUTATE TRANSMODATION IN ACTION.
I ASSUME, MOREAU, STORM'S WILL BEGIN WITH-OUT DELAY.
GENOSHA'S HEAD SCIENTIST, DAVID MOREAU-- THE GENEGINEER--MAY HAVE SPARED YOUNG 'RO'S LIFE FROM THE NATION'S MAD DICTATOR, CAMERON HODGE...
...BUT SOME FATES ARE FAR WORSE THAN DEATH!
WE SHAVE THE HEAD FOR THE SAME REASON WE CLAD THEM IN THIS UNIFORM:
TO MAKE THEM EASILY IDENTIFIABLE.
BUT THE UNIFORM ALSO HELPS SUSTAIN AND TRACK THEM.
QUITE BRILLIANT, ACTUALLY.
WHAT HAPPENS NEXT?
MY MUTATE ASSISTANT WILL ABSORB HER MEMORY...
...REDUCING HER MIND TO A BLANK SLATE.
AFTER THAT, WE CAN--
--IS SOMETHING WRONG?
NOTHING OF CONSEQUENCE.
APPARENTLY, WE HAVE SOME INTRUDERS--
--THE X-MEN, WOLVERINE AND PSYLOCKE.
DEALING WITH THEM SHOULD ONLY TAKE A MOMENT.
BY ALL MEANS, TAKE YOUR TIME.
WE MUST ACT QUICKLY, MY DEAR.
I'LL EXPLAIN AS WE GO, BUT IN THE END...
...I'M AFRAID YOU'LL HAVE TO TRUST ME.

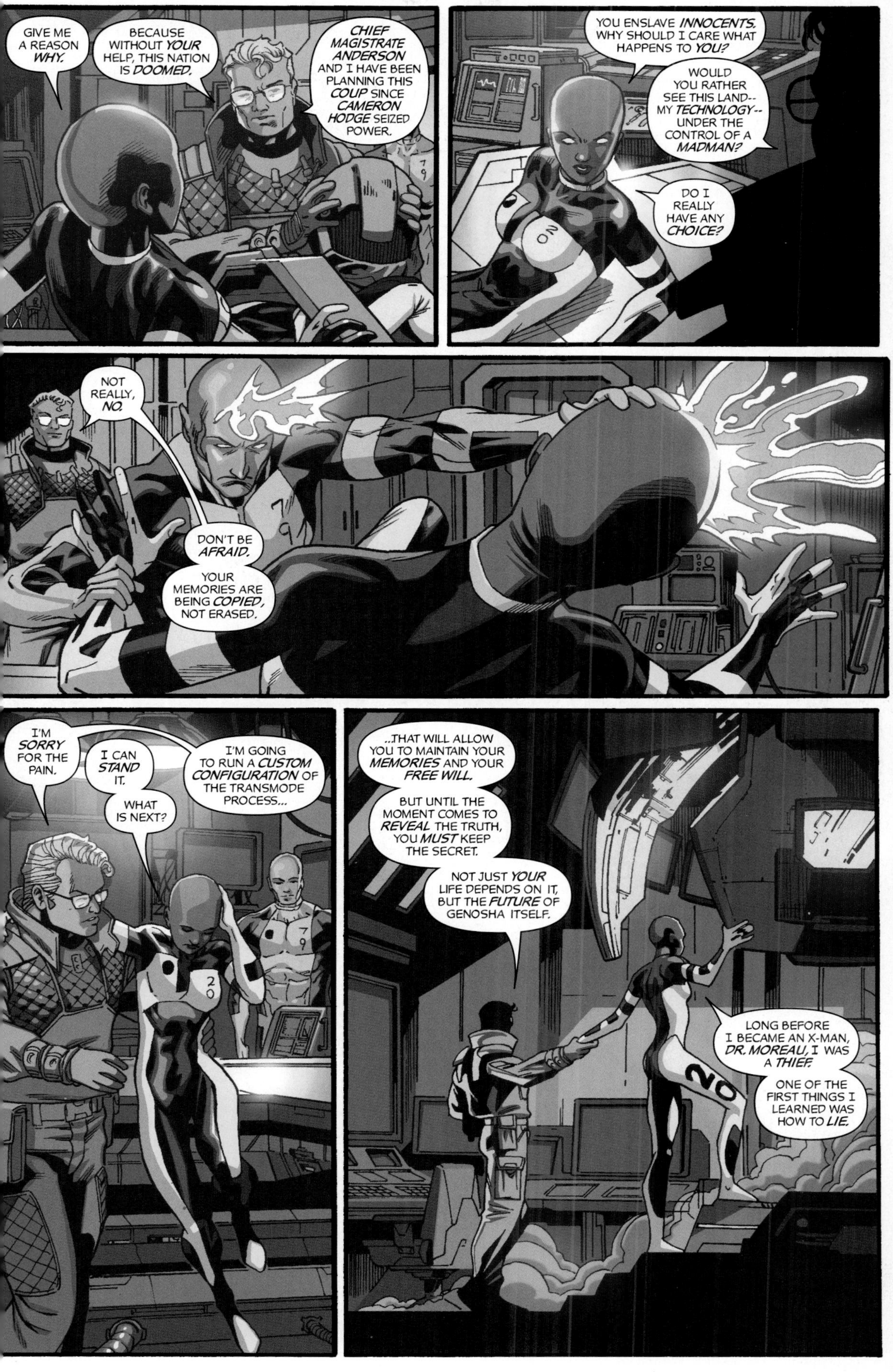
GIVE ME A REASON WHY.
BECAUSE WITHOUT YOUR HELP, THIS NATION IS DOOMED.
CHIEF MAGISTRATE ANDERSON AND I HAVE BEEN PLANNING THIS COUP SINCE CAMERON HODGE SEIZED POWER.
YOU ENSLAVE INNOCENTS. WHY SHOULD I CARE WHAT HAPPENS TO YOU?
WOULD YOU RATHER SEE THIS LAND-- MY TECHNOLOGY-- UNDER THE CONTROL OF A MADMAN?
DO I REALLY HAVE ANY CHOICE?
NOT REALLY, NO.
DON'T BE AFRAID.
YOUR MEMORIES ARE BEING COPIED, NOT ERASED.
I'M SORRY FOR THE PAIN.
I CAN STAND IT.
WHAT IS NEXT?
I'M GOING TO RUN A CUSTOM CONFIGURATION OF THE TRANSMODE PROCESS...
...THAT WILL ALLOW YOU TO MAINTAIN YOUR MEMORIES AND YOUR FREE WILL.
BUT UNTIL THE MOMENT COMES TO REVEAL THE TRUTH, YOU MUST KEEP THE SECRET.
NOT JUST YOUR LIFE DEPENDS ON IT, BUT THE FUTURE OF GENOSHA ITSELF.
LONG BEFORE I BECAME AN X-MAN, DR. MOREAU, I WAS A THIEF.
ONE OF THE FIRST THINGS I LEARNED WAS HOW TO LIE.

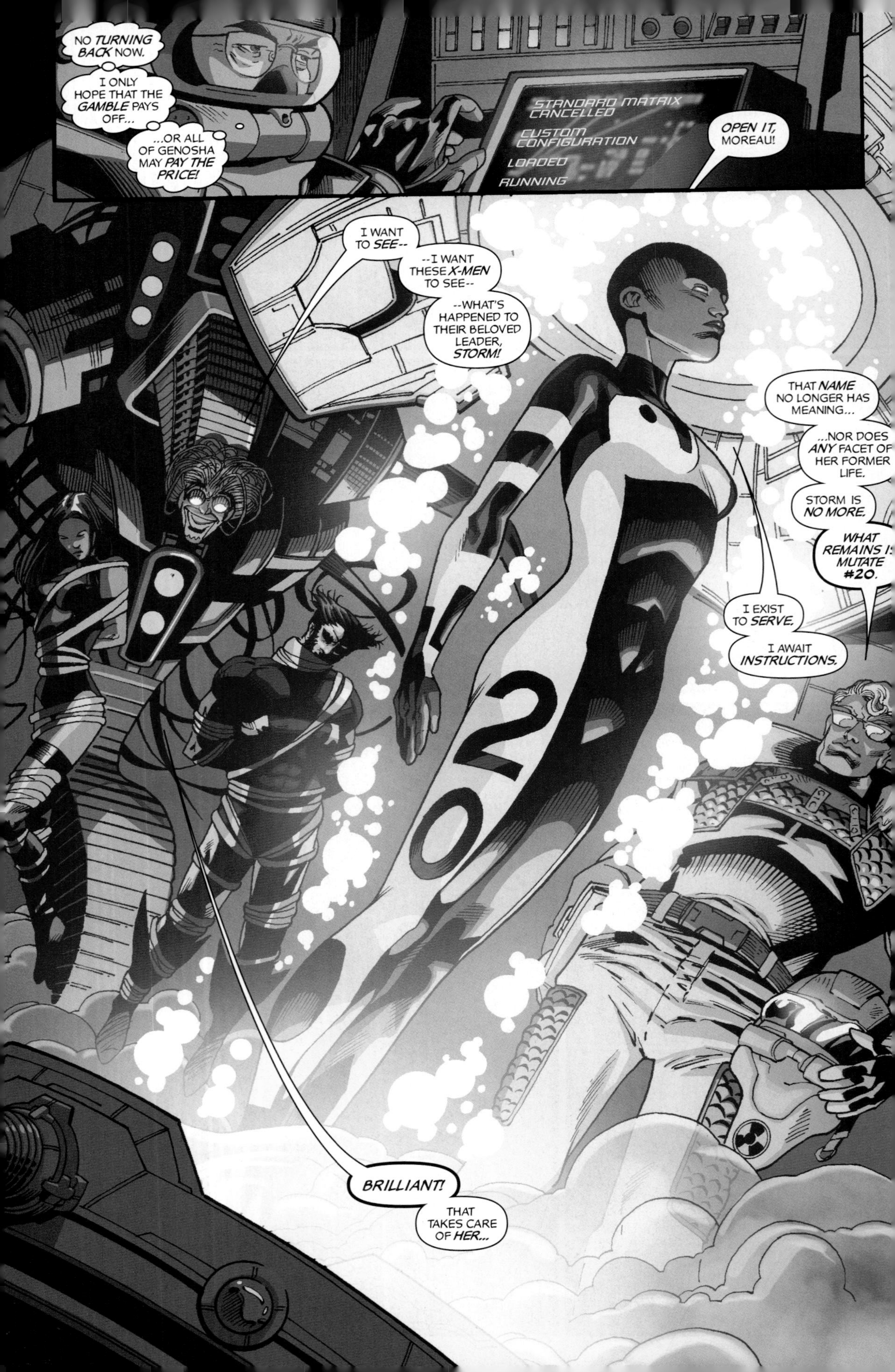
NO TURNING BACK NOW.
I ONLY HOPE THAT THE GAMBLE PAYS OFF...
...OR ALL OF GENOSHA MAY PAY THE PRICE!
STANDARD MATRIX CANCELLED
CUSTOM CONFIGURATION
LOADED
RUNNING
OPEN IT, MOREAU!
I WANT TO SEE--
--I WANT THESE X-MEN TO SEE--
--WHAT'S HAPPENED TO THEIR BELOVED LEADER, STORM!
THAT NAME NO LONGER HAS MEANING...
...NOR DOES ANY FACET OF HER FORMER LIFE.
STORM IS NO MORE.
WHAT REMAINS IS MUTATE #20.
I EXIST TO SERVE.
I AWAIT INSTRUCTIONS.
BRILLIANT!
THAT TAKES CARE OF HER...

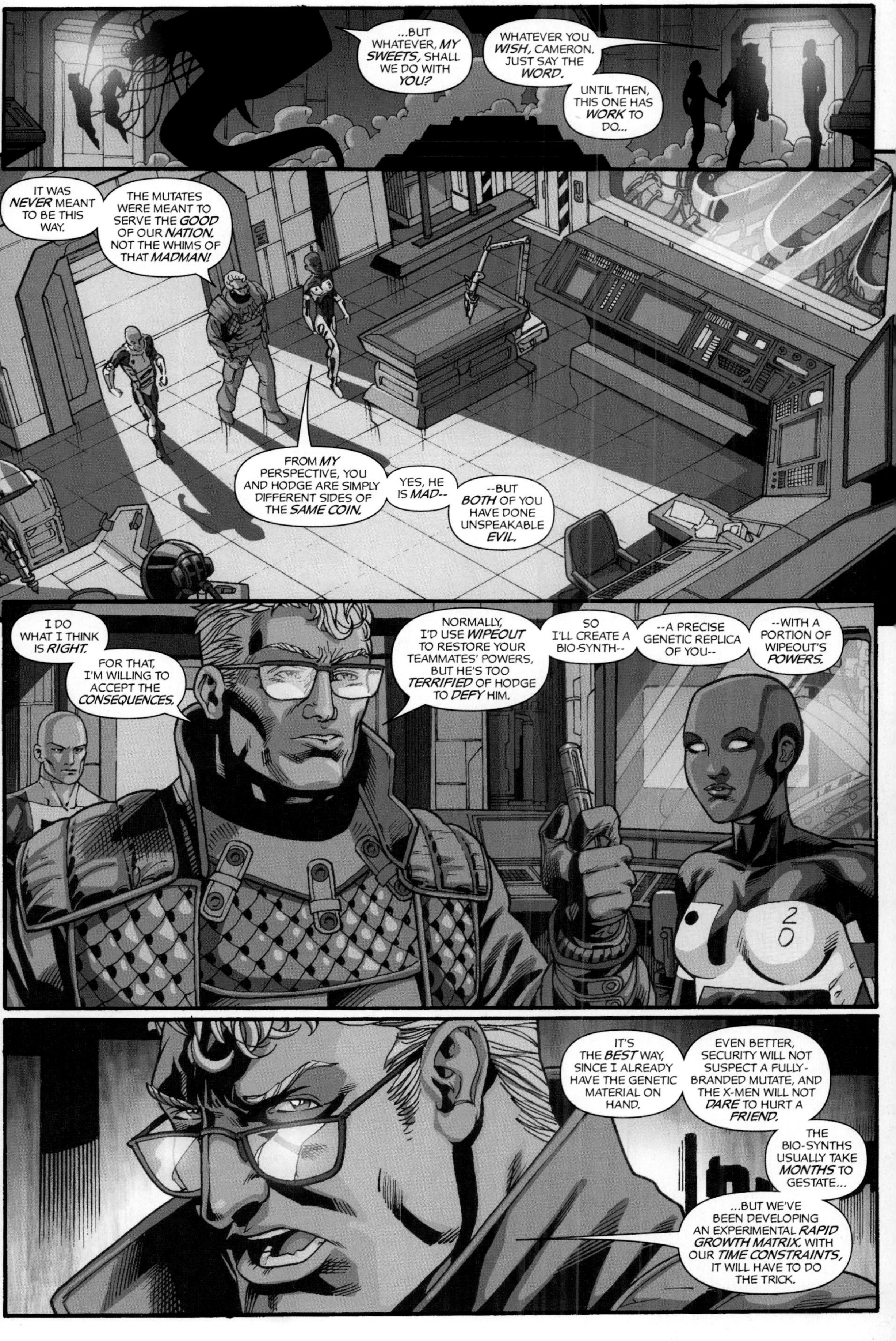
...BUT WHATEVER, MY SWEETS, SHALL WE DO WITH YOU?
WHATEVER YOU WISH, CAMERON. JUST SAY THE WORD.
UNTIL THEN, THIS ONE HAS WORK TO DO...
IT WAS NEVER MEANT TO BE THIS WAY.
THE MUTATES WERE MEANT TO SERVE THE GOOD OF OUR NATION. NOT THE WHIMS OF THAT MADMAN!
FROM MY PERSPECTIVE, YOU AND HODGE ARE SIMPLY DIFFERENT SIDES OF THE SAME COIN.
YES, HE IS MAD--
--BUT BOTH OF YOU HAVE DONE UNSPEAKABLE EVIL.
I DO WHAT I THINK IS RIGHT.
FOR THAT, I'M WILLING TO ACCEPT THE CONSEQUENCES.
NORMALLY, I'D USE WIPEOUT TO RESTORE YOUR TEAMMATES' POWERS, BUT HE'S TOO TERRIFIED OF HODGE TO DEFY HIM.
SO I'LL CREATE A BIO-SYNTH--
--A PRECISE GENETIC REPLICA OF YOU--
--WITH A PORTION OF WIPEOUT'S POWERS.
20
IT'S THE BEST WAY, SINCE I ALREADY HAVE THE GENETIC MATERIAL ON HAND.
EVEN BETTER, SECURITY WILL NOT SUSPECT A FULLY-BRANDED MUTATE, AND THE X-MEN WILL NOT DARE TO HURT A FRIEND.
THE BIO-SYNTHS USUALLY TAKE MONTHS TO GESTATE...
...BUT WE'VE BEEN DEVELOPING AN EXPERIMENTAL RAPID GROWTH MATRIX. WITH OUR TIME CONSTRAINTS, IT WILL HAVE TO DO THE TRICK.

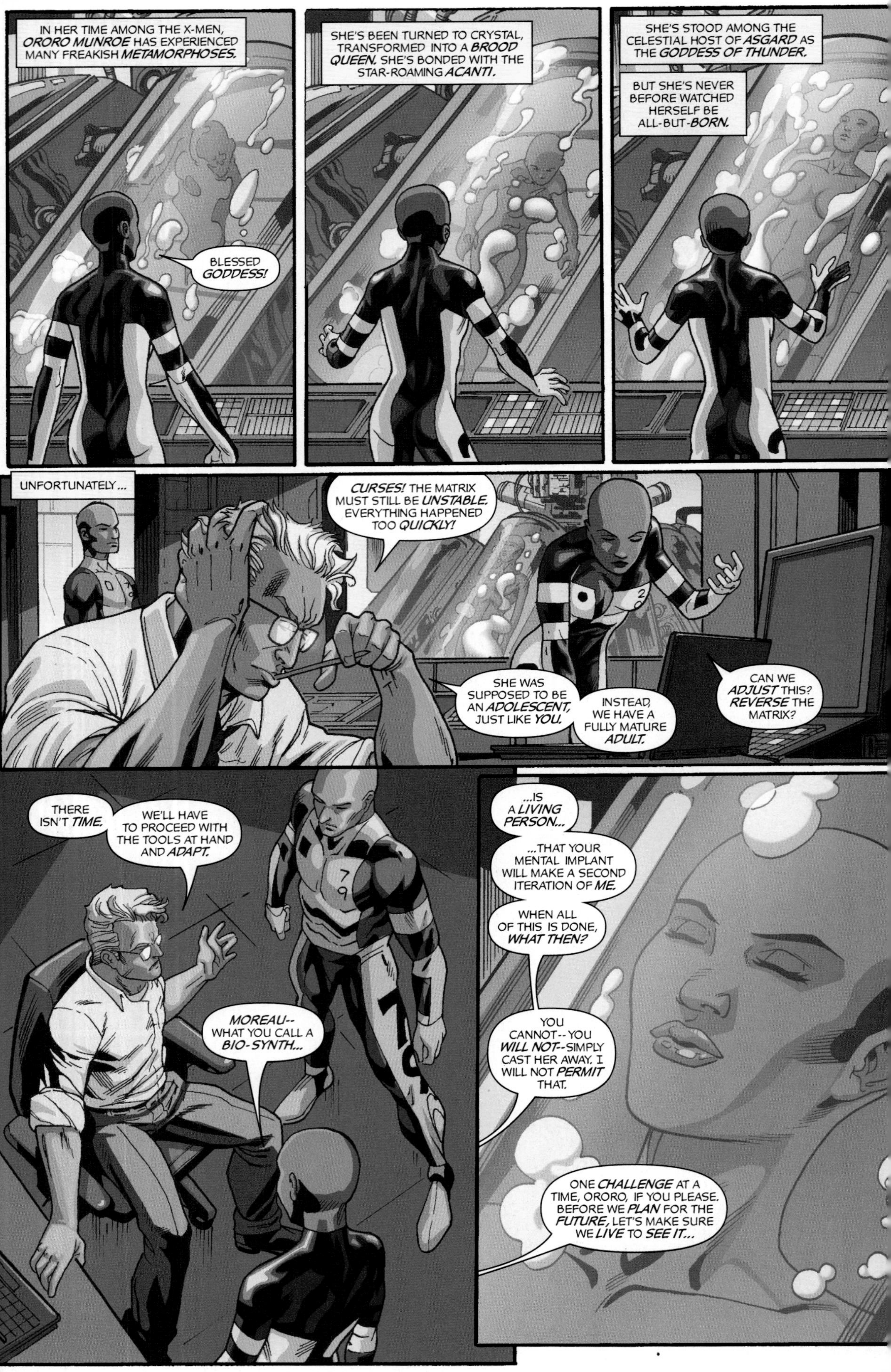

IN HER TIME AMONG THE X-MEN, ORORO MUNROE HAS EXPERIENCED MANY FREAKISH METAMORPHOSES.
BLESSED GODDESS!
SHE'S BEEN TURNED TO CRYSTAL, TRANSFORMED INTO A BROOD QUEEN. SHE'S BONDED WITH THE STAR-ROAMING ACANTI.
SHE'S STOOD AMONG THE CELESTIAL HOST OF ASGARD AS THE GODDESS OF THUNDER.
BUT SHE'S NEVER BEFORE WATCHED HERSELF BE ALL-BUT-BORN.
UNFORTUNATELY...
CURSES! THE MATRIX MUST STILL BE UNSTABLE. EVERYTHING HAPPENED TOO QUICKLY!
SHE WAS SUPPOSED TO BE AN ADOLESCENT, JUST LIKE YOU.
INSTEAD, WE HAVE A FULLY MATURE ADULT.
CAN WE ADJUST THIS? REVERSE THE MATRIX?
THERE ISN'T TIME.
WE'LL HAVE TO PROCEED WITH THE TOOLS AT HAND AND ADAPT.
MOREAU-- WHAT YOU CALL A BIO-SYNTH...
...IS A LIVING PERSON...
...THAT YOUR MENTAL IMPLANT WILL MAKE A SECOND ITERATION OF ME.
WHEN ALL OF THIS IS DONE, WHAT THEN?
YOU CANNOT--YOU WILL NOT--SIMPLY CAST HER AWAY. I WILL NOT PERMIT THAT.
ONE CHALLENGE AT A TIME, ORORO, IF YOU PLEASE. BEFORE WE PLAN FOR THE FUTURE, LET'S MAKE SURE WE LIVE TO SEE IT...

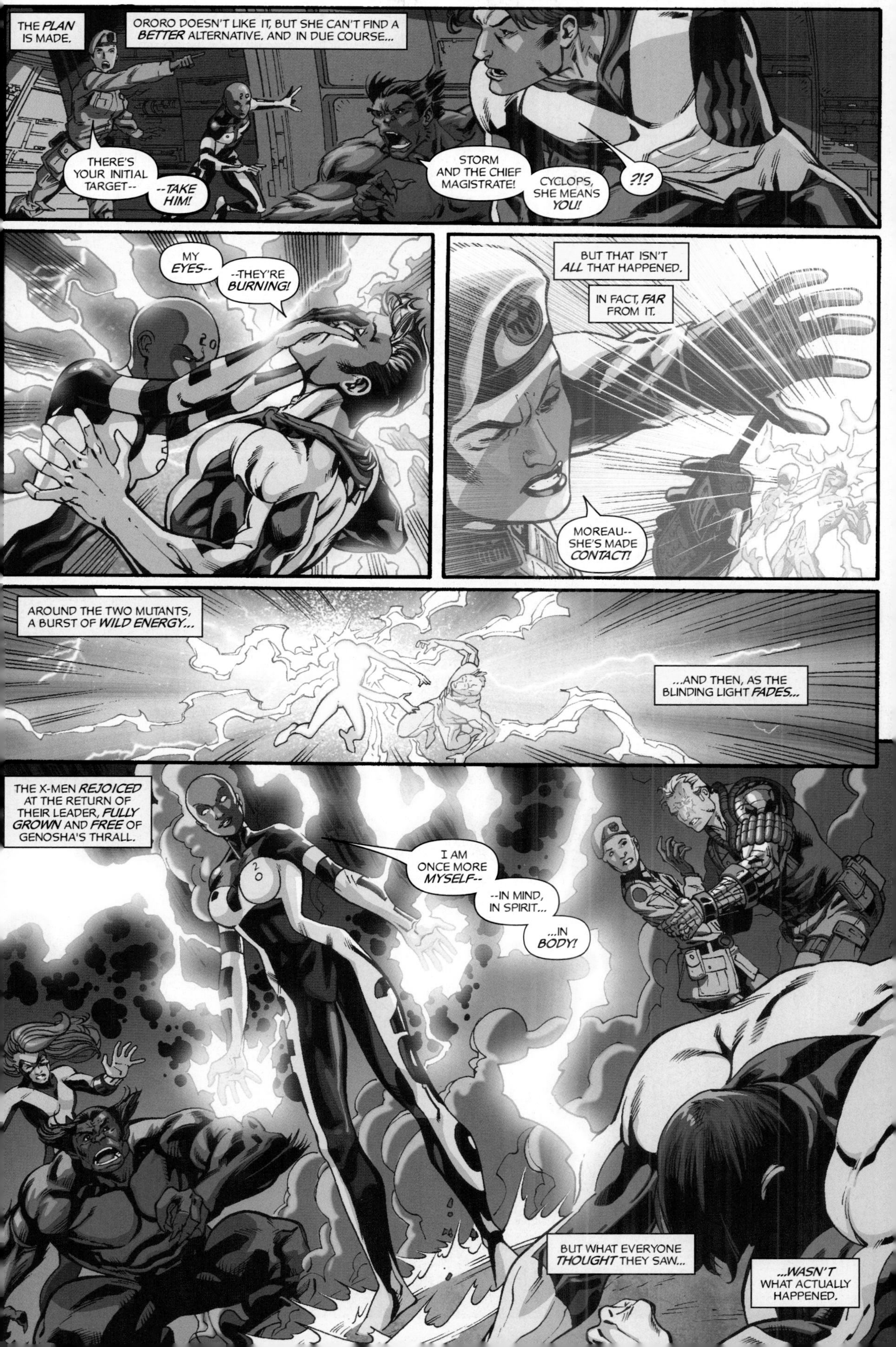
THE PLAN IS MADE.
ORORO DOESN'T LIKE IT, BUT SHE CAN'T FIND A BETTER ALTERNATIVE. AND IN DUE COURSE...
THERE'S YOUR INITIAL TARGET--
--TAKE HIM!
STORM AND THE CHIEF MAGISTRATE!
CYCLOPS, SHE MEANS YOU!
?!?
MY EYES--
--THEY'RE BURNING!
BUT THAT ISN'T ALL THAT HAPPENED.
IN FACT, FAR FROM IT.
MOREAU--SHE'S MADE CONTACT!
AROUND THE TWO MUTANTS, A BURST OF WILD ENERGY...
...AND THEN, AS THE BLINDING LIGHT FADES...
THE X-MEN REJOICED AT THE RETURN OF THEIR LEADER, FULLY GROWN AND FREE OF GENOSHA'S THRALL.
I AM ONCE MORE MYSELF--
--IN MIND, IN SPIRIT...
...IN BODY!
BUT WHAT EVERYONE THOUGHT THEY SAW...
...WASN'T WHAT ACTUALLY HAPPENED.

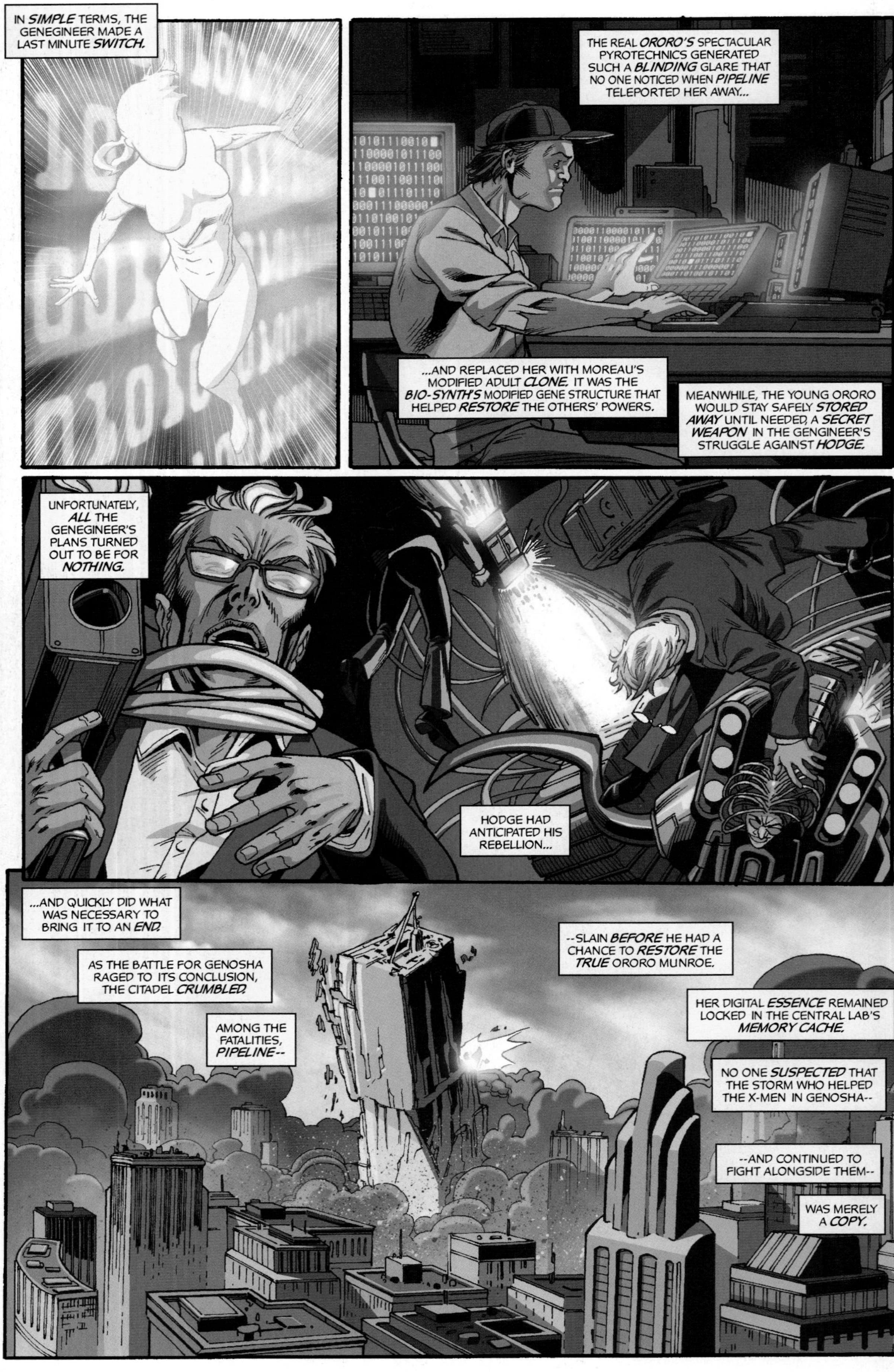
IN SIMPLE TERMS, THE GENEGINEER MADE A LAST MINUTE SWITCH.
THE REAL ORORO'S SPECTACULAR PYROTECHNICS GENERATED SUCH A BLINDING GLARE THAT NO ONE NOTICED WHEN PIPELINE TELEPORTED HER AWAY...
...AND REPLACED HER WITH MOREAU'S MODIFIED ADULT CLONE. IT WAS THE BIO-SYNTH'S MODIFIED GENE STRUCTURE THAT HELPED RESTORE THE OTHERS' POWERS.
MEANWHILE, THE YOUNG ORORO WOULD STAY SAFELY STORED AWAY UNTIL NEEDED, A SECRET WEAPON IN THE GENGINEER'S STRUGGLE AGAINST HODGE.
UNFORTUNATELY, ALL THE GENEGINEER'S PLANS TURNED OUT TO BE FOR NOTHING.
HODGE HAD ANTICIPATED HIS REBELLION...
...AND QUICKLY DID WHAT WAS NECESSARY TO BRING IT TO AN END.
AS THE BATTLE FOR GENOSHA RAGED TO ITS CONCLUSION, THE CITADEL CRUMBLED.
AMONG THE FATALITIES, PIPELINE--
--SLAIN BEFORE HE HAD A CHANCE TO RESTORE THE TRUE ORORO MUNROE.
HER DIGITAL ESSENCE REMAINED LOCKED IN THE CENTRAL LAB'S MEMORY CACHE.
NO ONE SUSPECTED THAT THE STORM WHO HELPED THE X-MEN IN GENOSHA--
--AND CONTINUED TO FIGHT ALONGSIDE THEM--
WAS MERELY A COPY.

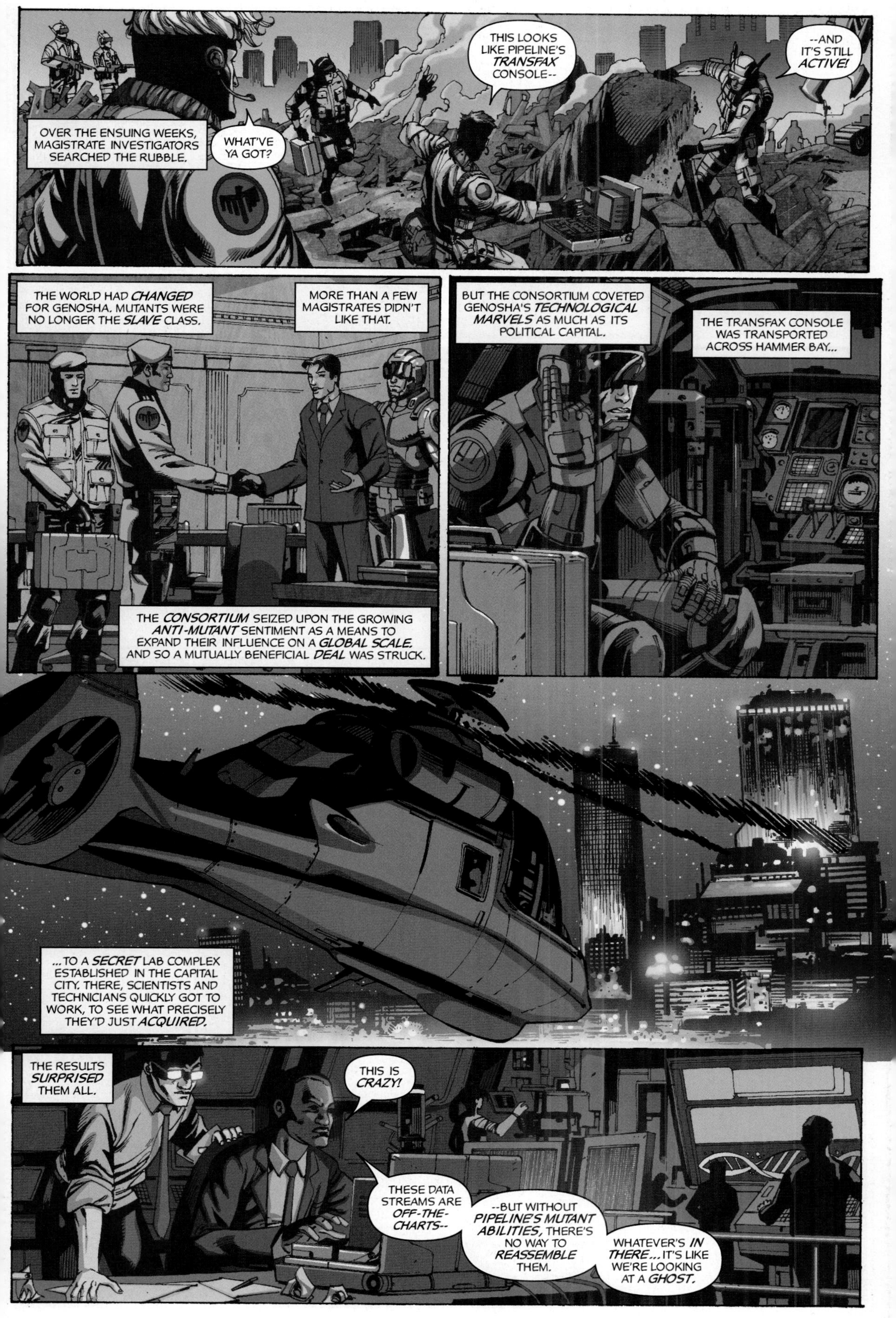
OVER THE ENSUING WEEKS, MAGISTRATE INVESTIGATORS SEARCHED THE RUBBLE.
WHAT'VE YA GOT?
THIS LOOKS LIKE PIPELINE'S *TRANSFAX* CONSOLE--
--AND IT'S STILL *ACTIVE!*
THE WORLD HAD *CHANGED* FOR GENOSHA. MUTANTS WERE NO LONGER THE *SLAVE* CLASS.
MORE THAN A FEW MAGISTRATES DIDN'T LIKE THAT.
THE *CONSORTIUM* SEIZED UPON THE GROWING *ANTI-MUTANT* SENTIMENT AS A MEANS TO EXPAND THEIR INFLUENCE ON A *GLOBAL SCALE.* AND SO A MUTUALLY BENEFICIAL *DEAL* WAS STRUCK.
BUT THE CONSORTIUM COVETED GENOSHA'S *TECHNOLOGICAL MARVELS* AS MUCH AS ITS POLITICAL CAPITAL.
THE TRANSFAX CONSOLE WAS TRANSPORTED ACROSS HAMMER BAY...
...TO A *SECRET* LAB COMPLEX ESTABLISHED IN THE CAPITAL CITY. THERE, SCIENTISTS AND TECHNICIANS QUICKLY GOT TO WORK, TO SEE WHAT PRECISELY THEY'D JUST *ACQUIRED.*
THE RESULTS *SURPRISED* THEM ALL.
THIS IS *CRAZY!*
THESE DATA STREAMS ARE *OFF-THE-CHARTS--*
--BUT WITHOUT *PIPELINE'S MUTANT ABILITIES,* THERE'S NO WAY TO *REASSEMBLE* THEM.
WHATEVER'S *IN THERE...* IT'S LIKE WE'RE LOOKING AT A *GHOST.*

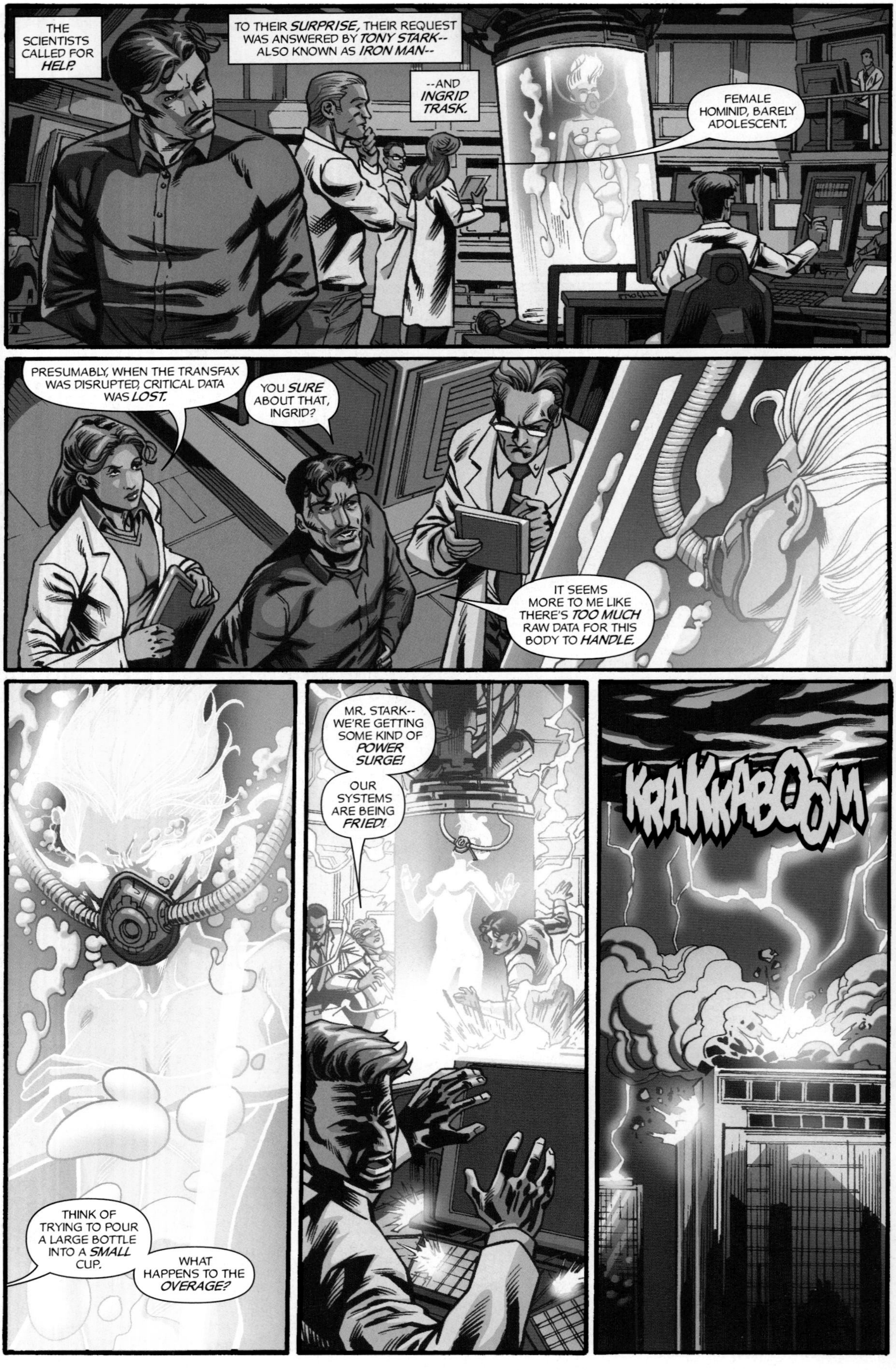
THE SCIENTISTS CALLED FOR HELP.
TO THEIR SURPRISE, THEIR REQUEST WAS ANSWERED BY TONY STARK-- ALSO KNOWN AS IRON MAN--
--AND INGRID TRASK.
FEMALE HOMINID, BARELY ADOLESCENT.
PRESUMABLY, WHEN THE TRANSFAX WAS DISRUPTED, CRITICAL DATA WAS LOST.
YOU SURE ABOUT THAT, INGRID?
IT SEEMS MORE TO ME LIKE THERE'S TOO MUCH RAW DATA FOR THIS BODY TO HANDLE.
THINK OF TRYING TO POUR A LARGE BOTTLE INTO A SMALL CUP.
WHAT HAPPENS TO THE OVERAGE?
MR. STARK-- WE'RE GETTING SOME KIND OF POWER SURGE!
OUR SYSTEMS ARE BEING FRIED!
KRAKKABOOM

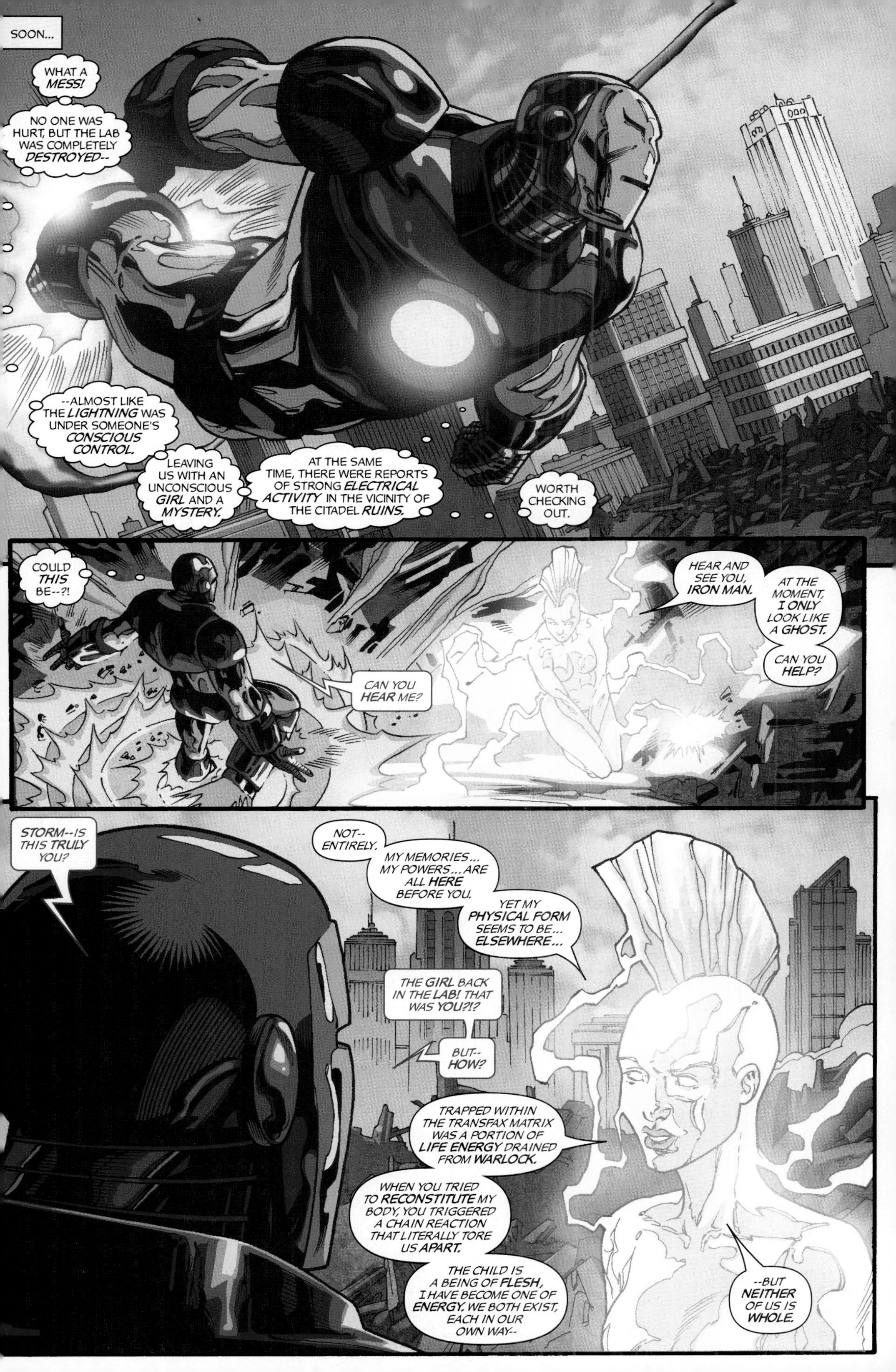

SOON...
WHAT A *MESS!*
NO ONE WAS HURT, BUT THE LAB WAS COMPLETELY *DESTROYED--*
--ALMOST LIKE THE *LIGHTNING* WAS UNDER SOMEONE'S *CONSCIOUS CONTROL.*
LEAVING US WITH AN UNCONSCIOUS *GIRL* AND A *MYSTERY.*
AT THE SAME TIME, THERE WERE REPORTS OF STRONG *ELECTRICAL ACTIVITY* IN THE VICINITY OF THE CITADEL *RUINS.*
WORTH CHECKING OUT.
COULD *THIS* BE--?!
CAN YOU *HEAR* ME?
HEAR AND SEE YOU, **IRON MAN.**
AT THE MOMENT, **I ONLY** LOOK LIKE A **GHOST.**
CAN YOU **HELP?**
STORM--IS THIS *TRULY* YOU?
NOT-- ENTIRELY.
MY MEMORIES... MY POWERS... ARE ALL **HERE** BEFORE YOU.
YET MY **PHYSICAL FORM** SEEMS TO BE... **ELSEWHERE...**
THE *GIRL* BACK IN THE *LAB!* THAT WAS *YOU?!?*
BUT-- *HOW?*
TRAPPED WITHIN THE TRANSFAX MATRIX WAS A PORTION OF **LIFE ENERGY** DRAINED FROM **WARLOCK.**
WHEN YOU TRIED TO **RECONSTITUTE** MY BODY, YOU TRIGGERED A CHAIN REACTION THAT LITERALLY TORE US **APART.**
THE CHILD IS A BEING OF **FLESH,** I HAVE BECOME ONE OF **ENERGY.** WE BOTH EXIST, EACH IN OUR OWN WAY--
--BUT **NEITHER** OF US IS **WHOLE.**

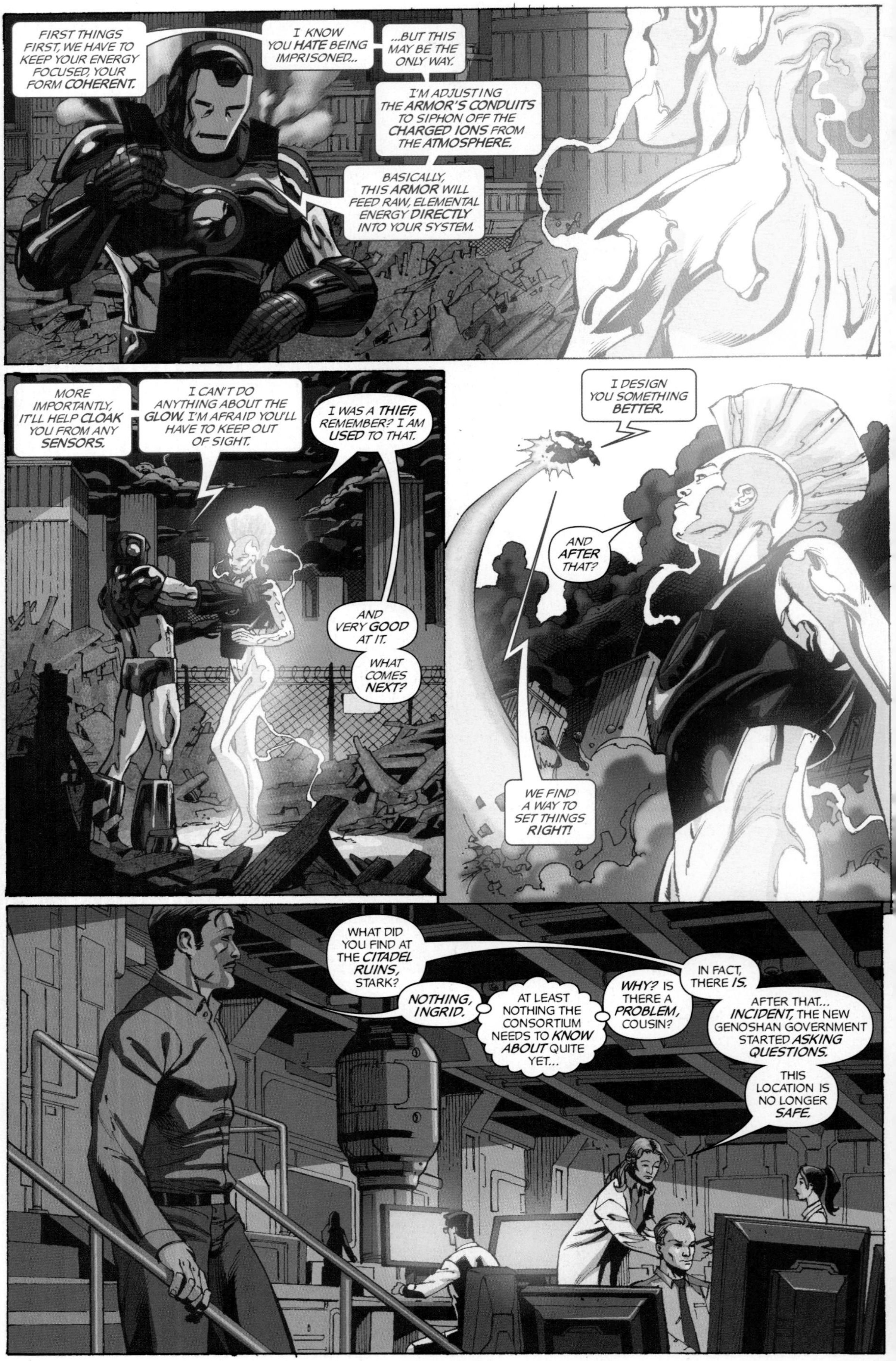

FIRST THINGS FIRST, WE HAVE TO KEEP YOUR ENERGY FOCUSED, YOUR FORM COHERENT.
I KNOW YOU HATE BEING IMPRISONED...
...BUT THIS MAY BE THE ONLY WAY.
I'M ADJUSTING THE ARMOR'S CONDUITS TO SIPHON OFF THE CHARGED IONS FROM THE ATMOSPHERE.
BASICALLY, THIS ARMOR WILL FEED RAW, ELEMENTAL ENERGY DIRECTLY INTO YOUR SYSTEM.
MORE IMPORTANTLY, IT'LL HELP CLOAK YOU FROM ANY SENSORS.
I CAN'T DO ANYTHING ABOUT THE GLOW. I'M AFRAID YOU'LL HAVE TO KEEP OUT OF SIGHT.
I WAS A THIEF, REMEMBER? I AM USED TO THAT.
AND VERY GOOD AT IT.
WHAT COMES NEXT?
I DESIGN YOU SOMETHING BETTER.
AND AFTER THAT?
WE FIND A WAY TO SET THINGS RIGHT!
WHAT DID YOU FIND AT THE CITADEL RUINS, STARK?
NOTHING, INGRID.
AT LEAST NOTHING THE CONSORTIUM NEEDS TO KNOW ABOUT QUITE YET...
WHY? IS THERE A PROBLEM, COUSIN?
IN FACT, THERE IS.
AFTER THAT... INCIDENT, THE NEW GENOSHAN GOVERNMENT STARTED ASKING QUESTIONS.
THIS LOCATION IS NO LONGER SAFE.

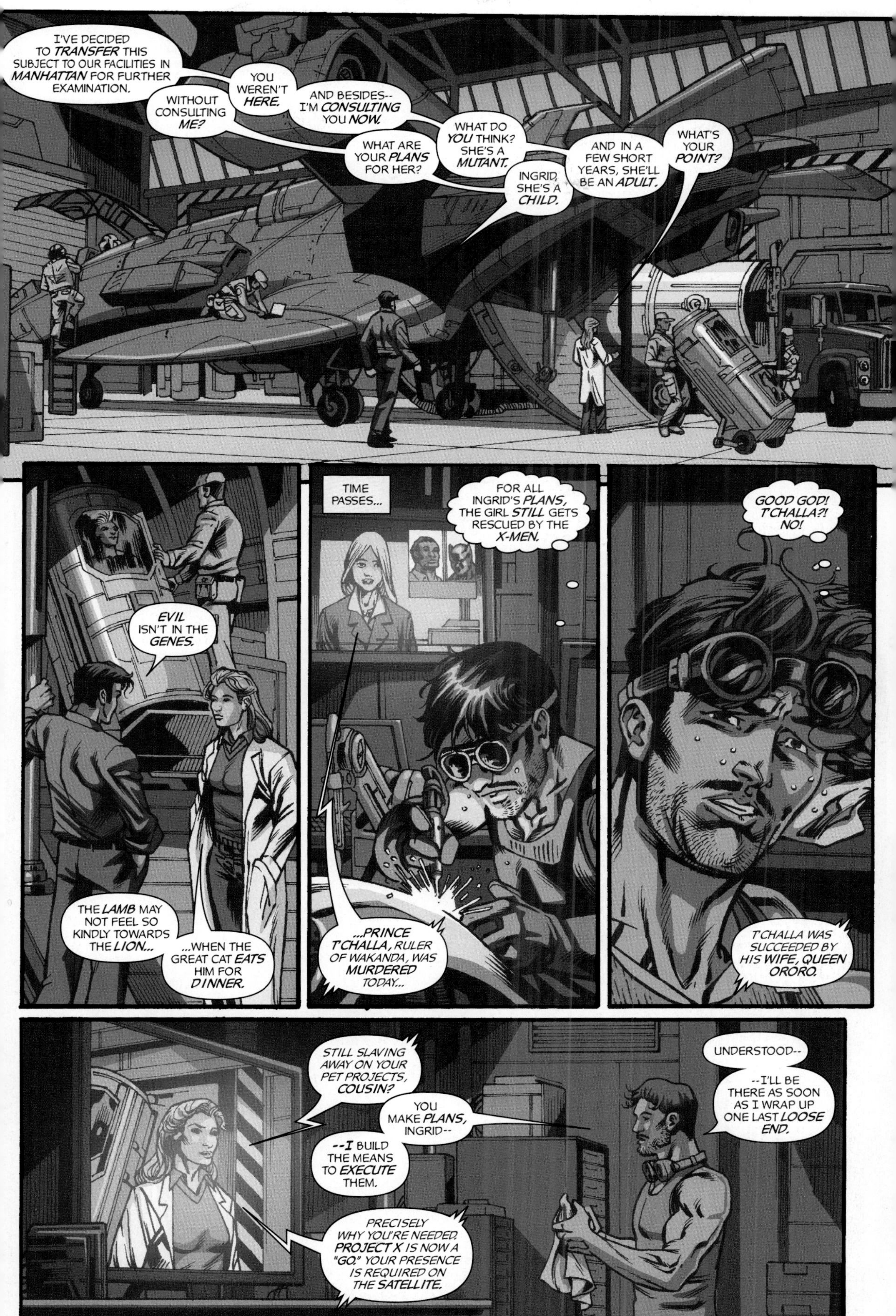
I'VE DECIDED TO TRANSFER THIS SUBJECT TO OUR FACILITIES IN MANHATTAN FOR FURTHER EXAMINATION.
WITHOUT CONSULTING ME?
YOU WEREN'T HERE.
AND BESIDES-- I'M CONSULTING YOU NOW.
WHAT ARE YOUR PLANS FOR HER?
WHAT DO YOU THINK? SHE'S A MUTANT.
INGRID, SHE'S A CHILD.
AND IN A FEW SHORT YEARS, SHE'LL BE AN ADULT.
WHAT'S YOUR POINT?
EVIL ISN'T IN THE GENES.
THE LAMB MAY NOT FEEL SO KINDLY TOWARDS THE LION...
...WHEN THE GREAT CAT EATS HIM FOR DINNER.
TIME PASSES...
FOR ALL INGRID'S PLANS, THE GIRL STILL GETS RESCUED BY THE X-MEN.
...PRINCE T'CHALLA, RULER OF WAKANDA, WAS MURDERED TODAY...
GOOD GOD! T'CHALLA?! NO!
T'CHALLA WAS SUCCEEDED BY HIS WIFE, QUEEN ORORO.
STILL SLAVING AWAY ON YOUR PET PROJECTS, COUSIN?
YOU MAKE PLANS, INGRID--
--I BUILD THE MEANS TO EXECUTE THEM.
PRECISELY WHY YOU'RE NEEDED. PROJECT X IS NOW A "GO." YOUR PRESENCE IS REQUIRED ON THE SATELLITE.
UNDERSTOOD--
--I'LL BE THERE AS SOON AS I WRAP UP ONE LAST LOOSE END.

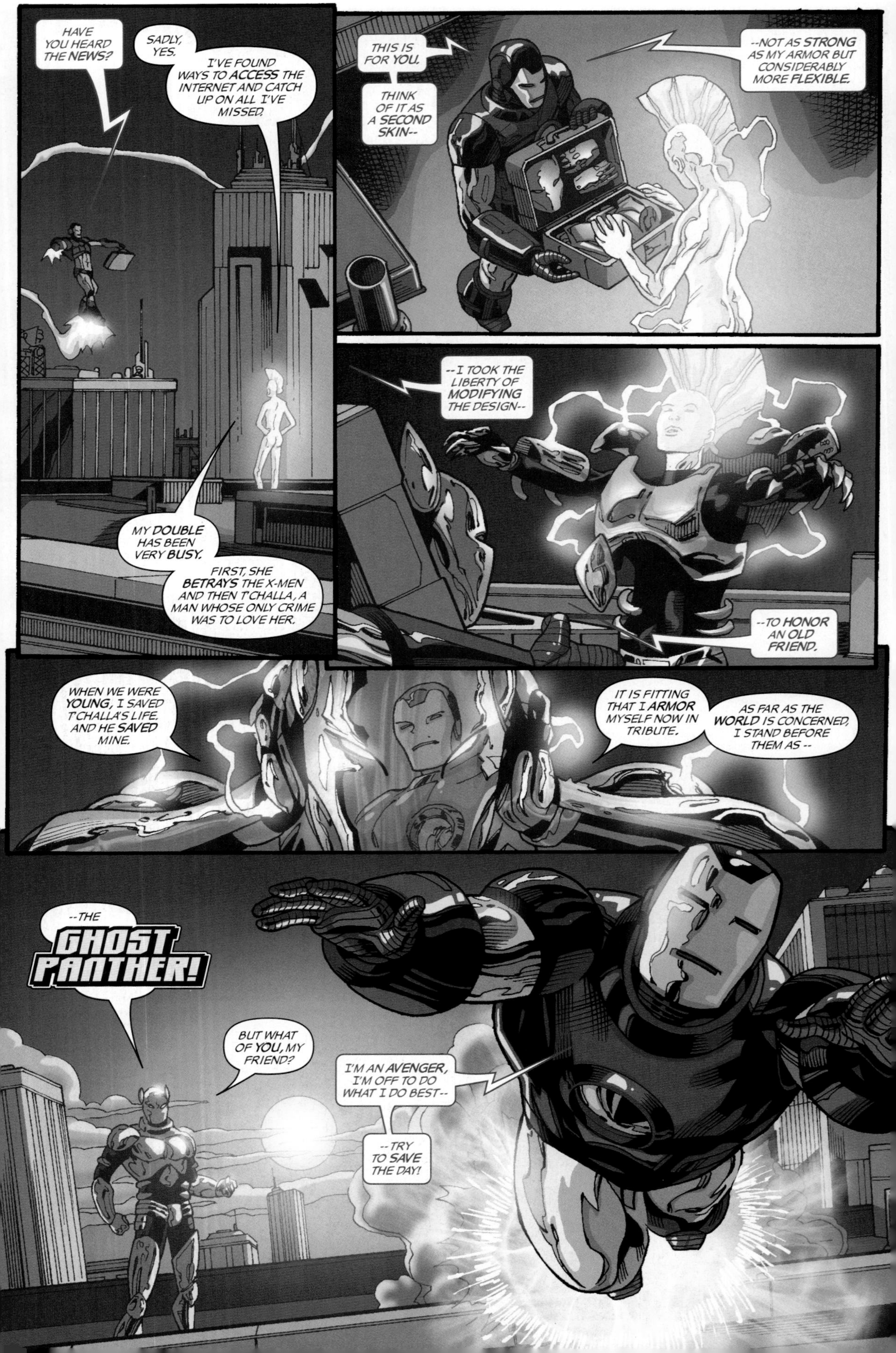
HAVE YOU HEARD THE NEWS?
SADLY, YES.
I'VE FOUND WAYS TO ACCESS THE INTERNET AND CATCH UP ON ALL I'VE MISSED.
MY DOUBLE HAS BEEN VERY BUSY.
FIRST, SHE BETRAYS THE X-MEN AND THEN T'CHALLA, A MAN WHOSE ONLY CRIME WAS TO LOVE HER.
THIS IS FOR YOU.
THINK OF IT AS A SECOND SKIN--
--NOT AS STRONG AS MY ARMOR BUT CONSIDERABLY MORE FLEXIBLE.
--I TOOK THE LIBERTY OF MODIFYING THE DESIGN--
--TO HONOR AN OLD FRIEND.
WHEN WE WERE YOUNG, I SAVED T'CHALLA'S LIFE. AND HE SAVED MINE.
IT IS FITTING THAT I ARMOR MYSELF NOW IN TRIBUTE.
AS FAR AS THE WORLD IS CONCERNED, I STAND BEFORE THEM AS --
--THE
GHOST PANTHER!
BUT WHAT OF YOU, MY FRIEND?
I'M AN AVENGER, I'M OFF TO DO WHAT I DO BEST--
--TRY TO SAVE THE DAY!

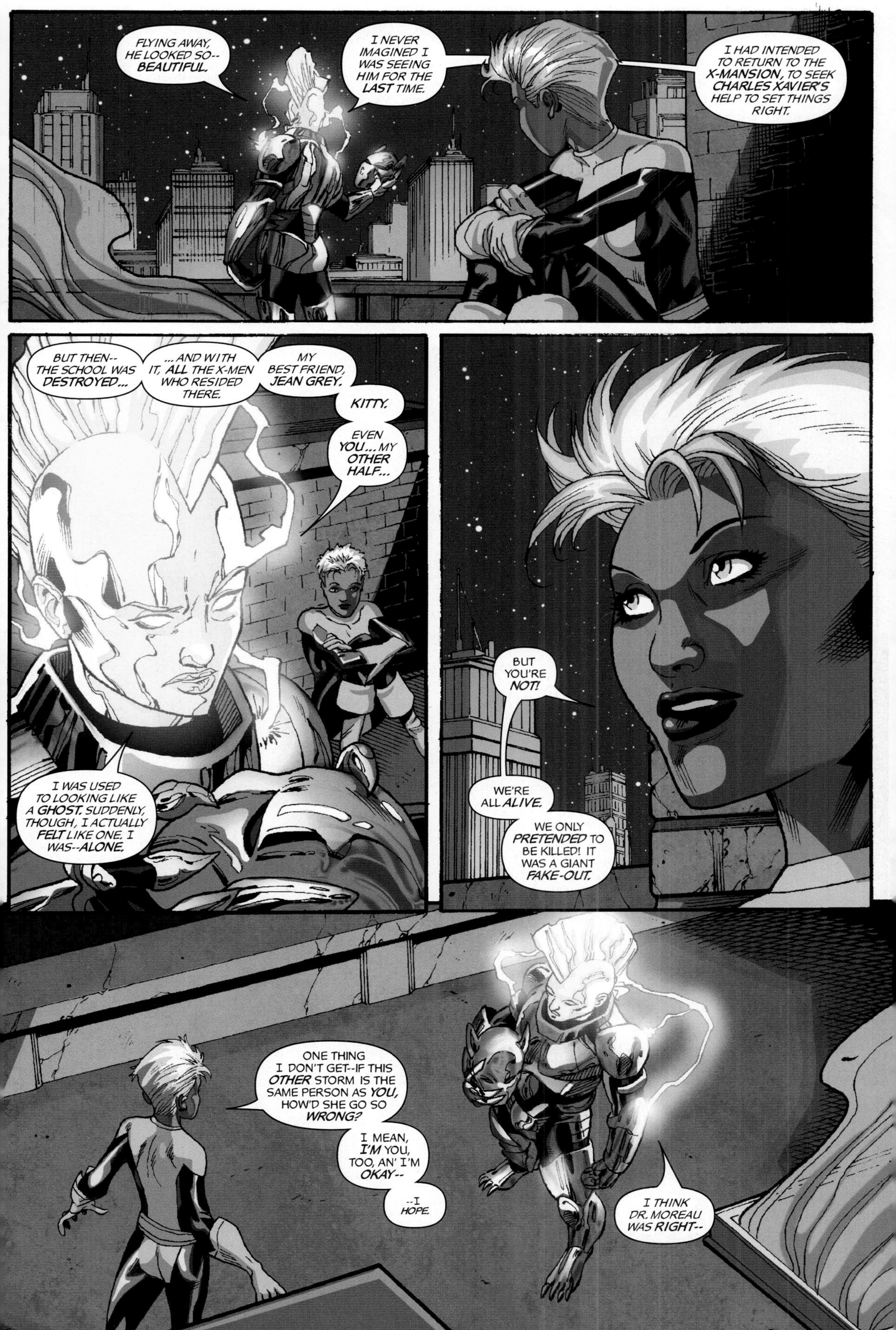
FLYING AWAY, HE LOOKED SO-- BEAUTIFUL.
I NEVER IMAGINED I WAS SEEING HIM FOR THE LAST TIME.
I HAD INTENDED TO RETURN TO THE X-MANSION, TO SEEK CHARLES XAVIER'S HELP TO SET THINGS RIGHT.
BUT THEN-- THE SCHOOL WAS DESTROYED...
...AND WITH IT, ALL THE X-MEN WHO RESIDED THERE.
MY BEST FRIEND, JEAN GREY.
KITTY.
EVEN YOU... MY OTHER HALF...
I WAS USED TO LOOKING LIKE A GHOST. SUDDENLY, THOUGH, I ACTUALLY FELT LIKE ONE. I WAS--ALONE.
BUT YOU'RE NOT!
WE'RE ALL ALIVE.
WE ONLY PRETENDED TO BE KILLED! IT WAS A GIANT FAKE-OUT.
ONE THING I DON'T GET--IF THIS OTHER STORM IS THE SAME PERSON AS YOU, HOW'D SHE GO SO WRONG?
I MEAN, I'M YOU, TOO, AN' I'M OKAY--
--I HOPE.
I THINK DR. MOREAU WAS RIGHT--

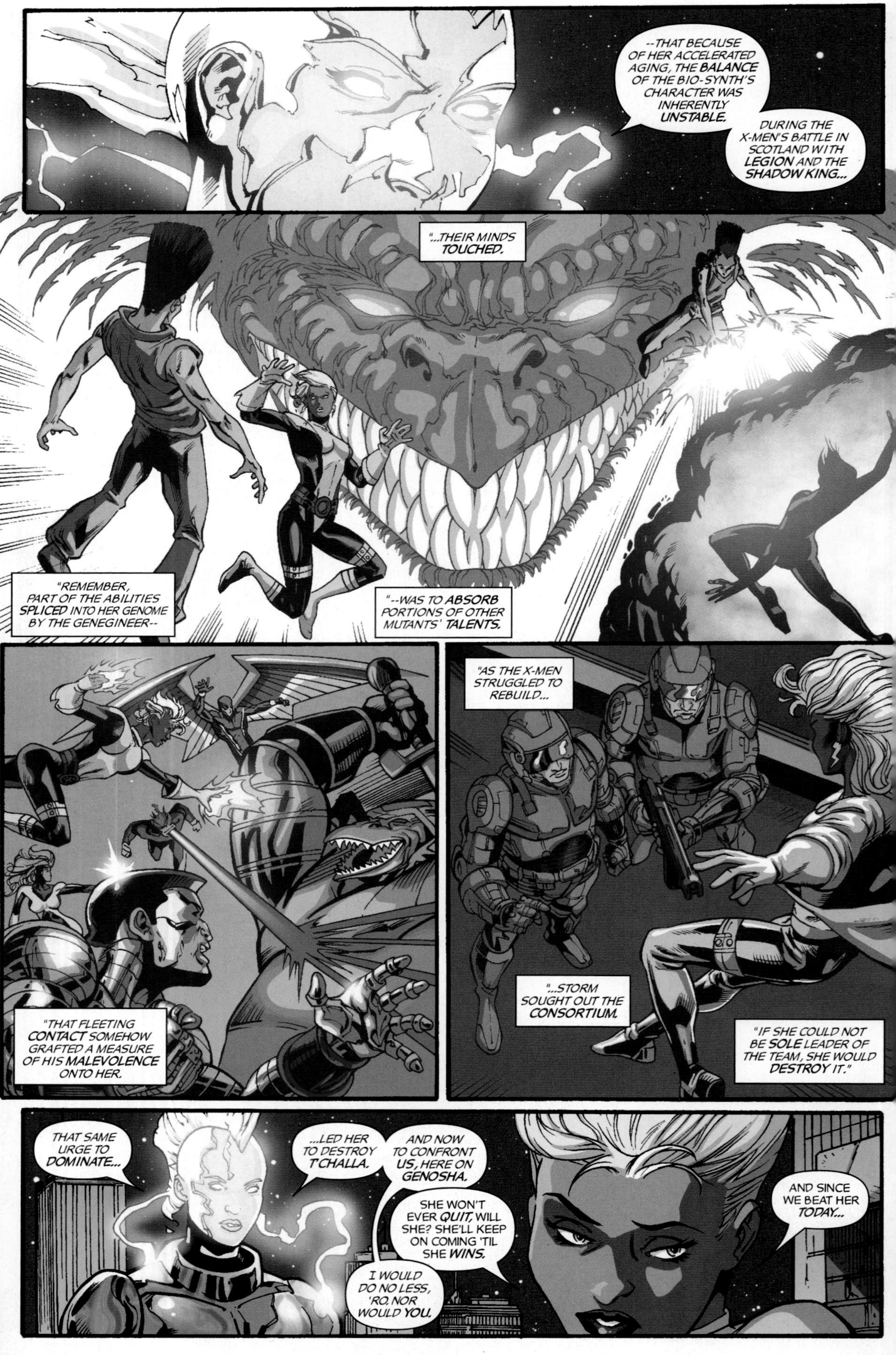
--THAT BECAUSE OF HER ACCELERATED AGING, THE BALANCE OF THE BIO-SYNTH'S CHARACTER WAS INHERENTLY UNSTABLE.
DURING THE X-MEN'S BATTLE IN SCOTLAND WITH LEGION AND THE SHADOW KING...
"...THEIR MINDS TOUCHED.
"REMEMBER, PART OF THE ABILITIES SPLICED INTO HER GENOME BY THE GENEGINEER--
"--WAS TO ABSORB PORTIONS OF OTHER MUTANTS' TALENTS.
"THAT FLEETING CONTACT SOMEHOW GRAFTED A MEASURE OF HIS MALEVOLENCE ONTO HER.
"AS THE X-MEN STRUGGLED TO REBUILD...
"...STORM SOUGHT OUT THE CONSORTIUM.
"IF SHE COULD NOT BE SOLE LEADER OF THE TEAM, SHE WOULD DESTROY IT."
THAT SAME URGE TO DOMINATE...
...LED HER TO DESTROY T'CHALLA.
AND NOW TO CONFRONT US, HERE ON GENOSHA.
SHE WON'T EVER QUIT, WILL SHE? SHE'LL KEEP ON COMING 'TIL SHE WINS.
I WOULD DO NO LESS, 'RO. NOR WOULD YOU.
AND SINCE WE BEAT HER TODAY...

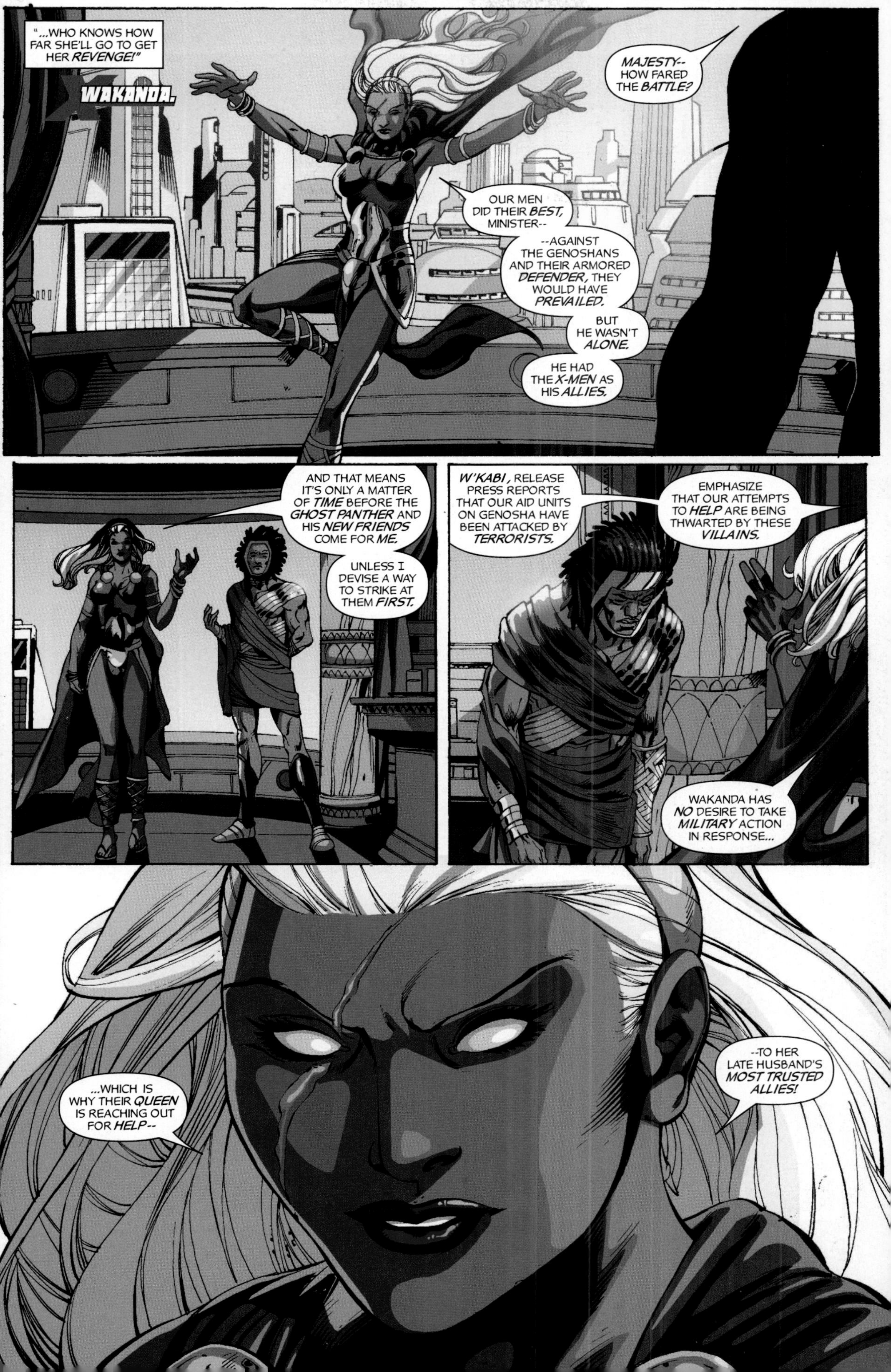
"...WHO KNOWS HOW FAR SHE'LL GO TO GET HER REVENGE!"
WAKANDA.
MAJESTY-- HOW FARED THE BATTLE?
OUR MEN DID THEIR BEST, MINISTER--
--AGAINST THE GENOSHANS AND THEIR ARMORED DEFENDER, THEY WOULD HAVE PREVAILED.
BUT HE WASN'T ALONE.
HE HAD THE X-MEN AS HIS ALLIES.
AND THAT MEANS IT'S ONLY A MATTER OF TIME BEFORE THE GHOST PANTHER AND HIS NEW FRIENDS COME FOR ME.
UNLESS I DEVISE A WAY TO STRIKE AT THEM FIRST.
W'KABI, RELEASE PRESS REPORTS THAT OUR AID UNITS ON GENOSHA HAVE BEEN ATTACKED BY TERRORISTS.
EMPHASIZE THAT OUR ATTEMPTS TO HELP ARE BEING THWARTED BY THESE VILLAINS.
WAKANDA HAS NO DESIRE TO TAKE MILITARY ACTION IN RESPONSE...
...WHICH IS WHY THEIR QUEEN IS REACHING OUT FOR HELP--
--TO HER LATE HUSBAND'S MOST TRUSTED ALLIES!

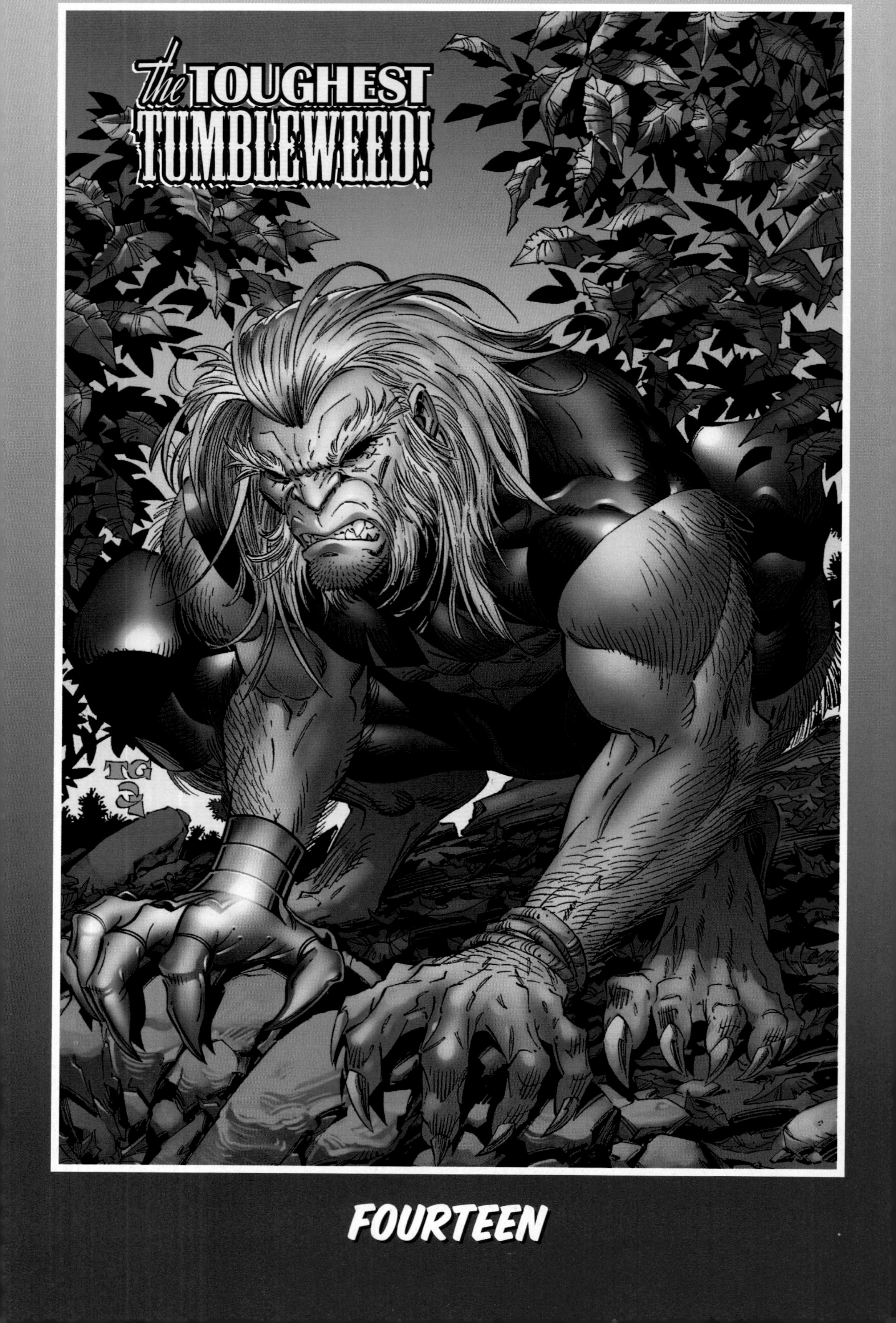
the TOUGHEST
TUMBLEWEED!
TG

FOURTEEN

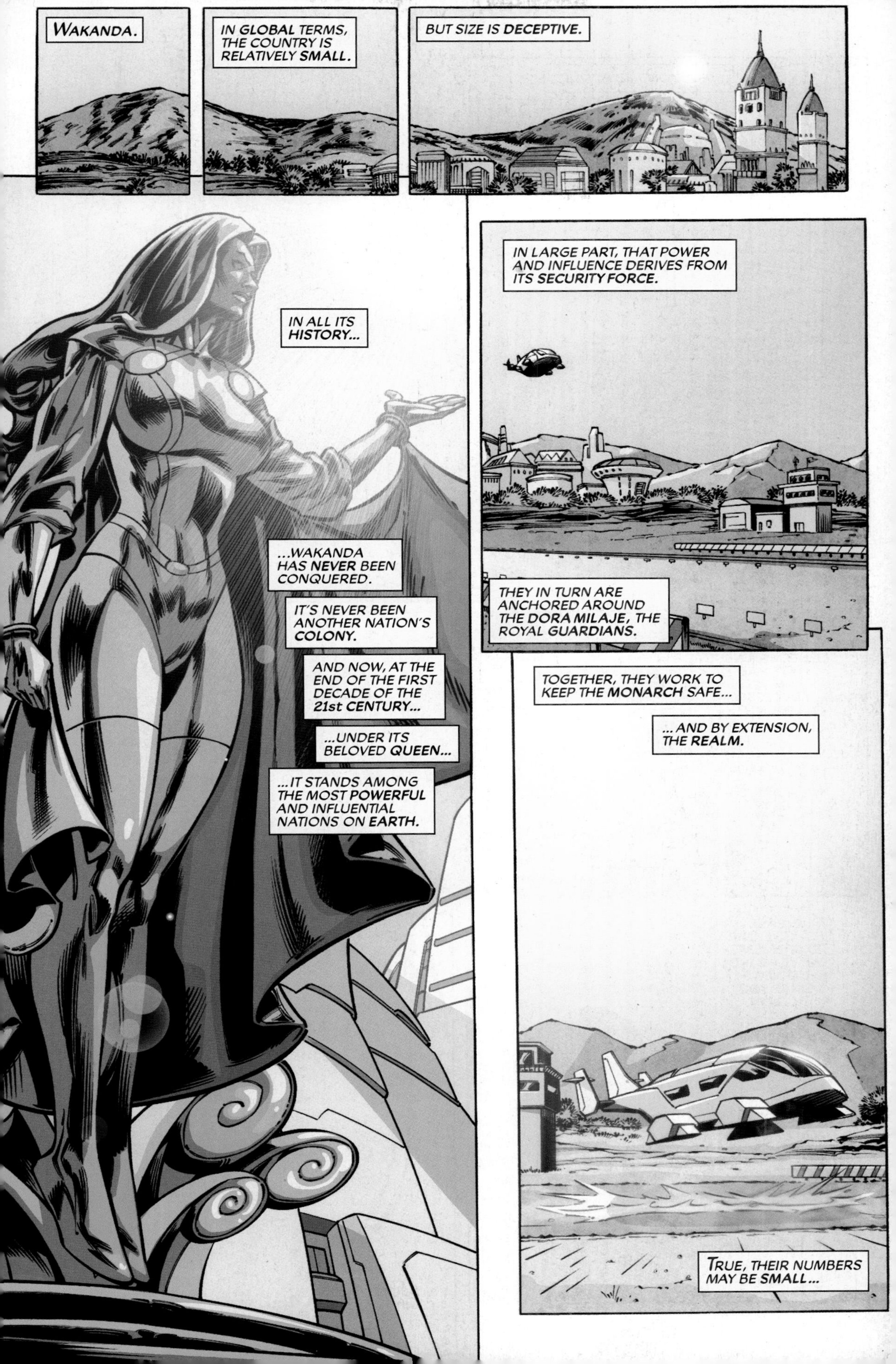
WAKANDA.
IN GLOBAL TERMS, THE COUNTRY IS RELATIVELY SMALL.
BUT SIZE IS DECEPTIVE.
IN ALL ITS HISTORY...
...WAKANDA HAS NEVER BEEN CONQUERED.
IT'S NEVER BEEN ANOTHER NATION'S COLONY.
AND NOW, AT THE END OF THE FIRST DECADE OF THE 21st CENTURY...
...UNDER ITS BELOVED QUEEN...
...IT STANDS AMONG THE MOST POWERFUL AND INFLUENTIAL NATIONS ON EARTH.
IN LARGE PART, THAT POWER AND INFLUENCE DERIVES FROM ITS SECURITY FORCE.
THEY IN TURN ARE ANCHORED AROUND THE DORA MILAJE, THE ROYAL GUARDIANS.
TOGETHER, THEY WORK TO KEEP THE MONARCH SAFE...
...AND BY EXTENSION, THE REALM.
TRUE, THEIR NUMBERS MAY BE SMALL...

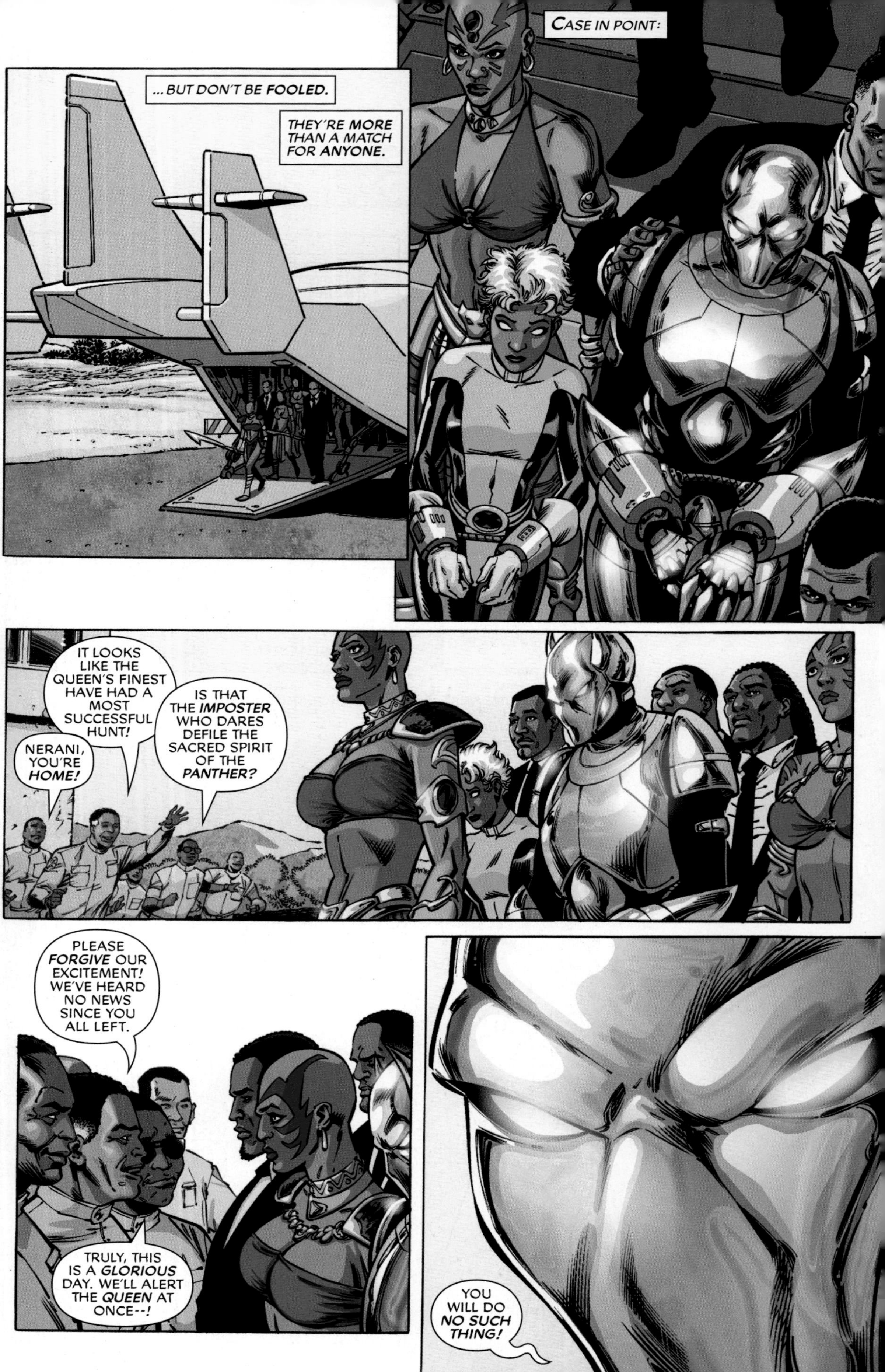
CASE IN POINT:
... BUT DON'T BE FOOLED.
THEY'RE MORE THAN A MATCH FOR ANYONE.
NERANI, YOU'RE HOME!
IT LOOKS LIKE THE QUEEN'S FINEST HAVE HAD A MOST SUCCESSFUL HUNT!
IS THAT THE IMPOSTER WHO DARES DEFILE THE SACRED SPIRIT OF THE PANTHER?
PLEASE FORGIVE OUR EXCITEMENT! WE'VE HEARD NO NEWS SINCE YOU ALL LEFT.
TRULY, THIS IS A GLORIOUS DAY. WE'LL ALERT THE QUEEN AT ONCE--!
YOU WILL DO NO SUCH THING!

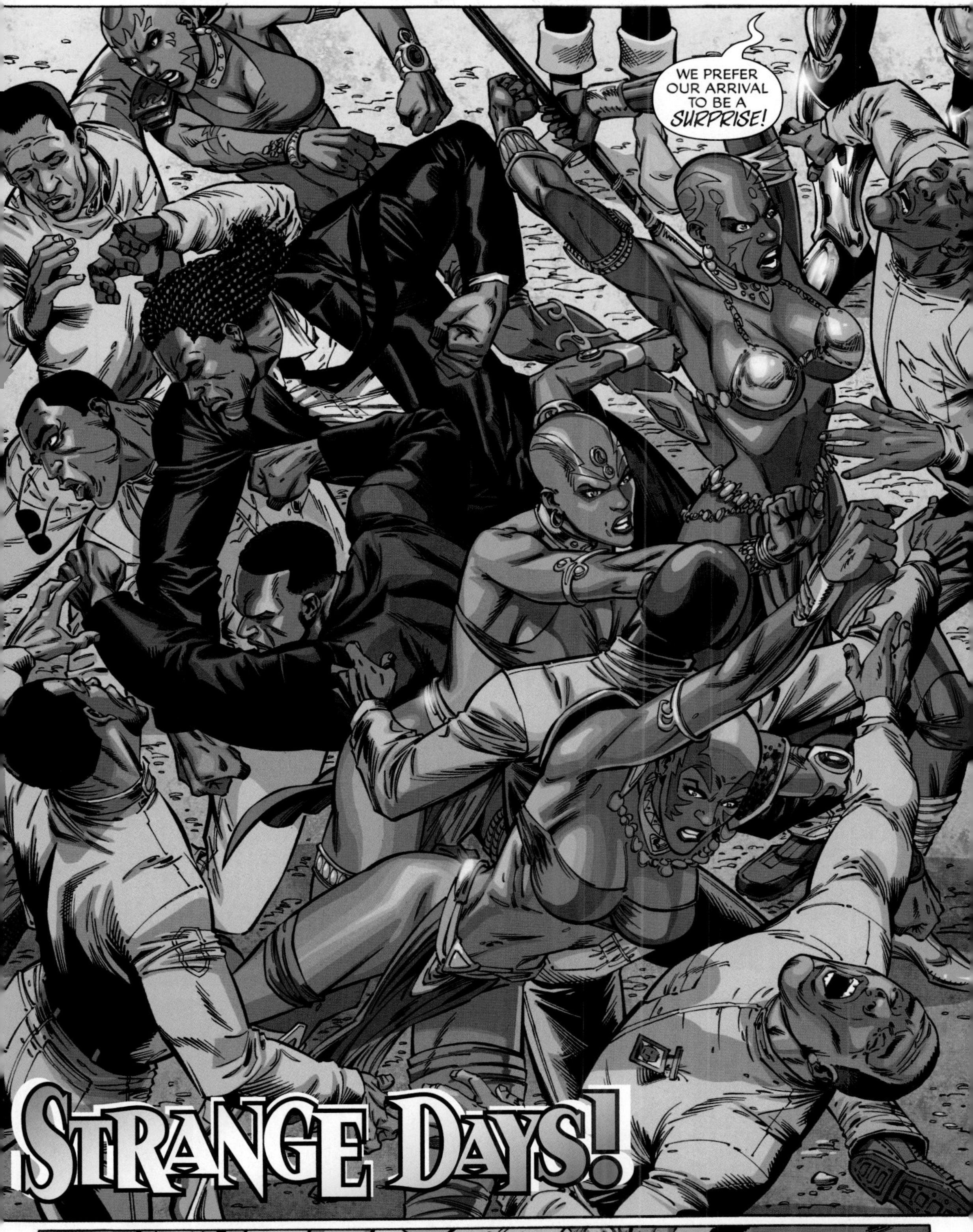
WE PREFER OUR ARRIVAL TO BE A SURPRISE!
STRANGE DAYS!

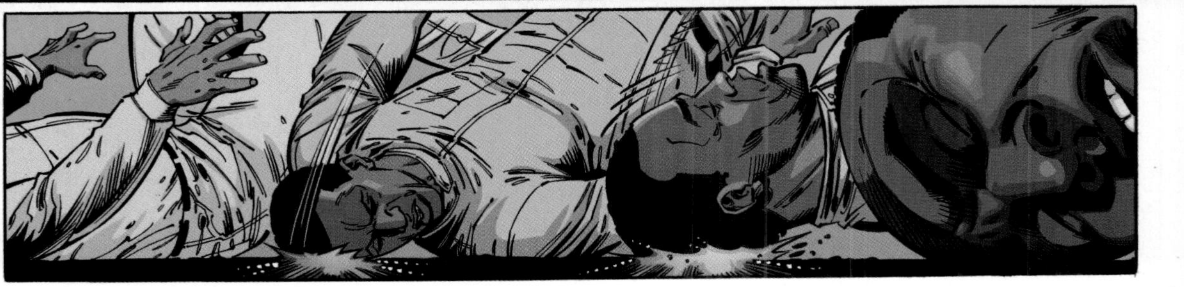

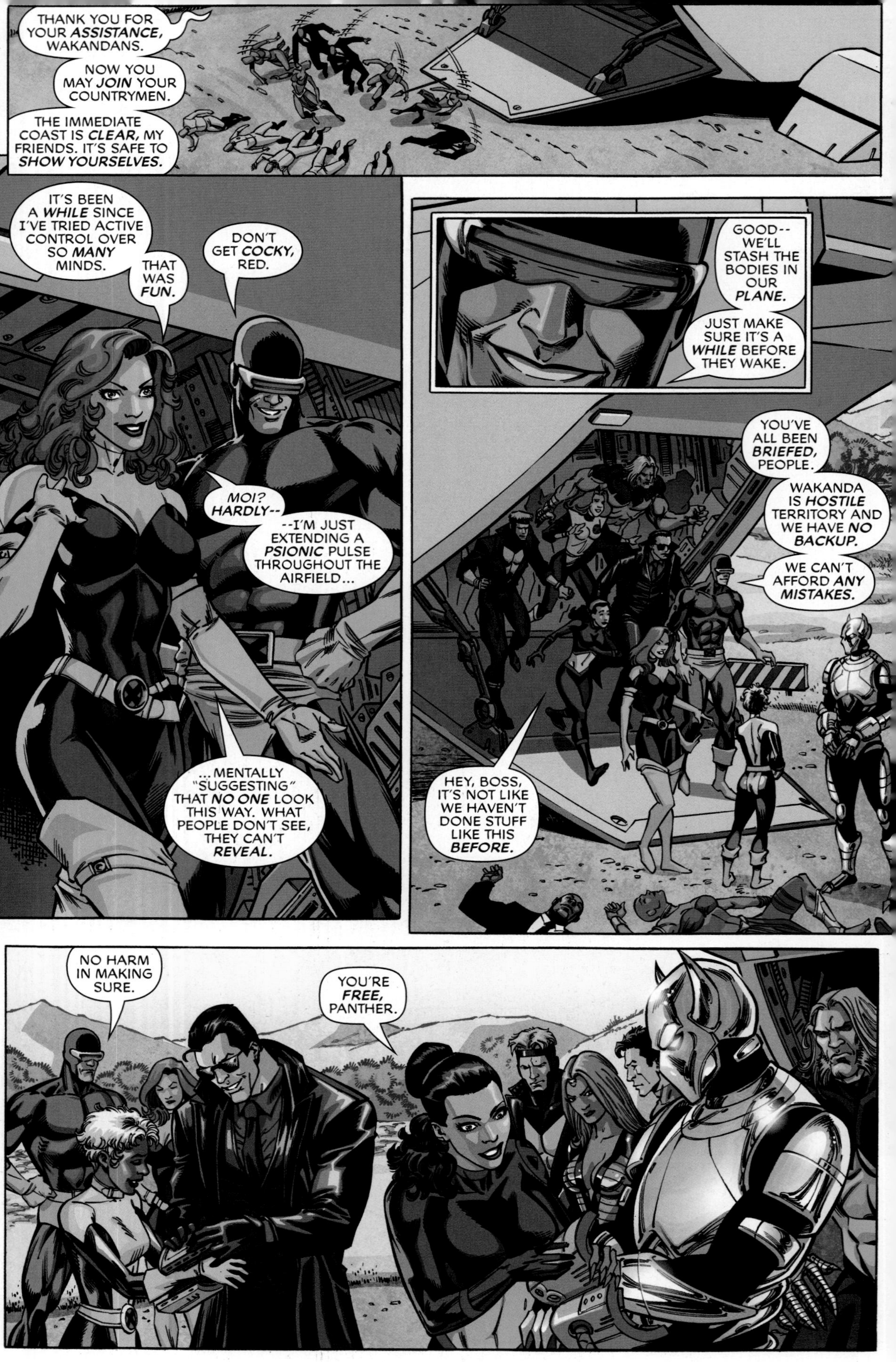
THANK YOU FOR YOUR ASSISTANCE, WAKANDANS.
NOW YOU MAY JOIN YOUR COUNTRYMEN.
THE IMMEDIATE COAST IS CLEAR, MY FRIENDS. IT'S SAFE TO SHOW YOURSELVES.
IT'S BEEN A WHILE SINCE I'VE TRIED ACTIVE CONTROL OVER SO MANY MINDS.
THAT WAS FUN.
DON'T GET COCKY, RED.
MOI? HARDLY--
--I'M JUST EXTENDING A PSIONIC PULSE THROUGHOUT THE AIRFIELD...
...MENTALLY "SUGGESTING" THAT NO ONE LOOK THIS WAY. WHAT PEOPLE DON'T SEE, THEY CAN'T REVEAL.
GOOD--WE'LL STASH THE BODIES IN OUR PLANE.
JUST MAKE SURE IT'S A WHILE BEFORE THEY WAKE.
YOU'VE ALL BEEN BRIEFED, PEOPLE.
WAKANDA IS HOSTILE TERRITORY AND WE HAVE NO BACKUP.
WE CAN'T AFFORD ANY MISTAKES.
HEY, BOSS, IT'S NOT LIKE WE HAVEN'T DONE STUFF LIKE THIS BEFORE.
NO HARM IN MAKING SURE.
YOU'RE FREE, PANTHER.

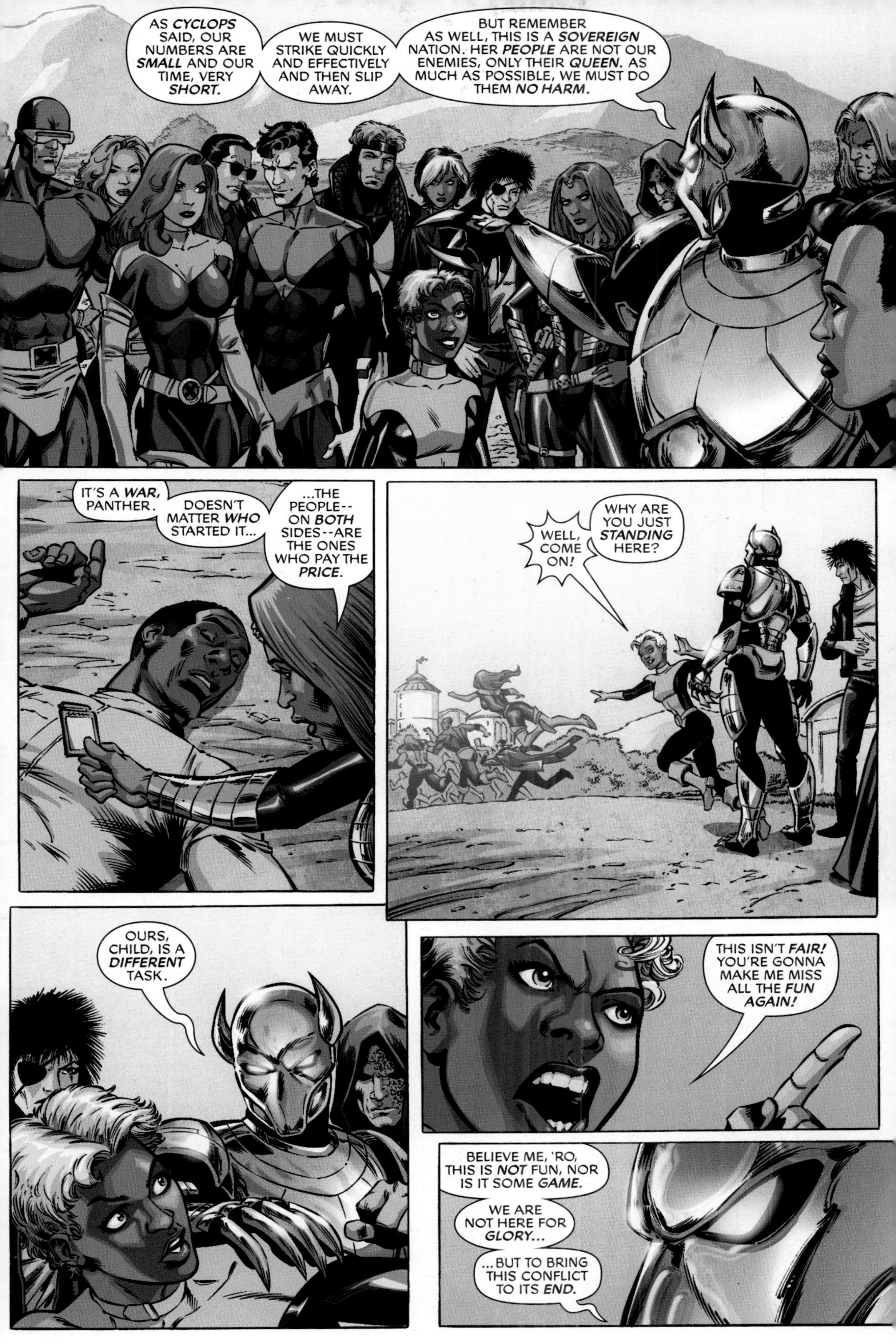
AS *CYCLOPS* SAID, OUR NUMBERS ARE *SMALL* AND OUR TIME, VERY *SHORT.*
WE MUST STRIKE QUICKLY AND EFFECTIVELY AND THEN SLIP AWAY.
BUT REMEMBER AS WELL, THIS IS A *SOVEREIGN* NATION. HER *PEOPLE* ARE NOT OUR ENEMIES, ONLY THEIR *QUEEN.* AS MUCH AS POSSIBLE, WE MUST DO THEM *NO HARM.*
IT'S A *WAR,* PANTHER.
DOESN'T MATTER *WHO* STARTED IT...
...THE PEOPLE-- ON *BOTH* SIDES--ARE THE ONES WHO PAY THE *PRICE.*
WHY ARE YOU JUST *STANDING* HERE?
WELL, COME ON*!*
OURS, CHILD, IS A *DIFFERENT* TASK.
THIS ISN'T *FAIR!* YOU'RE GONNA MAKE ME MISS ALL THE *FUN AGAIN!*
BELIEVE ME, 'RO, THIS IS *NOT* FUN, NOR IS IT SOME *GAME.*
WE ARE NOT HERE FOR *GLORY...*
...BUT TO BRING THIS CONFLICT TO ITS *END.*

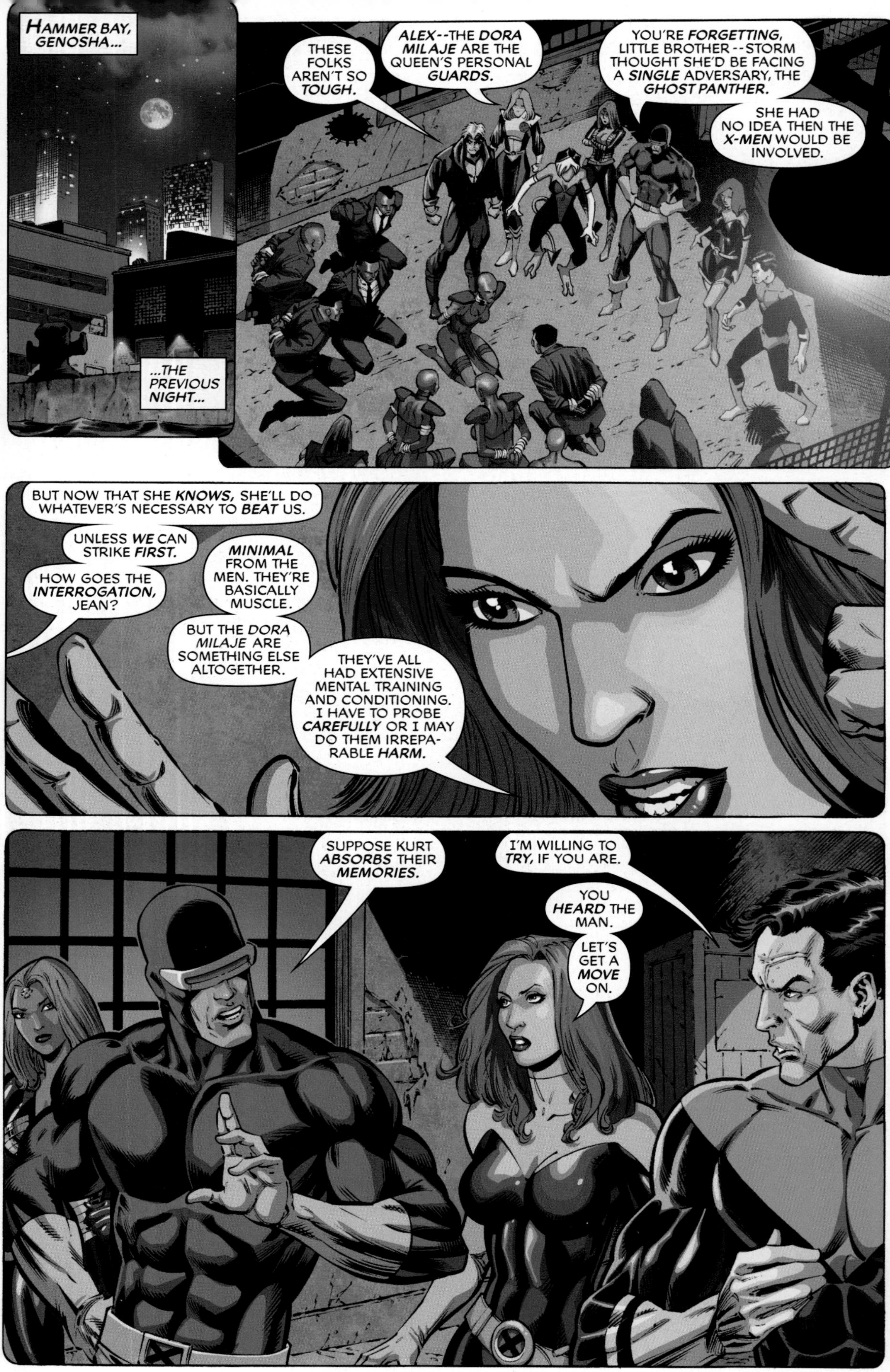
HAMMER BAY, GENOSHA...
...THE PREVIOUS NIGHT...
THESE FOLKS AREN'T SO TOUGH.
ALEX--THE DORA MILAJE ARE THE QUEEN'S PERSONAL GUARDS.
YOU'RE FORGETTING, LITTLE BROTHER--STORM THOUGHT SHE'D BE FACING A SINGLE ADVERSARY, THE GHOST PANTHER.
SHE HAD NO IDEA THEN THE X-MEN WOULD BE INVOLVED.
BUT NOW THAT SHE KNOWS, SHE'LL DO WHATEVER'S NECESSARY TO BEAT US.
UNLESS WE CAN STRIKE FIRST.
HOW GOES THE INTERROGATION, JEAN?
MINIMAL FROM THE MEN. THEY'RE BASICALLY MUSCLE.
BUT THE DORA MILAJE ARE SOMETHING ELSE ALTOGETHER.
THEY'VE ALL HAD EXTENSIVE MENTAL TRAINING AND CONDITIONING. I HAVE TO PROBE CAREFULLY OR I MAY DO THEM IRREPARABLE HARM.
SUPPOSE KURT ABSORBS THEIR MEMORIES.
I'M WILLING TO TRY, IF YOU ARE.
YOU HEARD THE MAN.
LET'S GET A MOVE ON.

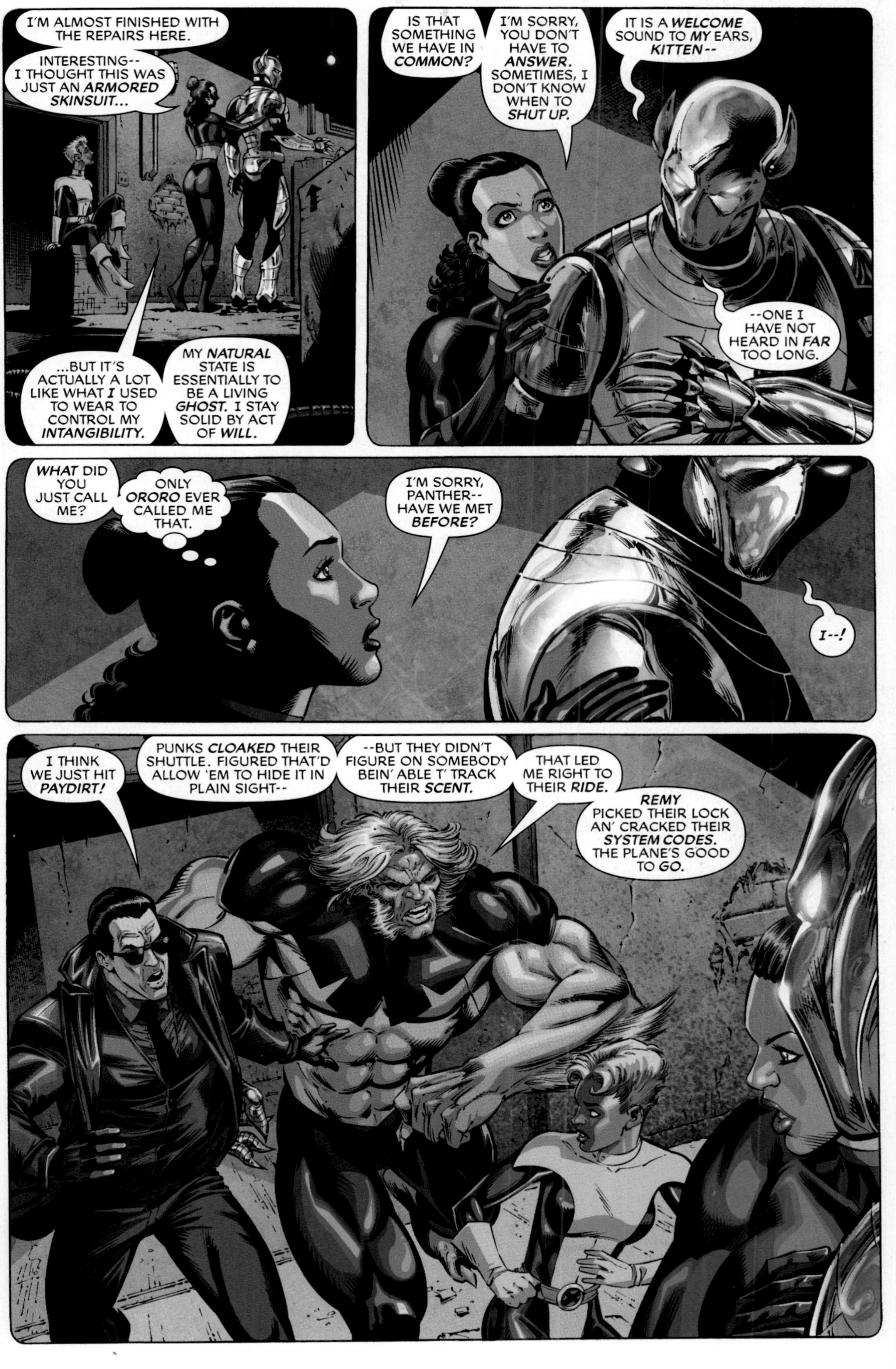

I'M ALMOST FINISHED WITH THE REPAIRS HERE.
INTERESTING-- I THOUGHT THIS WAS JUST AN ARMORED SKINSUIT...
...BUT IT'S ACTUALLY A LOT LIKE WHAT I USED TO WEAR TO CONTROL MY INTANGIBILITY.
MY NATURAL STATE IS ESSENTIALLY TO BE A LIVING GHOST. I STAY SOLID BY ACT OF WILL.
IS THAT SOMETHING WE HAVE IN COMMON?
I'M SORRY, YOU DON'T HAVE TO ANSWER. SOMETIMES, I DON'T KNOW WHEN TO SHUT UP.
IT IS A WELCOME SOUND TO MY EARS, KITTEN--
--ONE I HAVE NOT HEARD IN FAR TOO LONG.
WHAT DID YOU JUST CALL ME?
ONLY ORORO EVER CALLED ME THAT.
I'M SORRY, PANTHER-- HAVE WE MET BEFORE?
I--!
I THINK WE JUST HIT PAYDIRT!
PUNKS CLOAKED THEIR SHUTTLE. FIGURED THAT'D ALLOW 'EM TO HIDE IT IN PLAIN SIGHT--
--BUT THEY DIDN'T FIGURE ON SOMEBODY BEIN' ABLE T' TRACK THEIR SCENT.
THAT LED ME RIGHT TO THEIR RIDE.
REMY PICKED THEIR LOCK AN' CRACKED THEIR SYSTEM CODES. THE PLANE'S GOOD TO GO.

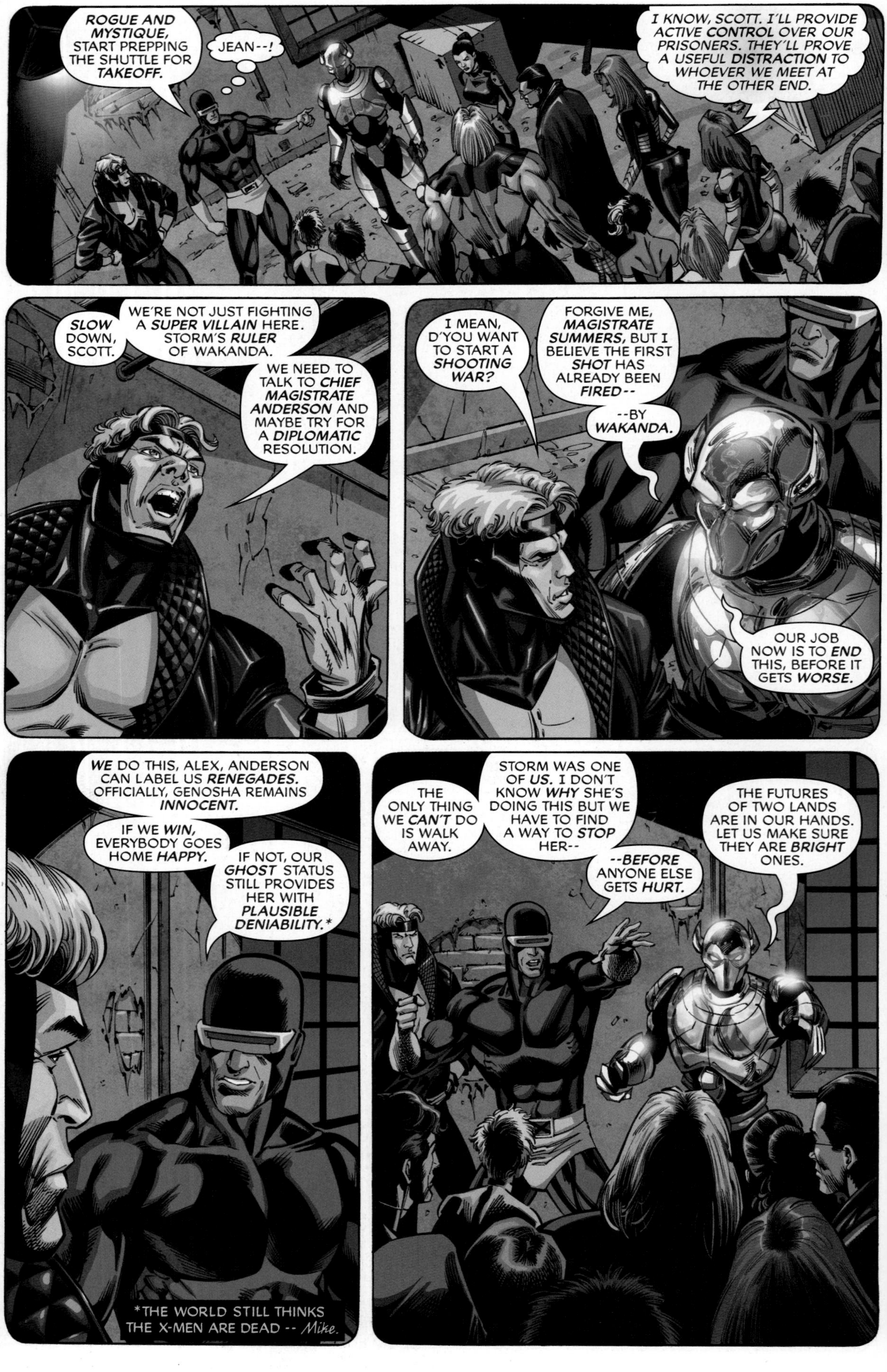
ROGUE AND MYSTIQUE, START PREPPING THE SHUTTLE FOR TAKEOFF.
JEAN--!
I KNOW, SCOTT. I'LL PROVIDE ACTIVE CONTROL OVER OUR PRISONERS. THEY'LL PROVE A USEFUL DISTRACTION TO WHOEVER WE MEET AT THE OTHER END.
SLOW DOWN, SCOTT.
WE'RE NOT JUST FIGHTING A SUPER VILLAIN HERE. STORM'S RULER OF WAKANDA.
WE NEED TO TALK TO CHIEF MAGISTRATE ANDERSON AND MAYBE TRY FOR A DIPLOMATIC RESOLUTION.
I MEAN, D'YOU WANT TO START A SHOOTING WAR?
FORGIVE ME, MAGISTRATE SUMMERS, BUT I BELIEVE THE FIRST SHOT HAS ALREADY BEEN FIRED--
--BY WAKANDA.
OUR JOB NOW IS TO END THIS, BEFORE IT GETS WORSE.
WE DO THIS, ALEX, ANDERSON CAN LABEL US RENEGADES. OFFICIALLY, GENOSHA REMAINS INNOCENT.
IF WE WIN, EVERYBODY GOES HOME HAPPY.
IF NOT, OUR GHOST STATUS STILL PROVIDES HER WITH PLAUSIBLE DENIABILITY.*
*THE WORLD STILL THINKS THE X-MEN ARE DEAD -- Mike.
THE ONLY THING WE CAN'T DO IS WALK AWAY.
STORM WAS ONE OF US. I DON'T KNOW WHY SHE'S DOING THIS BUT WE HAVE TO FIND A WAY TO STOP HER--
--BEFORE ANYONE ELSE GETS HURT.
THE FUTURES OF TWO LANDS ARE IN OUR HANDS. LET US MAKE SURE THEY ARE BRIGHT ONES.

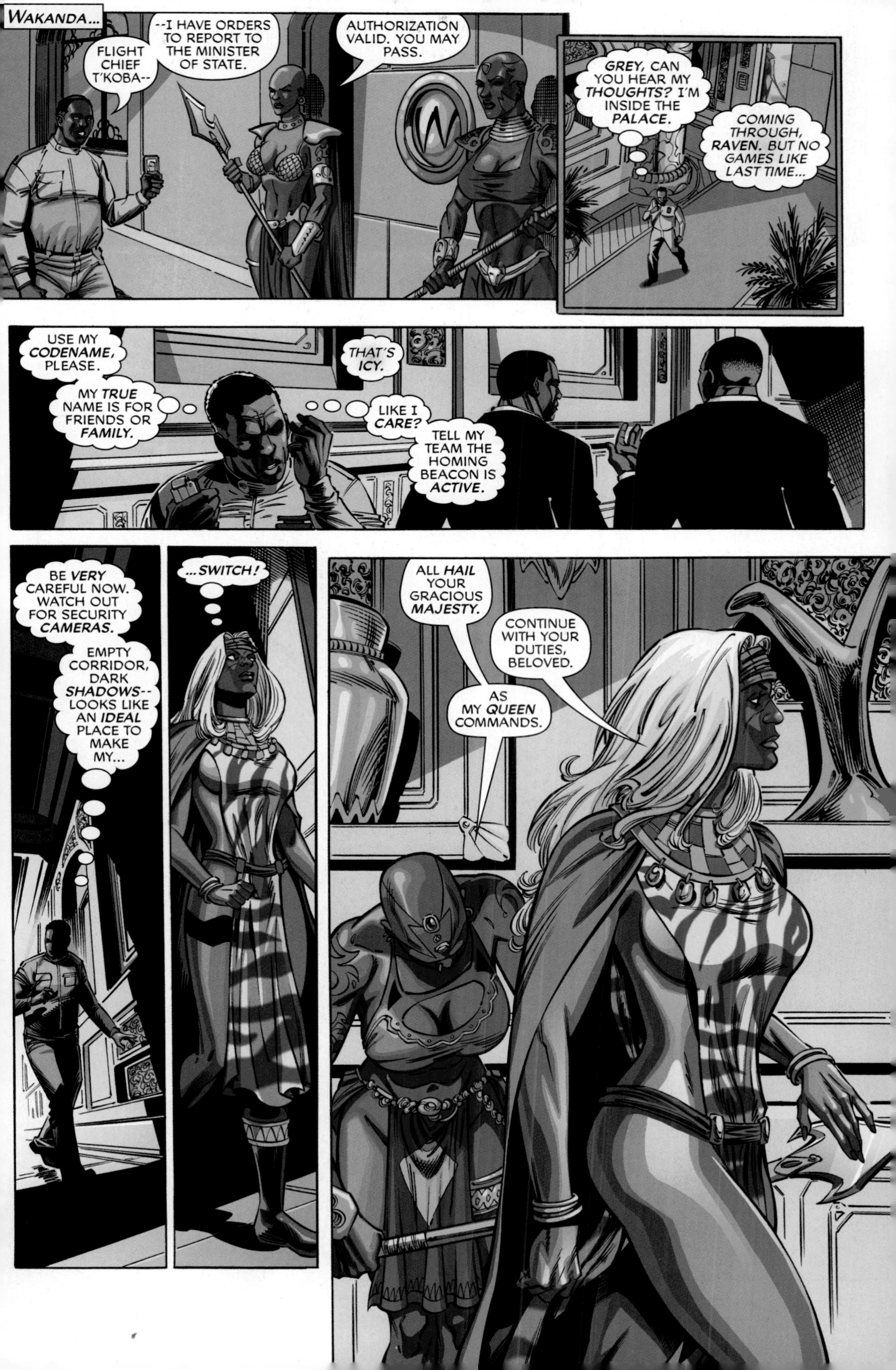
WAKANDA...
FLIGHT CHIEF T'KOBA--
--I HAVE ORDERS TO REPORT TO THE MINISTER OF STATE.
AUTHORIZATION VALID. YOU MAY PASS.
GREY, CAN YOU HEAR MY THOUGHTS? I'M INSIDE THE PALACE.
COMING THROUGH, RAVEN. BUT NO GAMES LIKE LAST TIME...
USE MY CODENAME, PLEASE.
MY TRUE NAME IS FOR FRIENDS OR FAMILY.
THAT'S ICY.
LIKE I CARE?
TELL MY TEAM THE HOMING BEACON IS ACTIVE.
BE VERY CAREFUL NOW. WATCH OUT FOR SECURITY CAMERAS.
EMPTY CORRIDOR, DARK SHADOWS--LOOKS LIKE AN IDEAL PLACE TO MAKE MY...
...SWITCH!
ALL HAIL YOUR GRACIOUS MAJESTY.
CONTINUE WITH YOUR DUTIES, BELOVED.
AS MY QUEEN COMMANDS.

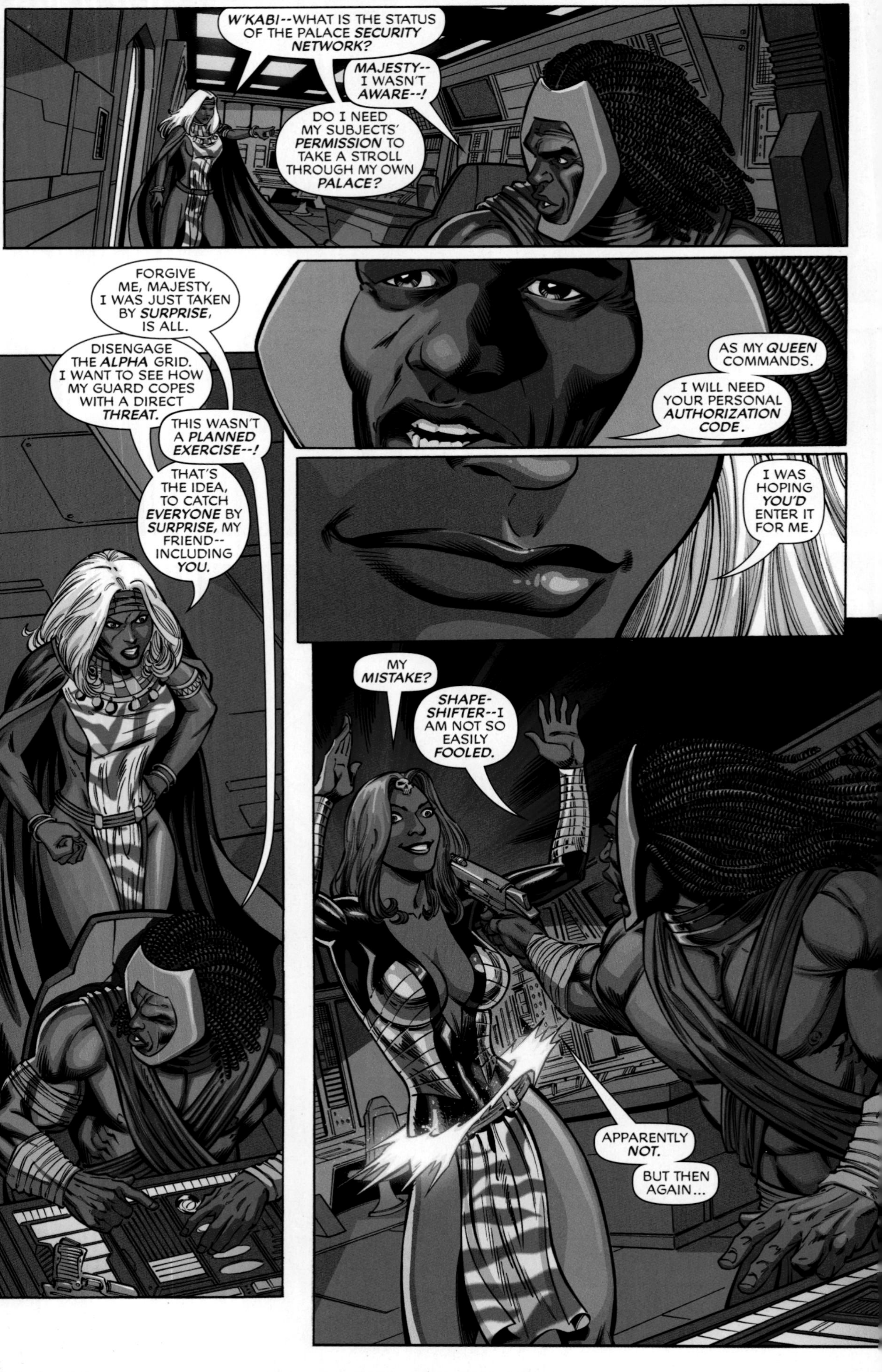
W'KABI--WHAT IS THE STATUS OF THE PALACE SECURITY NETWORK?
MAJESTY--I WASN'T AWARE--!
DO I NEED MY SUBJECTS' PERMISSION TO TAKE A STROLL THROUGH MY OWN PALACE?
FORGIVE ME, MAJESTY, I WAS JUST TAKEN BY SURPRISE, IS ALL.
DISENGAGE THE ALPHA GRID. I WANT TO SEE HOW MY GUARD COPES WITH A DIRECT THREAT.
THIS WASN'T A PLANNED EXERCISE--!
THAT'S THE IDEA, TO CATCH EVERYONE BY SURPRISE, MY FRIEND--INCLUDING YOU.
AS MY QUEEN COMMANDS.
I WILL NEED YOUR PERSONAL AUTHORIZATION CODE.
I WAS HOPING YOU'D ENTER IT FOR ME.
MY MISTAKE?
SHAPE-SHIFTER--I AM NOT SO EASILY FOOLED.
APPARENTLY NOT.
BUT THEN AGAIN...

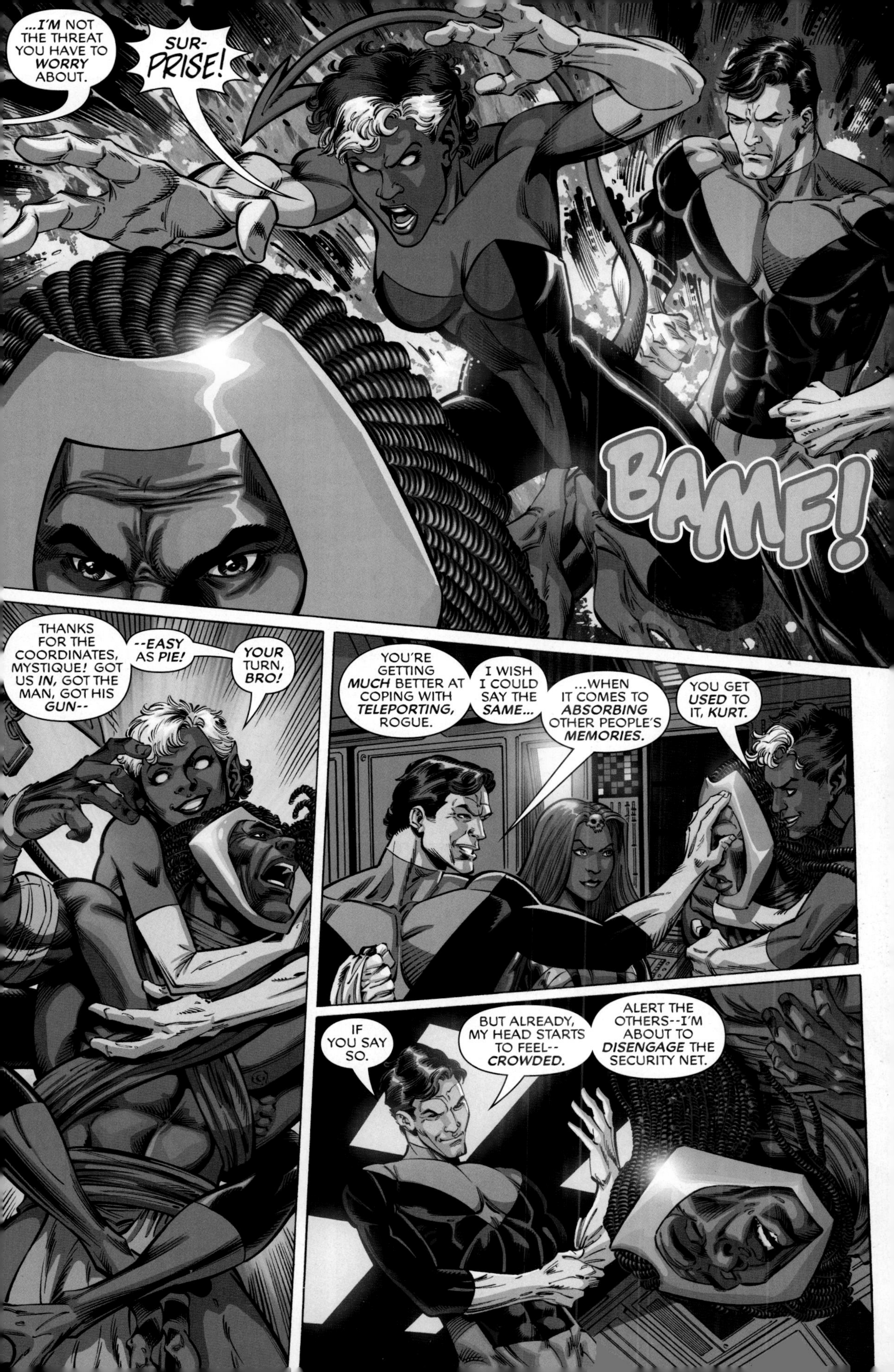
...I'M NOT THE THREAT YOU HAVE TO WORRY ABOUT.
SUR-PRISE!
BAMF!
THANKS FOR THE COORDINATES, MYSTIQUE! GOT US IN, GOT THE MAN, GOT HIS GUN--
--EASY AS PIE!
YOUR TURN, BRO!
YOU'RE GETTING MUCH BETTER AT COPING WITH TELEPORTING, ROGUE.
I WISH I COULD SAY THE SAME...
...WHEN IT COMES TO ABSORBING OTHER PEOPLE'S MEMORIES.
YOU GET USED TO IT, KURT.
IF YOU SAY SO.
BUT ALREADY, MY HEAD STARTS TO FEEL-- CROWDED.
ALERT THE OTHERS--I'M ABOUT TO DISENGAGE THE SECURITY NET.

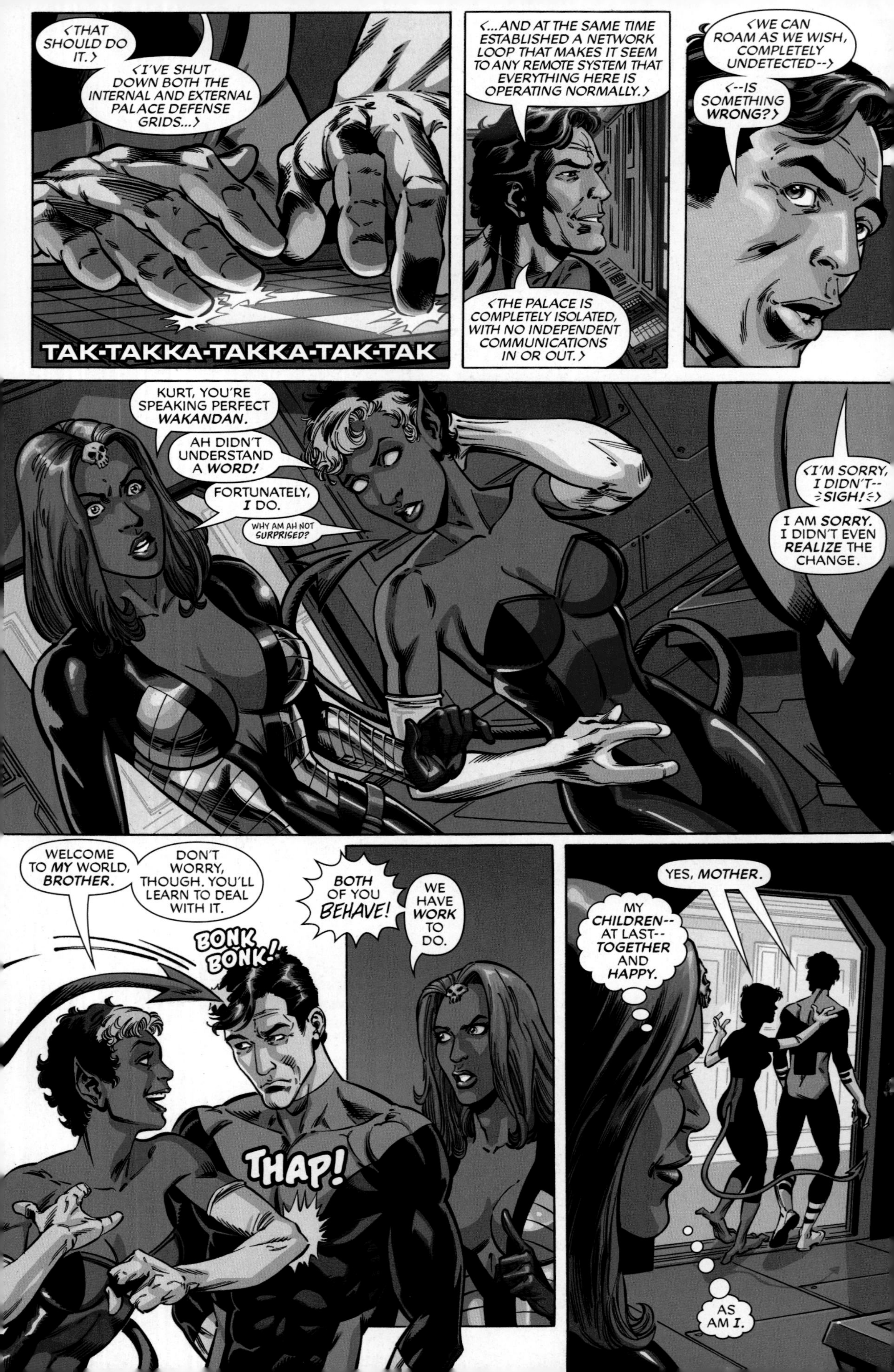
‹THAT SHOULD DO IT.›
‹I'VE SHUT DOWN BOTH THE INTERNAL AND EXTERNAL PALACE DEFENSE GRIDS...›
TAK-TAKKA-TAKKA-TAK-TAK
‹...AND AT THE SAME TIME ESTABLISHED A NETWORK LOOP THAT MAKES IT SEEM TO ANY REMOTE SYSTEM THAT EVERYTHING HERE IS OPERATING NORMALLY.›
‹THE PALACE IS COMPLETELY ISOLATED, WITH NO INDEPENDENT COMMUNICATIONS IN OR OUT.›
‹WE CAN ROAM AS WE WISH, COMPLETELY UNDETECTED--›
‹--IS SOMETHING WRONG?›
KURT, YOU'RE SPEAKING PERFECT WAKANDAN.
AH DIDN'T UNDERSTAND A WORD!
FORTUNATELY, I DO.
WHY AM AH NOT SURPRISED?
‹I'M SORRY, I DIDN'T-- ›SIGH!‹›
I AM SORRY. I DIDN'T EVEN REALIZE THE CHANGE.
WELCOME TO MY WORLD, BROTHER.
DON'T WORRY, THOUGH. YOU'LL LEARN TO DEAL WITH IT.
BOTH OF YOU BEHAVE!
WE HAVE WORK TO DO.
BONK BONK!
THAP!
YES, MOTHER.
MY CHILDREN-- AT LAST-- TOGETHER AND HAPPY.
AS AM I.

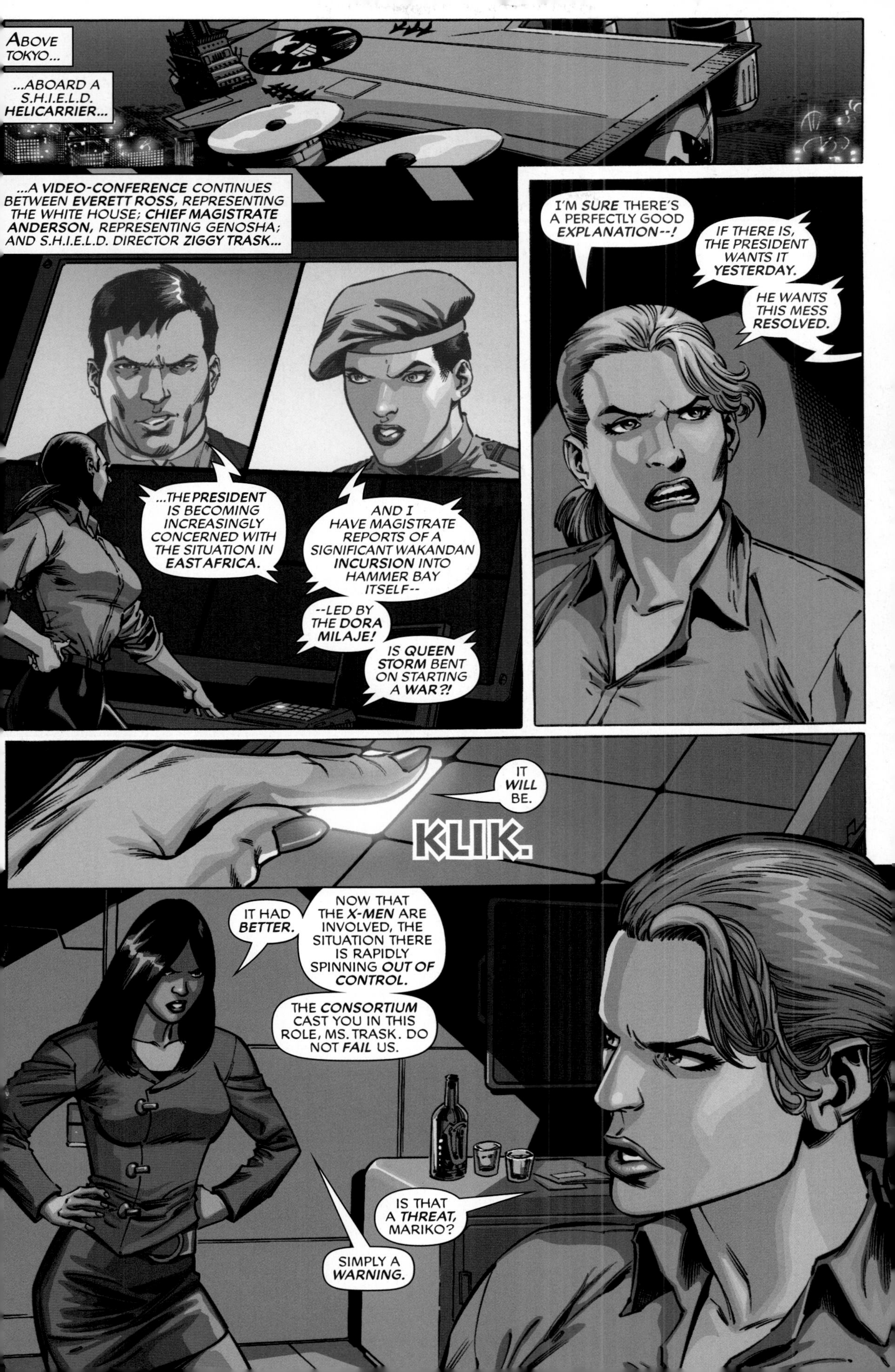
ABOVE TOKYO...
...ABOARD A S.H.I.E.L.D. HELICARRIER...
...A VIDEO-CONFERENCE CONTINUES BETWEEN EVERETT ROSS, REPRESENTING THE WHITE HOUSE; CHIEF MAGISTRATE ANDERSON, REPRESENTING GENOSHA; AND S.H.I.E.L.D. DIRECTOR ZIGGY TRASK...
...THE PRESIDENT IS BECOMING INCREASINGLY CONCERNED WITH THE SITUATION IN EAST AFRICA.
AND I HAVE MAGISTRATE REPORTS OF A SIGNIFICANT WAKANDAN INCURSION INTO HAMMER BAY ITSELF--
--LED BY THE DORA MILAJE!
IS QUEEN STORM BENT ON STARTING A WAR?!
I'M SURE THERE'S A PERFECTLY GOOD EXPLANATION--!
IF THERE IS, THE PRESIDENT WANTS IT YESTERDAY.
HE WANTS THIS MESS RESOLVED.
IT WILL BE.
KLIK.
IT HAD BETTER.
NOW THAT THE X-MEN ARE INVOLVED, THE SITUATION THERE IS RAPIDLY SPINNING OUT OF CONTROL.
THE CONSORTIUM CAST YOU IN THIS ROLE, MS. TRASK. DO NOT FAIL US.
IS THAT A THREAT, MARIKO?
SIMPLY A WARNING.

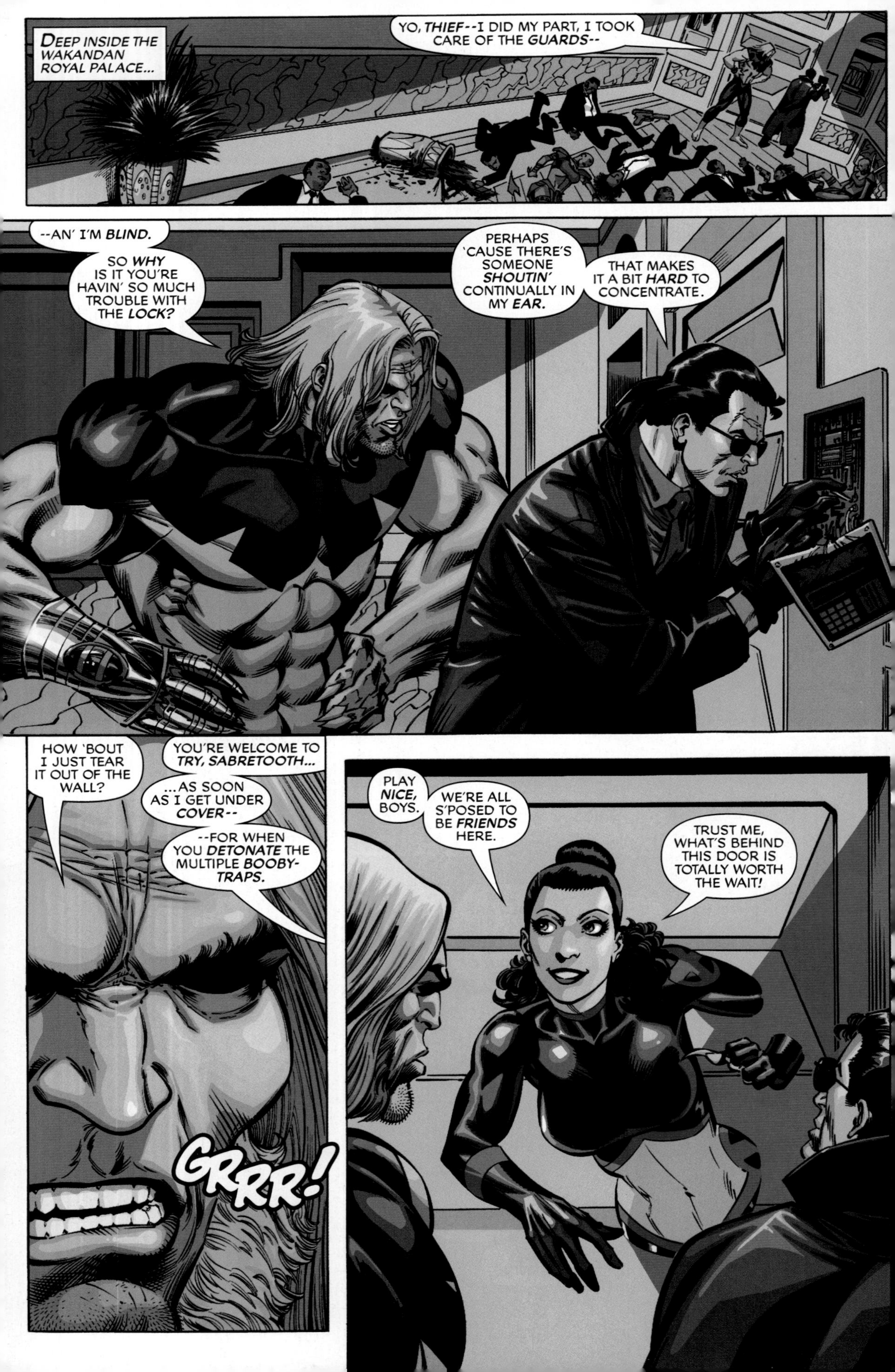
DEEP INSIDE THE WAKANDAN ROYAL PALACE...
YO, THIEF--I DID MY PART, I TOOK CARE OF THE GUARDS--
--AN' I'M BLIND.
SO WHY IS IT YOU'RE HAVIN' SO MUCH TROUBLE WITH THE LOCK?
PERHAPS 'CAUSE THERE'S SOMEONE SHOUTIN' CONTINUALLY IN MY EAR.
THAT MAKES IT A BIT HARD TO CONCENTRATE.
HOW 'BOUT I JUST TEAR IT OUT OF THE WALL?
YOU'RE WELCOME TO TRY, SABRETOOTH...
...AS SOON AS I GET UNDER COVER--
--FOR WHEN YOU DETONATE THE MULTIPLE BOOBY-TRAPS.
GRRR!
PLAY NICE, BOYS.
WE'RE ALL S'POSED TO BE FRIENDS HERE.
TRUST ME, WHAT'S BEHIND THIS DOOR IS TOTALLY WORTH THE WAIT!

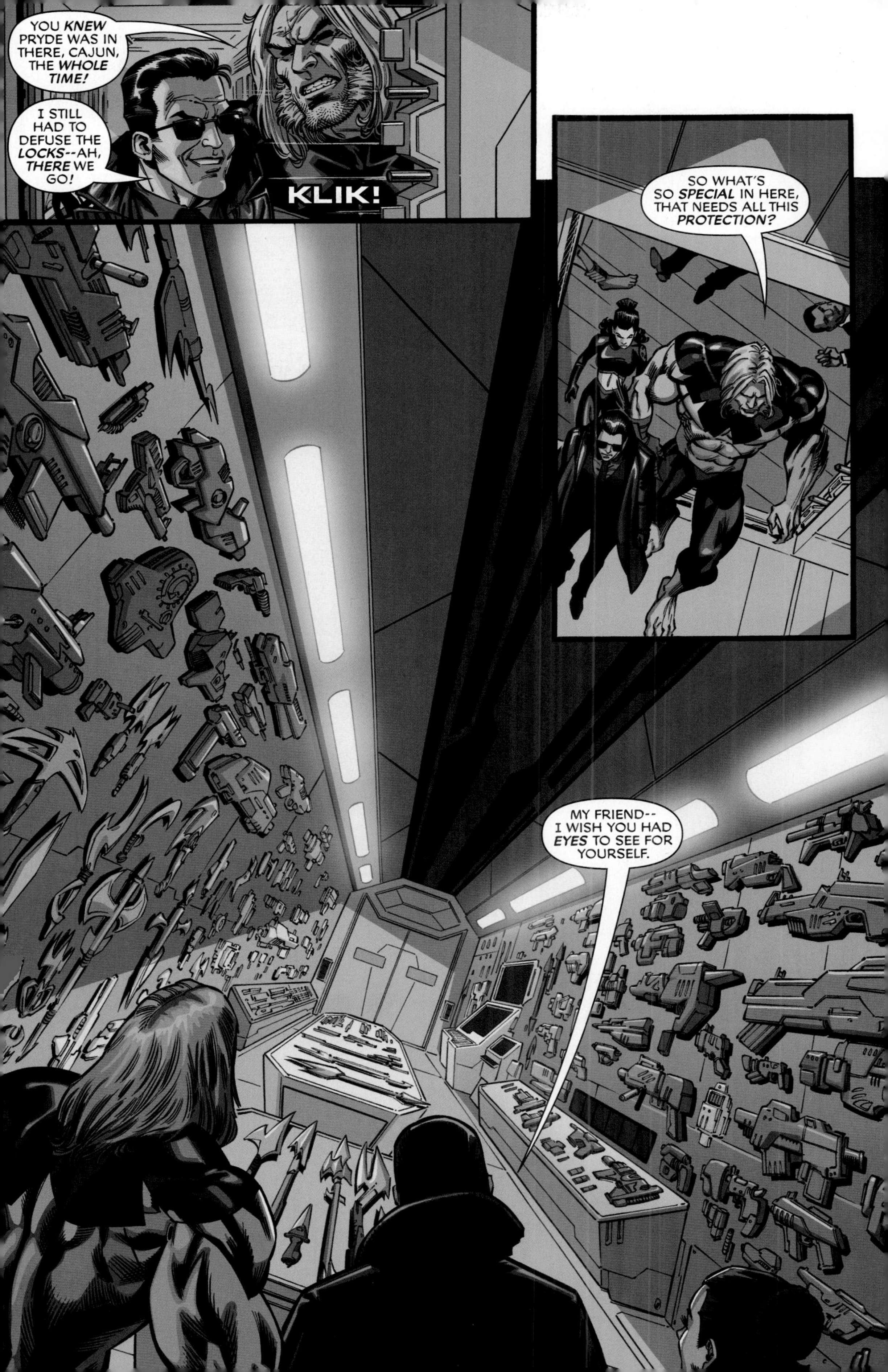
YOU KNEW PRYDE WAS IN THERE, CAJUN, THE WHOLE TIME!
I STILL HAD TO DEFUSE THE LOCKS--AH, THERE WE GO!
KLIK!
SO WHAT'S SO SPECIAL IN HERE, THAT NEEDS ALL THIS PROTECTION?
MY FRIEND-- I WISH YOU HAD EYES TO SEE FOR YOURSELF.

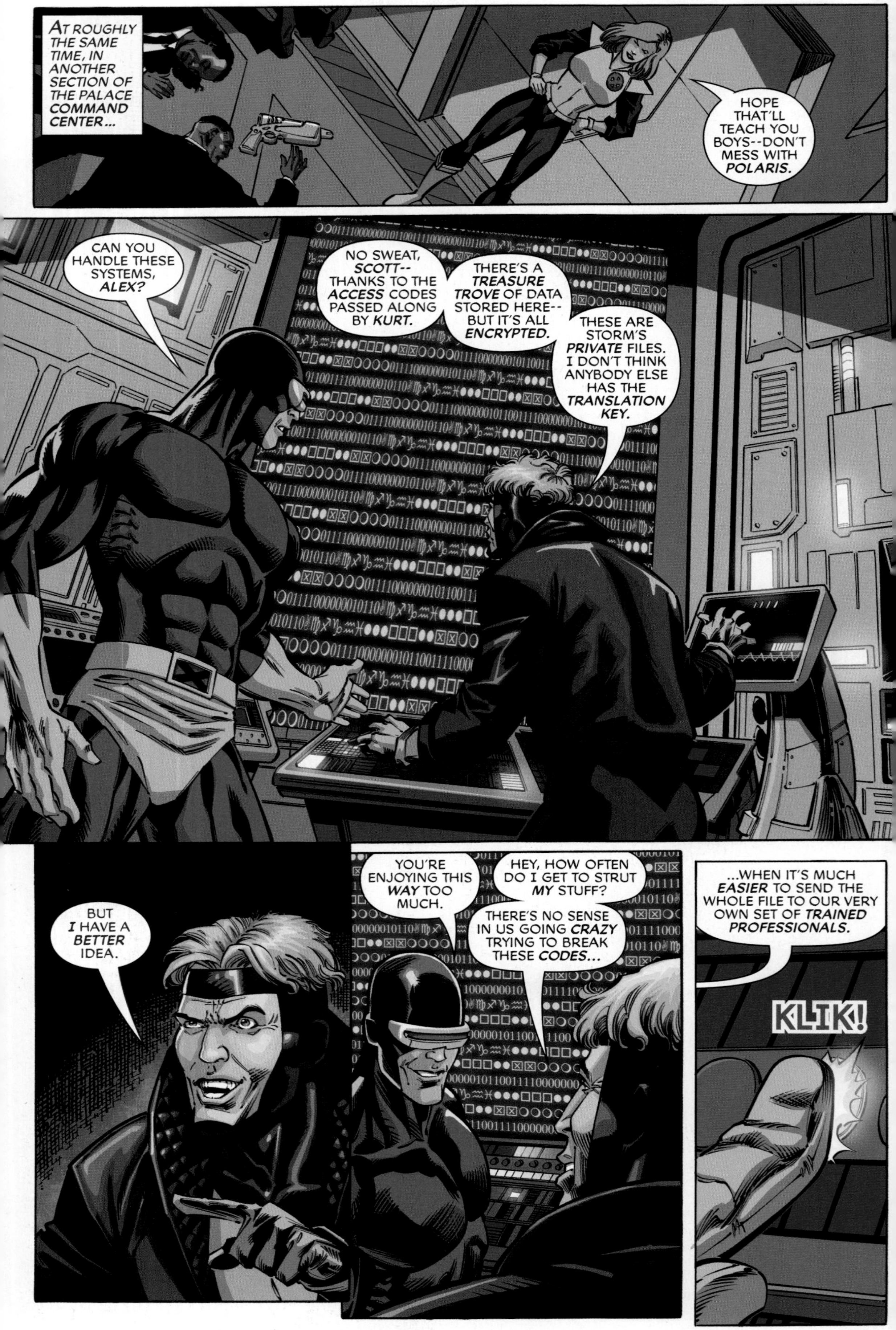
AT ROUGHLY THE SAME TIME, IN ANOTHER SECTION OF THE PALACE COMMAND CENTER...
HOPE THAT'LL TEACH YOU BOYS--DON'T MESS WITH POLARIS.
CAN YOU HANDLE THESE SYSTEMS, ALEX?
NO SWEAT, SCOTT-- THANKS TO THE ACCESS CODES PASSED ALONG BY KURT.
THERE'S A TREASURE TROVE OF DATA STORED HERE-- BUT IT'S ALL ENCRYPTED.
THESE ARE STORM'S PRIVATE FILES. I DON'T THINK ANYBODY ELSE HAS THE TRANSLATION KEY.
BUT I HAVE A BETTER IDEA.
YOU'RE ENJOYING THIS WAY TOO MUCH.
HEY, HOW OFTEN DO I GET TO STRUT MY STUFF?
THERE'S NO SENSE IN US GOING CRAZY TRYING TO BREAK THESE CODES...
...WHEN IT'S MUCH EASIER TO SEND THE WHOLE FILE TO OUR VERY OWN SET OF TRAINED PROFESSIONALS.
KLIK!

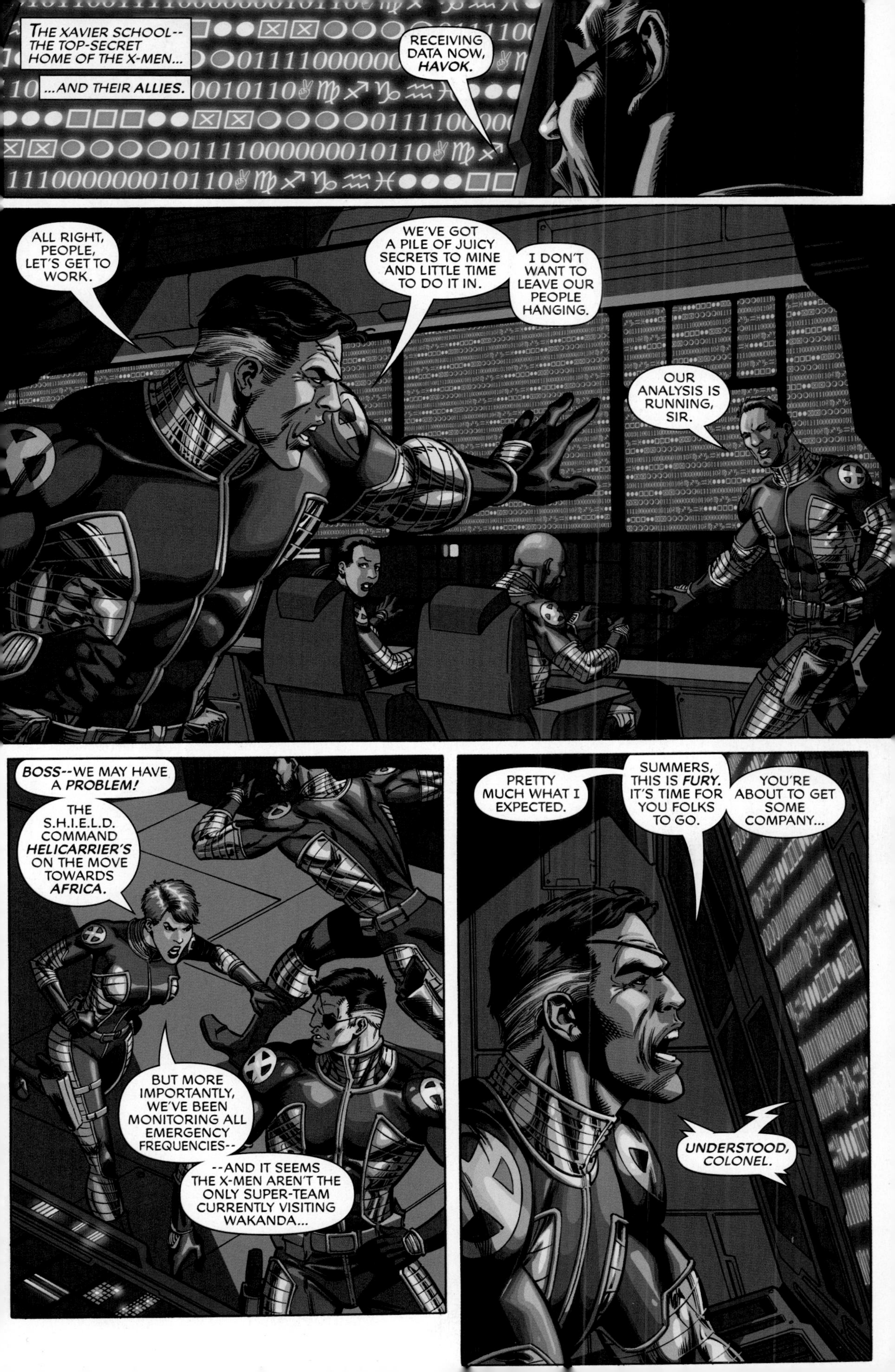
THE XAVIER SCHOOL-- THE TOP-SECRET HOME OF THE X-MEN...
...AND THEIR ALLIES.
RECEIVING DATA NOW, HAVOK.
ALL RIGHT, PEOPLE, LET'S GET TO WORK.
WE'VE GOT A PILE OF JUICY SECRETS TO MINE AND LITTLE TIME TO DO IT IN.
I DON'T WANT TO LEAVE OUR PEOPLE HANGING.
OUR ANALYSIS IS RUNNING, SIR.
BOSS--WE MAY HAVE A PROBLEM!
THE S.H.I.E.L.D. COMMAND HELICARRIER'S ON THE MOVE TOWARDS AFRICA.
BUT MORE IMPORTANTLY, WE'VE BEEN MONITORING ALL EMERGENCY FREQUENCIES--
--AND IT SEEMS THE X-MEN AREN'T THE ONLY SUPER-TEAM CURRENTLY VISITING WAKANDA...
PRETTY MUCH WHAT I EXPECTED.
SUMMERS, THIS IS FURY. IT'S TIME FOR YOU FOLKS TO GO.
YOU'RE ABOUT TO GET SOME COMPANY...
UNDERSTOOD, COLONEL.

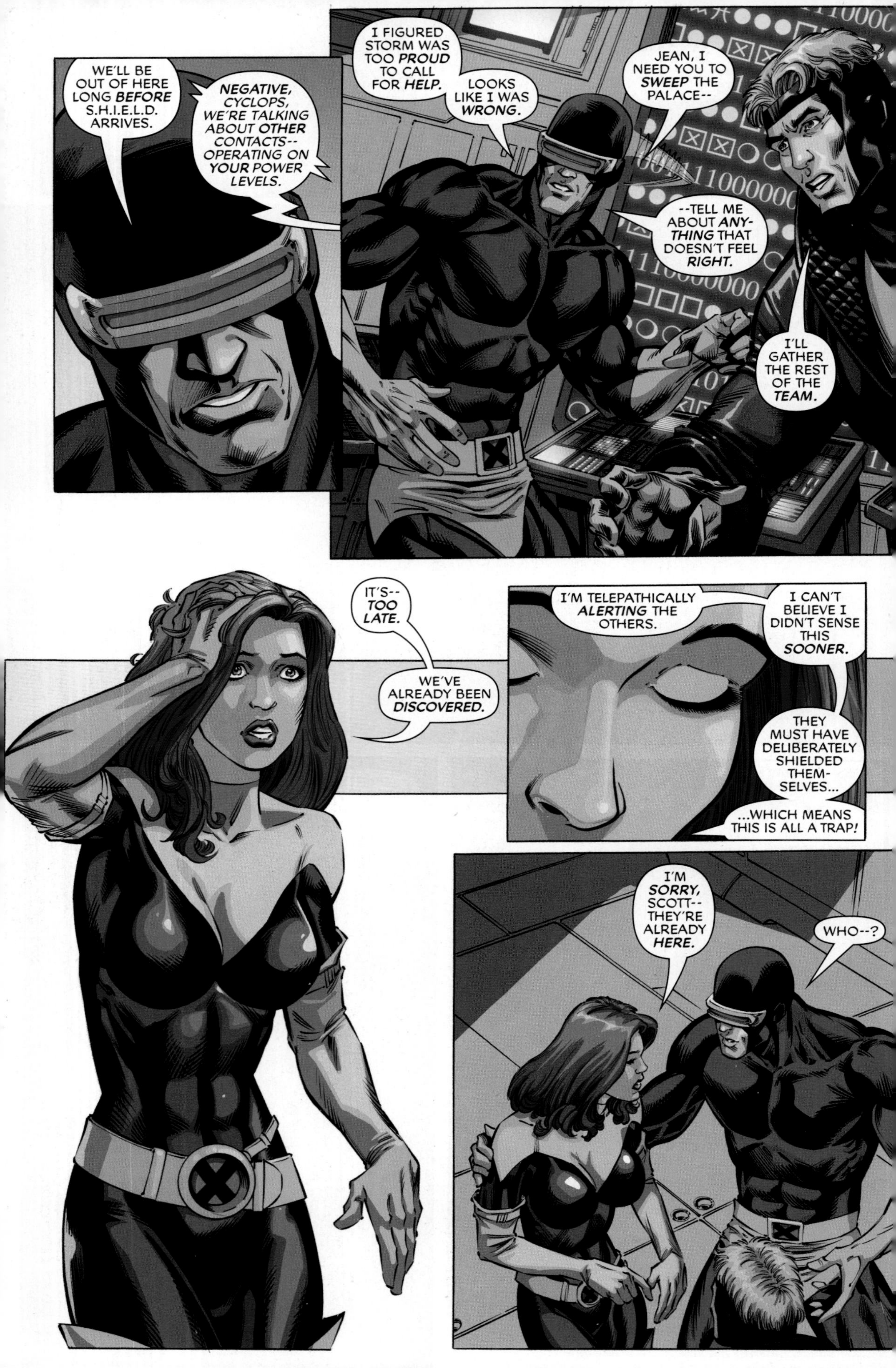
WE'LL BE OUT OF HERE LONG BEFORE S.H.I.E.L.D. ARRIVES.
NEGATIVE, CYCLOPS, WE'RE TALKING ABOUT OTHER CONTACTS-- OPERATING ON YOUR POWER LEVELS.
I FIGURED STORM WAS TOO PROUD TO CALL FOR HELP.
LOOKS LIKE I WAS WRONG.
JEAN, I NEED YOU TO SWEEP THE PALACE--
--TELL ME ABOUT ANY-THING THAT DOESN'T FEEL RIGHT.
I'LL GATHER THE REST OF THE TEAM.
IT'S-- TOO LATE.
WE'VE ALREADY BEEN DISCOVERED.
I'M TELEPATHICALLY ALERTING THE OTHERS.
I CAN'T BELIEVE I DIDN'T SENSE THIS SOONER.
THEY MUST HAVE DELIBERATELY SHIELDED THEM-SELVES...
...WHICH MEANS THIS IS ALL A TRAP!
I'M SORRY, SCOTT-- THEY'RE ALREADY HERE.
WHO--?

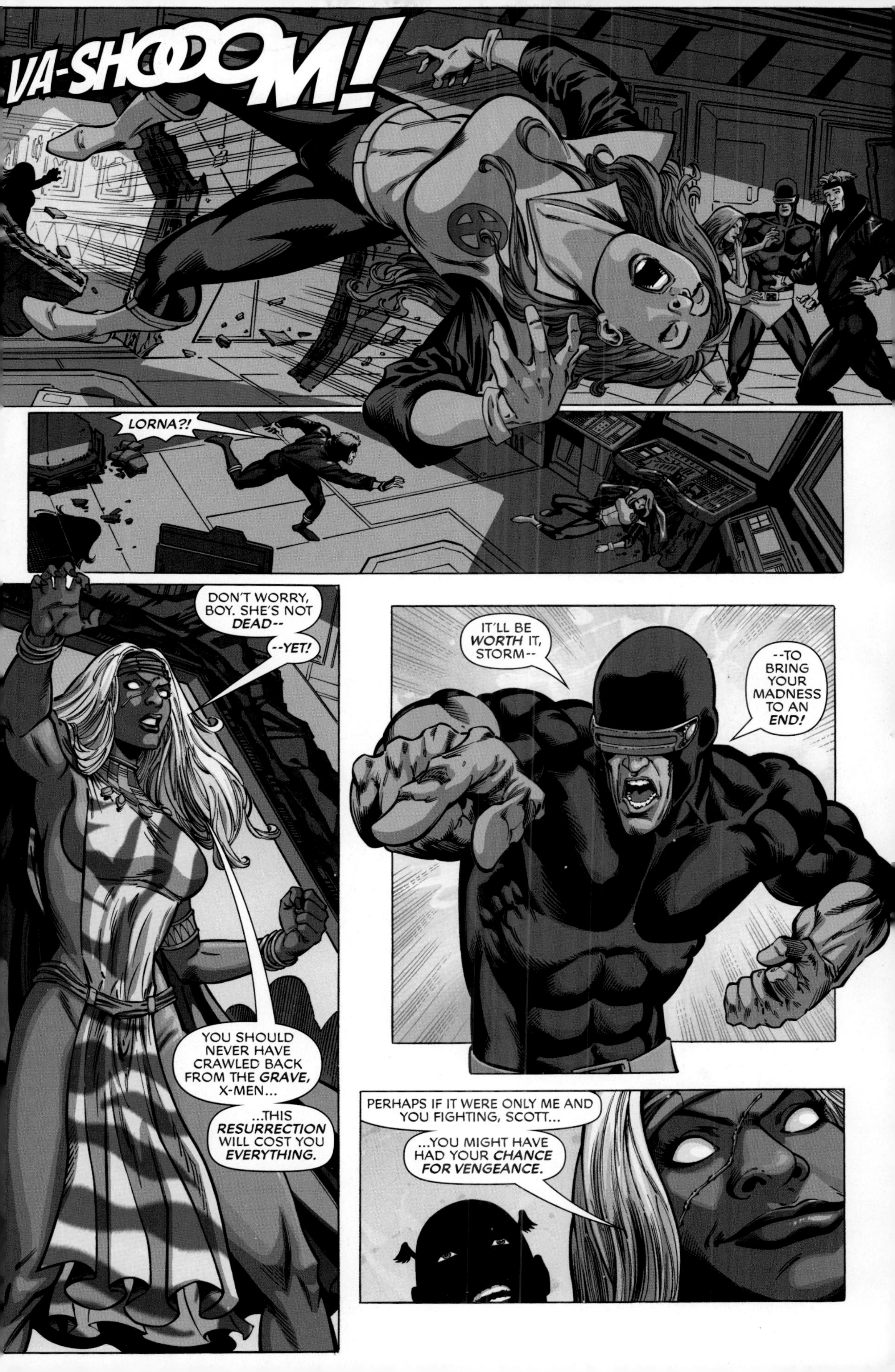
VA-SHOOOM!
LORNA?!
DON'T WORRY, BOY. SHE'S NOT DEAD--
--YET!
YOU SHOULD NEVER HAVE CRAWLED BACK FROM THE GRAVE, X-MEN...
...THIS RESURRECTION WILL COST YOU EVERYTHING.
IT'LL BE WORTH IT, STORM--
--TO BRING YOUR MADNESS TO AN END!
PERHAPS IF IT WERE ONLY ME AND YOU FIGHTING, SCOTT...
...YOU MIGHT HAVE HAD YOUR CHANCE FOR VENGEANCE.

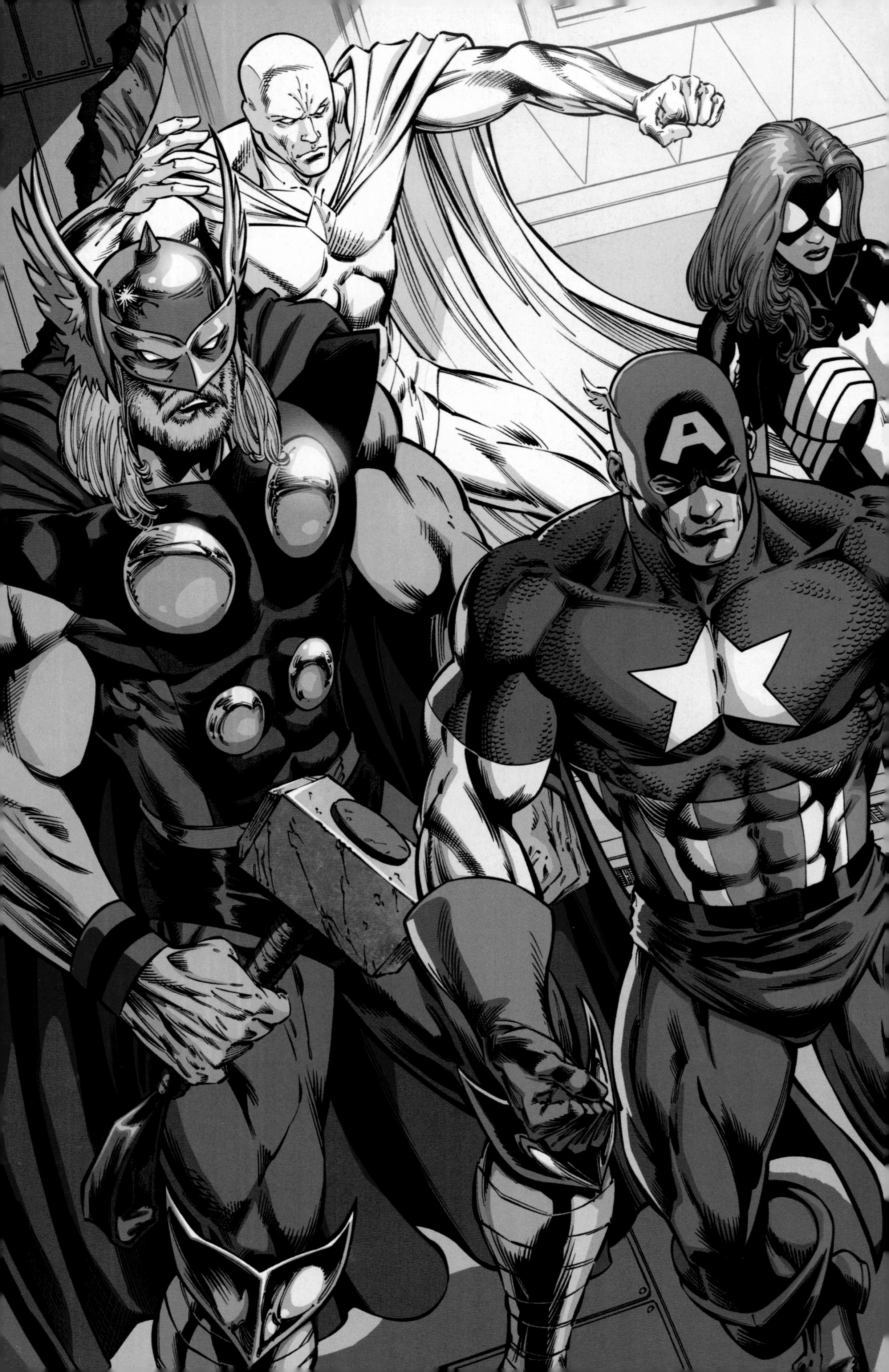

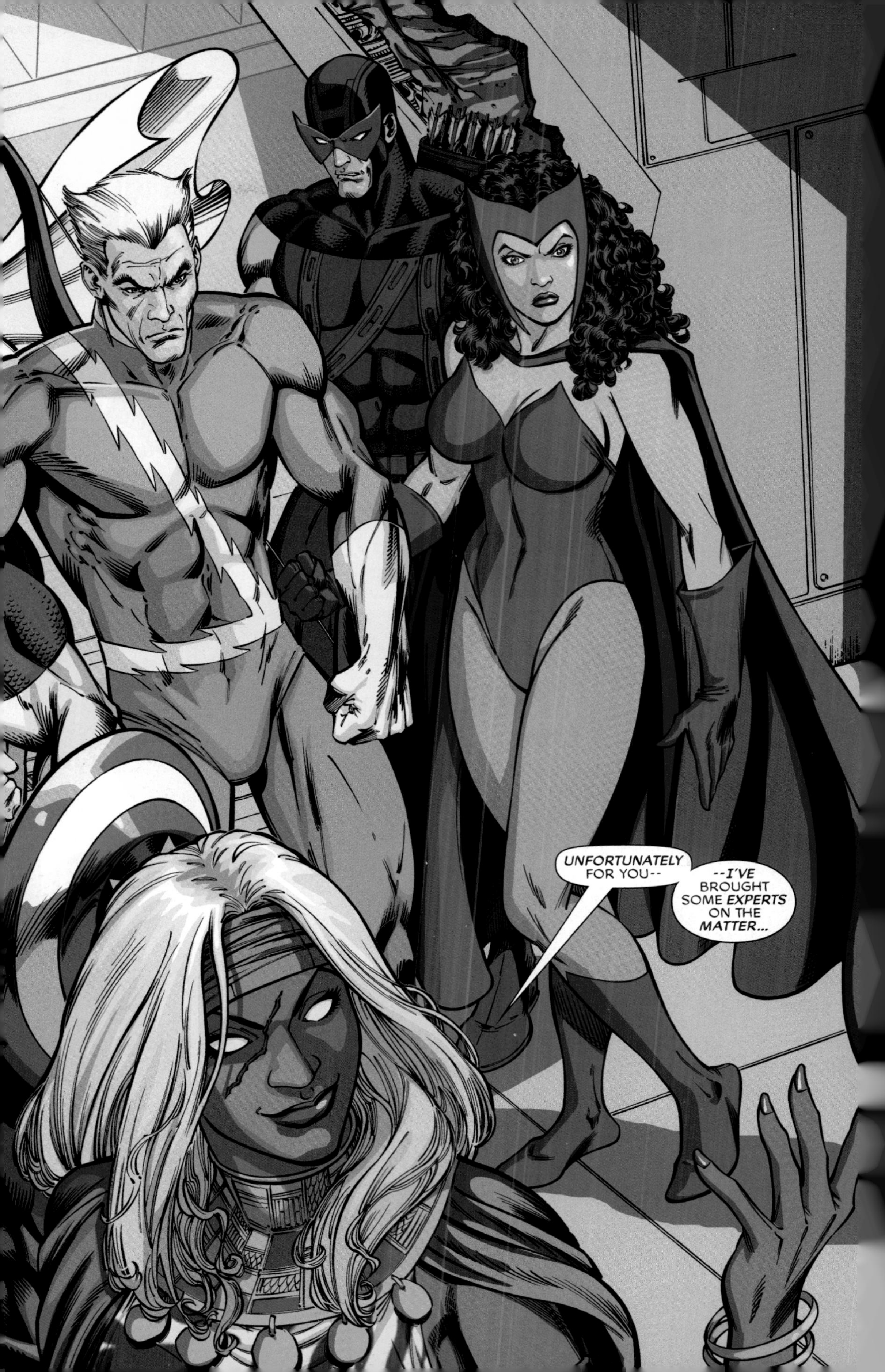
UNFORTUNATELY FOR YOU--
--I'VE BROUGHT SOME EXPERTS ON THE MATTER...

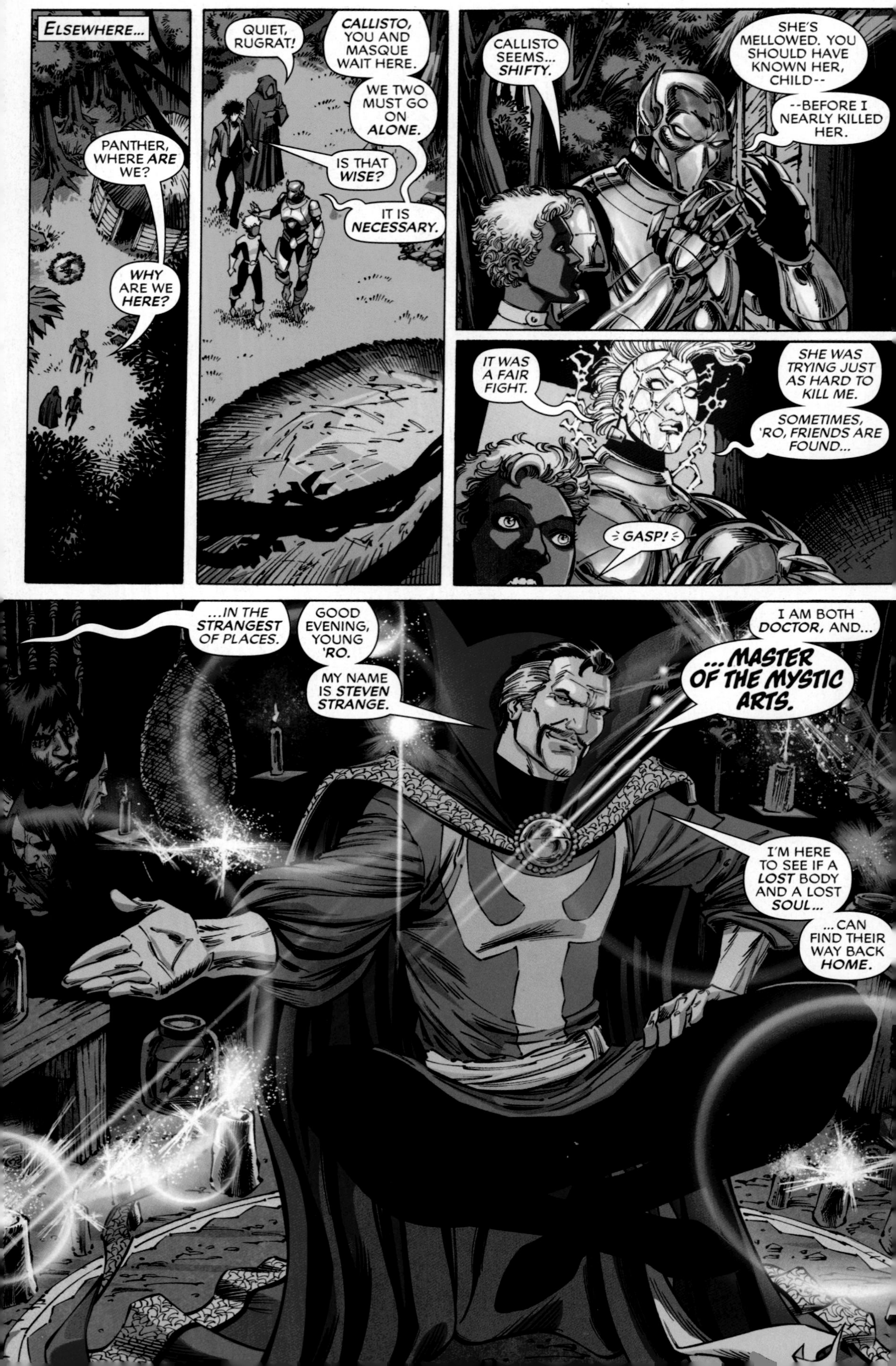
ELSEWHERE...
PANTHER, WHERE ARE WE?
WHY ARE WE HERE?
QUIET, RUGRAT!
CALLISTO, YOU AND MASQUE WAIT HERE.
WE TWO MUST GO ON ALONE.
IS THAT WISE?
IT IS NECESSARY.
CALLISTO SEEMS... SHIFTY.
SHE'S MELLOWED. YOU SHOULD HAVE KNOWN HER, CHILD--
--BEFORE I NEARLY KILLED HER.
IT WAS A FAIR FIGHT.
SHE WAS TRYING JUST AS HARD TO KILL ME.
SOMETIMES, 'RO, FRIENDS ARE FOUND...
GASP!
...IN THE STRANGEST OF PLACES.
GOOD EVENING, YOUNG 'RO.
MY NAME IS STEVEN STRANGE.
I AM BOTH DOCTOR, AND...
...MASTER OF THE MYSTIC ARTS.
I'M HERE TO SEE IF A LOST BODY AND A LOST SOUL...
...CAN FIND THEIR WAY BACK HOME.

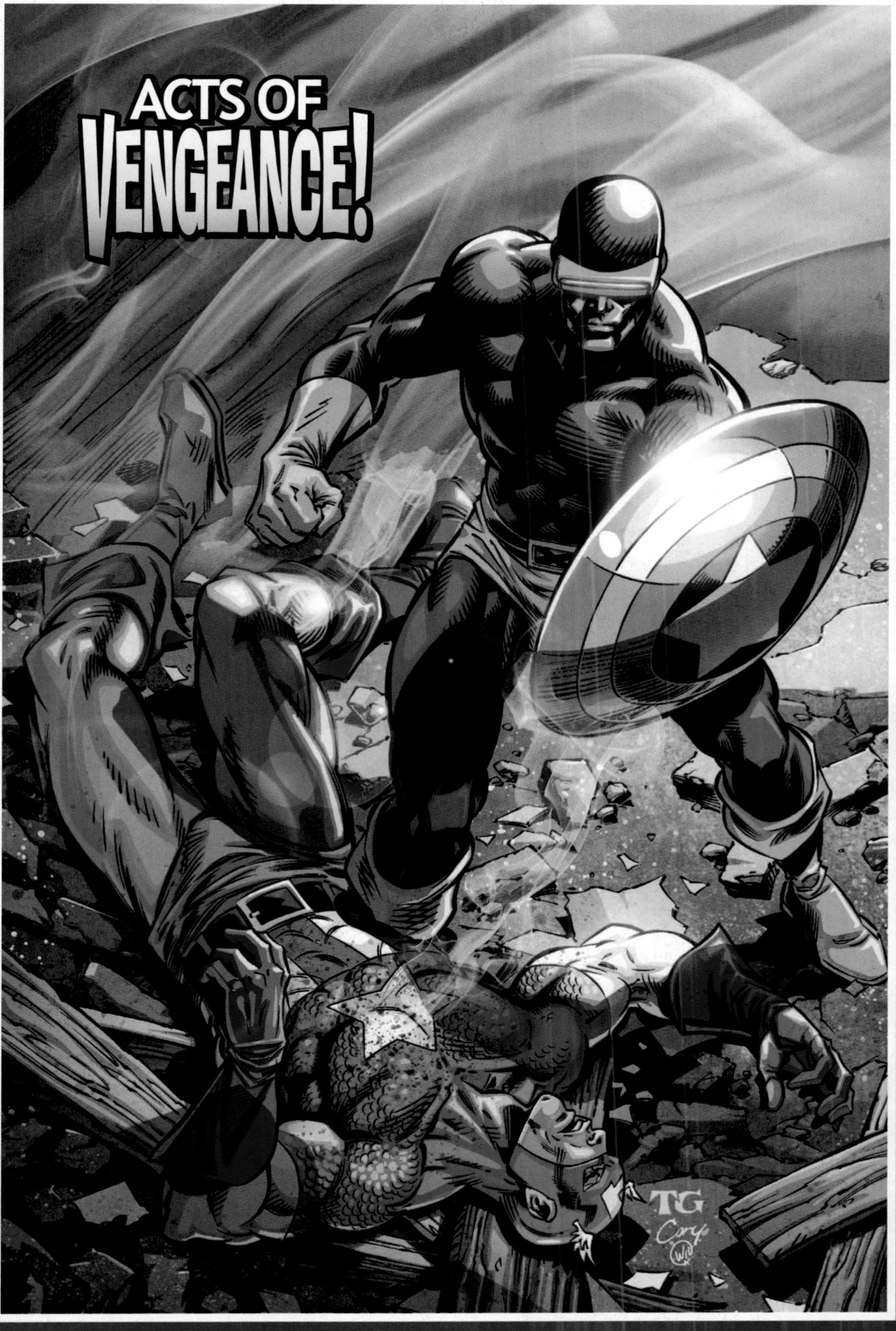
ACTS OF
VENGEANCE!
TG

FIFTEEN

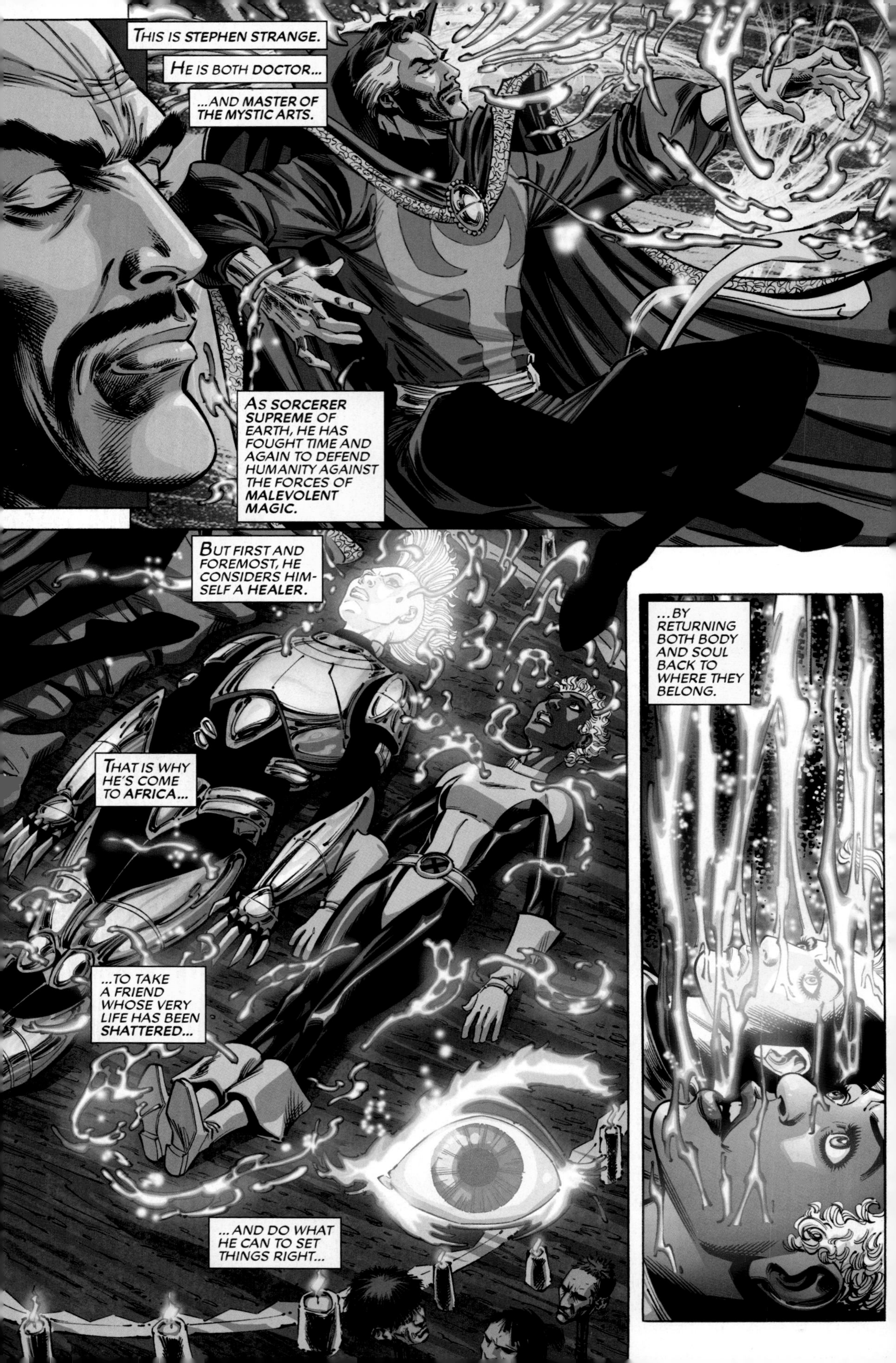
THIS IS STEPHEN STRANGE.
HE IS BOTH DOCTOR...
...AND MASTER OF THE MYSTIC ARTS.
AS SORCERER SUPREME OF EARTH, HE HAS FOUGHT TIME AND AGAIN TO DEFEND HUMANITY AGAINST THE FORCES OF MALEVOLENT MAGIC.
BUT FIRST AND FOREMOST, HE CONSIDERS HIM-SELF A HEALER.
THAT IS WHY HE'S COME TO AFRICA...
...TO TAKE A FRIEND WHOSE VERY LIFE HAS BEEN SHATTERED...
...AND DO WHAT HE CAN TO SET THINGS RIGHT...
...BY RETURNING BOTH BODY AND SOUL BACK TO WHERE THEY BELONG.

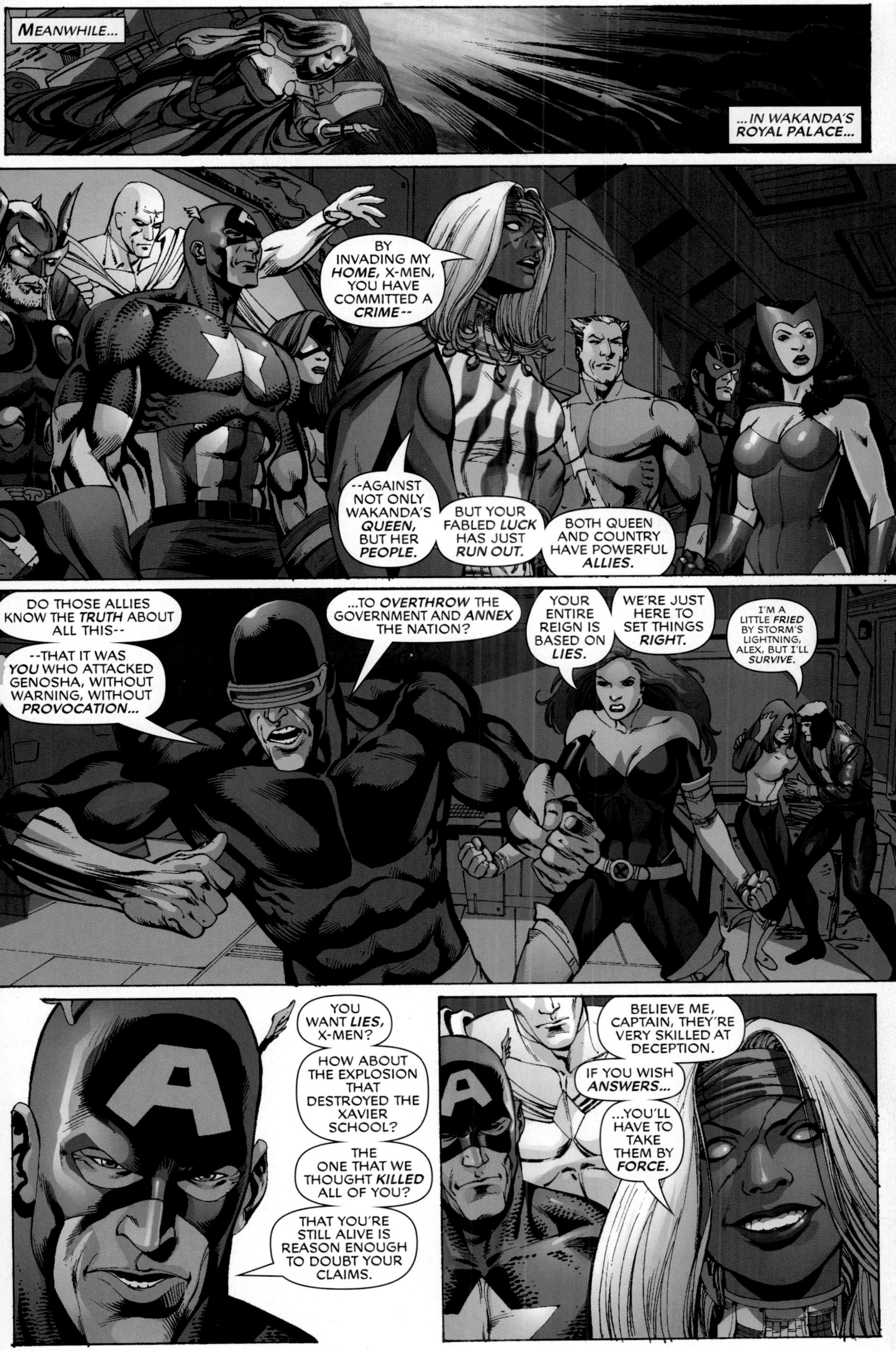
MEANWHILE...
...IN WAKANDA'S ROYAL PALACE...
BY INVADING MY HOME, X-MEN, YOU HAVE COMMITTED A CRIME--
--AGAINST NOT ONLY WAKANDA'S QUEEN, BUT HER PEOPLE.
BUT YOUR FABLED LUCK HAS JUST RUN OUT.
BOTH QUEEN AND COUNTRY HAVE POWERFUL ALLIES.
DO THOSE ALLIES KNOW THE TRUTH ABOUT ALL THIS--
--THAT IT WAS YOU WHO ATTACKED GENOSHA, WITHOUT WARNING, WITHOUT PROVOCATION...
...TO OVERTHROW THE GOVERNMENT AND ANNEX THE NATION?
YOUR ENTIRE REIGN IS BASED ON LIES.
WE'RE JUST HERE TO SET THINGS RIGHT.
I'M A LITTLE FRIED BY STORM'S LIGHTNING, ALEX, BUT I'LL SURVIVE.
YOU WANT LIES, X-MEN?
HOW ABOUT THE EXPLOSION THAT DESTROYED THE XAVIER SCHOOL?
THE ONE THAT WE THOUGHT KILLED ALL OF YOU?
THAT YOU'RE STILL ALIVE IS REASON ENOUGH TO DOUBT YOUR CLAIMS.
BELIEVE ME, CAPTAIN, THEY'RE VERY SKILLED AT DECEPTION.
IF YOU WISH ANSWERS...
...YOU'LL HAVE TO TAKE THEM BY FORCE.

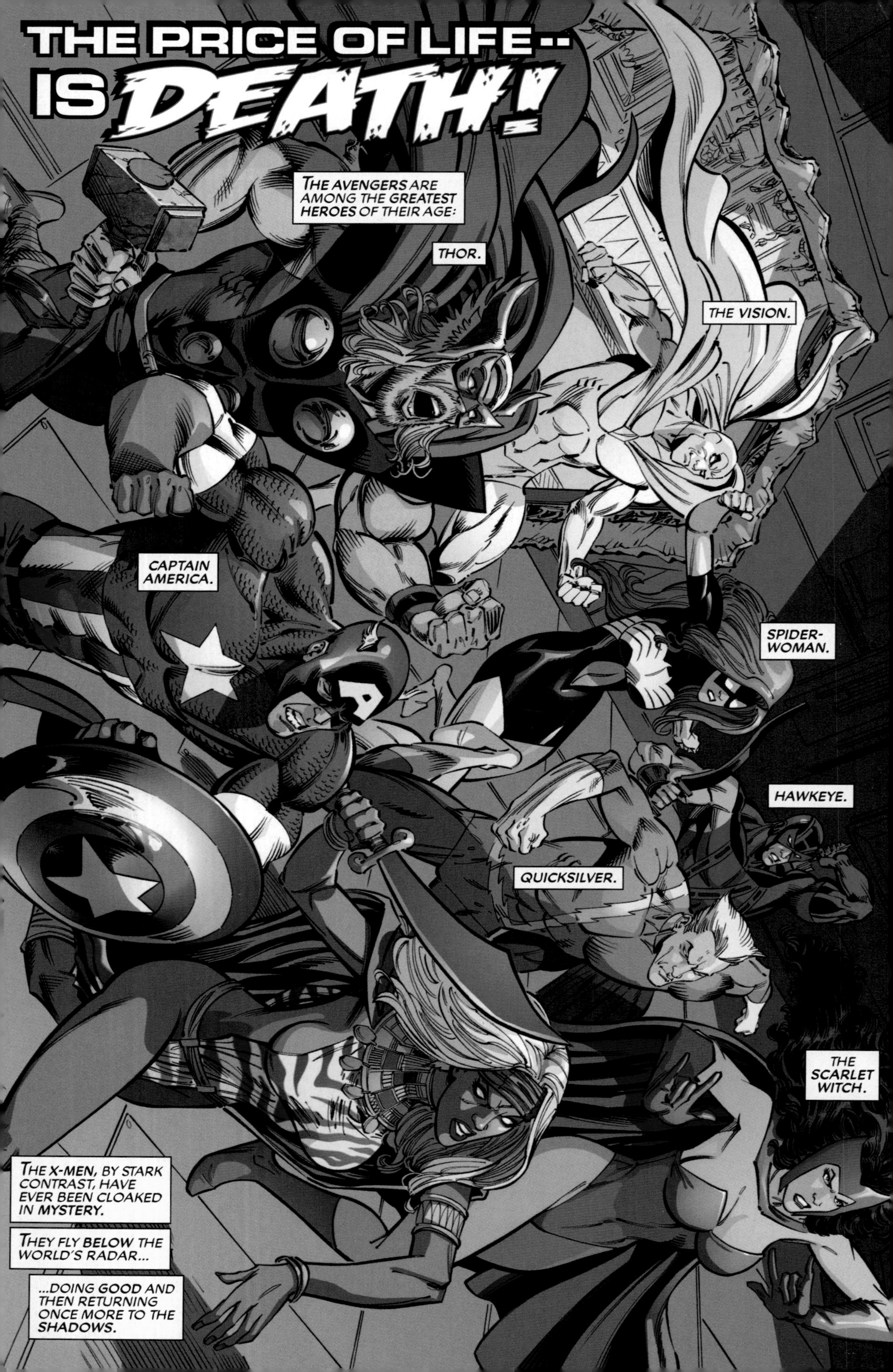
THE PRICE OF LIFE -- IS DEATH!
THE AVENGERS ARE AMONG THE GREATEST HEROES OF THEIR AGE:
THOR.
THE VISION.
CAPTAIN AMERICA.
SPIDER-WOMAN.
HAWKEYE.
QUICKSILVER.
THE SCARLET WITCH.
THE X-MEN, BY STARK CONTRAST, HAVE EVER BEEN CLOAKED IN MYSTERY.
THEY FLY BELOW THE WORLD'S RADAR...
...DOING GOOD AND THEN RETURNING ONCE MORE TO THE SHADOWS.

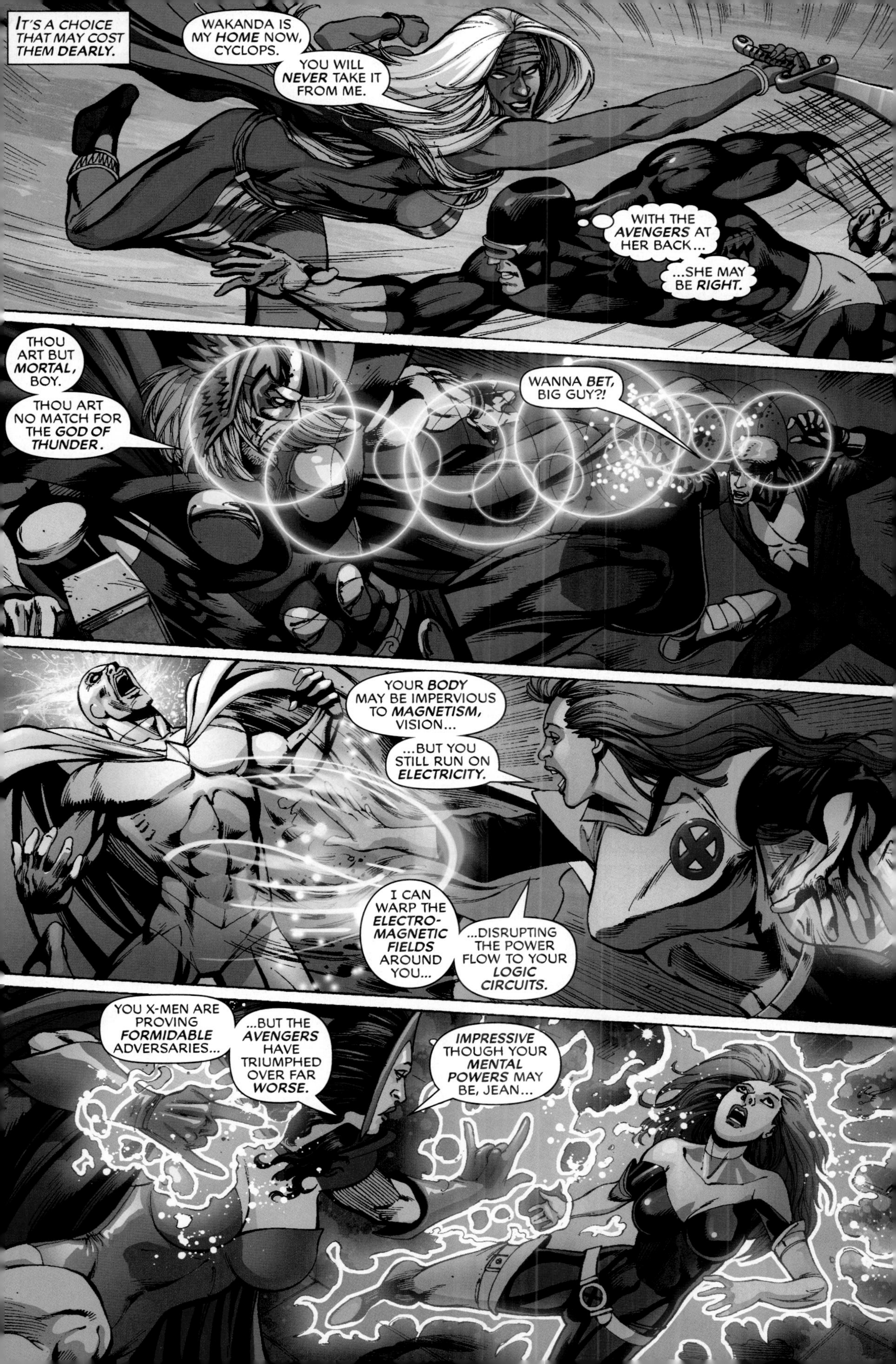

IT'S A CHOICE THAT MAY COST THEM DEARLY.
WAKANDA IS MY HOME NOW, CYCLOPS.
YOU WILL NEVER TAKE IT FROM ME.
WITH THE AVENGERS AT HER BACK...
...SHE MAY BE RIGHT.
THOU ART BUT MORTAL, BOY.
THOU ART NO MATCH FOR THE GOD OF THUNDER.
WANNA BET, BIG GUY?!
YOUR BODY MAY BE IMPERVIOUS TO MAGNETISM, VISION...
...BUT YOU STILL RUN ON ELECTRICITY.
I CAN WARP THE ELECTRO-MAGNETIC FIELDS AROUND YOU...
...DISRUPTING THE POWER FLOW TO YOUR LOGIC CIRCUITS.
YOU X-MEN ARE PROVING FORMIDABLE ADVERSARIES...
...BUT THE AVENGERS HAVE TRIUMPHED OVER FAR WORSE.
IMPRESSIVE THOUGH YOUR MENTAL POWERS MAY BE, JEAN...

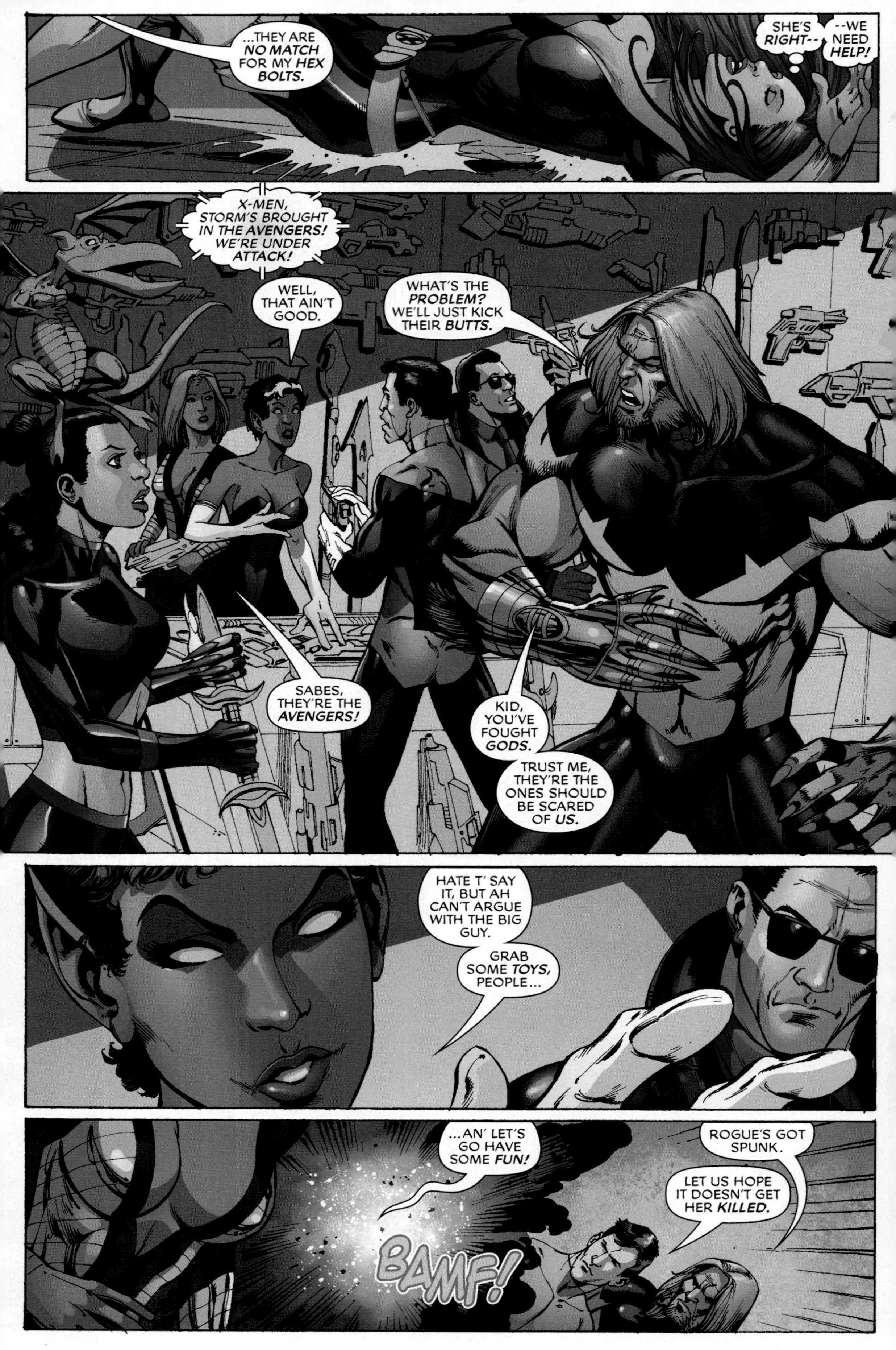

...THEY ARE NO MATCH FOR MY HEX BOLTS.
SHE'S RIGHT--
--WE NEED HELP!
X-MEN, STORM'S BROUGHT IN THE AVENGERS! WE'RE UNDER ATTACK!
WELL, THAT AIN'T GOOD.
WHAT'S THE PROBLEM? WE'LL JUST KICK THEIR BUTTS.
SABES, THEY'RE THE AVENGERS!
KID, YOU'VE FOUGHT GODS.
TRUST ME, THEY'RE THE ONES SHOULD BE SCARED OF US.
HATE T' SAY IT, BUT AH CAN'T ARGUE WITH THE BIG GUY.
GRAB SOME TOYS, PEOPLE...
...AN' LET'S GO HAVE SOME FUN!
BAMF!
ROGUE'S GOT SPUNK.
LET US HOPE IT DOESN'T GET HER KILLED.

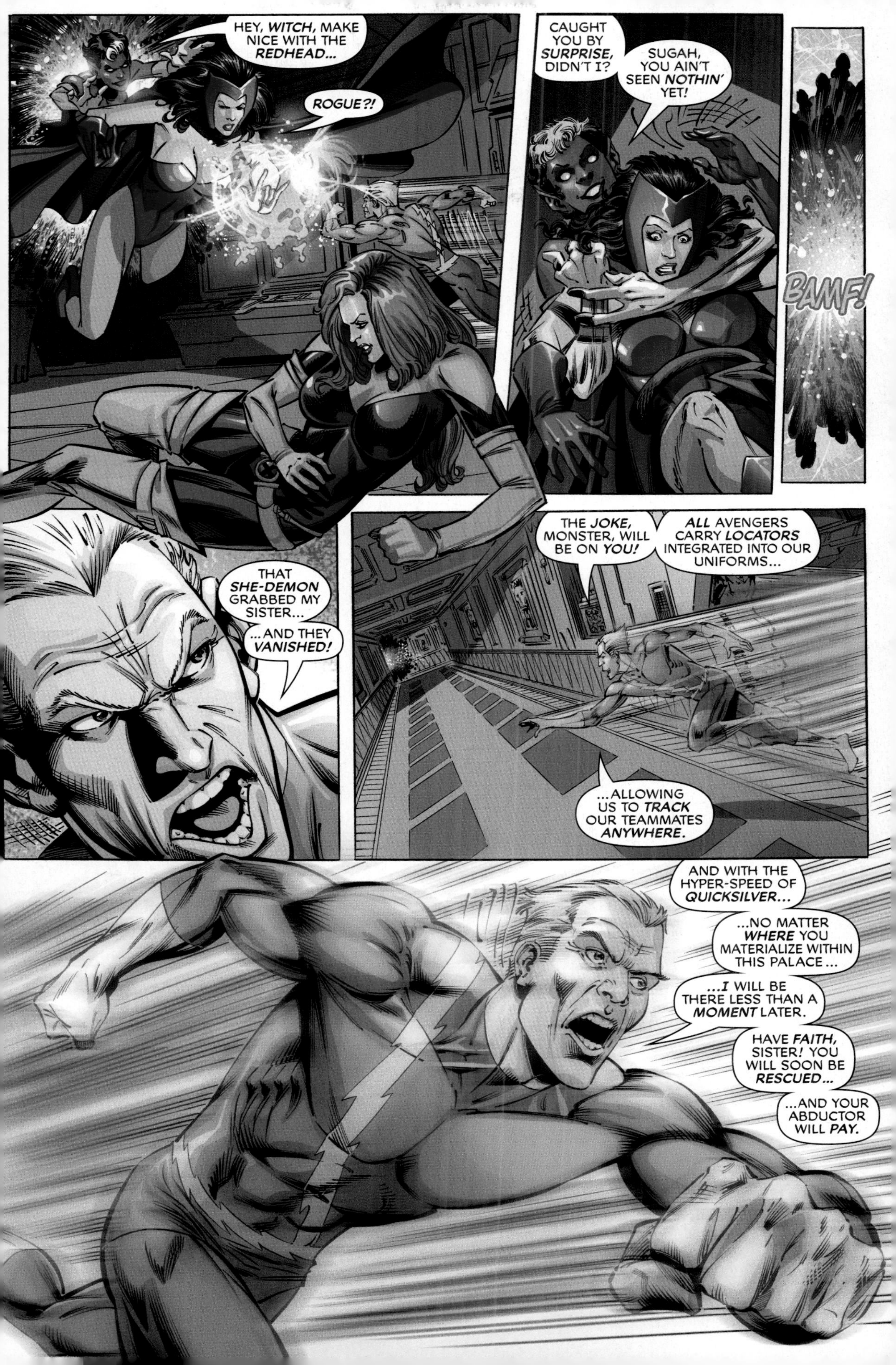
HEY, WITCH, MAKE NICE WITH THE REDHEAD...
ROGUE?!
CAUGHT YOU BY SURPRISE, DIDN'T I?
SUGAH, YOU AIN'T SEEN NOTHIN' YET!
BAMF!
THAT SHE-DEMON GRABBED MY SISTER...
...AND THEY VANISHED!
THE JOKE, MONSTER, WILL BE ON YOU!
ALL AVENGERS CARRY LOCATORS INTEGRATED INTO OUR UNIFORMS...
...ALLOWING US TO TRACK OUR TEAMMATES ANYWHERE.
AND WITH THE HYPER-SPEED OF QUICKSILVER...
...NO MATTER WHERE YOU MATERIALIZE WITHIN THIS PALACE...
...I WILL BE THERE LESS THAN A MOMENT LATER.
HAVE FAITH, SISTER! YOU WILL SOON BE RESCUED...
...AND YOUR ABDUCTOR WILL PAY.

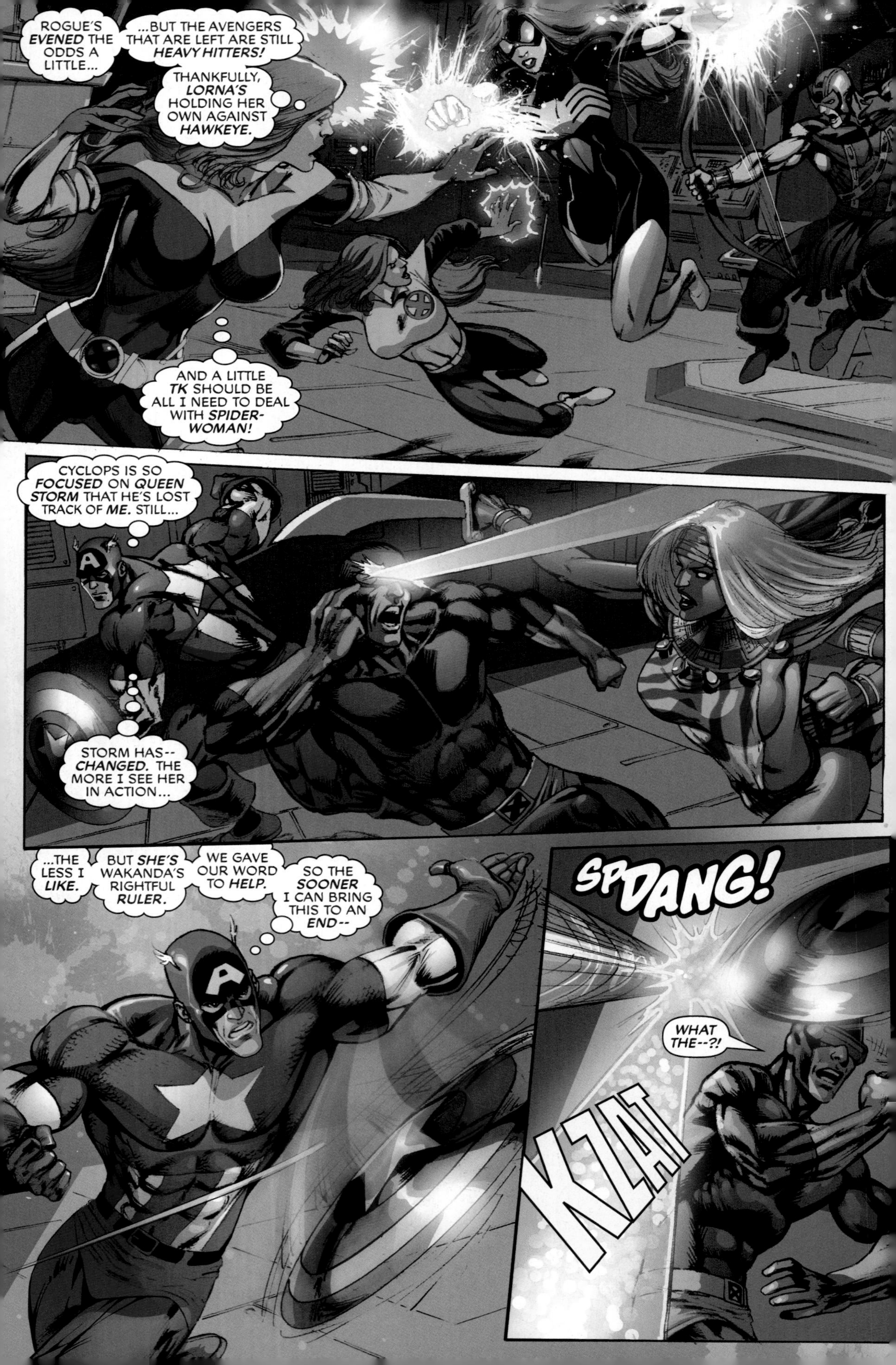
ROGUE'S EVENED THE ODDS A LITTLE...
...BUT THE AVENGERS THAT ARE LEFT ARE STILL HEAVY HITTERS!
THANKFULLY, LORNA'S HOLDING HER OWN AGAINST HAWKEYE.
AND A LITTLE TK SHOULD BE ALL I NEED TO DEAL WITH SPIDER-WOMAN!
CYCLOPS IS SO FOCUSED ON QUEEN STORM THAT HE'S LOST TRACK OF ME. STILL...
STORM HAS--CHANGED. THE MORE I SEE HER IN ACTION...
...THE LESS I LIKE.
BUT SHE'S WAKANDA'S RIGHTFUL RULER.
WE GAVE OUR WORD TO HELP.
SO THE SOONER I CAN BRING THIS TO AN END--
SPDANG!
WHAT THE--?!
KZAT

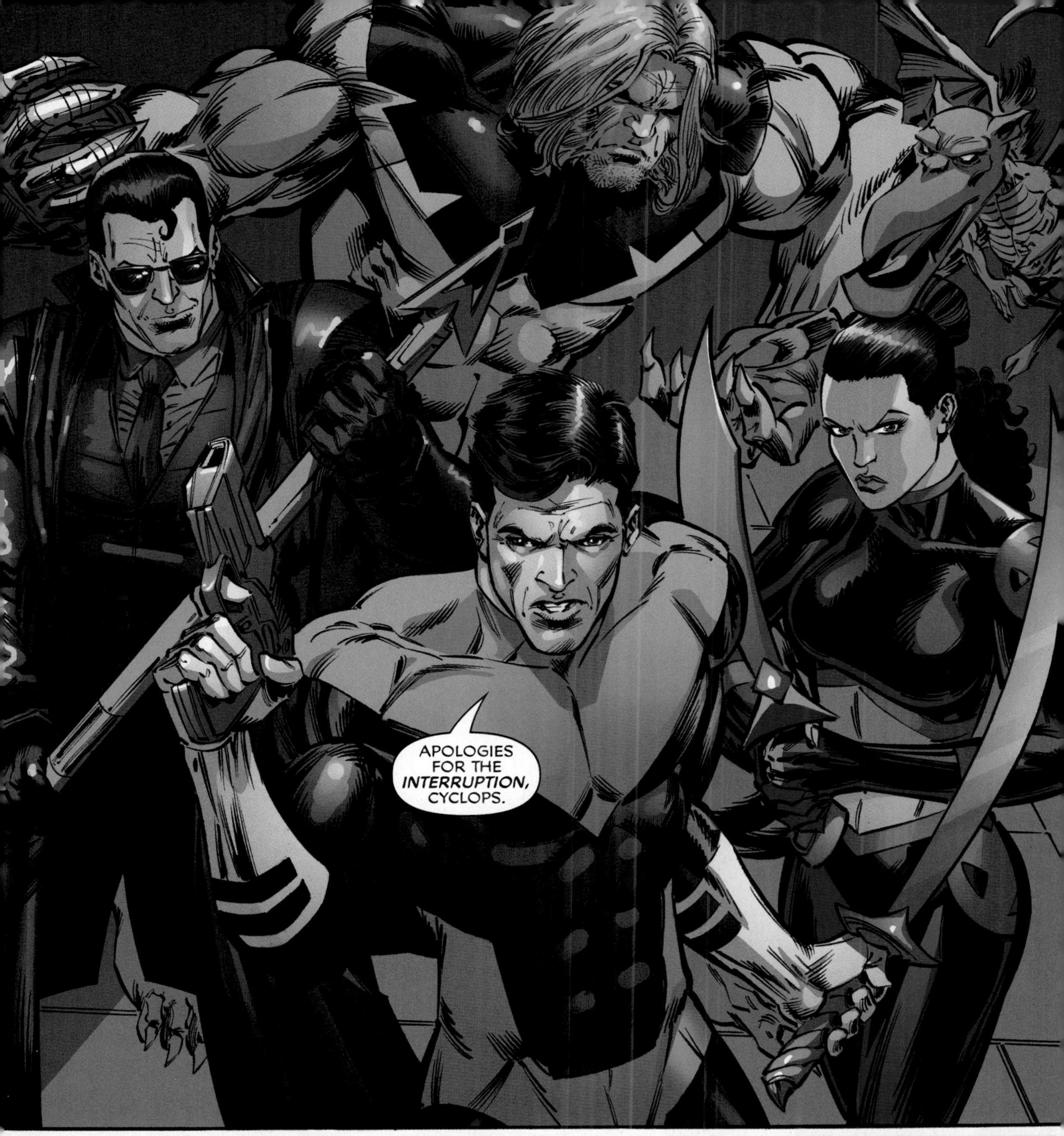
APOLOGIES FOR THE *INTERRUPTION,* CYCLOPS.

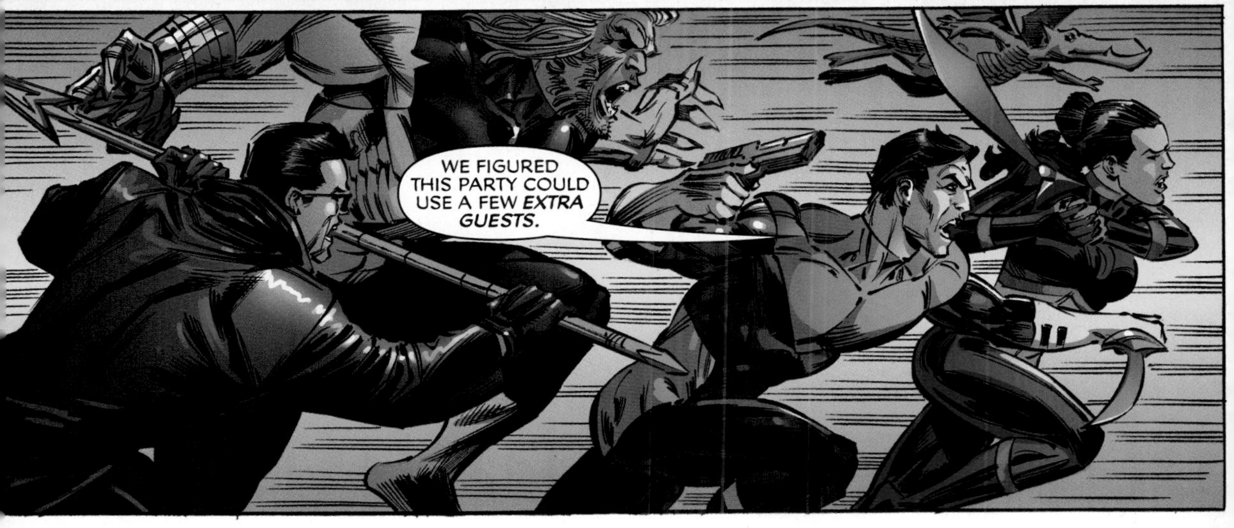
WE FIGURED THIS PARTY COULD USE A FEW *EXTRA GUESTS.*

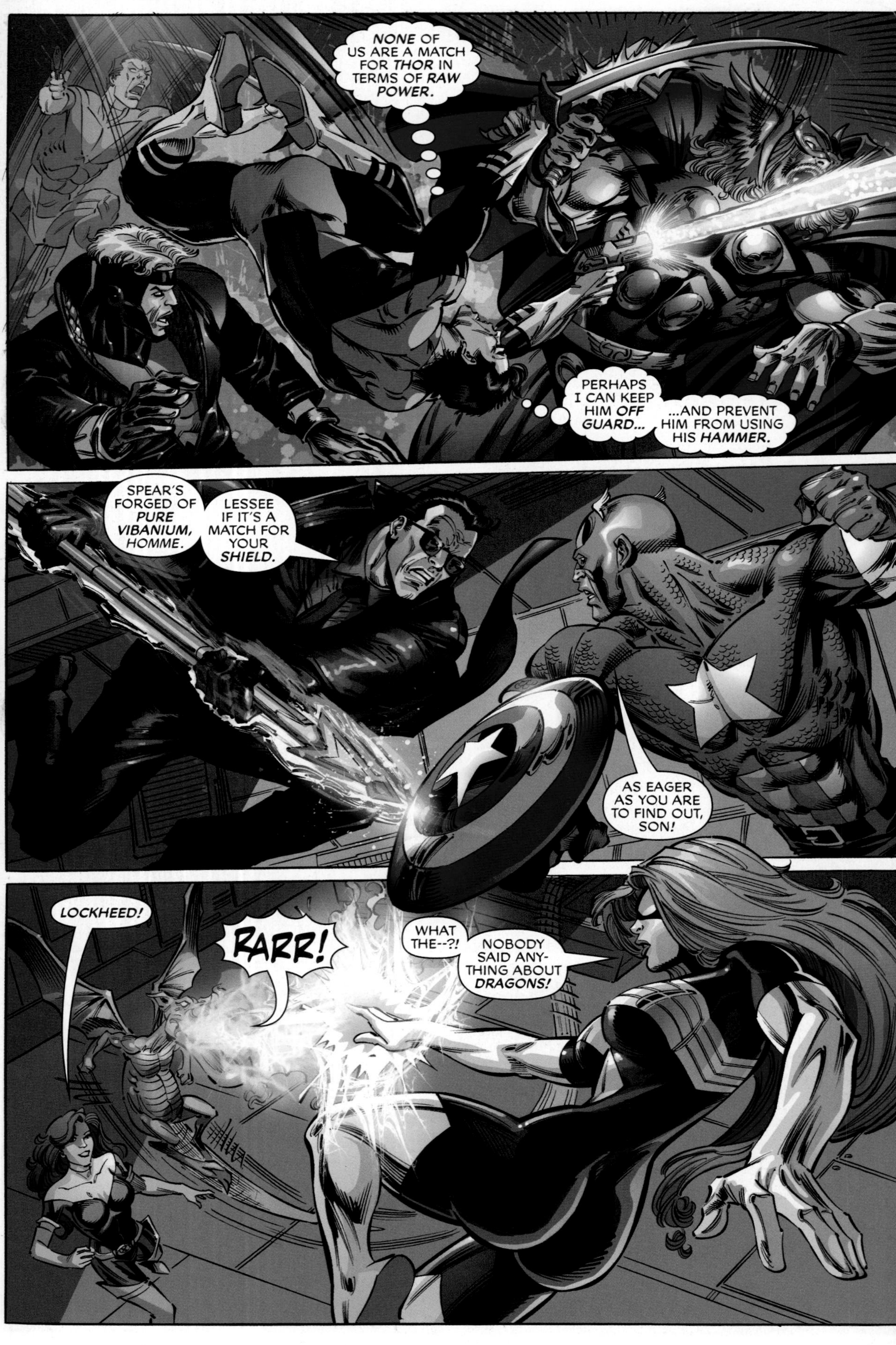
NONE OF US ARE A MATCH FOR THOR IN TERMS OF RAW POWER.
PERHAPS I CAN KEEP HIM OFF GUARD...
...AND PREVENT HIM FROM USING HIS HAMMER.
SPEAR'S FORGED OF PURE VIBANIUM, HOMME.
LESSEE IF IT'S A MATCH FOR YOUR SHIELD.
AS EAGER AS YOU ARE TO FIND OUT, SON!
LOCKHEED!
RARR!
WHAT THE--?!
NOBODY SAID ANY-THING ABOUT DRAGONS!

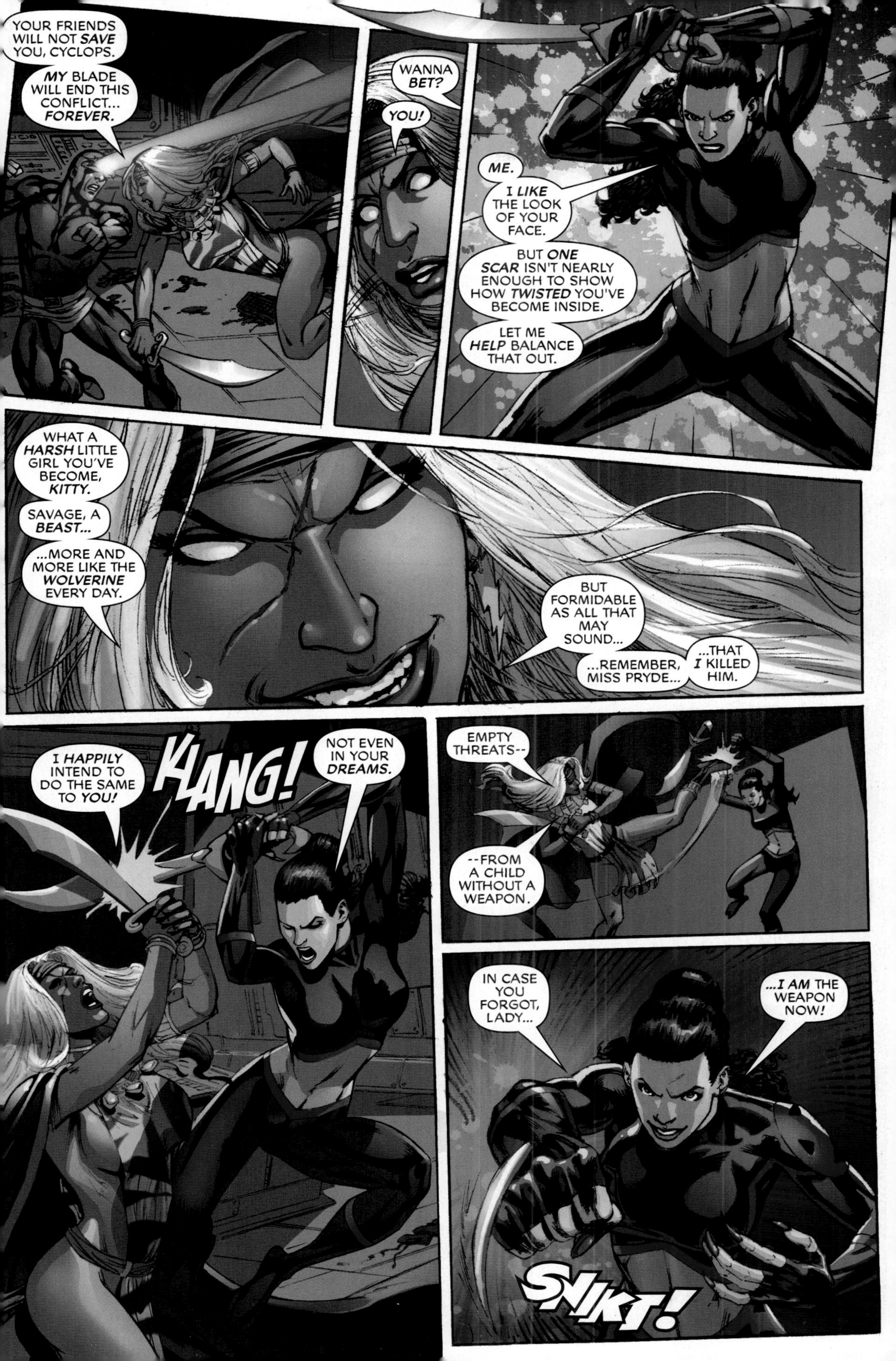

YOUR FRIENDS WILL NOT SAVE YOU, CYCLOPS.
MY BLADE WILL END THIS CONFLICT... FOREVER.
WANNA BET?
YOU!
ME.
I LIKE THE LOOK OF YOUR FACE.
BUT ONE SCAR ISN'T NEARLY ENOUGH TO SHOW HOW TWISTED YOU'VE BECOME INSIDE.
LET ME HELP BALANCE THAT OUT.
WHAT A HARSH LITTLE GIRL YOU'VE BECOME, KITTY.
SAVAGE, A BEAST...
...MORE AND MORE LIKE THE WOLVERINE EVERY DAY.
BUT FORMIDABLE AS ALL THAT MAY SOUND...
...REMEMBER, MISS PRYDE...
...THAT I KILLED HIM.
I HAPPILY INTEND TO DO THE SAME TO YOU!
KLANG!
NOT EVEN IN YOUR DREAMS.
EMPTY THREATS--
--FROM A CHILD WITHOUT A WEAPON.
IN CASE YOU FORGOT, LADY...
...I AM THE WEAPON NOW!
SNIKT!

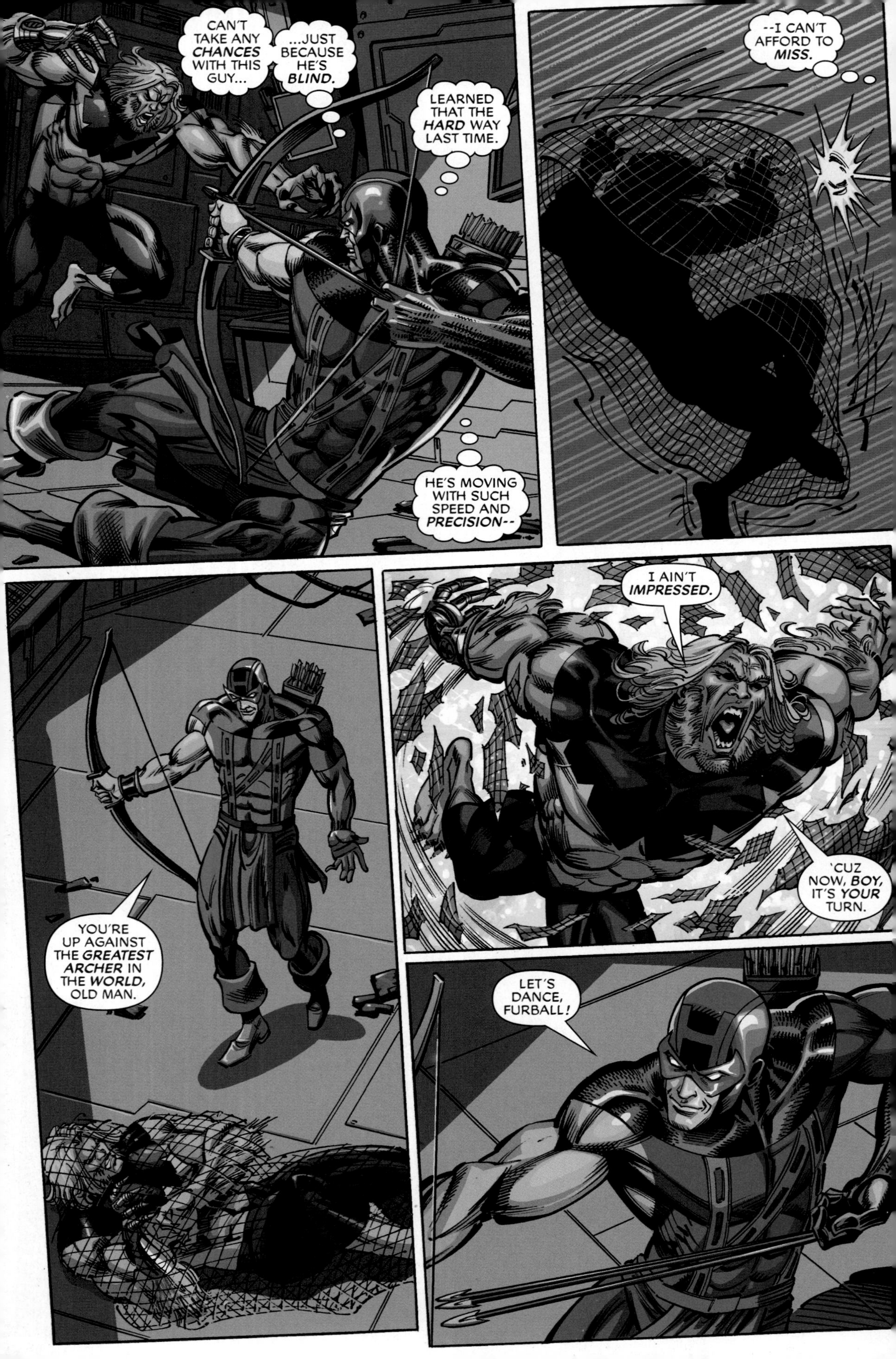
CAN'T TAKE ANY CHANCES WITH THIS GUY...
...JUST BECAUSE HE'S BLIND.
LEARNED THAT THE HARD WAY LAST TIME.
HE'S MOVING WITH SUCH SPEED AND PRECISION--
--I CAN'T AFFORD TO MISS.
YOU'RE UP AGAINST THE GREATEST ARCHER IN THE WORLD, OLD MAN.
I AIN'T IMPRESSED.
'CUZ NOW, BOY, IT'S YOUR TURN.
LET'S DANCE, FURBALL!

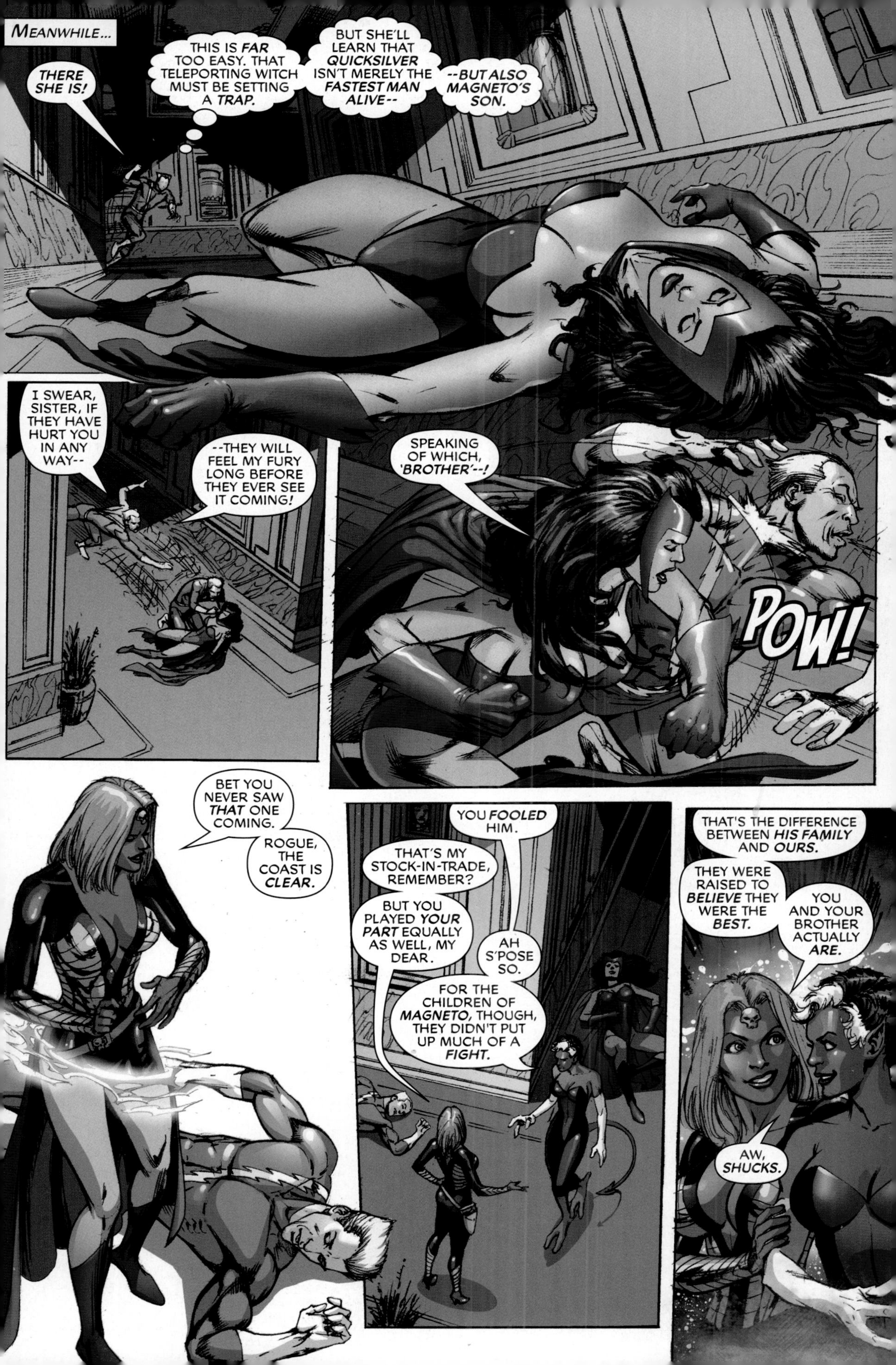
MEANWHILE...
THERE SHE IS!
THIS IS FAR TOO EASY. THAT TELEPORTING WITCH MUST BE SETTING A TRAP.
BUT SHE'LL LEARN THAT QUICKSILVER ISN'T MERELY THE FASTEST MAN ALIVE--
--BUT ALSO MAGNETO'S SON.
I SWEAR, SISTER, IF THEY HAVE HURT YOU IN ANY WAY--
--THEY WILL FEEL MY FURY LONG BEFORE THEY EVER SEE IT COMING!
SPEAKING OF WHICH, 'BROTHER'--!
POW!
BET YOU NEVER SAW THAT ONE COMING.
ROGUE, THE COAST IS CLEAR.
YOU FOOLED HIM.
THAT'S MY STOCK-IN-TRADE, REMEMBER?
BUT YOU PLAYED YOUR PART EQUALLY AS WELL, MY DEAR.
AH S'POSE SO.
FOR THE CHILDREN OF MAGNETO, THOUGH, THEY DIDN'T PUT UP MUCH OF A FIGHT.
THAT'S THE DIFFERENCE BETWEEN HIS FAMILY AND OURS.
THEY WERE RAISED TO BELIEVE THEY WERE THE BEST.
YOU AND YOUR BROTHER ACTUALLY ARE.
AW, SHUCKS.

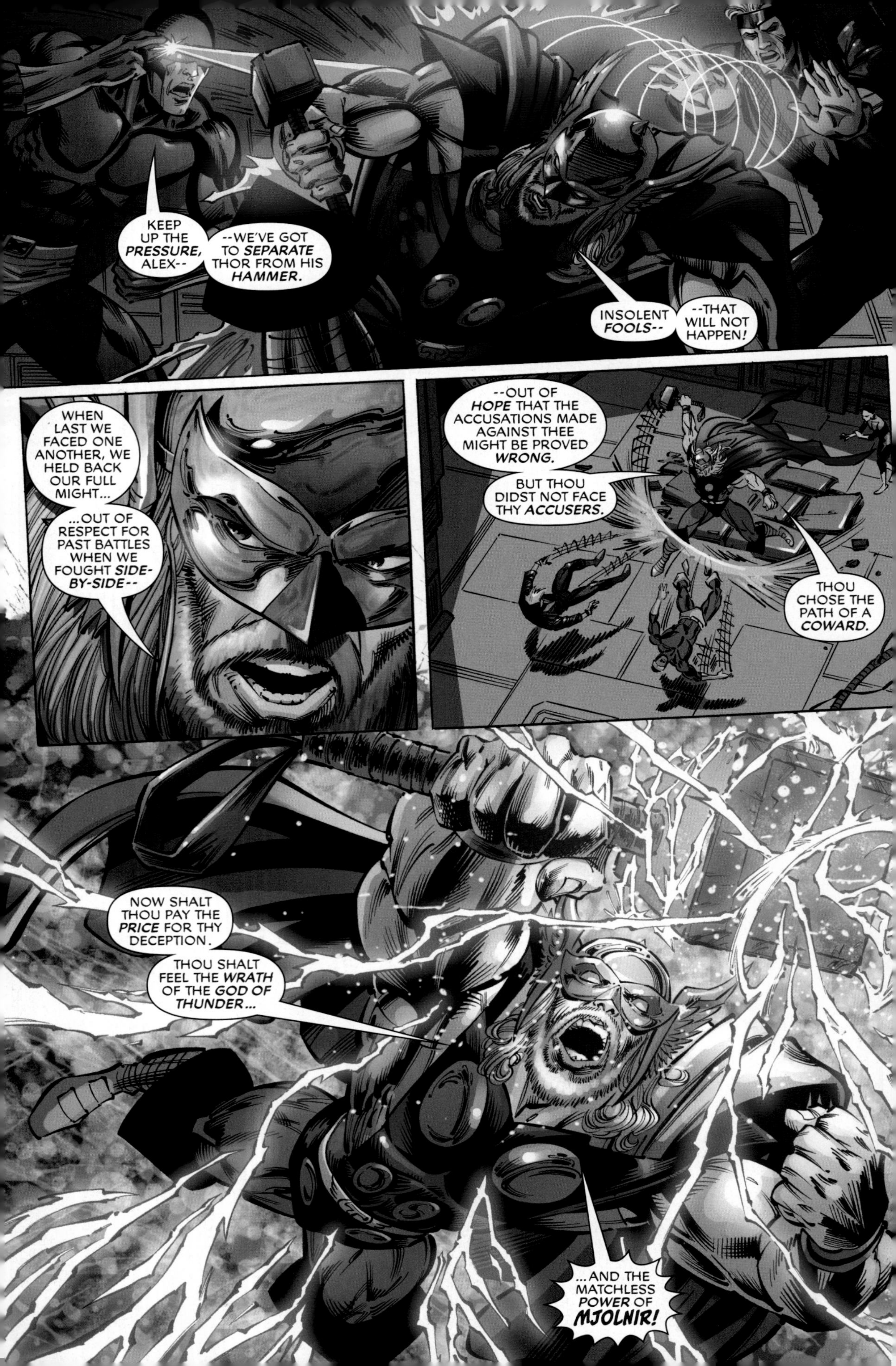
KEEP UP THE PRESSURE, ALEX--
--WE'VE GOT TO SEPARATE THOR FROM HIS HAMMER.
INSOLENT FOOLS--
--THAT WILL NOT HAPPEN!
WHEN LAST WE FACED ONE ANOTHER, WE HELD BACK OUR FULL MIGHT...
...OUT OF RESPECT FOR PAST BATTLES WHEN WE FOUGHT SIDE-BY-SIDE--
--OUT OF HOPE THAT THE ACCUSATIONS MADE AGAINST THEE MIGHT BE PROVED WRONG.
BUT THOU DIDST NOT FACE THY ACCUSERS.
THOU CHOSE THE PATH OF A COWARD.
NOW SHALT THOU PAY THE PRICE FOR THY DECEPTION.
THOU SHALT FEEL THE WRATH OF THE GOD OF THUNDER...
...AND THE MATCHLESS POWER OF MJOLNIR!

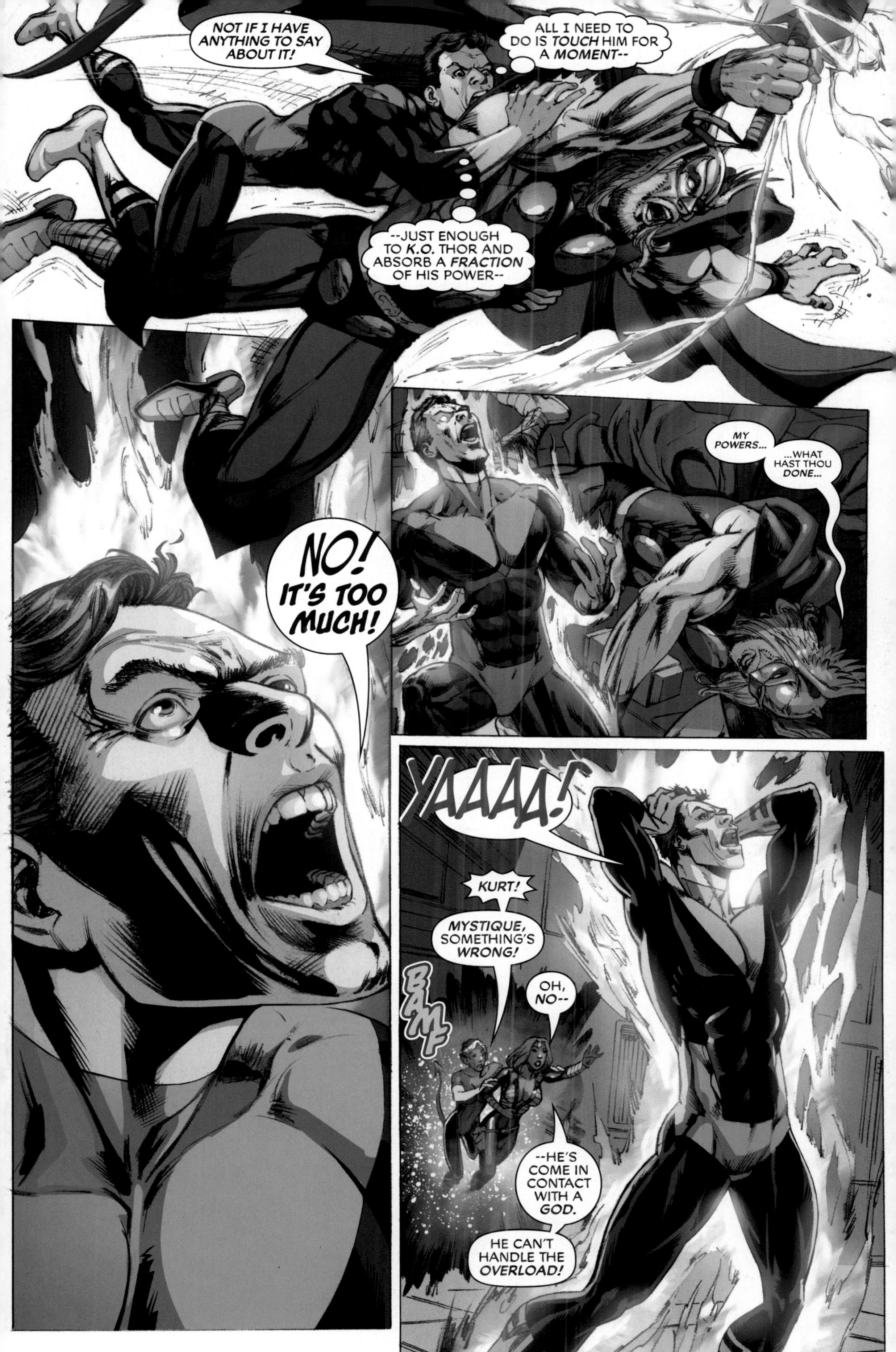
NOT IF I HAVE ANYTHING TO SAY ABOUT IT!
ALL I NEED TO DO IS TOUCH HIM FOR A MOMENT--
--JUST ENOUGH TO K.O. THOR AND ABSORB A FRACTION OF HIS POWER--
NO! IT'S TOO MUCH!
MY POWERS...
...WHAT HAST THOU DONE...
YAAAA!
KURT!
MYSTIQUE, SOMETHING'S WRONG!
BAMF
OH, NO--
--HE'S COME IN CONTACT WITH A GOD.
HE CAN'T HANDLE THE OVERLOAD!

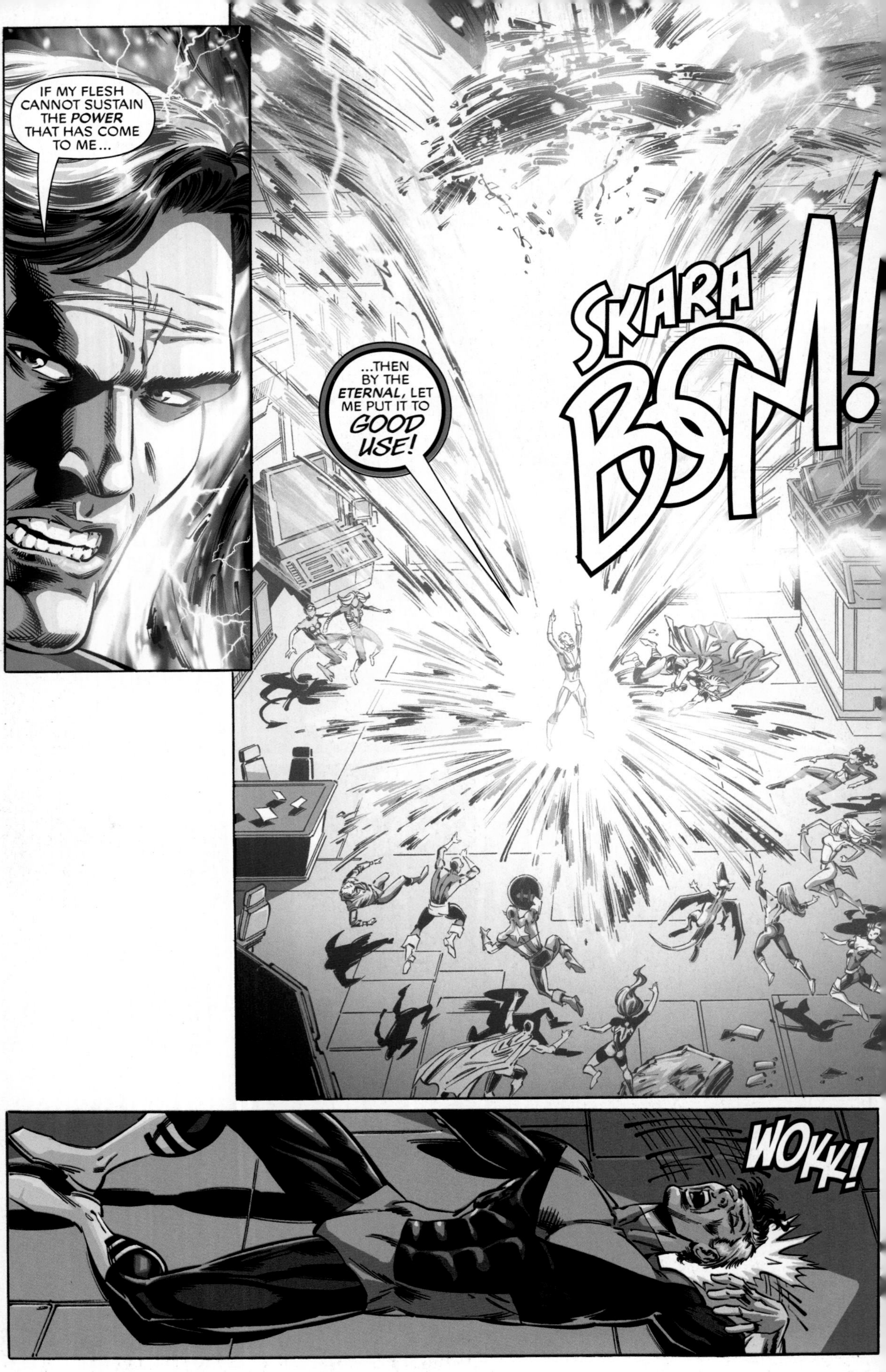
IF MY FLESH CANNOT SUSTAIN THE *POWER* THAT HAS COME TO ME...
...THEN BY THE *ETERNAL*, LET ME PUT IT TO *GOOD USE!*
SKARA BOOM!
WOKK!

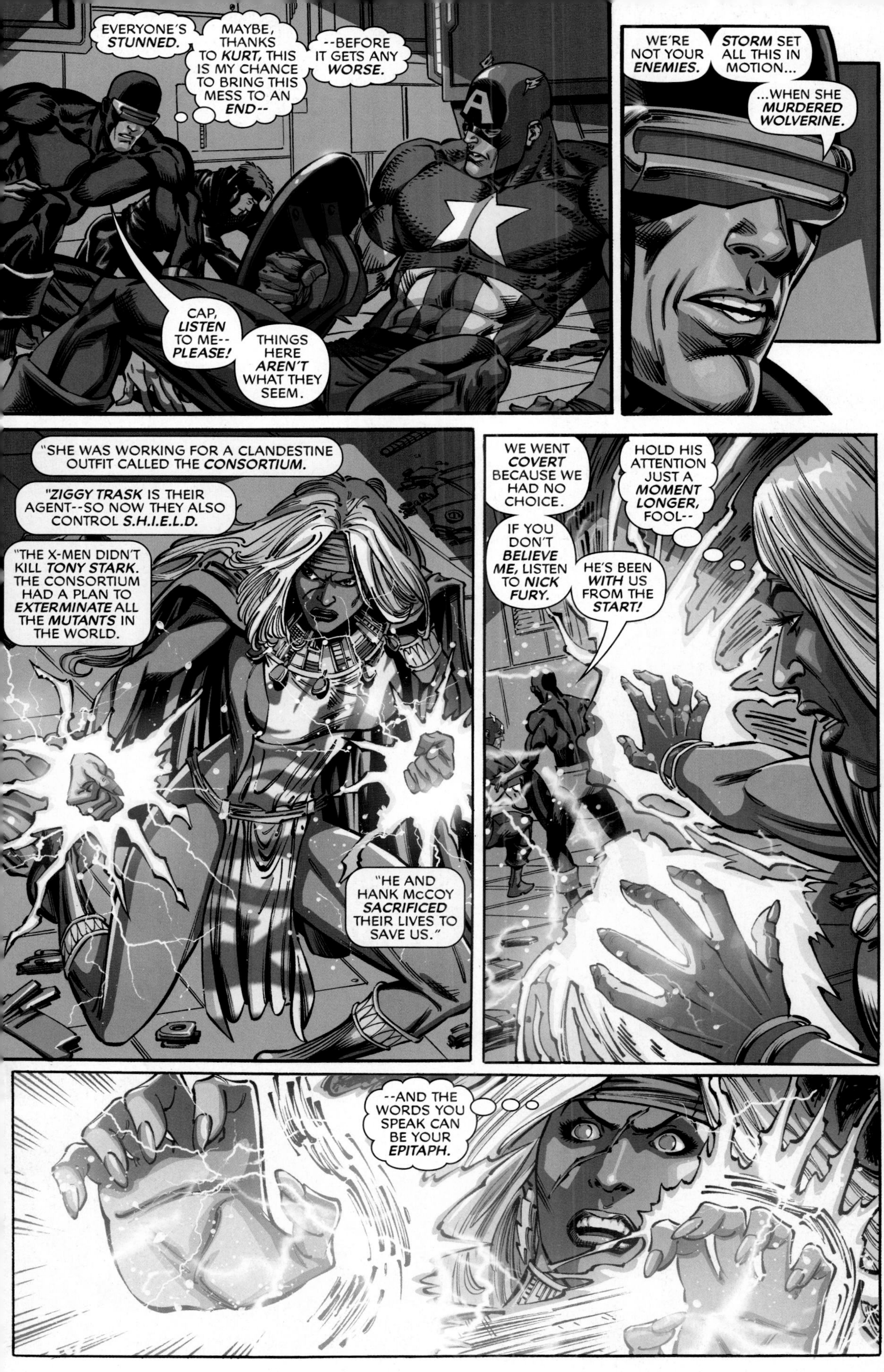
EVERYONE'S STUNNED.
MAYBE, THANKS TO KURT, THIS IS MY CHANCE TO BRING THIS MESS TO AN END--
--BEFORE IT GETS ANY WORSE.
CAP, LISTEN TO ME-- PLEASE!
THINGS HERE AREN'T WHAT THEY SEEM.
WE'RE NOT YOUR ENEMIES.
STORM SET ALL THIS IN MOTION...
...WHEN SHE MURDERED WOLVERINE.
"SHE WAS WORKING FOR A CLANDESTINE OUTFIT CALLED THE CONSORTIUM.
"ZIGGY TRASK IS THEIR AGENT--SO NOW THEY ALSO CONTROL S.H.I.E.L.D.
"THE X-MEN DIDN'T KILL TONY STARK. THE CONSORTIUM HAD A PLAN TO EXTERMINATE ALL THE MUTANTS IN THE WORLD.
"HE AND HANK McCOY SACRIFICED THEIR LIVES TO SAVE US."
WE WENT COVERT BECAUSE WE HAD NO CHOICE.
IF YOU DON'T BELIEVE ME, LISTEN TO NICK FURY.
HE'S BEEN WITH US FROM THE START!
HOLD HIS ATTENTION JUST A MOMENT LONGER, FOOL--
--AND THE WORDS YOU SPEAK CAN BE YOUR EPITAPH.

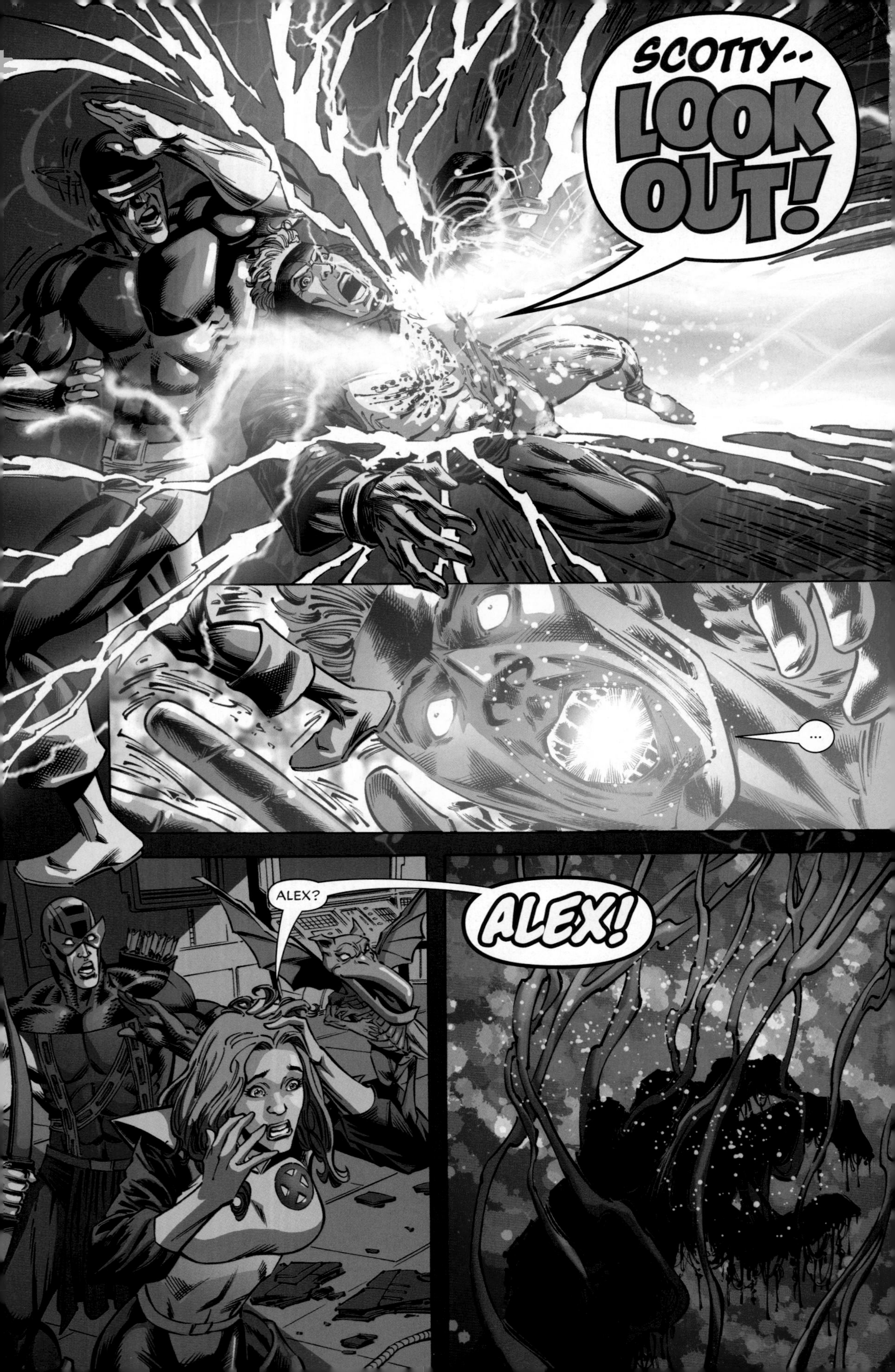
SCOTTY--
LOOK OUT!
...
ALEX?
ALEX!

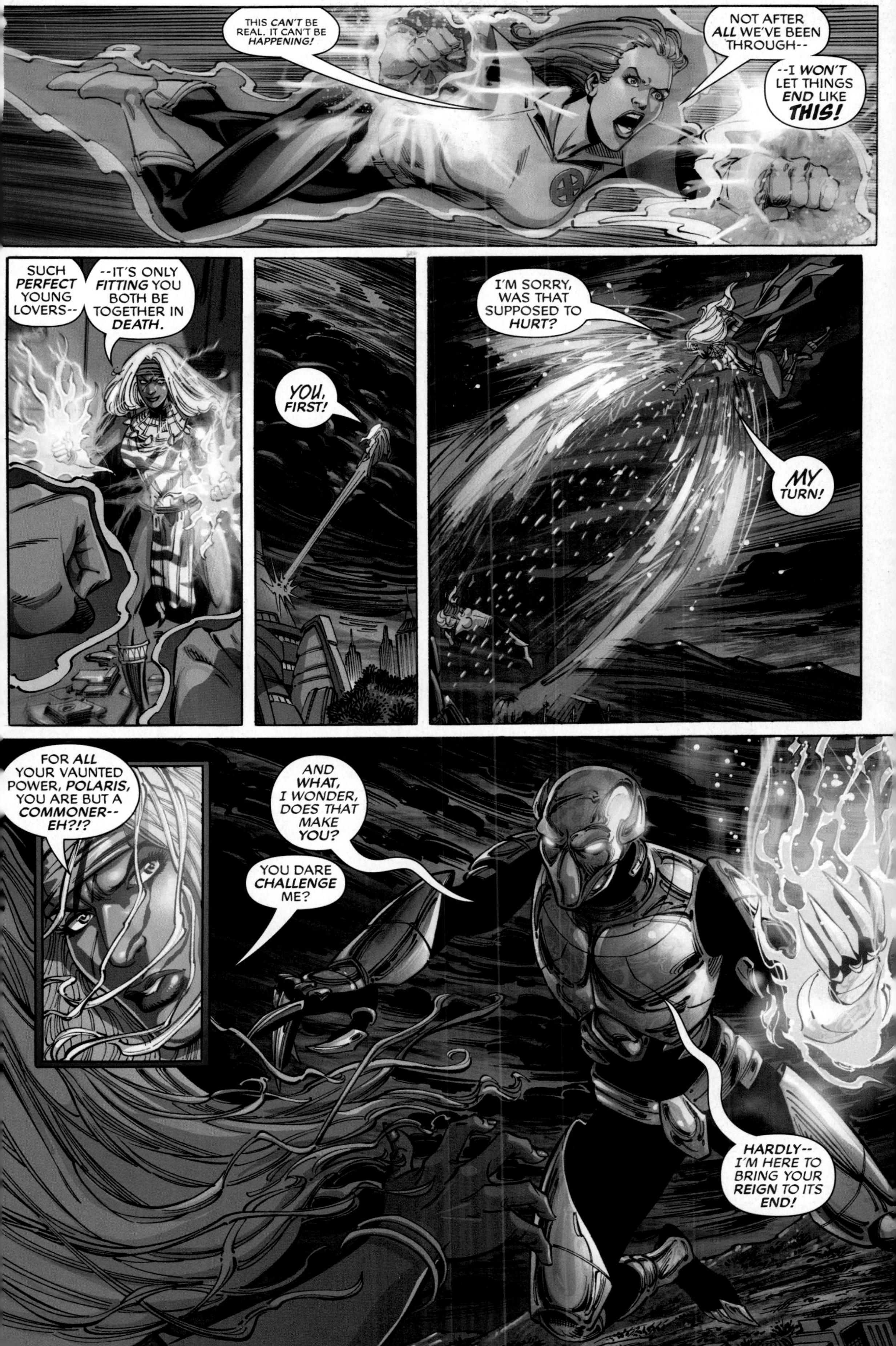
THIS CAN'T BE REAL. IT CAN'T BE HAPPENING!
NOT AFTER ALL WE'VE BEEN THROUGH--
--I WON'T LET THINGS END LIKE THIS!
SUCH PERFECT YOUNG LOVERS--
--IT'S ONLY FITTING YOU BOTH BE TOGETHER IN DEATH.
YOU, FIRST!
I'M SORRY, WAS THAT SUPPOSED TO HURT?
MY TURN!
FOR ALL YOUR VAUNTED POWER, POLARIS, YOU ARE BUT A COMMONER--
EH?!?
AND WHAT, I WONDER, DOES THAT MAKE YOU?
YOU DARE CHALLENGE ME?
HARDLY-- I'M HERE TO BRING YOUR REIGN TO ITS END!

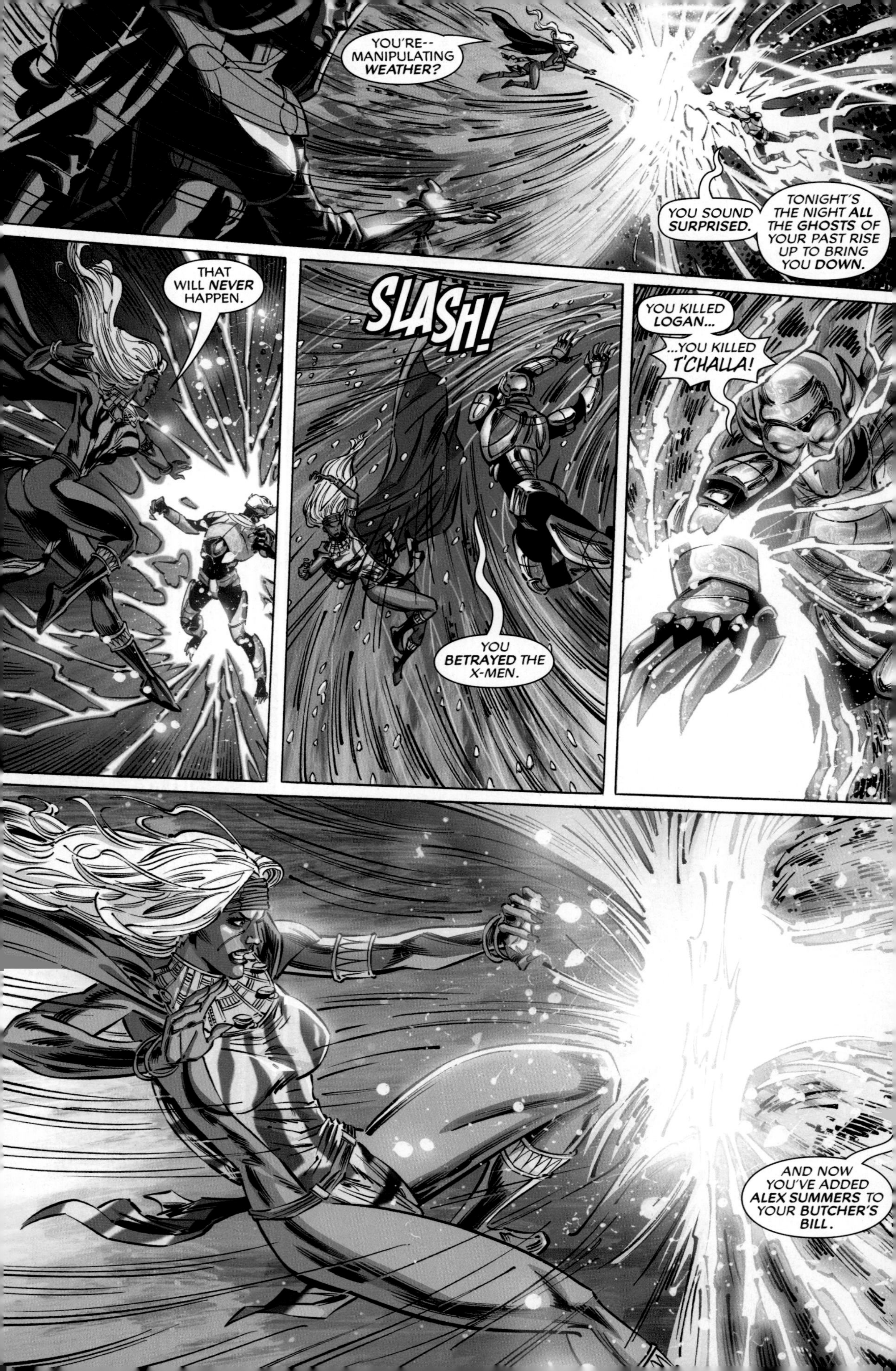
YOU'RE-- MANIPULATING WEATHER?
YOU SOUND SURPRISED.
TONIGHT'S THE NIGHT ALL THE GHOSTS OF YOUR PAST RISE UP TO BRING YOU DOWN.
THAT WILL NEVER HAPPEN.
SLASH!
YOU BETRAYED THE X-MEN.
YOU KILLED LOGAN...
...YOU KILLED T'CHALLA!
AND NOW YOU'VE ADDED ALEX SUMMERS TO YOUR BUTCHER'S BILL.

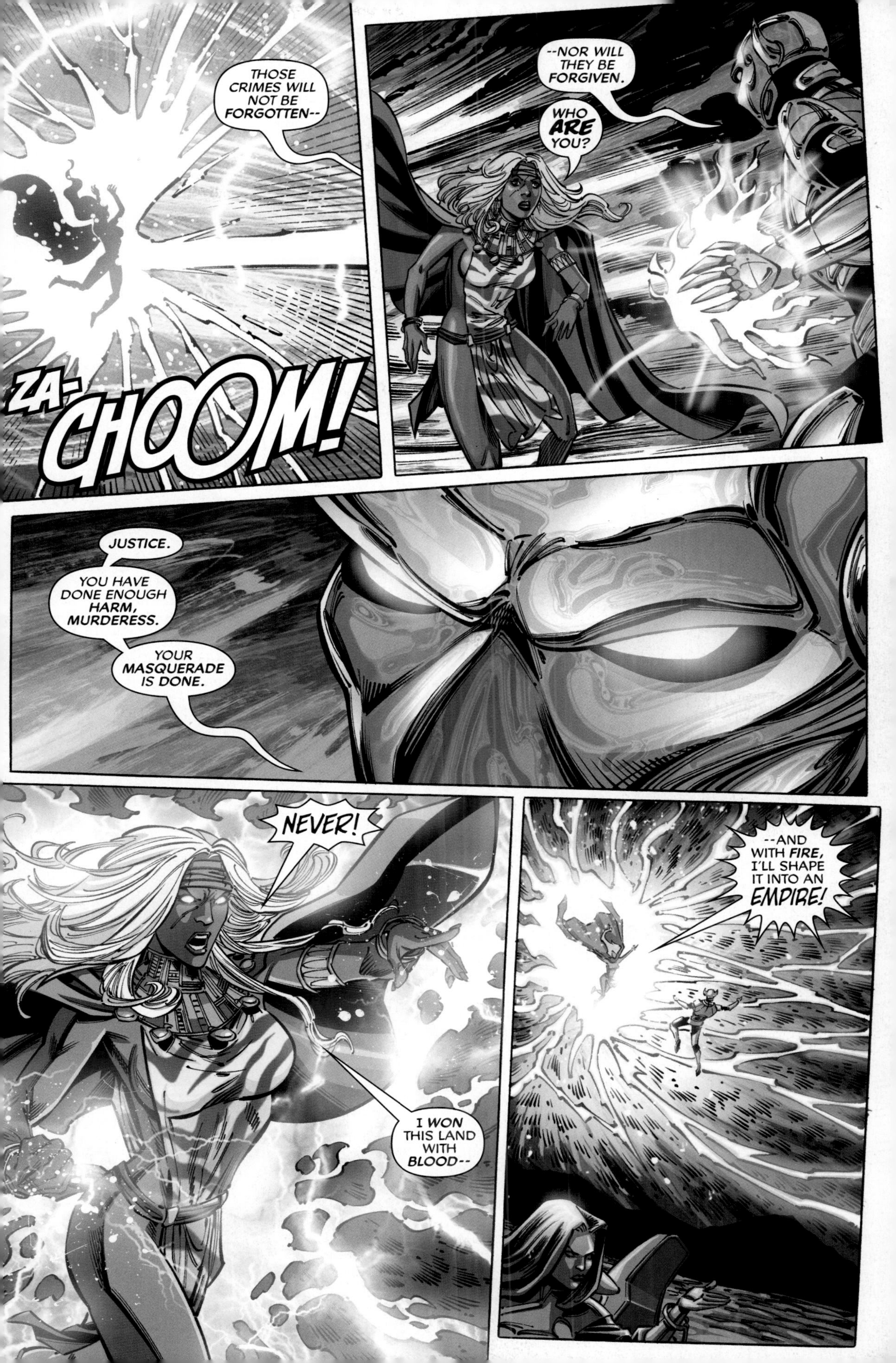
THOSE CRIMES WILL NOT BE FORGOTTEN--
ZA-CHOOM!
--NOR WILL THEY BE FORGIVEN.
WHO ARE YOU?
JUSTICE.
YOU HAVE DONE ENOUGH HARM, MURDERESS.
YOUR MASQUERADE IS DONE.
NEVER!
I WON THIS LAND WITH BLOOD--
--AND WITH FIRE, I'LL SHAPE IT INTO AN EMPIRE!

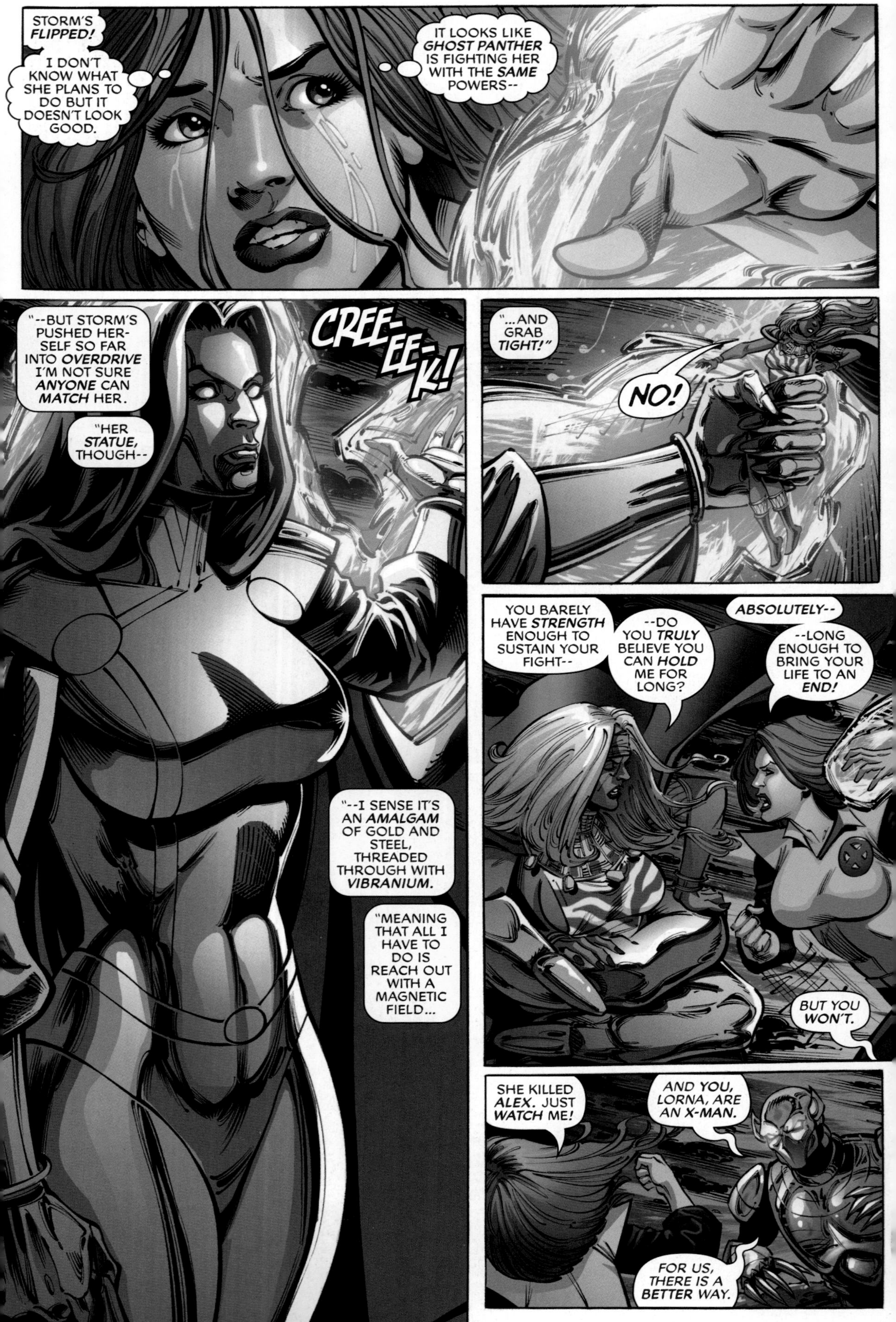

STORM'S FLIPPED!
I DON'T KNOW WHAT SHE PLANS TO DO BUT IT DOESN'T LOOK GOOD.
IT LOOKS LIKE GHOST PANTHER IS FIGHTING HER WITH THE SAME POWERS--
"--BUT STORM'S PUSHED HER-SELF SO FAR INTO OVERDRIVE I'M NOT SURE ANYONE CAN MATCH HER.
"HER STATUE, THOUGH--
CREE-EE-K!
"--I SENSE IT'S AN AMALGAM OF GOLD AND STEEL, THREADED THROUGH WITH VIBRANIUM.
"MEANING THAT ALL I HAVE TO DO IS REACH OUT WITH A MAGNETIC FIELD...
"...AND GRAB TIGHT!"
NO!
YOU BARELY HAVE STRENGTH ENOUGH TO SUSTAIN YOUR FIGHT--
--DO YOU TRULY BELIEVE YOU CAN HOLD ME FOR LONG?
ABSOLUTELY--
--LONG ENOUGH TO BRING YOUR LIFE TO AN END!
BUT YOU WON'T.
SHE KILLED ALEX. JUST WATCH ME!
AND YOU, LORNA, ARE AN X-MAN.
FOR US, THERE IS A BETTER WAY.

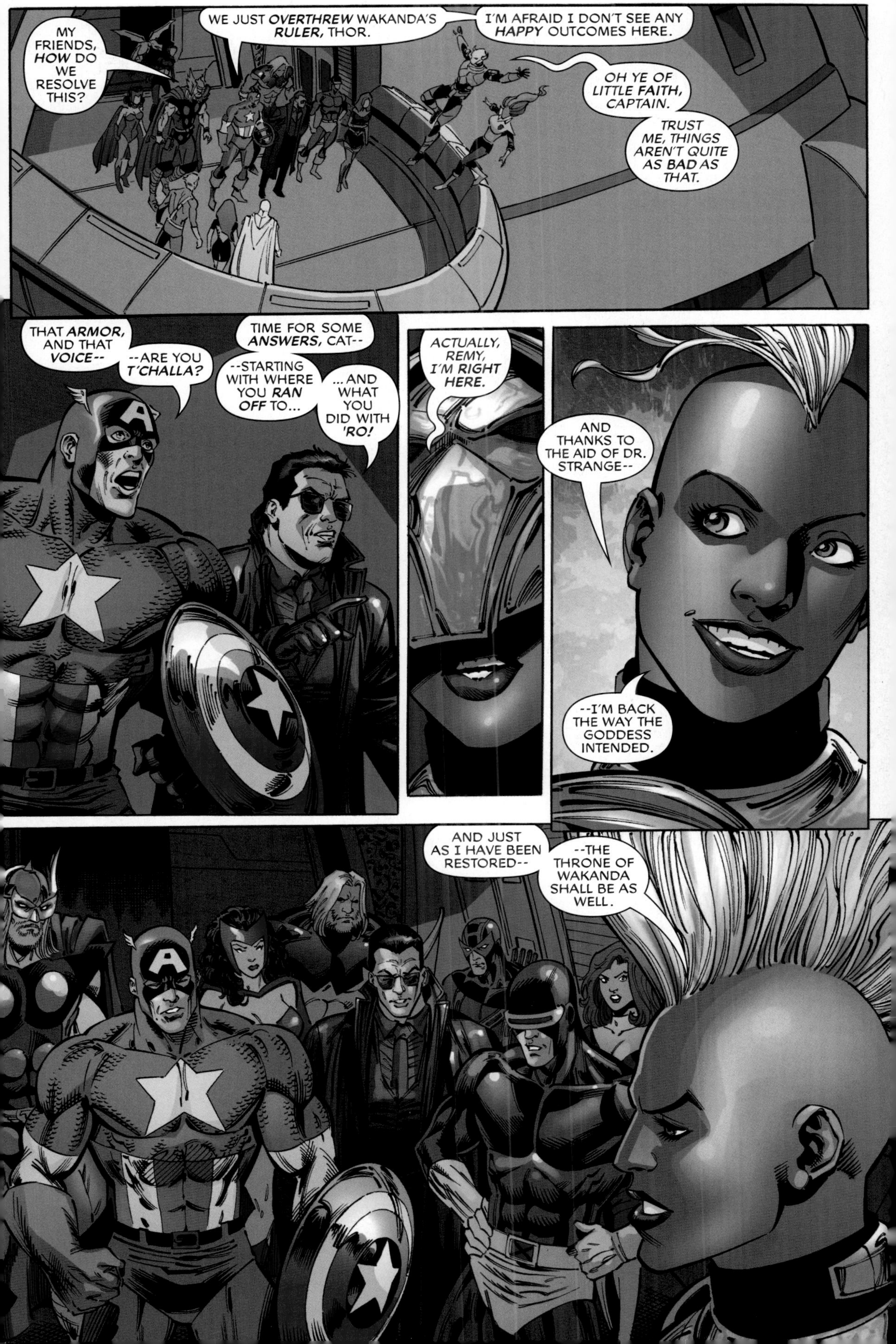
MY FRIENDS, HOW DO WE RESOLVE THIS?
WE JUST OVERTHREW WAKANDA'S RULER, THOR.
I'M AFRAID I DON'T SEE ANY HAPPY OUTCOMES HERE.
OH YE OF LITTLE FAITH, CAPTAIN.
TRUST ME, THINGS AREN'T QUITE AS BAD AS THAT.
THAT ARMOR, AND THAT VOICE--
--ARE YOU T'CHALLA?
TIME FOR SOME ANSWERS, CAT--
--STARTING WITH WHERE YOU RAN OFF TO...
...AND WHAT YOU DID WITH 'RO!
ACTUALLY, REMY, I'M RIGHT HERE.
AND THANKS TO THE AID OF DR. STRANGE--
--I'M BACK THE WAY THE GODDESS INTENDED.
AND JUST AS I HAVE BEEN RESTORED--
--THE THRONE OF WAKANDA SHALL BE AS WELL.

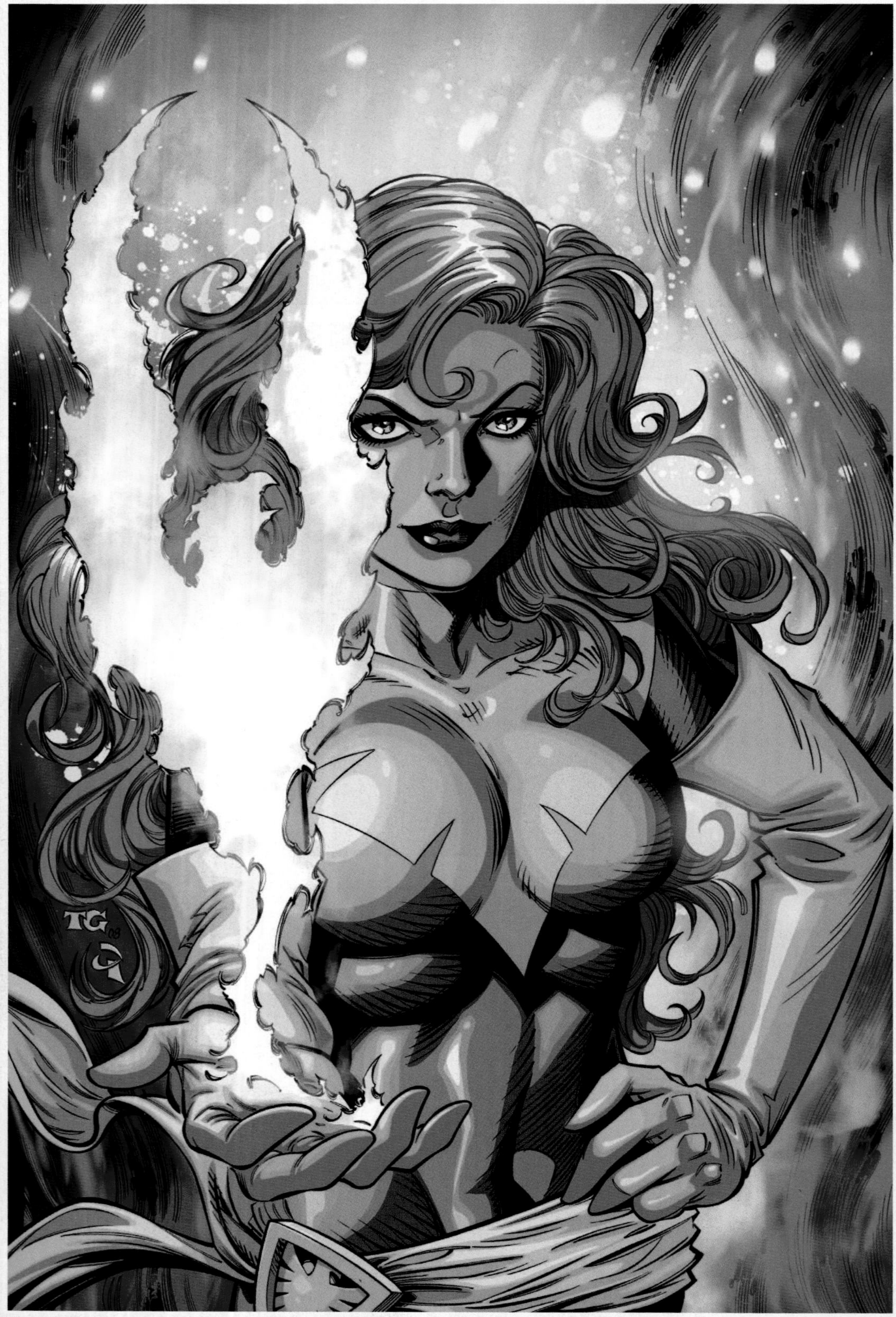
TG 08

SIXTEEN

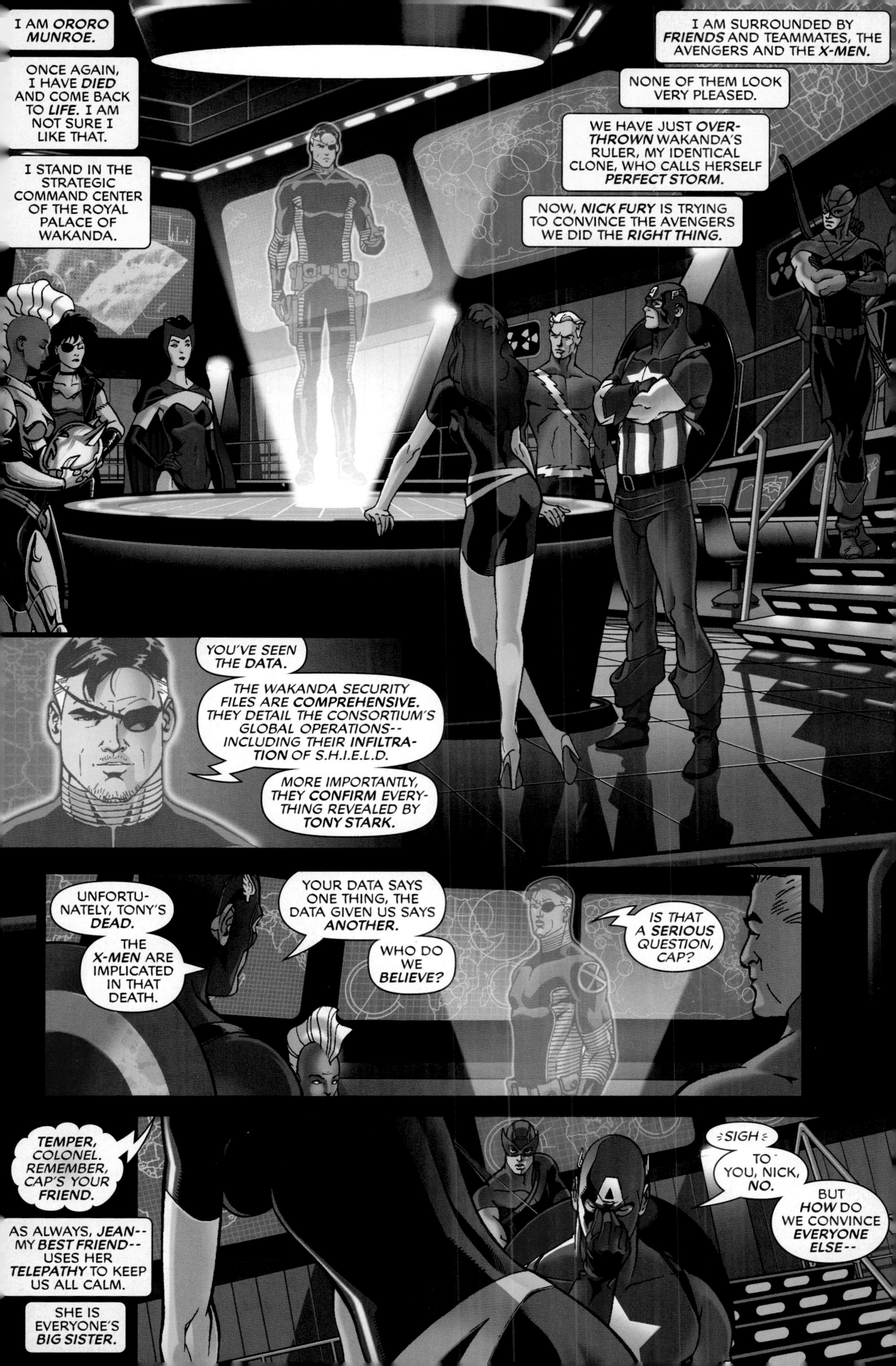
I AM ORORO MUNROE.
ONCE AGAIN, I HAVE DIED AND COME BACK TO LIFE. I AM NOT SURE I LIKE THAT.
I STAND IN THE STRATEGIC COMMAND CENTER OF THE ROYAL PALACE OF WAKANDA.
I AM SURROUNDED BY FRIENDS AND TEAMMATES, THE AVENGERS AND THE X-MEN.
NONE OF THEM LOOK VERY PLEASED.
WE HAVE JUST OVERTHROWN WAKANDA'S RULER, MY IDENTICAL CLONE, WHO CALLS HERSELF PERFECT STORM.
NOW, NICK FURY IS TRYING TO CONVINCE THE AVENGERS WE DID THE RIGHT THING.
YOU'VE SEEN THE DATA.
THE WAKANDA SECURITY FILES ARE COMPREHENSIVE. THEY DETAIL THE CONSORTIUM'S GLOBAL OPERATIONS-- INCLUDING THEIR INFILTRATION OF S.H.I.E.L.D.
MORE IMPORTANTLY, THEY CONFIRM EVERYTHING REVEALED BY TONY STARK.
UNFORTUNATELY, TONY'S DEAD.
THE X-MEN ARE IMPLICATED IN THAT DEATH.
YOUR DATA SAYS ONE THING, THE DATA GIVEN US SAYS ANOTHER.
WHO DO WE BELIEVE?
IS THAT A SERIOUS QUESTION, CAP?
TEMPER, COLONEL. REMEMBER, CAP'S YOUR FRIEND.
AS ALWAYS, JEAN-- MY BEST FRIEND-- USES HER TELEPATHY TO KEEP US ALL CALM.
SHE IS EVERYONE'S BIG SISTER.
SIGH
TO YOU, NICK, NO.
BUT HOW DO WE CONVINCE EVERYONE ELSE--

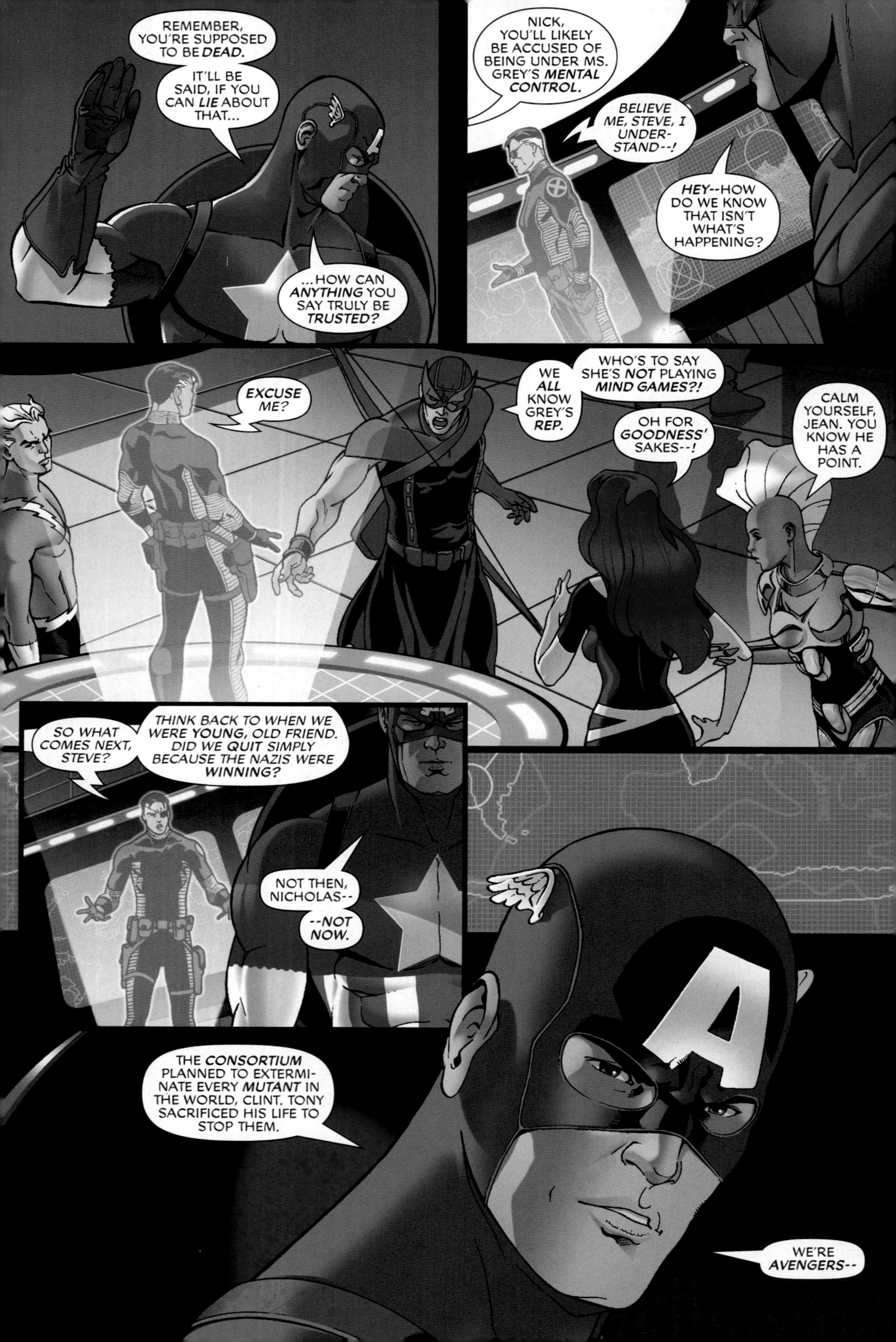
REMEMBER, YOU'RE SUPPOSED TO BE DEAD.
IT'LL BE SAID, IF YOU CAN LIE ABOUT THAT...
...HOW CAN ANYTHING YOU SAY TRULY BE TRUSTED?
NICK, YOU'LL LIKELY BE ACCUSED OF BEING UNDER MS. GREY'S MENTAL CONTROL.
BELIEVE ME, STEVE, I UNDER-STAND--!
HEY--HOW DO WE KNOW THAT ISN'T WHAT'S HAPPENING?
EXCUSE ME?
WE ALL KNOW GREY'S REP.
WHO'S TO SAY SHE'S NOT PLAYING MIND GAMES?!
OH FOR GOODNESS' SAKES--!
CALM YOURSELF, JEAN. YOU KNOW HE HAS A POINT.
SO WHAT COMES NEXT, STEVE?
THINK BACK TO WHEN WE WERE YOUNG, OLD FRIEND. DID WE QUIT SIMPLY BECAUSE THE NAZIS WERE WINNING?
NOT THEN, NICHOLAS--
--NOT NOW.
THE CONSORTIUM PLANNED TO EXTERMINATE EVERY MUTANT IN THE WORLD, CLINT. TONY SACRIFICED HIS LIFE TO STOP THEM.
WE'RE AVENGERS--

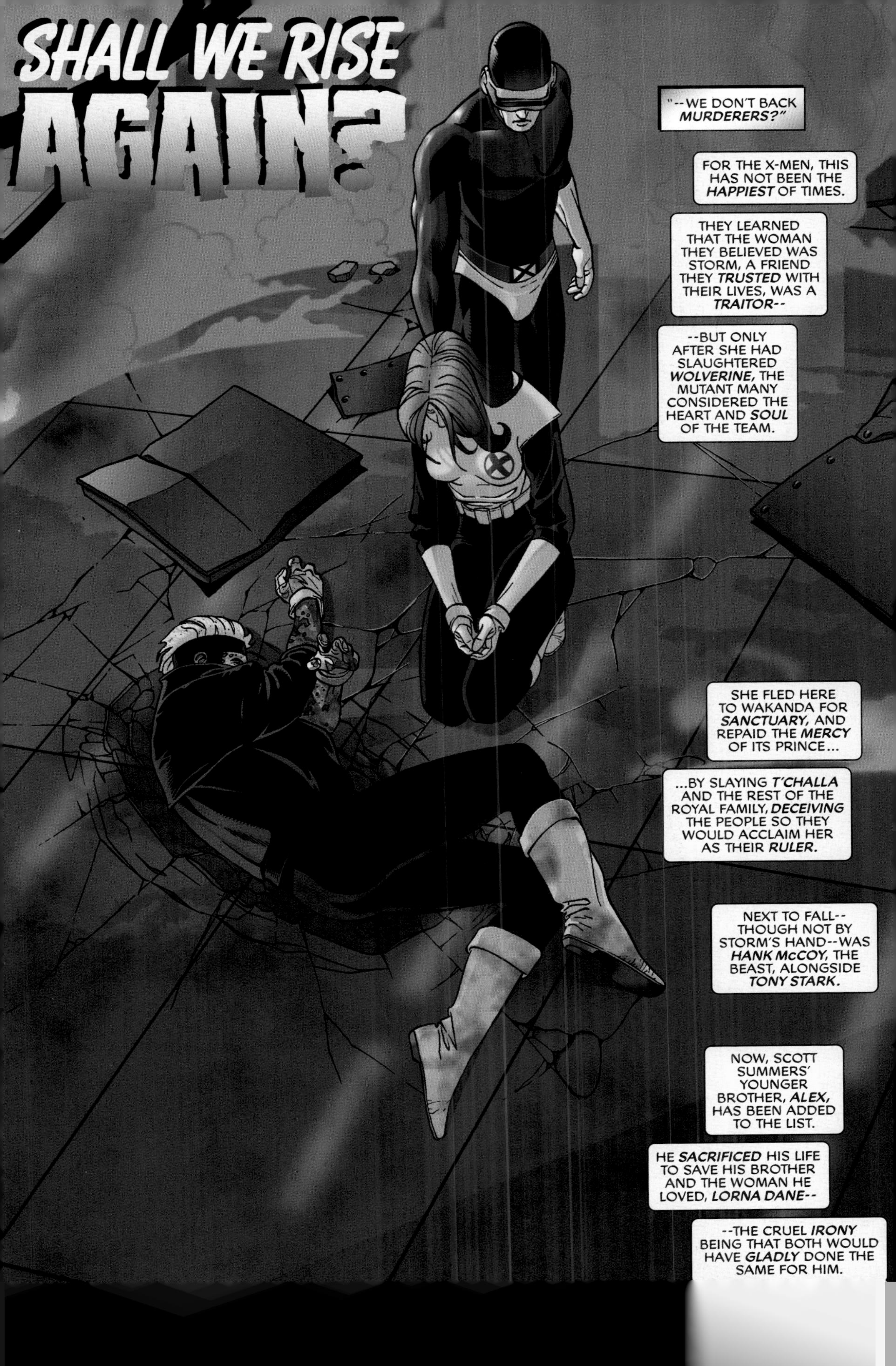

SHALL WE RISE AGAIN?
"--WE DON'T BACK MURDERERS?"
FOR THE X-MEN, THIS HAS NOT BEEN THE HAPPIEST OF TIMES.
THEY LEARNED THAT THE WOMAN THEY BELIEVED WAS STORM, A FRIEND THEY TRUSTED WITH THEIR LIVES, WAS A TRAITOR--
--BUT ONLY AFTER SHE HAD SLAUGHTERED WOLVERINE, THE MUTANT MANY CONSIDERED THE HEART AND SOUL OF THE TEAM.
SHE FLED HERE TO WAKANDA FOR SANCTUARY, AND REPAID THE MERCY OF ITS PRINCE...
...BY SLAYING T'CHALLA AND THE REST OF THE ROYAL FAMILY, DECEIVING THE PEOPLE SO THEY WOULD ACCLAIM HER AS THEIR RULER.
NEXT TO FALL--THOUGH NOT BY STORM'S HAND--WAS HANK McCOY, THE BEAST, ALONGSIDE TONY STARK.
NOW, SCOTT SUMMERS' YOUNGER BROTHER, ALEX, HAS BEEN ADDED TO THE LIST.
HE SACRIFICED HIS LIFE TO SAVE HIS BROTHER AND THE WOMAN HE LOVED, LORNA DANE--
--THE CRUEL IRONY BEING THAT BOTH WOULD HAVE GLADLY DONE THE SAME FOR HIM.

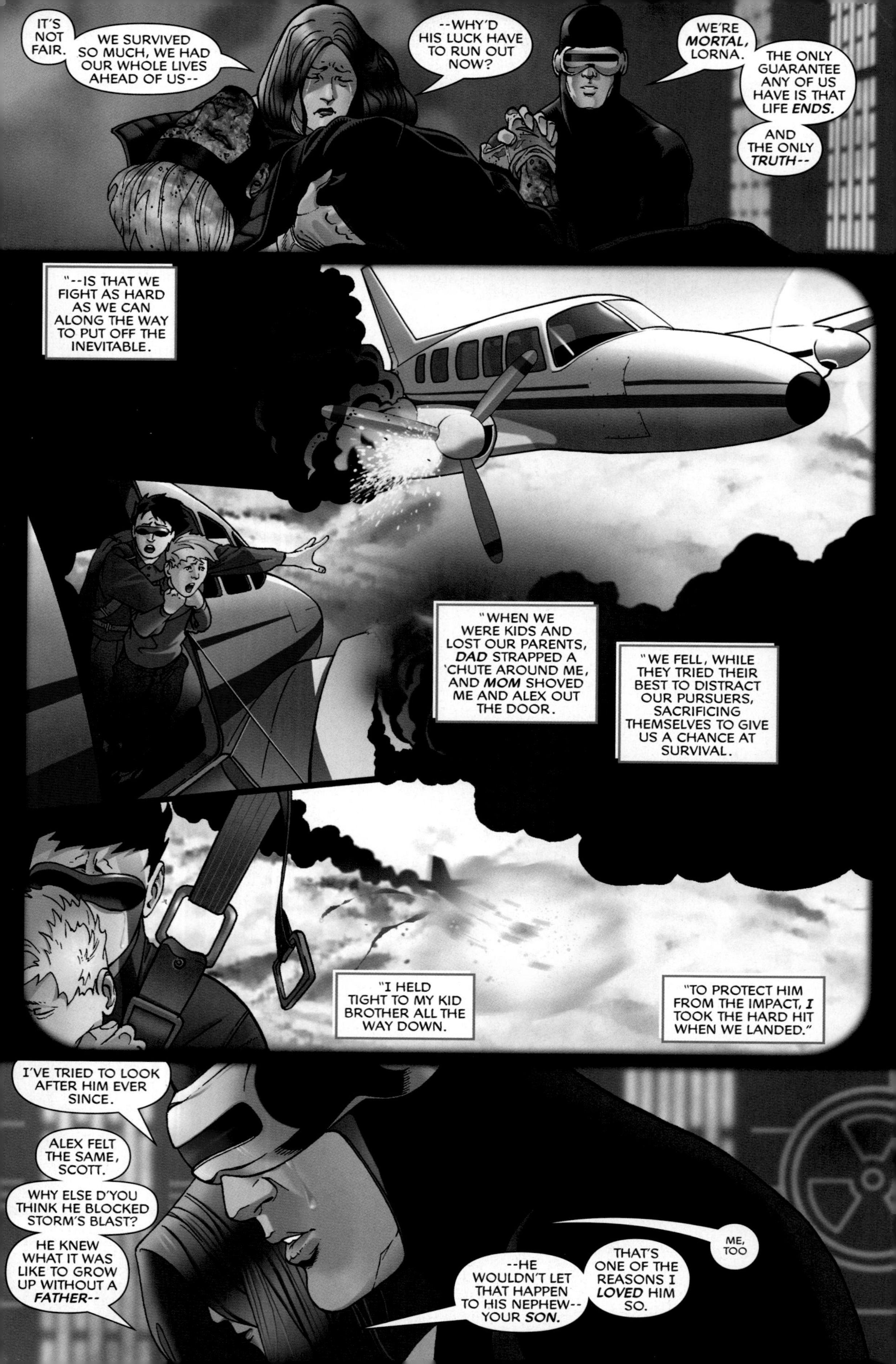
IT'S NOT FAIR.
WE SURVIVED SO MUCH, WE HAD OUR WHOLE LIVES AHEAD OF US--
--WHY'D HIS LUCK HAVE TO RUN OUT NOW?
WE'RE MORTAL, LORNA.
THE ONLY GUARANTEE ANY OF US HAVE IS THAT LIFE ENDS.
AND THE ONLY TRUTH--
"--IS THAT WE FIGHT AS HARD AS WE CAN ALONG THE WAY TO PUT OFF THE INEVITABLE.
"WHEN WE WERE KIDS AND LOST OUR PARENTS, DAD STRAPPED A 'CHUTE AROUND ME, AND MOM SHOVED ME AND ALEX OUT THE DOOR.
"WE FELL, WHILE THEY TRIED THEIR BEST TO DISTRACT OUR PURSUERS, SACRIFICING THEMSELVES TO GIVE US A CHANCE AT SURVIVAL.
"I HELD TIGHT TO MY KID BROTHER ALL THE WAY DOWN.
"TO PROTECT HIM FROM THE IMPACT, I TOOK THE HARD HIT WHEN WE LANDED."
I'VE TRIED TO LOOK AFTER HIM EVER SINCE.
ALEX FELT THE SAME, SCOTT.
WHY ELSE D'YOU THINK HE BLOCKED STORM'S BLAST?
HE KNEW WHAT IT WAS LIKE TO GROW UP WITHOUT A FATHER--
--HE WOULDN'T LET THAT HAPPEN TO HIS NEPHEW--YOUR SON.
THAT'S ONE OF THE REASONS I LOVED HIM SO.
ME, TOO

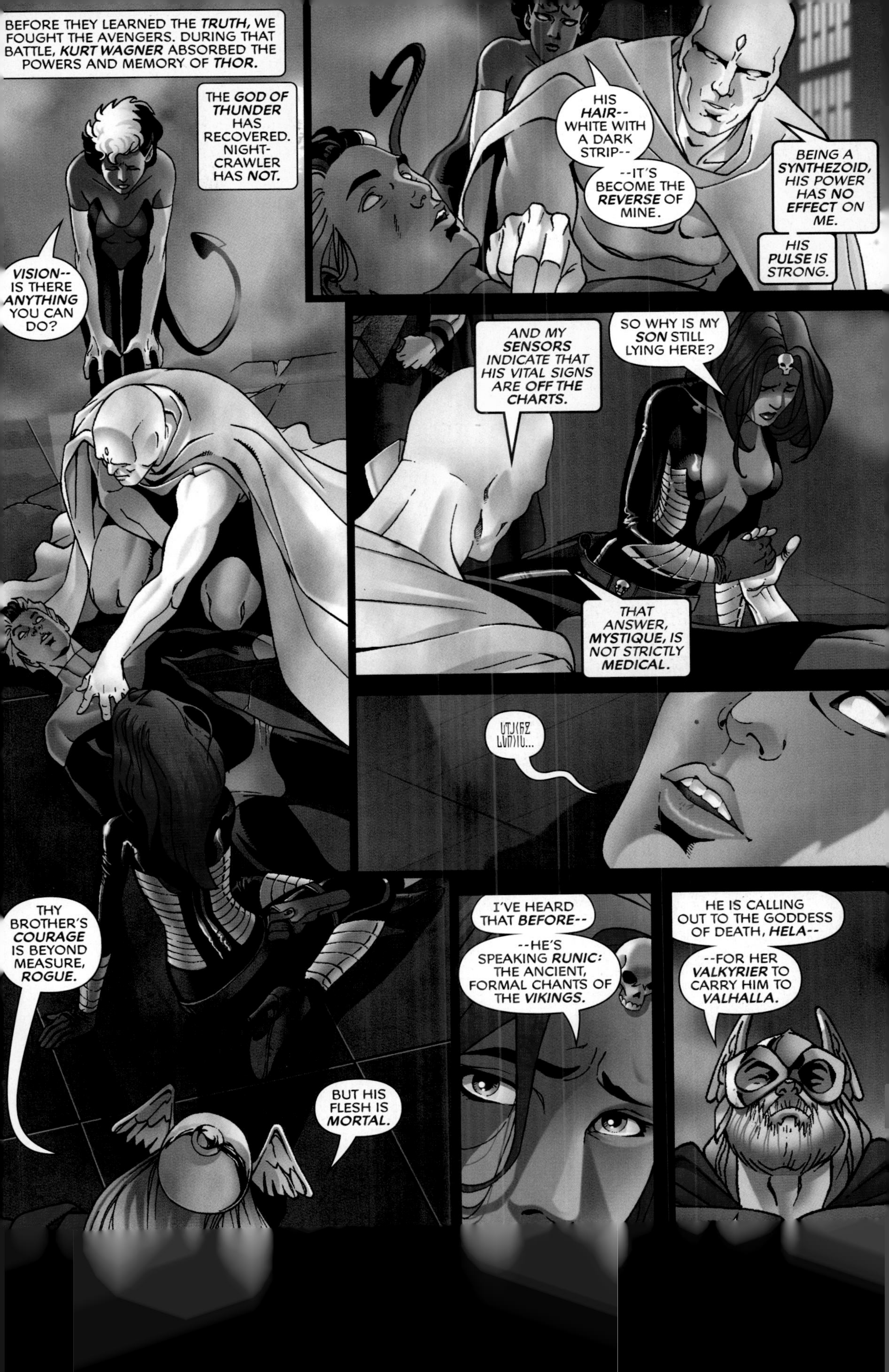

BEFORE THEY LEARNED THE *TRUTH,* WE FOUGHT THE AVENGERS. DURING THAT BATTLE, *KURT WAGNER* ABSORBED THE POWERS AND MEMORY OF *THOR.*
THE *GOD OF THUNDER* HAS RECOVERED. NIGHT-CRAWLER HAS *NOT.*
VISION-- IS THERE *ANYTHING* YOU CAN DO?
HIS *HAIR--* WHITE WITH A DARK STRIP--
--IT'S BECOME THE *REVERSE* OF MINE.
BEING A *SYNTHEZOID,* HIS POWER HAS *NO EFFECT* ON *ME.*
HIS *PULSE* IS *STRONG.*
AND MY *SENSORS* INDICATE THAT HIS VITAL SIGNS ARE *OFF THE CHARTS.*
SO WHY IS MY *SON* STILL LYING HERE?
THAT ANSWER, *MYSTIQUE,* IS NOT STRICTLY *MEDICAL.*
THY BROTHER'S *COURAGE* IS BEYOND MEASURE, *ROGUE.*
BUT HIS FLESH IS *MORTAL.*
I'VE HEARD THAT *BEFORE--*
--HE'S SPEAKING *RUNIC:* THE ANCIENT, FORMAL CHANTS OF THE *VIKINGS.*
HE IS CALLING OUT TO THE GODDESS OF DEATH, *HELA--*
--FOR HER *VALKYRIER* TO CARRY HIM TO *VALHALLA.*

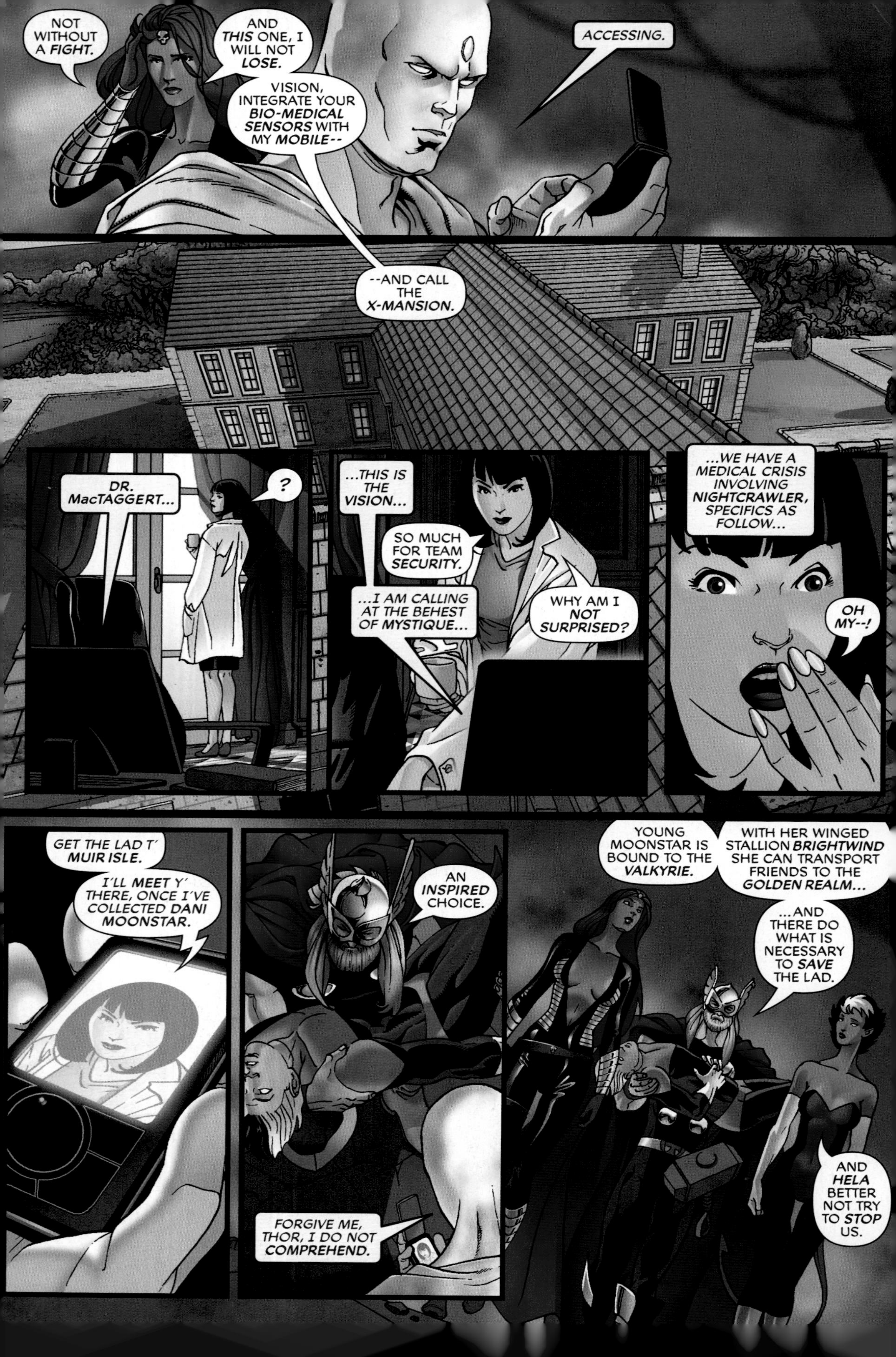
NOT WITHOUT A FIGHT.
AND THIS ONE, I WILL NOT LOSE.
VISION, INTEGRATE YOUR BIO-MEDICAL SENSORS WITH MY MOBILE--
ACCESSING.
--AND CALL THE X-MANSION.
DR. MacTAGGERT...
?
...THIS IS THE VISION...
SO MUCH FOR TEAM SECURITY.
...I AM CALLING AT THE BEHEST OF MYSTIQUE...
WHY AM I NOT SURPRISED?
...WE HAVE A MEDICAL CRISIS INVOLVING NIGHTCRAWLER, SPECIFICS AS FOLLOW...
OH MY--!
GET THE LAD T' MUIR ISLE.
I'LL MEET Y' THERE, ONCE I'VE COLLECTED DANI MOONSTAR.
AN INSPIRED CHOICE.
FORGIVE ME, THOR, I DO NOT COMPREHEND.
YOUNG MOONSTAR IS BOUND TO THE VALKYRIE.
WITH HER WINGED STALLION BRIGHTWIND SHE CAN TRANSPORT FRIENDS TO THE GOLDEN REALM...
...AND THERE DO WHAT IS NECESSARY TO SAVE THE LAD.
AND HELA BETTER NOT TRY TO STOP US.

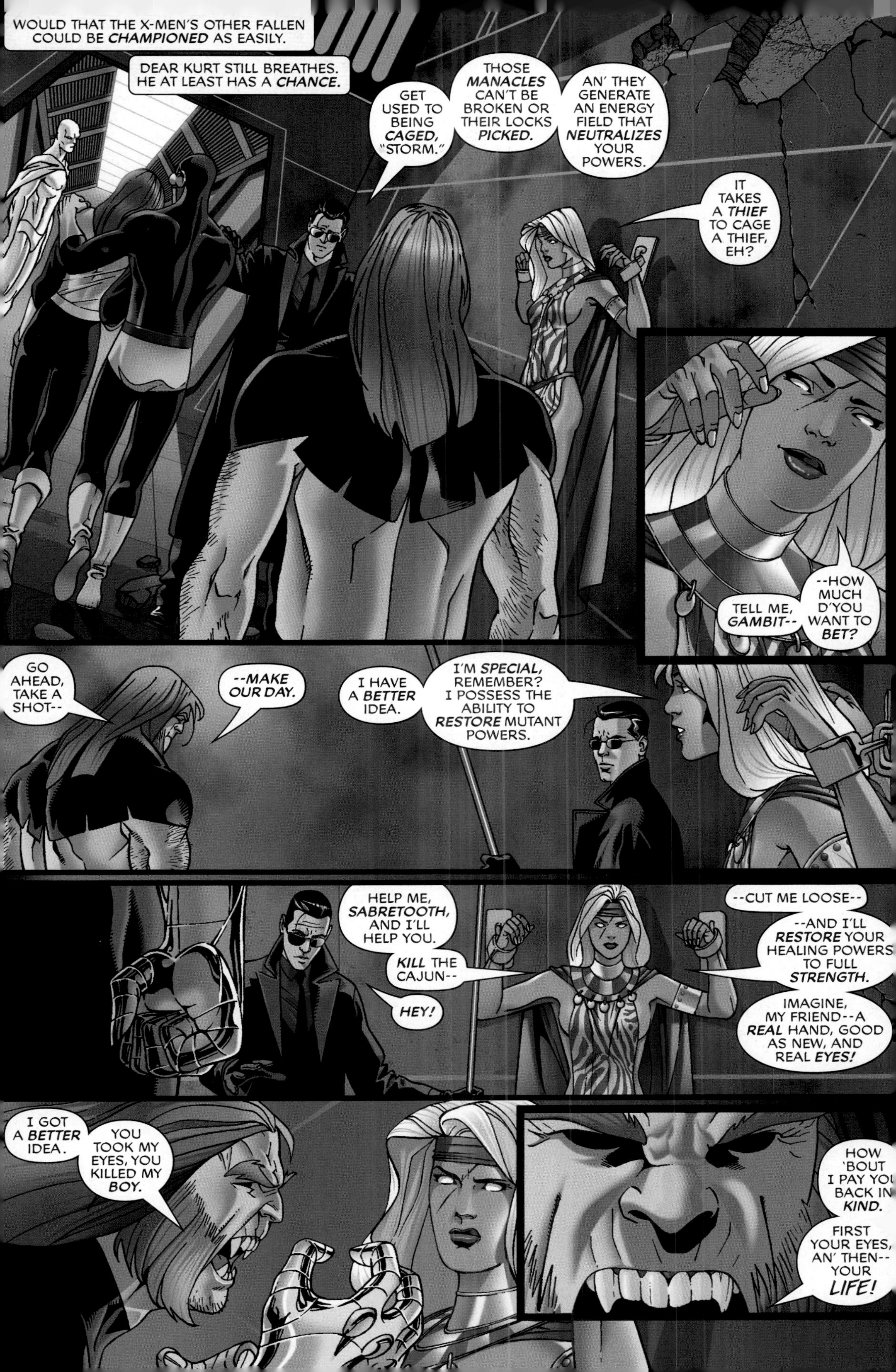
WOULD THAT THE X-MEN'S OTHER FALLEN COULD BE CHAMPIONED AS EASILY.
DEAR KURT STILL BREATHES. HE AT LEAST HAS A CHANCE.
GET USED TO BEING CAGED, "STORM."
THOSE MANACLES CAN'T BE BROKEN OR THEIR LOCKS PICKED.
AN' THEY GENERATE AN ENERGY FIELD THAT NEUTRALIZES YOUR POWERS.
IT TAKES A THIEF TO CAGE A THIEF, EH?
TELL ME, GAMBIT--
--HOW MUCH D'YOU WANT TO BET?
GO AHEAD, TAKE A SHOT--
--MAKE OUR DAY.
I HAVE A BETTER IDEA.
I'M SPECIAL, REMEMBER? I POSSESS THE ABILITY TO RESTORE MUTANT POWERS.
HELP ME, SABRETOOTH, AND I'LL HELP YOU.
KILL THE CAJUN--
HEY!
--CUT ME LOOSE--
--AND I'LL RESTORE YOUR HEALING POWERS TO FULL STRENGTH.
IMAGINE, MY FRIEND--A REAL HAND, GOOD AS NEW, AND REAL EYES!
I GOT A BETTER IDEA.
YOU TOOK MY EYES, YOU KILLED MY BOY.
HOW 'BOUT I PAY YOU BACK IN KIND.
FIRST YOUR EYES, AN' THEN--YOUR LIFE!

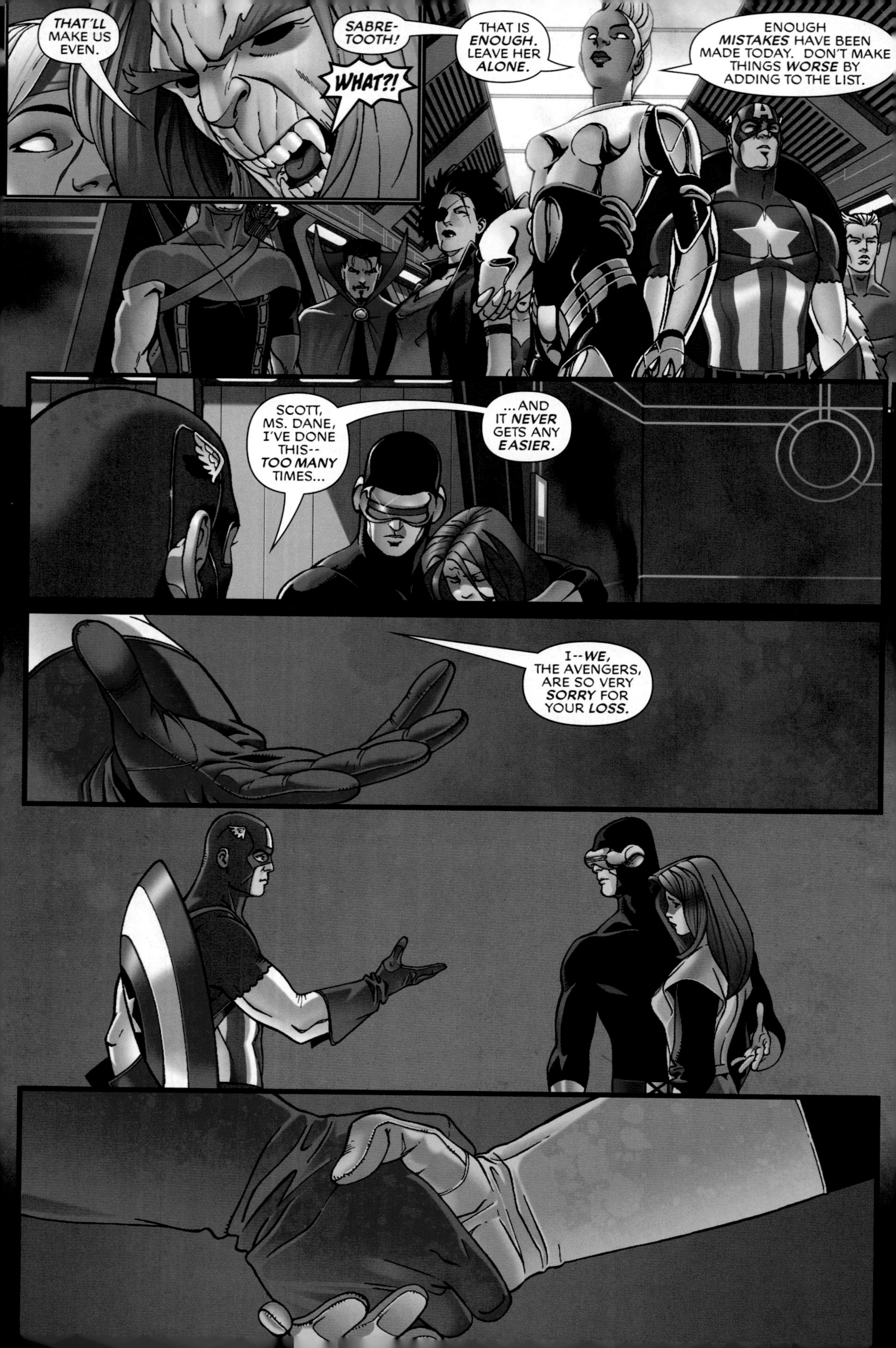

THAT'LL MAKE US EVEN.
SABRE-TOOTH!
WHAT?!
THAT IS ENOUGH. LEAVE HER ALONE.
ENOUGH MISTAKES HAVE BEEN MADE TODAY. DON'T MAKE THINGS WORSE BY ADDING TO THE LIST.
SCOTT, MS. DANE, I'VE DONE THIS--TOO MANY TIMES...
...AND IT NEVER GETS ANY EASIER.
I--WE, THE AVENGERS, ARE SO VERY SORRY FOR YOUR LOSS.

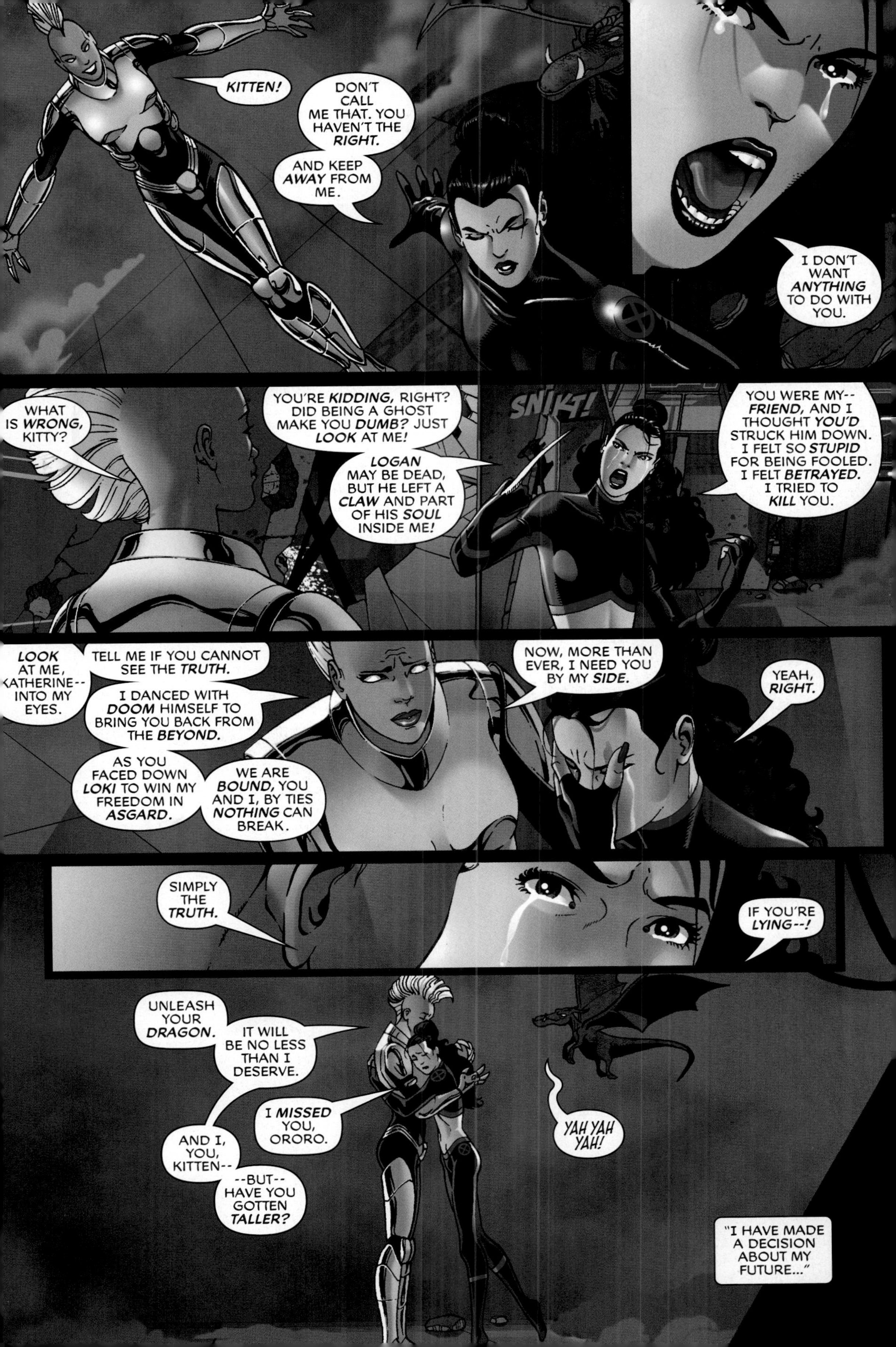
KITTEN!
DON'T CALL ME THAT. YOU HAVEN'T THE RIGHT.
AND KEEP AWAY FROM ME.
I DON'T WANT ANYTHING TO DO WITH YOU.
WHAT IS WRONG, KITTY?
YOU'RE KIDDING, RIGHT? DID BEING A GHOST MAKE YOU DUMB? JUST LOOK AT ME!
LOGAN MAY BE DEAD, BUT HE LEFT A CLAW AND PART OF HIS SOUL INSIDE ME!
SNIKT!
YOU WERE MY-- FRIEND, AND I THOUGHT YOU'D STRUCK HIM DOWN. I FELT SO STUPID FOR BEING FOOLED. I FELT BETRAYED. I TRIED TO KILL YOU.
LOOK AT ME, KATHERINE-- INTO MY EYES.
TELL ME IF YOU CANNOT SEE THE TRUTH.
I DANCED WITH DOOM HIMSELF TO BRING YOU BACK FROM THE BEYOND.
AS YOU FACED DOWN LOKI TO WIN MY FREEDOM IN ASGARD.
WE ARE BOUND, YOU AND I, BY TIES NOTHING CAN BREAK.
NOW, MORE THAN EVER, I NEED YOU BY MY SIDE.
YEAH, RIGHT.
SIMPLY THE TRUTH.
IF YOU'RE LYING--!
UNLEASH YOUR DRAGON.
IT WILL BE NO LESS THAN I DESERVE.
I MISSED YOU, ORORO.
AND I, YOU, KITTEN--
--BUT-- HAVE YOU GOTTEN TALLER?
YAH YAH YAH!
"I HAVE MADE A DECISION ABOUT MY FUTURE..."

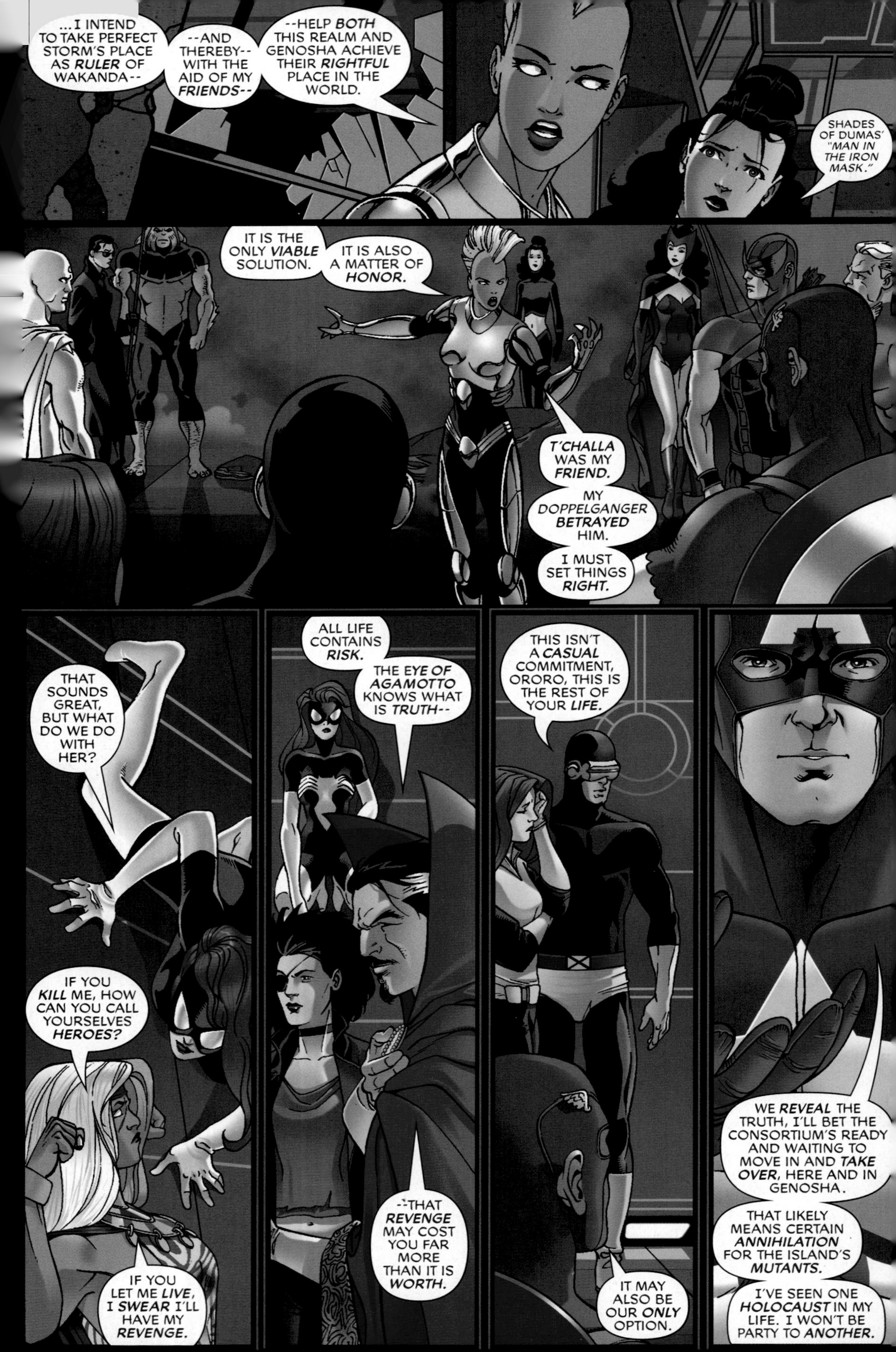
...I INTEND TO TAKE PERFECT STORM'S PLACE AS RULER OF WAKANDA--
--AND THEREBY--WITH THE AID OF MY FRIENDS--
--HELP BOTH THIS REALM AND GENOSHA ACHIEVE THEIR RIGHTFUL PLACE IN THE WORLD.
SHADES OF DUMAS' "MAN IN THE IRON MASK."
IT IS THE ONLY VIABLE SOLUTION.
IT IS ALSO A MATTER OF HONOR.
T'CHALLA WAS MY FRIEND.
MY DOPPELGANGER BETRAYED HIM.
I MUST SET THINGS RIGHT.
THAT SOUNDS GREAT, BUT WHAT DO WE DO WITH HER?
IF YOU KILL ME, HOW CAN YOU CALL YOURSELVES HEROES?
IF YOU LET ME LIVE, I SWEAR I'LL HAVE MY REVENGE.
ALL LIFE CONTAINS RISK.
THE EYE OF AGAMOTTO KNOWS WHAT IS TRUTH--
--THAT REVENGE MAY COST YOU FAR MORE THAN IT IS WORTH.
THIS ISN'T A CASUAL COMMITMENT, ORORO, THIS IS THE REST OF YOUR LIFE.
IT MAY ALSO BE OUR ONLY OPTION.
WE REVEAL THE TRUTH, I'LL BET THE CONSORTIUM'S READY AND WAITING TO MOVE IN AND TAKE OVER, HERE AND IN GENOSHA.
THAT LIKELY MEANS CERTAIN ANNIHILATION FOR THE ISLAND'S MUTANTS.
I'VE SEEN ONE HOLOCAUST IN MY LIFE. I WON'T BE PARTY TO ANOTHER.

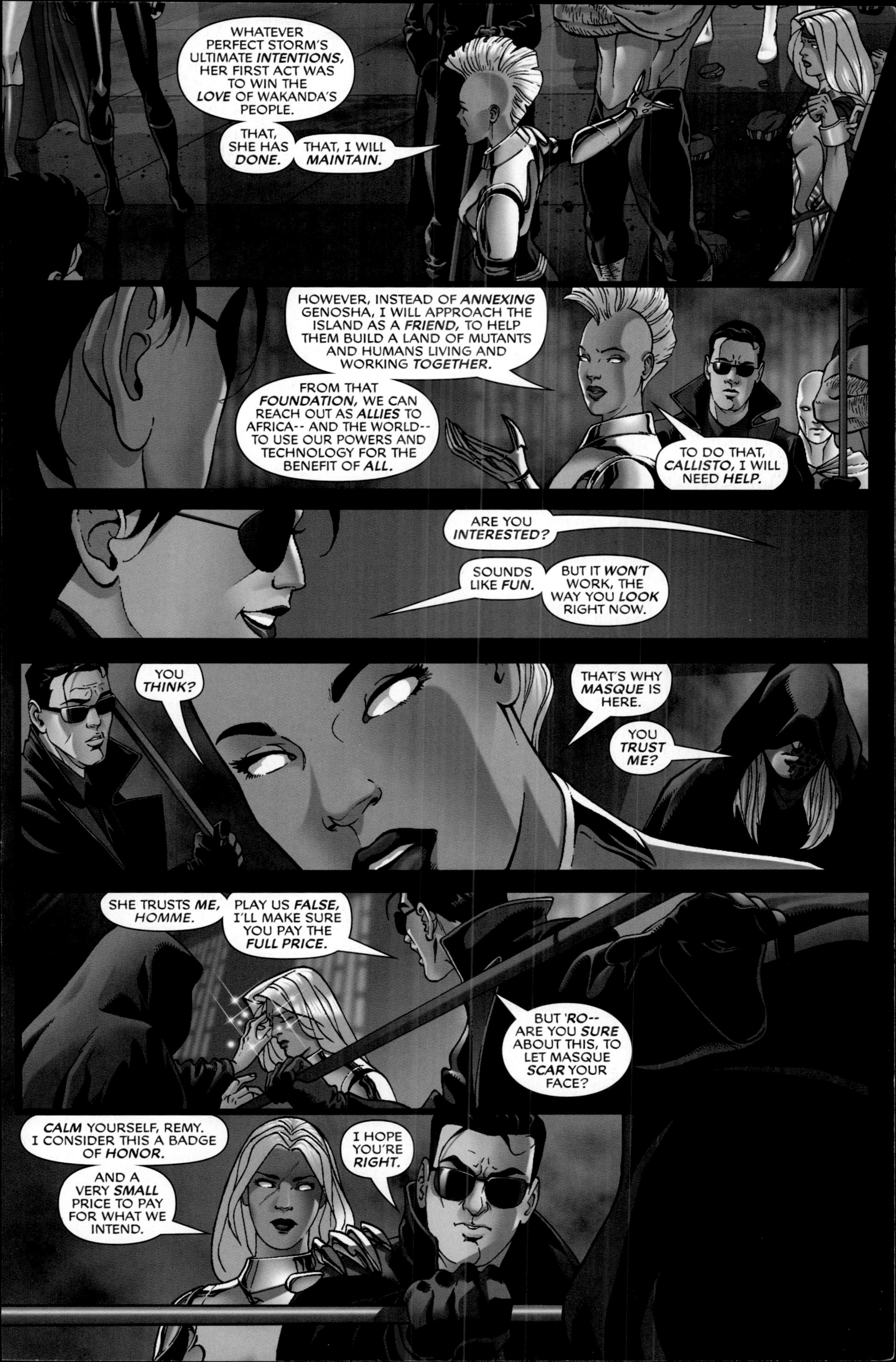
WHATEVER PERFECT STORM'S ULTIMATE INTENTIONS, HER FIRST ACT WAS TO WIN THE LOVE OF WAKANDA'S PEOPLE.
THAT, SHE HAS DONE.
THAT, I WILL MAINTAIN.
HOWEVER, INSTEAD OF ANNEXING GENOSHA, I WILL APPROACH THE ISLAND AS A FRIEND, TO HELP THEM BUILD A LAND OF MUTANTS AND HUMANS LIVING AND WORKING TOGETHER.
FROM THAT FOUNDATION, WE CAN REACH OUT AS ALLIES TO AFRICA-- AND THE WORLD-- TO USE OUR POWERS AND TECHNOLOGY FOR THE BENEFIT OF ALL.
TO DO THAT, CALLISTO, I WILL NEED HELP.
ARE YOU INTERESTED?
SOUNDS LIKE FUN.
BUT IT WON'T WORK, THE WAY YOU LOOK RIGHT NOW.
YOU THINK?
THAT'S WHY MASQUE IS HERE.
YOU TRUST ME?
SHE TRUSTS ME, HOMME.
PLAY US FALSE, I'LL MAKE SURE YOU PAY THE FULL PRICE.
BUT 'RO-- ARE YOU SURE ABOUT THIS, TO LET MASQUE SCAR YOUR FACE?
CALM YOURSELF, REMY. I CONSIDER THIS A BADGE OF HONOR.
AND A VERY SMALL PRICE TO PAY FOR WHAT WE INTEND.
I HOPE YOU'RE RIGHT.

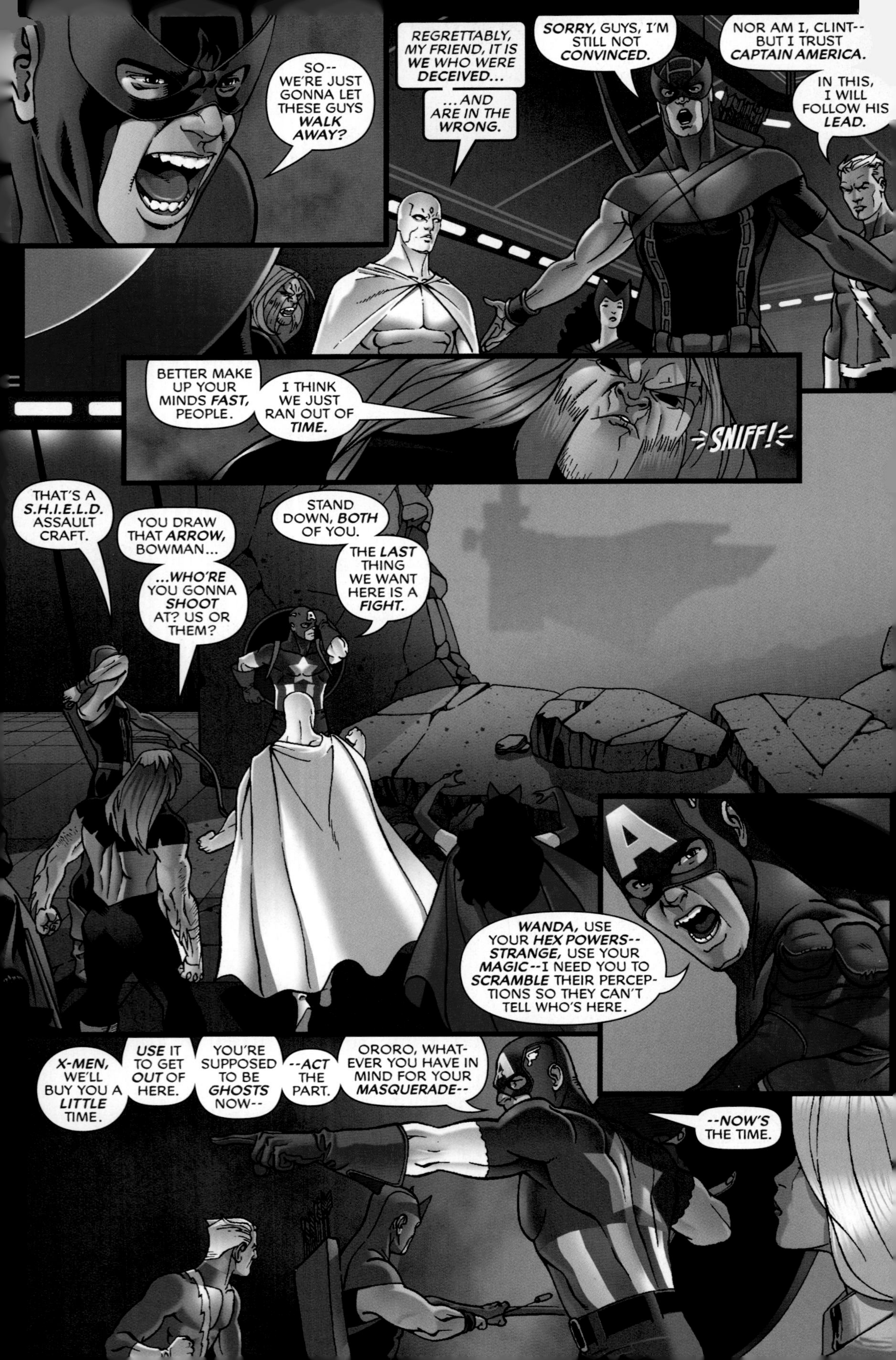
SO-- WE'RE JUST GONNA LET THESE GUYS WALK AWAY?
REGRETTABLY, MY FRIEND, IT IS WE WHO WERE DECEIVED...
...AND ARE IN THE WRONG.
SORRY, GUYS, I'M STILL NOT CONVINCED.
NOR AM I, CLINT-- BUT I TRUST CAPTAIN AMERICA.
IN THIS, I WILL FOLLOW HIS LEAD.
BETTER MAKE UP YOUR MINDS FAST, PEOPLE.
I THINK WE JUST RAN OUT OF TIME.
SNIFF!
THAT'S A S.H.I.E.L.D. ASSAULT CRAFT.
YOU DRAW THAT ARROW, BOWMAN...
...WHO'RE YOU GONNA SHOOT AT? US OR THEM?
STAND DOWN, BOTH OF YOU.
THE LAST THING WE WANT HERE IS A FIGHT.
WANDA, USE YOUR HEX POWERS-- STRANGE, USE YOUR MAGIC--I NEED YOU TO SCRAMBLE THEIR PERCEPTIONS SO THEY CAN'T TELL WHO'S HERE.
X-MEN, WE'LL BUY YOU A LITTLE TIME.
USE IT TO GET OUT OF HERE.
YOU'RE SUPPOSED TO BE GHOSTS NOW--
--ACT THE PART.
ORORO, WHATEVER YOU HAVE IN MIND FOR YOUR MASQUERADE--
--NOW'S THE TIME.

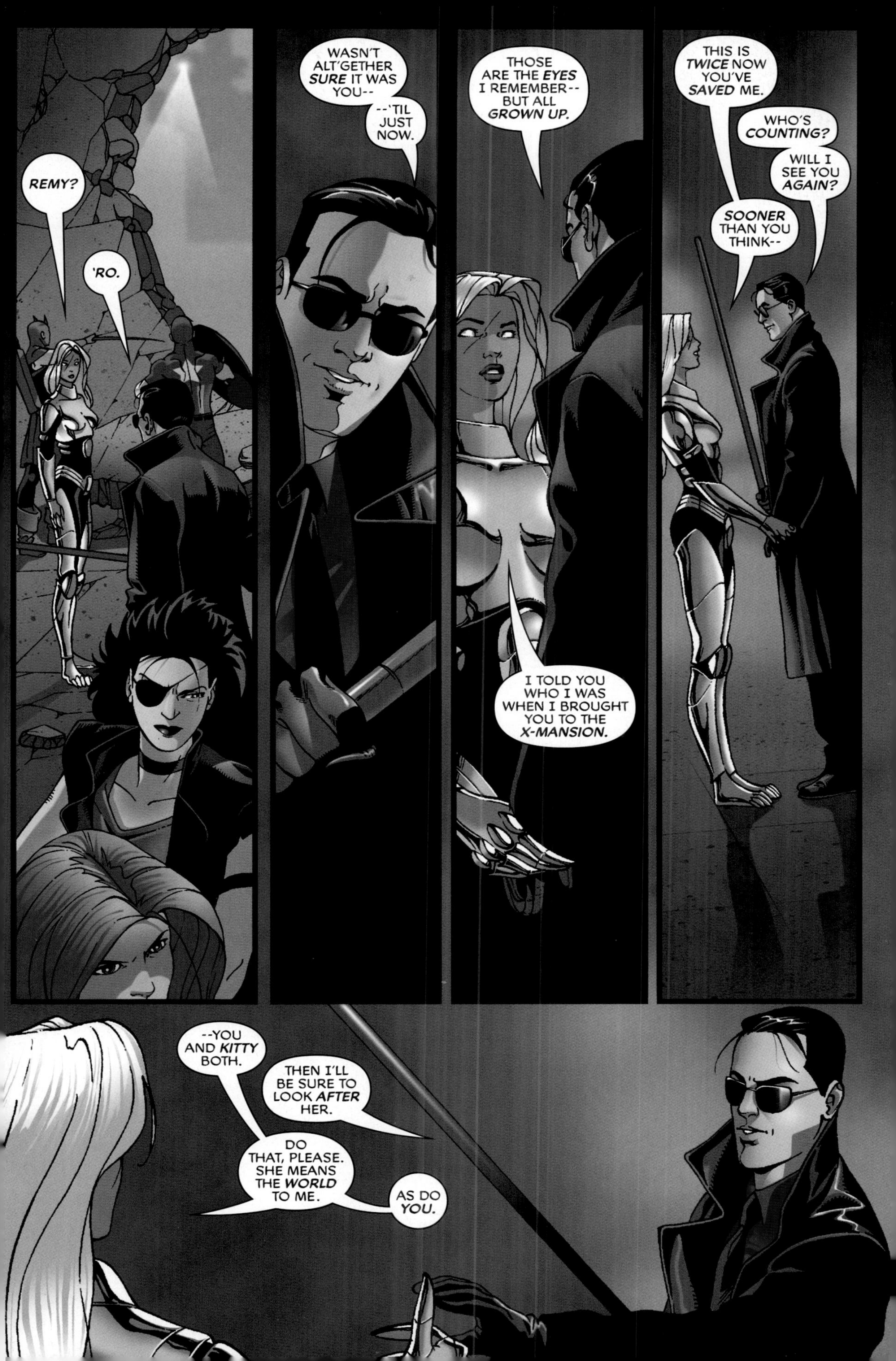
REMY?
'RO.
WASN'T ALT'GETHER SURE IT WAS YOU--
--'TIL JUST NOW.
THOSE ARE THE EYES I REMEMBER-- BUT ALL GROWN UP.
I TOLD YOU WHO I WAS WHEN I BROUGHT YOU TO THE X-MANSION.
THIS IS TWICE NOW YOU'VE SAVED ME.
WHO'S COUNTING?
WILL I SEE YOU AGAIN?
SOONER THAN YOU THINK--
--YOU AND KITTY BOTH.
THEN I'LL BE SURE TO LOOK AFTER HER.
DO THAT, PLEASE. SHE MEANS THE WORLD TO ME.
AS DO YOU.

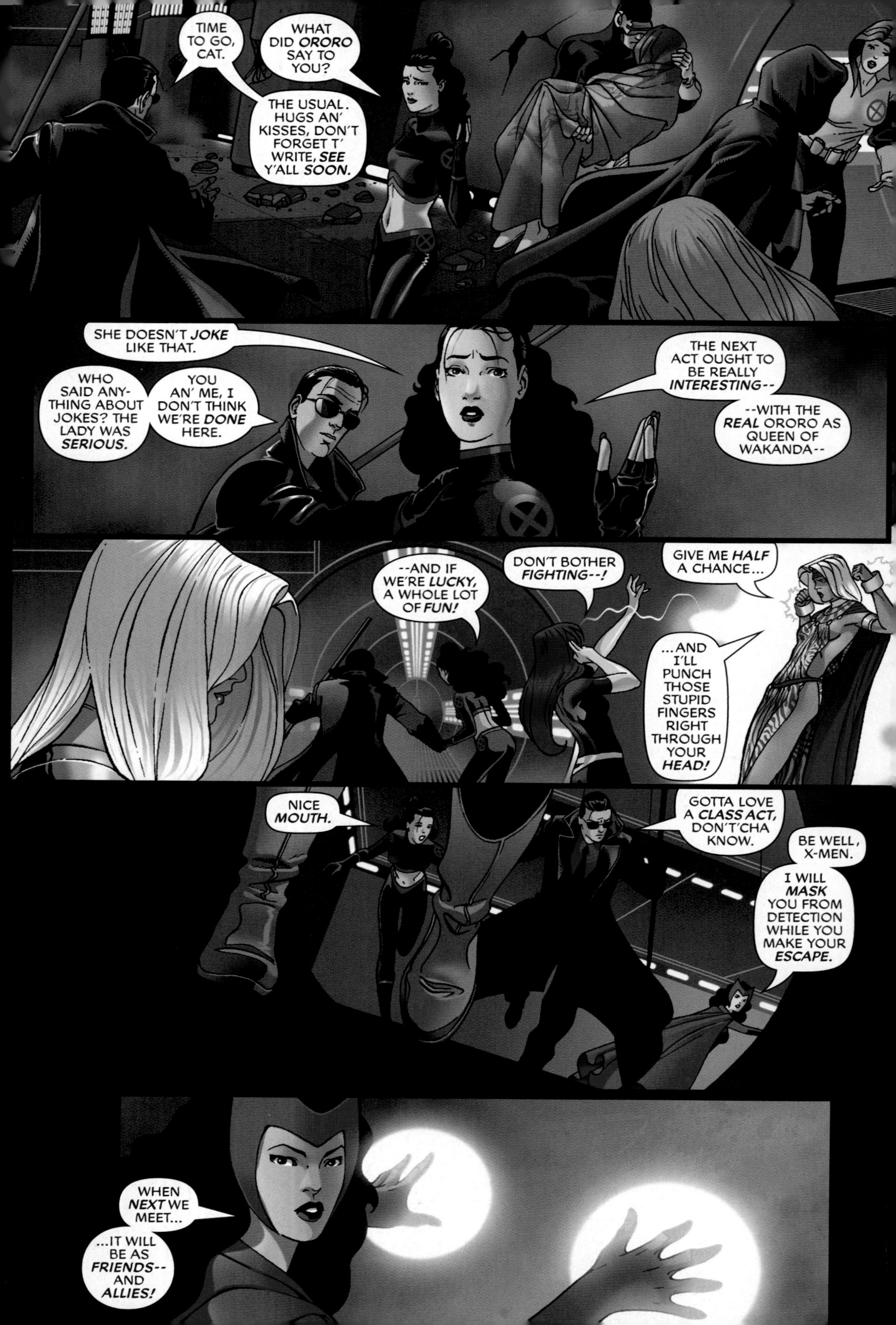
TIME TO GO, CAT.
WHAT DID ORORO SAY TO YOU?
THE USUAL. HUGS AN' KISSES, DON'T FORGET T' WRITE, SEE Y'ALL SOON.
SHE DOESN'T JOKE LIKE THAT.
WHO SAID ANY-THING ABOUT JOKES? THE LADY WAS SERIOUS.
YOU AN' ME, I DON'T THINK WE'RE DONE HERE.
THE NEXT ACT OUGHT TO BE REALLY INTERESTING--
--WITH THE REAL ORORO AS QUEEN OF WAKANDA--
--AND IF WE'RE LUCKY, A WHOLE LOT OF FUN!
DON'T BOTHER FIGHTING--!
GIVE ME HALF A CHANCE...
...AND I'LL PUNCH THOSE STUPID FINGERS RIGHT THROUGH YOUR HEAD!
NICE MOUTH.
GOTTA LOVE A CLASS ACT, DON'T'CHA KNOW.
BE WELL, X-MEN.
I WILL MASK YOU FROM DETECTION WHILE YOU MAKE YOUR ESCAPE.
WHEN NEXT WE MEET...
...IT WILL BE AS FRIENDS-- AND ALLIES!

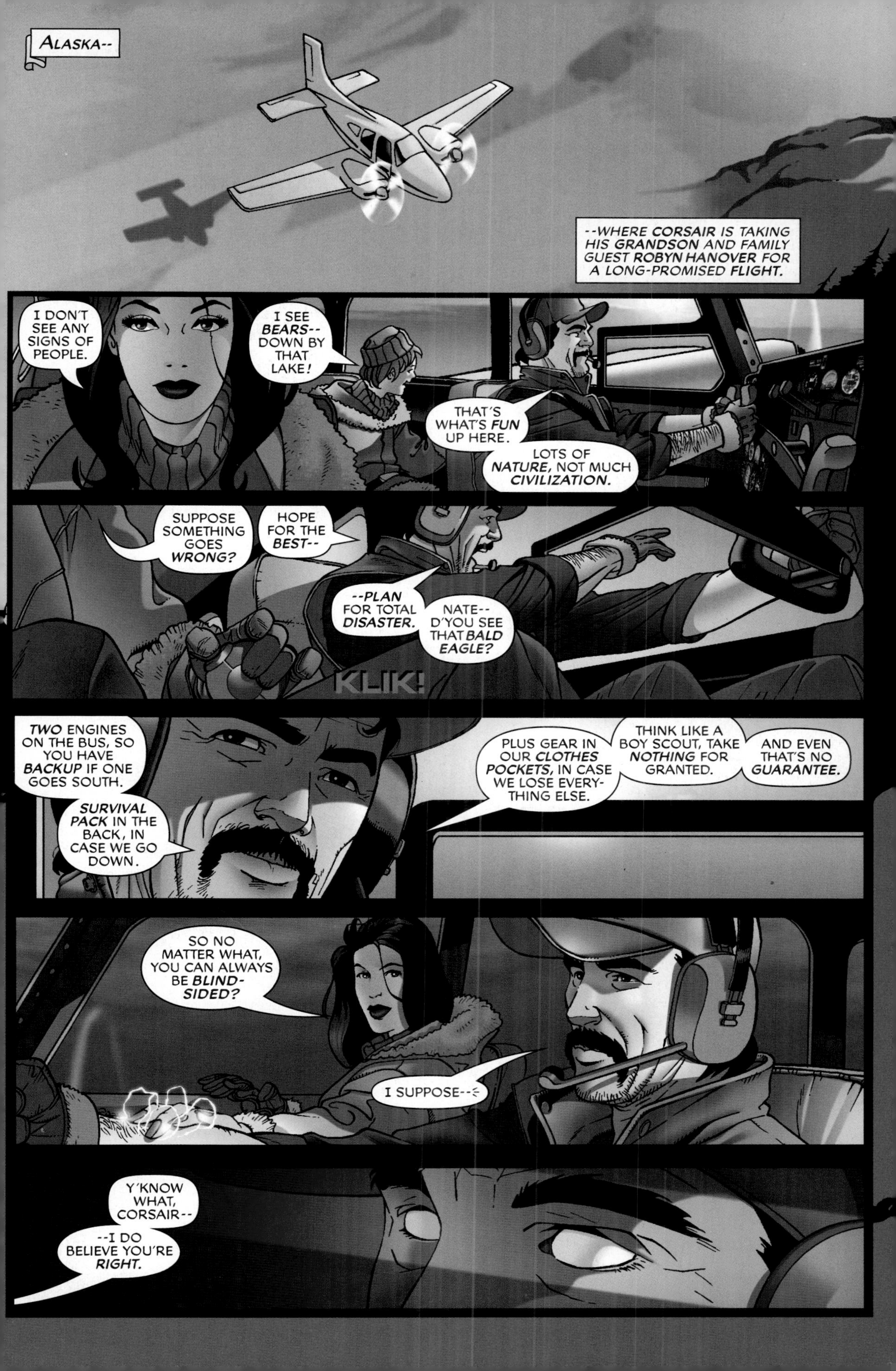
ALASKA--
--WHERE CORSAIR IS TAKING HIS GRANDSON AND FAMILY GUEST ROBYN HANOVER FOR A LONG-PROMISED FLIGHT.
I DON'T SEE ANY SIGNS OF PEOPLE.
I SEE BEARS--DOWN BY THAT LAKE!
THAT'S WHAT'S FUN UP HERE.
LOTS OF NATURE, NOT MUCH CIVILIZATION.
SUPPOSE SOMETHING GOES WRONG?
HOPE FOR THE BEST--
--PLAN FOR TOTAL DISASTER.
NATE--D'YOU SEE THAT BALD EAGLE?
KLIK!
TWO ENGINES ON THE BUS, SO YOU HAVE BACKUP IF ONE GOES SOUTH.
SURVIVAL PACK IN THE BACK, IN CASE WE GO DOWN.
PLUS GEAR IN OUR CLOTHES POCKETS, IN CASE WE LOSE EVERY-THING ELSE.
THINK LIKE A BOY SCOUT, TAKE NOTHING FOR GRANTED.
AND EVEN THAT'S NO GUARANTEE.
SO NO MATTER WHAT, YOU CAN ALWAYS BE BLIND-SIDED?
I SUPPOSE--
Y'KNOW WHAT, CORSAIR--
--I DO BELIEVE YOU'RE RIGHT.

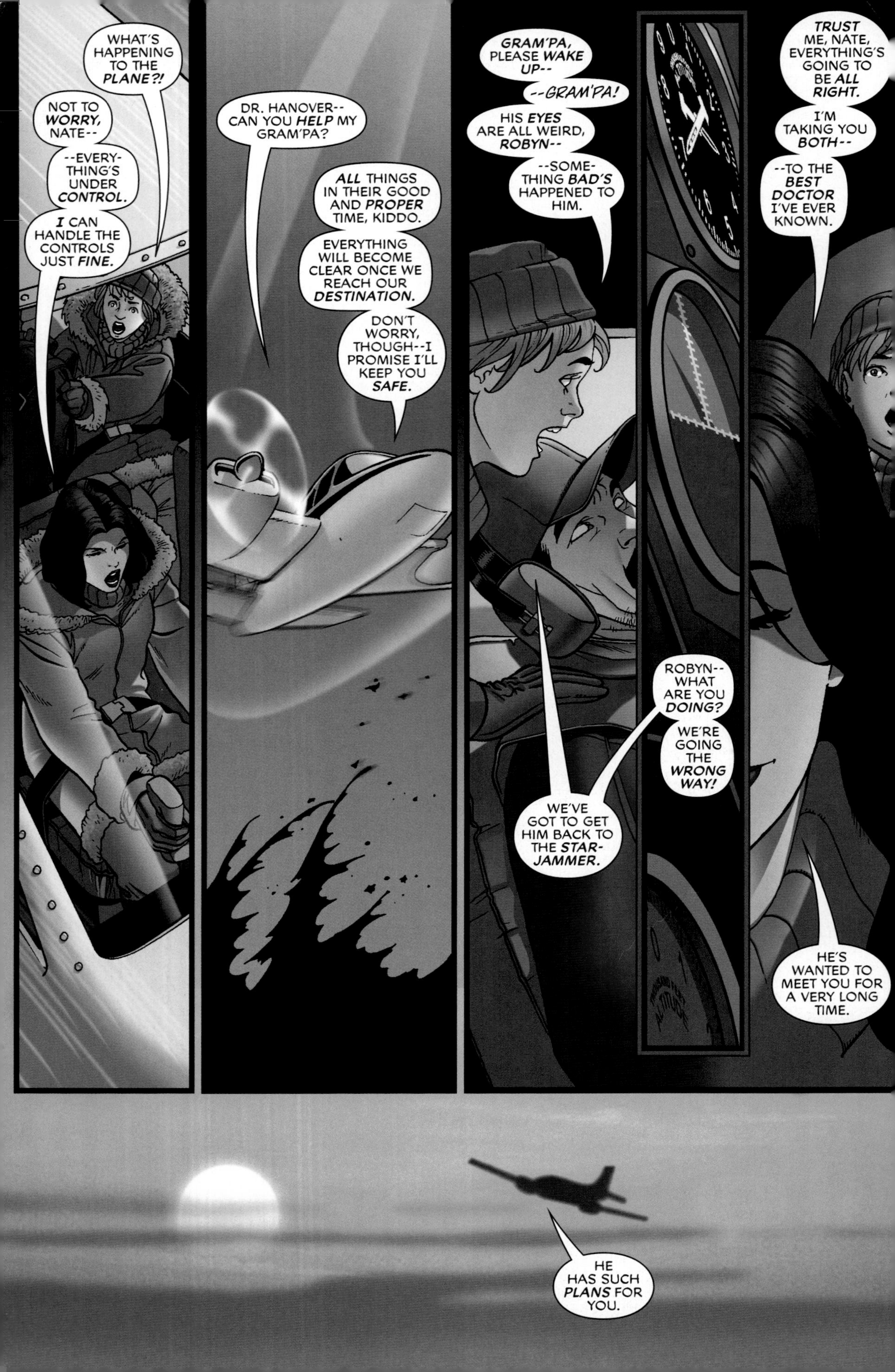

WHAT'S HAPPENING TO THE *PLANE?!*
NOT TO *WORRY,* NATE--
--EVERY-THING'S UNDER *CONTROL.*
I CAN HANDLE THE CONTROLS JUST *FINE.*
DR. HANOVER-- CAN YOU *HELP* MY GRAM'PA?
ALL THINGS IN THEIR GOOD AND *PROPER* TIME, KIDDO.
EVERYTHING WILL BECOME CLEAR ONCE WE REACH OUR *DESTINATION.*
DON'T WORRY, THOUGH--I PROMISE I'LL KEEP YOU *SAFE.*
GRAM'PA, PLEASE *WAKE UP--*
--GRAM'PA!
HIS *EYES* ARE ALL WEIRD, *ROBYN--*
--SOME-THING *BAD'S* HAPPENED TO HIM.
WE'VE GOT TO GET HIM BACK TO THE *STAR-JAMMER.*
ROBYN-- WHAT ARE YOU *DOING?*
WE'RE GOING THE *WRONG WAY!*
TRUST ME, NATE, EVERYTHING'S GOING TO BE *ALL RIGHT.*
I'M TAKING YOU *BOTH--*
--TO THE *BEST DOCTOR* I'VE EVER KNOWN.
HE'S WANTED TO MEET YOU FOR A VERY LONG TIME.
HE HAS SUCH *PLANS* FOR YOU.

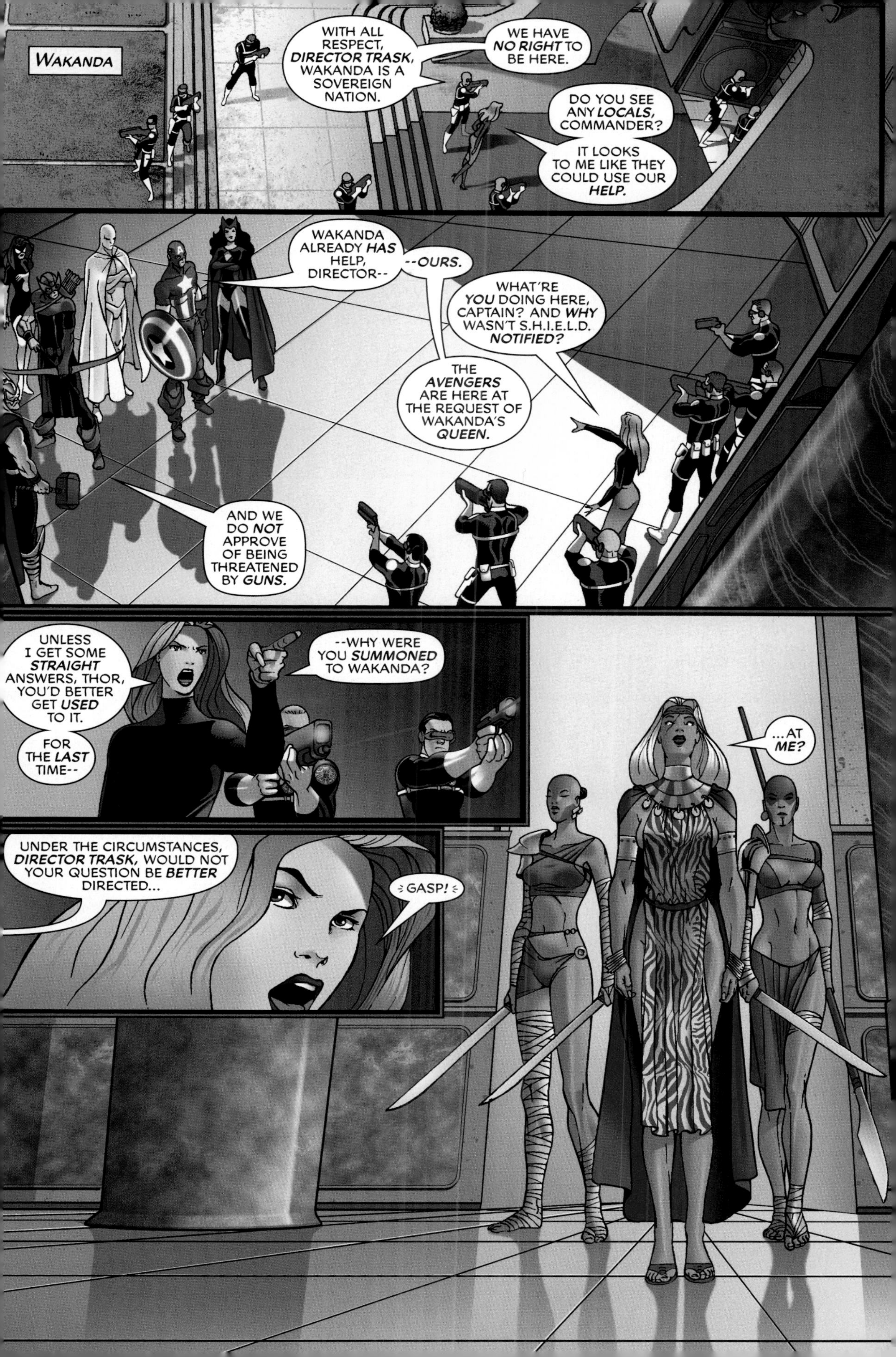
WAKANDA
WITH ALL RESPECT, DIRECTOR TRASK, WAKANDA IS A SOVEREIGN NATION.
WE HAVE NO RIGHT TO BE HERE.
DO YOU SEE ANY LOCALS, COMMANDER?
IT LOOKS TO ME LIKE THEY COULD USE OUR HELP.
WAKANDA ALREADY HAS HELP, DIRECTOR--
--OURS.
WHAT'RE YOU DOING HERE, CAPTAIN? AND WHY WASN'T S.H.I.E.L.D. NOTIFIED?
THE AVENGERS ARE HERE AT THE REQUEST OF WAKANDA'S QUEEN.
AND WE DO NOT APPROVE OF BEING THREATENED BY GUNS.
UNLESS I GET SOME STRAIGHT ANSWERS, THOR, YOU'D BETTER GET USED TO IT.
FOR THE LAST TIME--
--WHY WERE YOU SUMMONED TO WAKANDA?
UNDER THE CIRCUMSTANCES, DIRECTOR TRASK, WOULD NOT YOUR QUESTION BE BETTER DIRECTED...
GASP!
...AT ME?

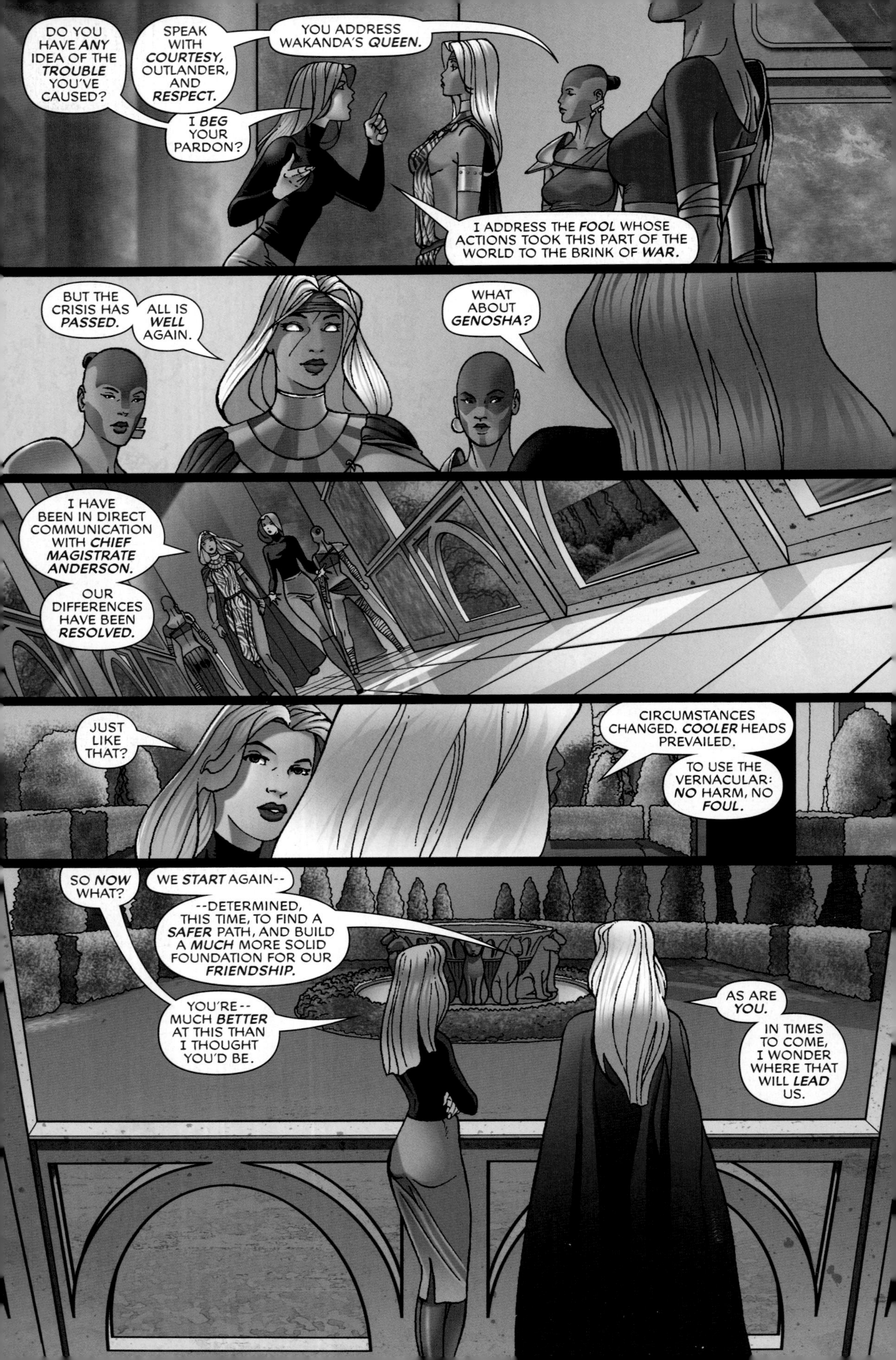
DO YOU HAVE ANY IDEA OF THE TROUBLE YOU'VE CAUSED?
SPEAK WITH COURTESY, OUTLANDER, AND RESPECT.
YOU ADDRESS WAKANDA'S QUEEN.
I BEG YOUR PARDON?
I ADDRESS THE FOOL WHOSE ACTIONS TOOK THIS PART OF THE WORLD TO THE BRINK OF WAR.
BUT THE CRISIS HAS PASSED.
ALL IS WELL AGAIN.
WHAT ABOUT GENOSHA?
I HAVE BEEN IN DIRECT COMMUNICATION WITH CHIEF MAGISTRATE ANDERSON.
OUR DIFFERENCES HAVE BEEN RESOLVED.
JUST LIKE THAT?
CIRCUMSTANCES CHANGED. COOLER HEADS PREVAILED.
TO USE THE VERNACULAR: NO HARM, NO FOUL.
SO NOW WHAT?
WE START AGAIN--
--DETERMINED, THIS TIME, TO FIND A SAFER PATH, AND BUILD A MUCH MORE SOLID FOUNDATION FOR OUR FRIENDSHIP.
YOU'RE-- MUCH BETTER AT THIS THAN I THOUGHT YOU'D BE.
AS ARE YOU.
IN TIMES TO COME, I WONDER WHERE THAT WILL LEAD US.

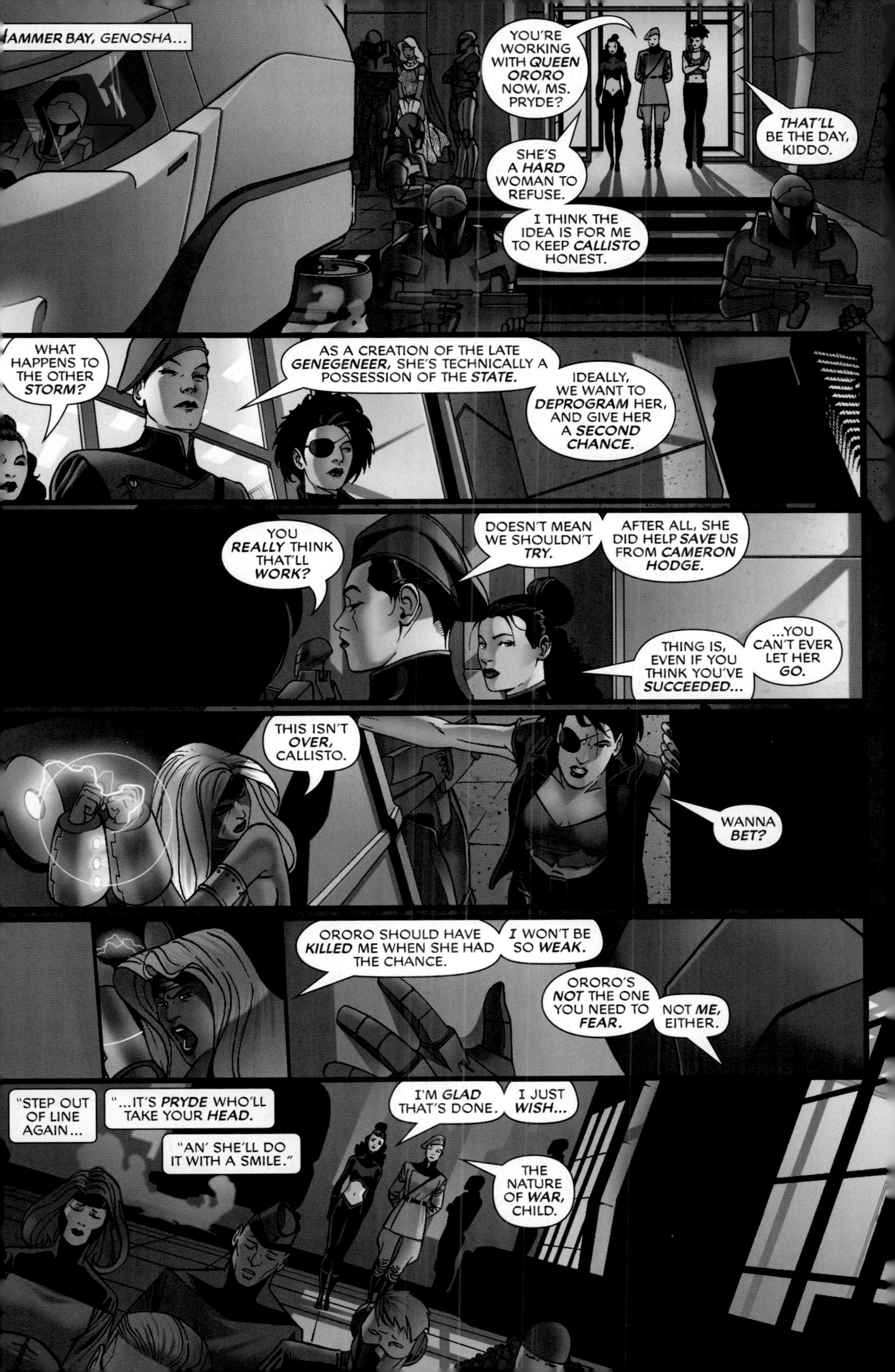
HAMMER BAY, GENOSHA...
YOU'RE WORKING WITH QUEEN ORORO NOW, MS. PRYDE?
THAT'LL BE THE DAY, KIDDO.
SHE'S A HARD WOMAN TO REFUSE.
I THINK THE IDEA IS FOR ME TO KEEP CALLISTO HONEST.
WHAT HAPPENS TO THE OTHER STORM?
AS A CREATION OF THE LATE GENEGENEER, SHE'S TECHNICALLY A POSSESSION OF THE STATE.
IDEALLY, WE WANT TO DEPROGRAM HER, AND GIVE HER A SECOND CHANCE.
YOU REALLY THINK THAT'LL WORK?
DOESN'T MEAN WE SHOULDN'T TRY.
AFTER ALL, SHE DID HELP SAVE US FROM CAMERON HODGE.
THING IS, EVEN IF YOU THINK YOU'VE SUCCEEDED...
...YOU CAN'T EVER LET HER GO.
THIS ISN'T OVER, CALLISTO.
WANNA BET?
ORORO SHOULD HAVE KILLED ME WHEN SHE HAD THE CHANCE.
I WON'T BE SO WEAK.
ORORO'S NOT THE ONE YOU NEED TO FEAR.
NOT ME, EITHER.
"STEP OUT OF LINE AGAIN...
"...IT'S PRYDE WHO'LL TAKE YOUR HEAD.
"AN' SHE'LL DO IT WITH A SMILE."
I'M GLAD THAT'S DONE.
I JUST WISH...
THE NATURE OF WAR, CHILD.

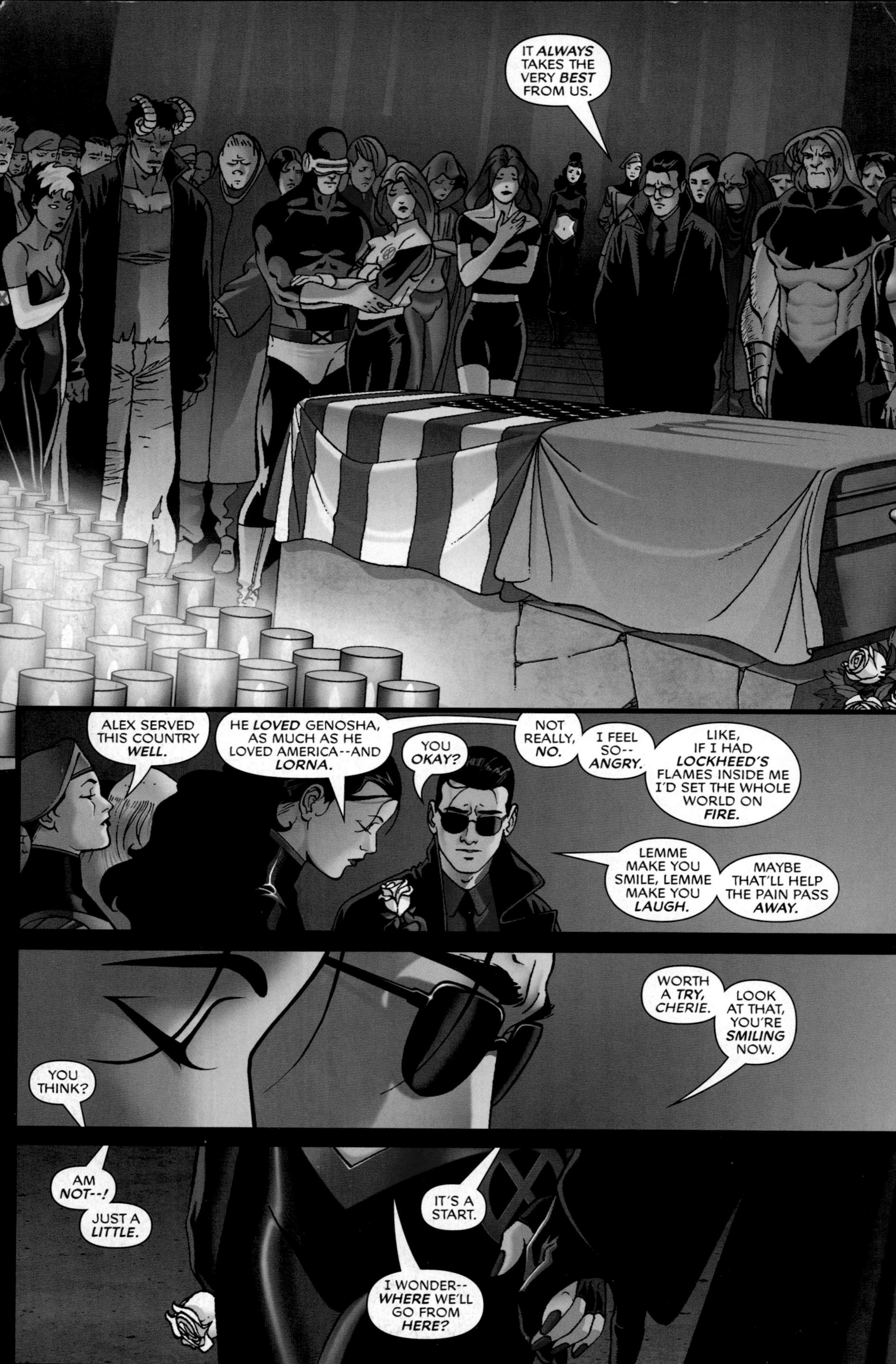
IT ALWAYS TAKES THE VERY BEST FROM US.
ALEX SERVED THIS COUNTRY WELL.
HE LOVED GENOSHA, AS MUCH AS HE LOVED AMERICA--AND LORNA.
YOU OKAY?
NOT REALLY, NO.
I FEEL SO-- ANGRY.
LIKE, IF I HAD LOCKHEED'S FLAMES INSIDE ME I'D SET THE WHOLE WORLD ON FIRE.
LEMME MAKE YOU SMILE, LEMME MAKE YOU LAUGH.
MAYBE THAT'LL HELP THE PAIN PASS AWAY.
WORTH A TRY, CHERIE.
LOOK AT THAT, YOU'RE SMILING NOW.
YOU THINK?
AM NOT--!
JUST A LITTLE.
IT'S A START.
I WONDER-- WHERE WE'LL GO FROM HERE?

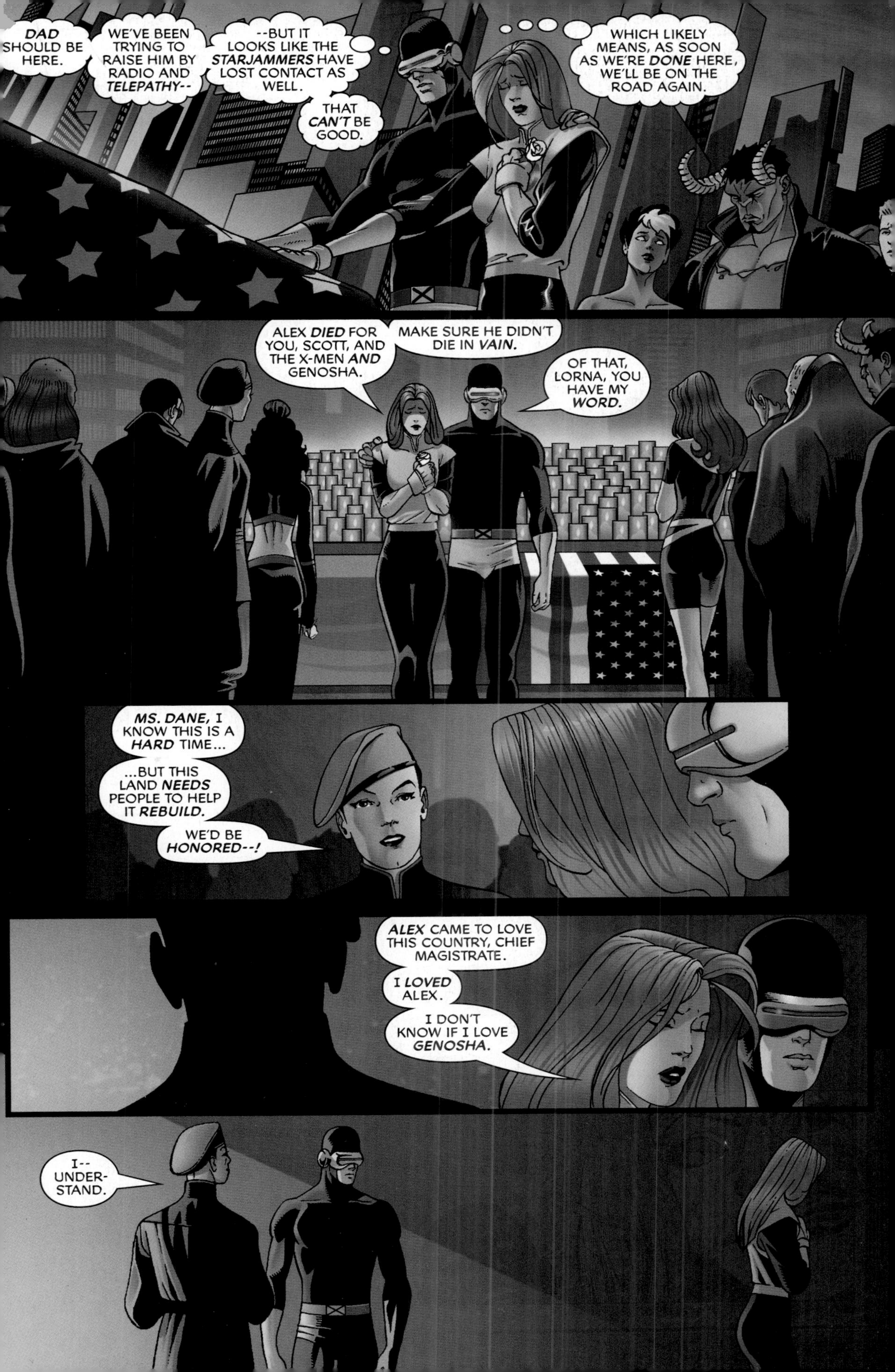
DAD SHOULD BE HERE.
WE'VE BEEN TRYING TO RAISE HIM BY RADIO AND TELEPATHY--
--BUT IT LOOKS LIKE THE STARJAMMERS HAVE LOST CONTACT AS WELL.
THAT CAN'T BE GOOD.
WHICH LIKELY MEANS, AS SOON AS WE'RE DONE HERE, WE'LL BE ON THE ROAD AGAIN.
ALEX DIED FOR YOU, SCOTT, AND THE X-MEN AND GENOSHA.
MAKE SURE HE DIDN'T DIE IN VAIN.
OF THAT, LORNA, YOU HAVE MY WORD.
MS. DANE, I KNOW THIS IS A HARD TIME...
...BUT THIS LAND NEEDS PEOPLE TO HELP IT REBUILD.
WE'D BE HONORED--!
ALEX CAME TO LOVE THIS COUNTRY, CHIEF MAGISTRATE.
I LOVED ALEX.
I DON'T KNOW IF I LOVE GENOSHA.
I-- UNDER-STAND.

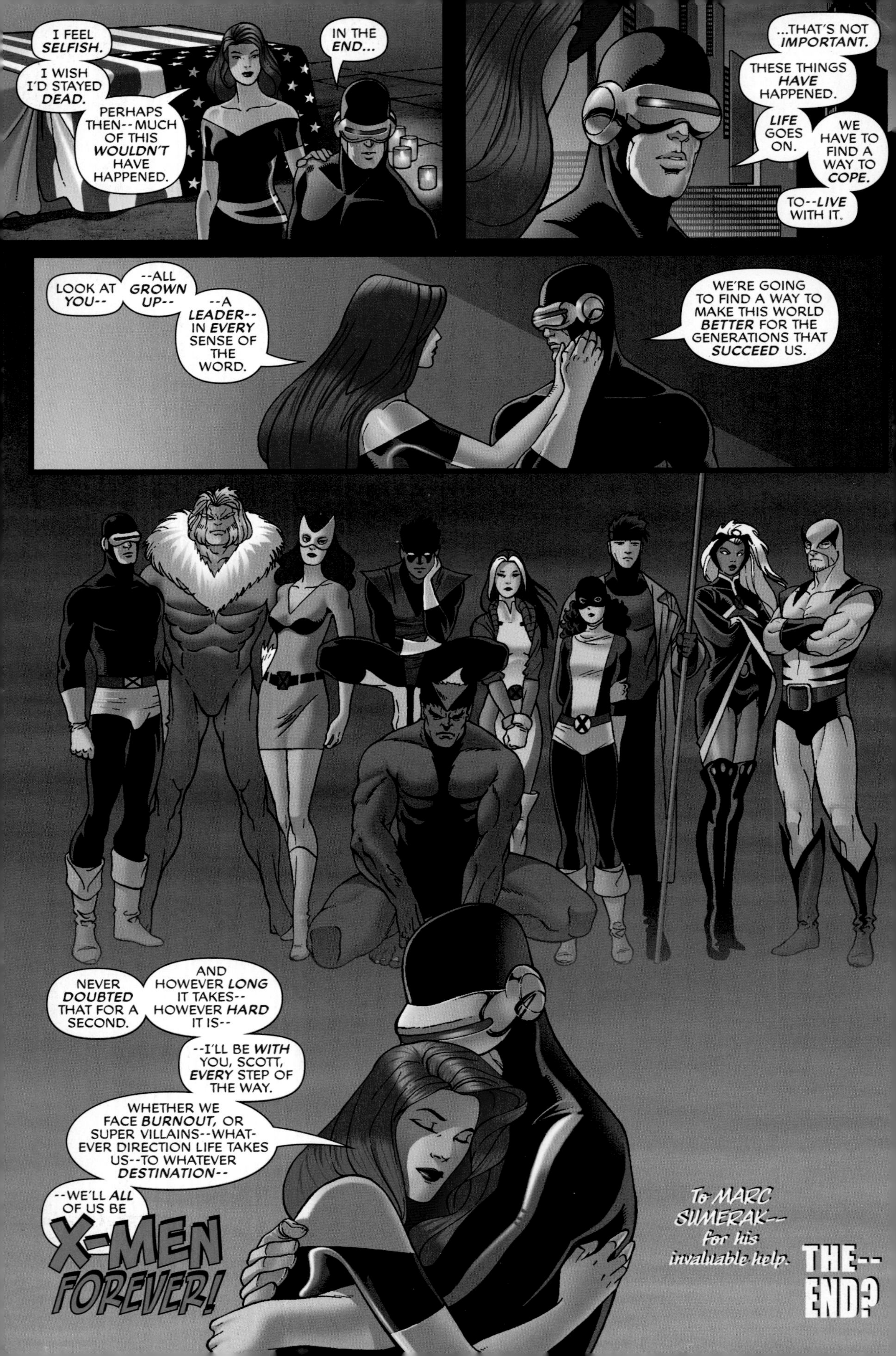
I FEEL SELFISH.
I WISH I'D STAYED DEAD.
PERHAPS THEN--MUCH OF THIS WOULDN'T HAVE HAPPENED.
IN THE END...
...THAT'S NOT IMPORTANT.
THESE THINGS HAVE HAPPENED.
LIFE GOES ON.
WE HAVE TO FIND A WAY TO COPE.
TO--LIVE WITH IT.
LOOK AT YOU--
--ALL GROWN UP--
--A LEADER--IN EVERY SENSE OF THE WORD.
WE'RE GOING TO FIND A WAY TO MAKE THIS WORLD BETTER FOR THE GENERATIONS THAT SUCCEED US.
NEVER DOUBTED THAT FOR A SECOND.
AND HOWEVER LONG IT TAKES--HOWEVER HARD IT IS--
--I'LL BE WITH YOU, SCOTT, EVERY STEP OF THE WAY.
WHETHER WE FACE BURNOUT, OR SUPER VILLAINS--WHATEVER DIRECTION LIFE TAKES US--TO WHATEVER DESTINATION--
--WE'LL ALL OF US BE
X-MEN FOREVER!
To MARC SUMERAK--for his invaluable help.
THE--END?